Savings Services
for the Poor

Savings Services for the Poor

An Operational Guide

Edited by
Madeline Hirschland

Kumarian
Press, Inc.

Deutsche Gesellschaft für
Technische Zusammenarbeit (GTZ) GmbH

commissioned by:

Federal Ministry
for Economic Cooperation
and Development

MicroSave
Market-led solutions for financial services

USAID
FROM THE AMERICAN PEOPLE

Savings Services for the Poor: An Operational Guide
Published in 2005 in the United States of America by Kumarian Press, Inc., 1294 Blue
Hills Avenue, Bloomfield, CT 06002 USA

The text of this book is set in 10/12 Times

Production and design by Joan Weber Laflamme, jml ediset
Proofread by Bob Land

Printed in the United States by McNaughton & Gunn, Inc. Text printed with vegetable oil-
based ink.

∞ The paper used in this publication meets the minimum requirements of the American
National Standard for Information Sciences—Permanence of Paper for printed Library Materials, ANSI Z39.48–1984

Library of Congress Cataloging-in-Publication Data

Savings services for the poor : an operational guide / edited by Madeline Hirschland.
    p. cm.
    Includes index.
    Summary: "Contains practical guidance for managing sound savings operations for
small and rural depositors. The book addresses two types of institutions: microfinance
institutions and mainstream banks"—Provided by publisher.
    Includes bibliographical references and index.
    ISBN 1–56549–209–9 (pbk. : alk. paper)
    1. Savings accounts. 2. Saving and investment. 3. Savings banks. 4. Banks and
banking. 5. Bank management. 6. Microfinance. 7. Poor. I.
Hirschland, Madeline.
HG1660.A3S28 2005
332.1'752'068—dc22

        2005018007

---

14 13 12 11 10 09 08 07 06 05   10 9 8 7 6 5 4 3 2 1   First Printing 2005

In the years since this book was conceived, our world has become increasingly fragmented. Not so within our book. We, its contributors, come from many places and perspectives yet are united in our pursuit of sustainable financial services—and all that that might mean for the lives of the poor. As it is within, so may it be without.

Contents

Part I
Overview

Part II
Services

Part III
Systems

Illustrations

Foreword

In 1976, when I was teaching economics at Chittagong University in Bangladesh, a small group of poor women taught me a lesson that has guided me ever since. It is the lesson that no one needs to remain poor, that every poor person can hope to escape from poverty if only we make sure that a few simple enabling conditions are in place. One of those conditions is access to basic affordable financial services. Those poor women in Chittagong, and since then millions more in Bangladesh and around the world, have been helped to fight poverty through the use of loans that can be paid back in easily managed small but frequent installments.

The Grameen Bank, the institution that I founded to work with women to defeat poverty, has over the years developed great expertise in collecting small payments from bank members scattered throughout the forty-one thousand villages of Bangladesh. Increasingly, Grameen has exploited this expertise to help its members deposit into a wide variety of voluntary savings schemes, including passbook savings, fixed deposits, and contractual savings. In "Grameen II," now in place in all our branches, the Grameen Pension Scheme, a contractual savings arrangement, has become one of our most popular and useful products, helping thousands of women secure their own futures by building up a substantial financial asset.

If they are managed soundly, saving services are a win-win proposition. They help the poor to secure themselves against the risks and uncertainties of their lives, and they can help microcredit nongovernmental organizations (NGOs) to capitalize their loan portfolio. In Grameen, we now have new branches that have been capitalized from day one by local deposits. *Grameen Bank has not accepted donor money since 1995. Now, with mobilization of local deposits, Grameen Bank does not even have to borrow money from the market.*

In most countries, however, microcredit NGOs are not allowed to take deposits by the regulatory bodies. If microcredit NGOs that are capable of managing the savings of the poor could open the doors for taking public deposits, expansion of outreach could be very rapid, because this would free them from dependence on donor money. It is a very strange phenomenon in many countries to see that conventional banks with repayment rates below 70 percent are allowed to take huge amounts of public deposits year after year, but microcredit institutions with an unbroken record of over 90 percent recovery are not allowed to take public deposits. It is often argued that since microcredit programs do not come under any law, it is highly risky to allow them to take deposits. This always seems to me a funny argument. Why don't we create a law to bring the microcredit programs under a legal cover, create a special regulatory commission to regulate them, and allow them to take public deposits? Of course, this should include a long and hard quality check of the microcredit operation of an NGO. Creating such a commission would help local deposits in the villages to work for local poor people instead of being siphoned off to the big cities to finance big businesses. This is the frustrating part of our experience. One feels like throwing one's arms in the air and screaming in protest.

That is why I am delighted to contribute to the publication you now hold in your hands. Here is a book that recognizes the potential of savings while at the same time soberly acknowledging that, to assure that the savings of the poor are secure, deposit mobilization requires skills and attitudes that are different from those needed just for lending. It offers clear guidance, including practical tools, on how to mobilize and intermediate voluntary savings, by drawing on the experience of institutions, large and small, from Africa, Asia, and Latin America. It will make a major contribution to what must remain the goal of microfinancial services—the total elimination of poverty worldwide.

MUHAMMAD YUNUS
Grameen Bank

Acknowledgments

So many people contributed to this book! First and foremost, I am grateful to Kate McKee of USAID's Office of Microenterprise Development. Her vision and support made this guide possible. Dirk Steinwand of GTZ, Graham Wright of *MicroSave*, and Chris Dunford of Freedom from Hunger gave essential support and were flexible and helpful to boot. Freedom from Hunger generously permitted me to adapt and use material I had prepared for them. Gary Garrison of the Fulbright Commission provided the stone that made the soup. Kumarian Press also committed itself to the book early on. Jim Lance patiently slogged through the details of publication with me while Joan Weber Laflamme skillfully turned it from manuscript to book, Marilyn Breiter and Jackie Bush eased the way, and Louise Rarick provided vital support in the final stages.

The authors deserve a mighty thanks. Despite busy schedules they marshaled the time to share their expertise and the patience to revise until we got it right. I am especially grateful for the good-natured perseverance of Monnie Biety, who single-handedly took on three of the book's most demanding chapters.

A picture is worth a thousand words. Particular value was added by those who contributed case material: Renée Chao-Béroff, José Luis Cisneros, David Cracknell, Mariko Dramane, Marie-Luise Haberberger, Alfred Hamadziripi, Lloyd Hardy, Jennifer Hoffmann, Prahlad Mali, Elsa Patricia Manrique, Godfried Odame-Asare, Madhav Poudyal, Stuart Rutherford, Khem Raj Sapkota, Christoph Schultz, Kathleen Stack, Mark Staehle, Cherie Tan, Hillary Miller Wise, Gamini Yapa, and Gabriela Zapata.

Each chapter was reviewed by experts in its topic area: Fawzia Abu-Hijleh, Ismail Adam, Dale Adams, Aris Alip, Sergio Antezana, Ken Appentang-Mensah, John Berry, Monnie Biety, David Cracknell, Carlos Cuevas, Carlos Danel, Mahendra Giri, Meryl Hirschland, Jennifer Hoffmann, Mohammed Azim Hossain, Annica Jansen, Fabian Kasi, Michael Kasibante, Kathryn Larcombe, Constance Larmie, Kate McKee, Margaret Mensah, Rochus Mommartz, Jonathan Morduch, Nthenya Mule, Leonard Mutesasira, Gokul Pyakurel, Stuart Rutherford, Jalan Sharma, Nav Raj Simkhada, Kathleen Stack, Mark Staehle, John Takacsy, Tulasi Prasad Uprety, and J. D. Von Pischke. These reviewers gave their time freely; their suggestions were invaluable.

The sage advice of Beth Rhyne helped launch this book on a sound course, and her incisive review helped guide it to a solid landing. Her suggestions have improved the book immeasurably. The book is also much stronger for the many insights and leads provided by David Cracknell, Kathryn Larcombe, and Stuart Rutherford. I called upon them often, and they always responded generously.

Sushila Gautam was an exceptional research assistant; her insights and resourcefulness ensured that our time in the field provided the book with a rich and sound basis. Shafiqual Chaudhury, Namrata Sharma, and S. K. Sinha provided all the support one could want during fieldwork, while Mohammed Azim Hossain was a fount of useful information and sharp analysis.

My understanding of what it takes to serve the rural poor was deepened by colleagues in Bangladesh and Nepal who generously shared their time and expertise: Md. Jamilur Rahman Chy, Abdu Sobahan, Shah Alam, and their staff at ASA; Imran Matin of BRAC; Zakir Hossain, Mosharrof Hossain, and the staff of BURO, Tangail; Edward Abbey and Md. Emrul Hasan of Plan International Bangladesh; S. K. Sinha, Hossin Islam, Mark Staehle, and the staff of *Safe*Save in Bangladesh; Md. Abdul Mannan of Sraban Engineering Works; and in Nepal, Ganesh Tamrakar and the board of the Bhumiraj Cooperative, and Bharat Prasad Sharma and the staff of the BISCOL Savings and Credit Cooperative; Prahlad Mali, formerly of CECI; Nav Raj Simkhada, formerly of the Centre for Micro-Finance; Gokul Pyakurel, formerly of the Center for Self-Help Development; Pitamber Pd. Acharya and Yuv Raj Bartaula of DEPROSC; Uli Wehnert of GTZ's Nepal office; Himalaya Bhakta Pradhananga of the Himalaya Finance and Savings Co. Ltd.; Tulasi Prasad Uprety of Nepal Rastra Bank; Harihar DevPant of Nirdhan Bank; Khem Raj Sapkota and Madhav Poudyal of VYCCU; Saraswati Shrestha of WEAN; and the managing directors of the Small Farmer Cooperative in Kumroj, the Navajeevan Cooperative, and the Far Western Multi-Purpose Cooperative.

To each of these colleagues, many, many thanks.

This guide builds on the work of leaders in the area of savings operations. Like many in this field, I owe my interest in savings to Marguerite Robinson. Her analysis of the Bank Rakyat Indonesia provides many of our most fundamental insights about savings operations. The World Council of Credit Unions (WOCCU) has promoted savings for decades. From Guatemala to Nepal, WOCCU affiliates confirm an important assumption—if they are managed rigorously, small not-for-profits can serve small depositors and cover costs. GTZ has led the way in shedding light on best practices. Cases, tools, and insights from its work enrich many of the chapters. Finally, *MicroSave* has been instrumental in developing institutional capacity. Its experience, tools, and research findings consistently break new ground and add value throughout this volume.

Lessons from pioneers in serving poor and rural clients also provide the foundation for much of the book. *Safe*Save has demonstrated that poor people will use services that are truly flexible and convenient. In so doing, *Safe*save compels us to grapple with the real challenge inherent in serving the poor: how to manage such services securely and recover costs. The work of ASA (Association for Social Advancement) exemplifies one answer to this challenge: ASA covers the costs of providing doorstep services to millions by relentlessly pursuing simplicity and efficiency. Finally, NABARD (National Bank for Agriculture and Rural Development), CARE, and numerous small cooperatives offer a powerful approach for reaching the rural poor: self-managed groups.

For helping me get to the point where I could birth this book, I am grateful to my mentors—David Feingold for his kind encouragement, intellectual guidance, and help in making critical decisions; Merilee Grindle for her confidence in my abilities and for opening doors; Jeff Ashe for bringing me into the field and modeling how to dream big and work hard; Diane Kwasnick for her gentle and wise guidance; and Deborah Hirschland-Fine for her ever-present support. For the perspective I bring to this work, I wish to thank Lois and Jerry Jenkins, who taught me to take crossing cultures for granted; Nangithia Mbogori, Mwiti Mbogori of blessed memory, Silas and Mwarania Muriuki, and Joseph and Mary Kiirania, who made me so welcome in rural Chugu; and G. Balagopal and Prassy Balagopal who enabled me to work far from air-conditioned bubbles.

I am deeply grateful to each of my friends and family. A special thanks to Henry Hirschland, Janet Hirschland, Evelyn Polk, Lee Moss, Eliot Moss, Lora Berg, Polly Bates, Shailaja Chopella, and my wonderful friends here in Bloomington for their support of this work. I so appreciate the intelligence, warmth, and humor that Sue Hicks, Jitka Horne, Abigail Katz, Regina Katz, Didi Kerler, and our cousin Lina Khawalda brought to the children; without their care, the book would not have been possible.

Above all, I am grateful to Larry for his ever-ready support, wisdom, love, and humor, to Daniel and Tamar for being patient and fun and for traveling with me, and to all three for making me so happy.

To the extent that this book is mine to dedicate, I dedicate it to my parents, Evelyn Polk and Henry Hirschland, with unbounded gratitude and love.

Abbreviations

ALM	asset liability management
ASA	Association for Social Advancement (Bangladesh)
ATM	automatic teller machine
BAAC	Bank for Agriculture and Agricultural Cooperatives (Thailand)
BRI	Bank Rakyat Indonesia
CVECAs	Caisses Villageoises d'Épargne et de Crédit Autogérées
GNI	gross national income
IT	information technology
MFI	microfinance institution
MIS	management information system(s)
NABARD	National Bank for Agriculture and Rural Development (India)
NGO	nongovernmental organization
NIM	net interest margin
PC GNI	per capita gross national income
POS	point of service
RSA	rate-sensitive assets
RSL	rate-sensitive liabilities
SHGs	self-help groups
WOCCU	World Council of Credit Unions

Introduction

During lean times, savings help people get by. Savings enable them to invest when opportunity knocks, to weather a sudden illness or flood, or to pay for school fees, a wedding, or a new roof. Savings may or may not provide a lift out of poverty. They do make people less vulnerable to poverty's worst effects.

For microfinance institutions, savings can be a key to growth and profitability. Savings can provide a stable, low-cost means to finance the loan portfolio, dramatically increase an institution's client base, and improve borrowers' capacity to repay. The challenges of attracting and retaining depositors also can force institutions to become more customer-oriented, efficient, and professional. And savings can fuel growth at the level of communities as well as nations.

So, savings services are important. It is good news that financial institutions are offering more savings services than we in the microfinance community had thought. A recent global study estimates that microfinance institutions now manage twice as many deposit accounts as loan accounts.[1] If we include postal savings banks, state banks, rural banks, and cooperatives—other institutions that reach lower-income clients than those served by commercial banks—the ratio is four to one. Together, these institutions hold an estimated 570 million deposit accounts—although we don't know how many low-income depositors these accounts represent.[2]

Whatever the precise numbers, the literature in our field has yet to catch up. Our pursuit of microfinance best practices has largely bypassed savings. In the course of producing this book I have leafed through scores of "microfinance" cases and tools only to find that they refer solely to credit. In fact, credit is still the focus of the vast majority of resources and training. This is a problem, because managing savings well is critically important and significantly different from managing credit alone.

Maintaining the security of savings is crucial. If savings are lost, it is the poor who are robbed of the means to buy food during the hungry season, to pay for a child's schooling, or to sustain themselves when they can no longer work. Therefore, an institution should engage in *financial intermediation*—mobilizing savings that it disburses as loans—only if it meets stringent standards.[3] Poorly

Many thanks to Kate McKee, Jonathan Morduch, Larry Moss, Evelyn Polk, Stuart Rutherford, Kathleen Stack, and J. D. Von Pischke for their insightful reviews of this chapter.

managing the savings of the poor is not acceptable. Yet, meeting these standards is not easy.

Savings operations and financial intermediation pose quite different management challenges from credit alone. Savings services, particularly liquid ones, typically involve many more—and less predictable—transactions. Internal controls are more important and more complex. Similarly, managing assets vis-à-vis liabilities, developing adequate information systems, and motivating high productivity also are more challenging. At the same time, attracting a volume of deposits that permits positive returns may require many more clients and, in most cases, a greater diversity of clients. And, whereas credit requires the institution to trust the client, savings require just the opposite: in order to convince savers to trust it with their cash an institution is compelled to develop responsive customer care, a professional image, demand-driven services, and sustainable operations. In short, managing savings well is critically important, distinctly demanding, and often neglected.

This book should help fill the gap. Drawing on the experience of savings institutions from across the globe, it provides practical, step-by-step guidance for developing and managing sound savings operations. This guidance is directed toward two types of institutions. The first are credit-led microfinance institutions that want to initiate or strengthen their savings operations. The second are regulated financial institutions that already have strong savings operations and want to extend these to smaller or more rural depositors. The book addresses the chief management challenges for each.

Its focus is the microfinance market—savers who are unlikely to be served by commercial banks. Throughout the book, we consider each topic from this perspective. In order to be viable, however, most institutions that aim to serve the "unbanked" must also compete in the commercial market. Therefore, we also examine the marketing and management issues involved in extending services to this upper-end market.

In addition, the book considers two subsets of the micro market: poor and rural savers. This raises an obvious question. Why particularly focus on these markets? This question is of great import to the field of microfinance today. So, before describing the book's contents in more depth, we will briefly look at two related issues: why poor and rural markets merit special attention, and what focusing on these markets implies for savings operations.

WHY FOCUS ON POOR AND RURAL MARKETS?

We consider poor and rural depositors separately because in many places they are barely being reached. Study after study has found that microfinance institutions primarily serve the upper poor and the near poor. In some cases the majority is not poor. A review of studies of the outreach of microfinance institutions (MFIs) found that "in general a majority of microfinance clients in the programs studied cluster just above and just below the poverty line."[4] Furthermore, the large majority of microfinance clients live in cities and towns. In only a few countries are MFIs serving poorer and rural clients on a large scale.

Some microfinance experts suggest that clients that are poorer than those that most MFIs are currently reaching would not benefit from financial services.[5] This is not true. As discussed in Chapter 1, financial services by themselves can be valuable to all but the destitute. However, poor and rural savers often require different types of services than most MFIs offer.

Before going further, let's clarify this discussion with some definitions. Because countries differ vastly, these will necessarily be rough and qualitative. That's all right—our aim is simply to identify who can be reached by what types of services (see Figure Intro-1). With this in mind, we consider three groups who cannot consistently meet their basic needs: the destitute, the poor, and the upper poor.[6]

By *destitute* we mean the typically small segment of the population that is not economically active and that does not have assets or other means that generate even an irregular source of income. For this group direct aid is appropriate and pure financial services are not. *Poor* refers to the mass of people who are economically active but whose incomes are small and irregular. At some times their income can cover their food and other recurring expenses with some amount to spare. At others they may not be able even to feed themselves adequately from their current income. Financial services can be particularly valuable to this group *if* these services are convenient and take the size and unreliability of this group's income into account. Typically, even where microfinance services are available, they are not designed well for the poor—who consequently use them for only a small fraction, if any, of their financial services. We define *upper poor* as people whose income is small but large and reliable enough to make the opening deposit or regular payments required by many existing microfinance services. Their standard of living places them below the poverty line.

Next, we have the *near poor*. As their name suggests, these people can consistently meet minimal standards for food, health care, and shelter but are vulnerable—a single accident can plunge them into poverty.

Finally, we will call people *rural* if they live farther than a quick trip from a town or city and *remote* if they live farther than a quick walk from a road.

Our typology asserts several important facts: in many countries, a large portion of the population is economically active and still has a small and, in many cases, unreliable income. With only current income, members of this group cannot consistently obtain sufficient food and health care. Little of their demand for financial services is met by MFIs or other financial institutions. In fact, they represent only a small fraction of these institutions' clientele. However, they can use appropriately designed financial services. How do we know this?

As Stuart Rutherford notes in Chapter 1, numerous studies and experience worldwide confirm that the poor already use financial services extensively—*informal* ones.[7] One study he cites is from a highly competitive microfinance market in rural Bangladesh. Over the course of one year, the sample households were

Figure Intro–1. Financial Services and the Poverty Spectrum

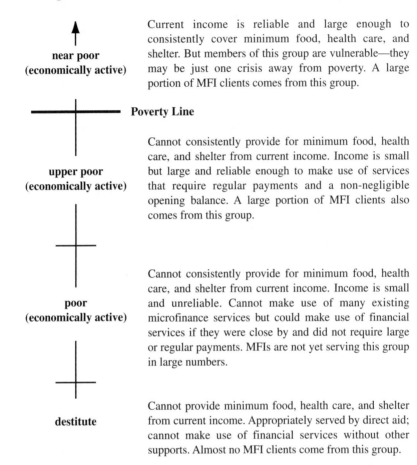

**near poor
(economically active)**

Current income is reliable and large enough to consistently cover minimum food, health care, and shelter. But members of this group are vulnerable—they may be just one crisis away from poverty. A large portion of MFI clients comes from this group.

Poverty Line

**upper poor
(economically active)**

Cannot consistently provide for minimum food, health care, and shelter from current income. Income is small but large and reliable enough to make use of services that require regular payments and a non-negligible opening balance. A large portion of MFI clients also comes from this group.

**poor
(economically active)**

Cannot consistently provide for minimum food, health care, and shelter from current income. Income is small and unreliable. Cannot make use of many existing microfinance services but could make use of financial services if they were close by and did not require large or regular payments. MFIs are not yet serving this group in large numbers.

destitute

Cannot provide minimum food, health care, and shelter from current income. Appropriately served by direct aid; cannot make use of financial services without other supports. Almost no MFI clients come from this group.

This schematic corresponds to the one in Cohen and Sebstad, *Microfinance Risk Management and Poverty*, 4. Our terminology differs slightly, and our categories are defined in terms of income streams rather than percentages of the poor population.

estimated to be "pushing or pulling three-quarters of their income through the informal money market" in an average of twenty-six informal lending or savings contracts. For the upper poor and poor households in the sample, MFIs were handling just 7 percent of these financial contracts; 30 percent of these households were not using any MFI services at all. Studies with a similar design in South Africa and India also found poor households using financial services intensively, with informal services representing the majority of their usage.

Indeed, even people in remote areas use financial services if they are convenient. One of our cases describes a 152–member financial cooperative in a mountain village almost two miles from a rough dirt road. Of the households in its catchment area, 72 percent are members; they own shares and make a monthly deposit in order to take advantage of the cooperative's financial services (see Box 8–2).

While poor and rural people are already saving in the informal sector, these services have some significant shortcomings. Although informal savings mechanisms are typically very convenient, they are often neither reliable nor secure. For example, a study in Uganda found that over the course of one year, 99 percent of respondents who saved informally lost a portion of these funds; on average, the portion lost was 22 percent.[8] For these savers secure formal services would likely be a step up.

WHAT IT TAKES TO SERVE THESE MARKETS: DELIVERY CHANNELS, PRODUCTS, AND INSTITUTIONS

If poor and rural savers demand financial services, why are we not already serving them? For potential clients, one of the biggest obstacles is distance.[9] For many poor and rural savers, walking or paying to travel even three miles to make a small deposit is not realistic. For example, a market survey, reported in Chapter 5, in a low-income suburban community in Malawi, found that 75 percent of respondents were willing to travel less than five kilometers to transact; over one-quarter would go no farther than two kilometers (Box 5–1). Yet, particularly in rural areas, MFI or bank branches are rarely so close by.

In theory we can overcome the distance challenge by offering services in central locations that people already frequent. But in fact, while many people travel regularly to places where a bank or MFI branch might be located, many do not. Poorer people, particularly women, are often among the less mobile. In the Malawi survey areas just cited, three-quarters of respondents reported traveling to market weekly, but the figure dropped to just half in the poorer communities.[10] It is no surprise then that from Ghana to the Philippines to Thailand institutions that have brought services closer to clients have seen huge increases in deposits—deposits that clients did not make when services were farther away (see Box 8–1, section 8.7, and Box 5–2).

With the poor, however, convenience is not the only barrier. Even where clients are served close to their homes, as in much of rural Bangladesh, the poor still are often excluded by the *terms*—rules—of products. For people with small unreliable incomes, regular fixed payments and non-negligible minimum balance requirements may not be feasible. In the Bangladesh study cited above, all the households that did not use MFI services gave the same basic reason: "the fixed weekly or monthly payments over a yearlong period would be either impossible or very difficult to meet." In order to recover their costs while meeting regulatory requirements, many institutions that are successfully mobilizing savings from the upper poor and near poor (including many cited in this book) employ product terms that de facto exclude the poor most of the time: they charge transaction fees that are equivalent to a significant portion of a laborer's daily wage or require a minimum deposit that is many times this wage. While the poor might pay such a fee for their rare large deposits, these product terms are prohibitive for their everyday savings desires. Similarly with distance: while they may be willing to travel to make a one-time large deposit, they are much less likely to do so to set aside their small daily or even weekly savings.

No wonder that most MFIs are not serving large numbers of rural and poor depositors. The features that are crucial to these savers—services that are close by and the opportunity to deposit amounts that are small and variable—raise operating costs. Providing services that are close by is particularly financially challenging in rural areas. But even in urban areas, establishing a network of conventional branches that offer poor-friendly services and are within a few miles of poor people's homes or work places is rarely feasible. To provide convenient, useful services to poor and rural depositors and remain financially viable, most MFIs must use different sorts of staffing and delivery channels.

This book is full of examples of banks, cooperatives, and NGOs that are doing precisely that. Their cost-effective delivery channels include mobile units in Kenya and Thailand, customized ATMs in Bolivia and South Africa, tiny offices in rural Indonesia and remote Nepal, self-help groups in Zimbabwe and Mexico, deposit collectors in Ghana and India, and services that are "piggybacked" onto postal or credit services throughout the world. The institutions that are employing these delivery channels are reaping the benefits, from a better public image and a bigger and more diverse market to greater profitability and a larger volume of stable funds for lending. At the same time these alternative staffing and delivery channels affect nearly every aspect of operations: they require simplicity and innovation in everything from products to controls.

The operations that result rarely look like conventional banking, but they innovate to make up the difference. For example, MFIs that deploy mobile collectors make up for the absence of traditional internal controls with a whole set of alternative controls. A small office or mobile unit that is open only a few hours a week has its sole employee or the parent branch accessible full time for a depositor faced with an emergency. Deposits may be illiquid because staff or volunteers cannot manage liquidity, but depositors are provided access to emergency loans. Of course, this sort of unconventional banking may not fit the requirements of conventional financial institutions.

In recent years the drive to extend services to massive numbers of the unbanked has led many of us to focus our attention on large for-profit institutions. As cases in this book illustrate, these institutions have tremendous potential to reach the unbanked (see Boxes 4–5, 5–4, 8–4, and 8–8). However, the cases also illustrate their limits for reaching poor and remote savers. Because of their cost structure and culture, large commercial institutions tend to have less potential than other types of institutions to accept very small liquid accounts and to manage less conventional, poor-focused delivery channels.

Throughout the book we find that most of the institutions that are serving poor and rural markets are cooperatives, NGOs, community banks, and state banks. The institutions driven to reach these markets—and the ones that do it best—have not been for-profits. Therefore, as the microfinance donor community concluded over a decade ago:

> It is desirable to encourage a range of institutions that use specialized methods to serve their particular market niches. These can include commercial and development banks, credit unions, mutual or community banks, non-governmental organizations (NGOs), finance companies, cooperatives, savings and credit associations, and other specialized intermediaries.[11]

If we want to serve poor and rural depositors, then donors and policymakers must continue to encourage a range of institutions.

THE BOOK ITSELF—
AND WHO SHOULD READ WHICH PARTS

Now that we've clarified why we devote some of our pages to poor and rural markets, let us turn our attention more broadly to the book's overall contents. Part I provides an overview to savings operations. Chapter 1 prepares the ground for what follows by considering the market for savings services—what poor people typically want and what they may already have. Chapters 2 and 3 examine the standards that institutions should meet before they engage in financial intermediation and provide some keys to developing operations that are financially viable. We then look at the steps and challenges involved for MFIs that do not have strong savings operations, in Chapter 4, and for regulated institutions that do and that want to extend them to smaller or more rural depositors, in Chapter 5.

Part II considers the building blocks of viable and valued services: market research, products, delivery channels, pricing, and promotion. After walking through the process of developing a new product in Chapter 6, we consider, in Chapter 7, how different types of products work for clients and institutions and some guidelines for choosing the mix of products offered. Chapter 8 looks at a variety of ways that institutions deliver services, their advantages and disadvantages, and where each might be most appropriate. Chapter 9 guides us through the process of setting interest rates and fees; it helps determine what is possible and what will best serve our interests. Chapter 10 gives pointers for developing a promotional strategy. Throughout Part II cases from a range of countries and institutions bring our guidelines to life.

Part III looks at how to manage risks and achieve high productivity—tasks that are essential to protect the deposits of the poor and the viability of our institutions. Chapter 11 explores managing the risks of fraud, theft, and mismanagement.

Chapters 12 and 13 consider how to manage liquidity risk and interest-rate risk. We examine how to assess our costs and efficiency in Chapter 14, and in Chapter 15 how to design an incentive scheme to improve the productivity of our staff. Each chapter provides simple tools to help with these tasks.

The book is intended as a reference guide for two sets of readers. The first are senior managers, board members, and technical-assistance providers who are directly involved in savings operations. This group should be interested in the entire book. The second group includes donors, regulators, and other policymakers whose work can make or break these efforts. These readers may be most interested in Chapters 1 through 5, which introduce the key financial and operational issues; Chapters 7 and 8, which explore appropriate services; and Chapters 11 through 13, which lay out the bottom-line requirements for keeping deposits safe. Chapters 1, 8, and 10—on the market for savings, delivery channels, and promotion, respectively—should be interesting to anyone concerned with financial services for poor and rural markets.

The book includes over forty cases that should be of interest to any reader. They provide valuable insights into the practical issues involved in mobilizing deposits from the perspective of a wide variety of institutions: large and small; savings-led and credit-led; state, commercial, and not-for-profit; those with broad outreach and those focused on poor or rural markets. Each case relates a particular institution's experience relative to a topic covered in the text, for example, the institutional challenges of developing savings operations, the use of ATMs to move down market, pricing, or managing a liquidity crisis.

The types of institutions toward which the book is directed face different sets of challenges. The first type—institutions that are already serving a "micro" market and wish to develop serious savings operations—must manage the shift from being credit-led to savings-led. This complex challenge is bigger than simply developing new products and adapting some management systems; it fundamentally changes an MFI. If the MFI is responsive to the market and vigilant about security, the sheer volume and growth in savings transactions can quickly dwarf its credit operations.[12] Furthermore, while managing the costs of savings is much easier if an MFI attracts large as well as small depositors, attracting large depositors requires fundamental changes in operations and culture. Chapter 4 describes these changes. With the exception of Chapter 5, the rest of the book is also relevant to institutions initiating or strengthening savings operations.

Institution of the second type—regulated financial institutions that already have strong savings operations and want to extend these to smaller or more rural depositors—already have the technical skills to manage financial intermediation. To succeed in going further down market, they typically need to develop ways to deliver services that are more convenient and cost less than their existing delivery channels. They will probably need to adjust their staffing, products, promotion, and management systems as well. Chapter 5 provides an overview of these changes, while the details are found in Chapters 3, 7, 8, 10, 11, and 15.

As noted above, serving poor and rural depositors often requires different services, staff, and management systems than serving higher-income urban markets. Guidance that is specific to serving poor and rural markets can be found in the final sections of Chapters 3, 4, and 7, much of Chapter 8, and sections of Chapters 11 and 12.

ENABLING SAVINGS MOBILIZATION: THE ROLE OF POLICYMAKERS AND DONORS

Although our book focuses on issues that managers can control, the success of savings initiatives is also strongly affected by the legal and regulatory environment. Interest rate caps on loans can make it impossible to invest savings at an interest rate that covers costs. High reserve requirements also make it difficult to generate sufficient revenues. In government institutions political interference in the lending process can lead to high default rates, while the lack of accountable results-oriented operations can make it difficult to achieve a sufficient volume of deposits. These policies and practices gravely threaten the viability of savings operations.

Other regulations that are intended to provide security can place services out of reach of rural and poor savers. High capital adequacy requirements make it difficult to establish small institutions that can serve more rural areas. Similarly, requiring branches to transact only in the office, have a strong room, or employ dual controls in traditional ways can make it impossible to employ some of the delivery channels we discussed above: mobile units, small offices, and deposit collectors. If meeting regulations puts services out of the reach of poor and rural depositors, then these depositors are left to save in the informal sector. This can be considerably less secure than saving with a mobile unit, small office, or formal-sector collector. Policymakers will serve poor and rural markets well by carefully considering how to balance providing security against providing access (see Chapter 2). And, they will serve all depositors by assuring that policies and practices enable savings operations to be viable.

Donors can also powerfully help—or hinder—savings operations. The soft loans that donors often provide can make it less attractive for a financial institution to mobilize deposits; if funding the loan portfolio with subsidized credit is cheaper than funding it with savings, then the MFI may have no place to profitably invest deposits. On the other hand, donors can help develop sound savings operations by providing technical assistance grants, helping strengthen prudential regulations and supervision, sponsoring exchange visits to institutions that successfully mobilize deposits, and supporting market research.[13] Investing in infrastructure, either technological, such as a national switch system, or physical, such as a rural branch network, can be key to jumpstarting savings mobilization in rural areas.[14] Finally, by supporting a range of institutions and delivery channels, donors can help extend services to poor and rural markets.

THE NEXT FRONTIER

We know how to reach large numbers of small savers. Our challenge now is to extend these services—on a massive scale—to poor and rural markets. To start, we need cheap and secure ways to deliver services that work for the poor. From savings groups in Mexico to collectors in Nepal, numerous institutions are leading the way. With their unconventional banking practices, these pioneers are pushing the "frontier of finance" to poorer and more rural markets.[15] Isn't this what microfinance is about?

Notes

[1] Robert Peck Christen, Richard Rosenberg, and Veena Jayadeva, "Financial Institutions with a 'Double Bottom Line': Implications for the Future of Microfinance," CGAP Occasional Paper No. 8 (Washington, DC: CGAP, 2004): 1, 5.

[2] Postal savings banks are the "heavy hitters." They hold nearly four-fifths of the accounts; microfinance institutions and state banks each hold about one-sixth. Although data for non-postal savings banks are not available, these institutions might hold another 150 million accounts. Of all these "alternative financial institutions," microfinance institutions probably serve the lowest-income clientele.

[3] These standards are discussed in Chapter 2.

[4] Monique Sebstad and Jennefer Cohen, *Microfinance, Risk Management, and Poverty* (Washington, DC: CGAP, 2001), 23, 27, 109–11. See also, Hege Gulli and Marguerite Berger, "Microfinance and Poverty Reduction—Evidence from Latin America," *Small Enterprise Development* 10, no. 3 (1999): 16–18; David Hulme, "Client Exits (Dropouts) from East African MicroFinance Institutions" (Nairobi: *MicroSave*, 1999); Sergio Navajas et al., "Microfinance and the Poorest of the Poor: Theory and Evidence from Bolivia," *World Development* 28, no. 2 (1999): 333–46; Hans D. Seibel, "Grameen Replicators: Do They Reach the Poor and Are They Sustainable?" Arbeitsstelle fur Entwicklungslanderforschung (AEF) Working Paper No. 1998–8 (Cologne: AEF, 1988).

[5] One version of this argument states that people who are not economically active cannot make use of financial services and should receive direct aid. This would make sense if the argument did not blur the distinction between this typically small segment of the population—people who are truly destitute—and the massive numbers of economically active poor whose incomes are small and unreliable.

[6] We avoid the term *extreme poor* for two reasons: First, it is sometimes used to refer to the destitute and other times is used to refer to the poor. Second, the word *extreme* connotes "outside of the mainstream" or "marginal." Confusing the poor with the destitute and calling them extreme makes it easier—though not correct—to dismiss them as a focus for mainstream microfinance.

[7] For a number of these studies, see Dale W. Adams and Delbert Fitchett, eds., *Informal Finance in Low-income Countries* (Boulder, CO: Westview Press, 1992). For some thinking on their significance, see Fritz J. A. Bouman, "Rotating and Accumulating Savings and Credit Associations: A Development Perspective," in *World Development* 23, no. 3 (1995): 371–84.

[8] Graham A. N. Wright and Leonard Mutesasira, "Relative Risk to the Savings of Poor People," in *Regulation: The Conventional View v. Poor People's Reality* (Nairobi: MicroSave, 2000), 6.

[9] Some microfinance practitioners argue that the chief obstacle is that the poor need more than financial services. Indeed, greater market access, business acumen, and skills may be necessary to increase their incomes significantly. But didn't we microfinance thinkers reject several years back the notion that microfinance was simply for microenterprises? Promises to donors that microfinance is the solution to poverty notwithstanding, financial services play not just a "promotional role"—increasing the incomes of the poor—but, just as important, a "protectional role," protecting them during harder times. Financial services enable people, *especially* poor people, to accumulate small sums to meet life's demands. See David Hulme and Paul Mosley, *Finance against Poverty* (London: Routledge, 1996), 1:106–7; Jean P. Druze and Amartya K. Sen, *Hunger and Public Action* (Oxford, UK: Clarendon Press, 1989), 60–61; and Stuart Rutherford, Chapter 1 herein.

[10] These market survey findings are summarized in Madeline Hirschland, "Opportunity International Bank of Malawi Microsavings Strategy," consultancy report (2003): 28–31.

[11] "Micro and Small Enterprise Finance: Guiding Principles for Selecting and Supporting Intermediaries" (Washington, DC: Committee of Donor Agencies for Small Enterprise Development and Donors' Working Group on Financial Sector Development, 1995).

[12] Marguerite S. Robinson, "Introducing Savings Mobilization in Microfinance Programs: When and How?" CGAP Focus Note 8 (1995), in *Are You Really Ready? The Potential Pitfalls of Savings Mobilisation* (Nairobi, Kenya: MicroSave, n.d.), 2.

[13] Dale Adams, "Filling the Deposit Gap in Microfinance," in *Best Practices in Savings Mobilization: November 5–6, 2002, Washington, D.C.* (Madison, WI: WOCCU, n.d.): 5–6.

[14] The governments of India and China have invested heavily in developing an infrastructure of rural branches. As a result, postal and state banks in these two countries hold fully half of the 570 million savings accounts cited at the beginning of this chapter.

[15] J. D. Von Pischke, *Finance at the Frontier* (Washington DC: World Bank, 1991).

PART I
OVERVIEW

1

Why Do the Poor Need Savings Services?

What They Get and What They Might Like

Stuart Rutherford

> *Money . . . is equally important to those who have it and those who don't.*
>
> —JOHN KENNETH GALBRAITH

This book is about adding *voluntary savings* to the money management services provided to poor people by microfinance institutions (MFIs).

The case for introducing voluntary savings, as for any other service, must convince us that two desirable outcomes are likely. First, it must show that the new service will be good for poor clients, making it easier for them to manage their money by expanding the range of financial intermediation options open to them. Second, it must show that the new service will be good for the MFIs, expanding their market among the poor, allowing them to do more business, profitably, with a larger number and broader range of clients. This introductory chapter provides reasons for believing that such market conditions exist, that is, that poor people's demand for savings services is substantial, and that the opportunities for MFIs to respond are large.

Voluntary savings should be understood in the context of why poor people need microfinance services and how they use them. The chapter begins, therefore, by reminding us of the fundamental role of savings in the lives of the poor. It then describes some of the informal microfinance services and devices that

The author is grateful to Dale Adams for his valuable comments, and to Daryl Collins for providing data from the South Africa Financial Diaries project.

have evolved to serve the poor, drawing attention to the way they work, how they respond to poor people's needs and wishes, and the key role played in them by savings.

The volume of financial transactions carried out by poor people in the informal sector is, we shall see, huge. But so far, MFIs, despite being generally more reliable and more secure than the informal sector, have managed to gain only a small foothold in this vast market. By learning from the informal sector and by delivering services, including voluntary savings, that are more convenient and better suited to poor people, MFIs have a wonderful opportunity to expand their work, to the benefit of themselves as well as their clients.

People who are not themselves poor are often skeptical about the poor's ability to save. It seems natural to argue that "poor people have barely enough money to survive—how can they possibly save?" In fact, for the poor, saving is crucial; they save because they must.

Indeed, their need to save may be even more urgent than for the not-so-poor. This is because their incomes are small (and often irregular and unreliable) and are spent almost immediately on basic survival—items like food, water, and cooking fuel—with the result that they suffer more often than the rest of us from being short of cash to buy anything else. So, when they need to pay for births, marriages, and deaths, or for education and health care, or for clothing or shelter, or when they need to recover from a storm or a drought or a fire or a theft or an accident, or when they want to buy some land, or set up a business, or make themselves more comfortable with a fan or a TV—they just don't have the money on hand.

When this happens, there are three common outcomes. One is that they go without. This may be merely inconvenient or it may be devastating. If the breadwinner's TB can't be cured because there's no money for treatment, he may be unable to go on working. The family's income drops sharply, perhaps to the point where family members don't even have enough to eat. This is the "vulnerability" of the poor that development economists describe. Poverty, as they say, is "dynamic"—it can happen suddenly, even to households that appeared to be doing well and pulling themselves out of poverty.

The second outcome is that the family may sell off its assets to raise the money. This may be better than going without, but it has obvious disadvantages. The assets that a family owns may be both few and vital to survival. Once sold, they may be extremely difficult to replace.

THE FINANCIAL SERVICES TRICK

But there's a third outcome. If you can't pay for something you urgently need out of today's resources, because you've spent all your current income, then you may be able to pay for it out of yesterday's income or out of tomorrow's income (or some mixture of the two). Financial services and devices make this trick possible—

the trick of paying for something *now* out of past or future income. Indeed, doing that trick is the main task of financial services from the perspective of the poor user. The trick depends on saving.

Paying for something out of past income is easily understood. It means you've successfully stored some savings somewhere and can now retrieve and spend them. In idiomatic English we say you have successfully "saved up."

Paying for something out of future income means that you need someone to give you an advance now against savings that you resolve to make in the future—I call this "saving down" (see Figure 1–1). A simpler word for such advances is, of course, a loan. But calling loans "advances against future savings" makes an important point: loans depend on savings. Taking a loan involves a promise to save some future income and thereby repay the loan. Nobody will give you a loan until they have extracted this promise from you. Often, they secure themselves against the risk that you'll break the promise by asking for collateral in some form.

Figure 1–1.

saving up: converting a series of savings into a usefully large lump sum
$$ \$\$\ \$\$\$ \quad \$\$\ \$\$\$\$ \quad \$\$\ \$\ \$\ \$\$\$\$ $$

time >

saving down: getting a usefully large lump sum as an advance against future savings

$$ \$\$\ \$\$\$ \quad \$\$\ \$\$\$\$ \quad \$\$\ \$\ \$\$\$\$\$ $$

So the poor *need* to save. But *can* they and *do* they? A brief review of informal financial services and devices should convince us that they do—in numerous ways. The features of these informal methods may suggest ways to design MFI services that meet their needs. What I have written in the following section is not hearsay; it is grounded in my own conversations over twenty-five years with thousands of poor people. Many of them live in South and Southeast Asia, and East Africa, but readers can find plenty of evidence in the literature[1] that what is described here is common around the world, and has been for generations.

Poor people universally try to *save at home*, in clay piggy banks, inside hollow bamboo sticks, tucked between roof sheets, buried in the earth, or sewn into pockets in petticoats. This is because, if you want to save, it helps if you can store these savings in *any amount*, at *any time*, *close by*, and *at no other cost*—things for us to bear in mind. But depositing the savings is one thing; keeping them there is another. These home banks are often too easy to withdraw from. Only too soon the men folk get at the cash for a night out, or your mother-in-law wheedles it out of you, or the children irresistibly demand candies or need cough medicine, or friends, relatives, and neighbors come with bad-luck stories—or it's just plain stolen or lost. So home savings score high for convenience of deposit, but very low for discipline and security.

TRY IT WITH A PARTNER

Neighbors can help. They can act as *money guards*. If I'm looking after a little of your money, it is much easier for me to resist spending it and to stop my family from spending it than if it were my own money. It makes sense, then, for you to hold some of my cash and for me to hold some of yours. Poor neighbors all over the world do this service for each other, with the result that "money guarding" is often indistinguishable from *interest-free lending and borrowing*, sometimes referred to as *reciprocal lending* because its users at one time lend to, and at another time borrow from, their neighbors and relatives. When I store my $5 with you, I don't mind much if you use the money, just as long as I can get it back from you when I need it or on the date that we agreed. These casual arrangements are extremely common and extremely convenient but, alas, they are not always reliable—as we shall see later.

In many parts of the world a more organized system flourishes. People set themselves up as professional money managers and charge for their services. *Deposit collectors* of this sort are common in West Africa, for example, where they collect savings on a daily basis and return the amount collected at the end of the month, minus one day's savings that the deposit collector keeps as his or her charge. Variations on this theme are found elsewhere. By paying for this service poor people demonstrate the value they place on a *secure* and *reliable* place to save; after all, they are accepting a negative rate of interest on their savings, something they obviously wouldn't do if they had good alternatives. A housewife in an Indian slum, with three school-age children and a casually employed laborer for a husband, knows she needs $10 next July to pay for school fees and books or she won't be able to keep the kids in school. If someone offers to take a few cents from her each day and then give it all back in July, she will gladly pay for such a service.

A similar service is provided by professional *moneylenders*. In many slums around the world you'll find poor people with scruffy bits of card ruled into a grid of cells, with some of the cells checked off. Depending on where you are, these may be the informal passbooks of the local deposit collector or of the local moneylender. In either case the process is the same. Someone comes each day (or each week, or whatever) and collects a few cents from you and marks your card to show you've paid. If it's a deposit collector's card, then you're saving up for a lump sum later. If it's a moneylender's card, then you've already had the lump sum and you are now "saving down" to repay it.

Deposit collectors and moneylenders offer a *local* service: poor people who would never think of traveling to a bank to deposit their small sums will happily give a few cents to someone who calls at their home or work place. As well as being small, the sums that deposit collectors and urban moneylenders collect are often *equal, frequent,* and *regular.* Each of these characteristics helps the saver to save either by making the savings convenient (the small size and frequency of the savings and the proximity of the service) or disciplined (the fixed values and regular daily or weekly paydays). Fixed values and regular intervals also help to keep the bookkeeping simple for both parties.

Many poor people, though, especially the irregularly employed, find equal-sized regular payments difficult. Their preferred moneylender is not a professional who visits them regularly, but a better-off neighbor—perhaps a retired schoolteacher or a prosperous farmer or trader—who will give them a casual *loan on interest* but will accept *irregular repayments.* The motive for such lenders may be their own desire to save—to get spare cash out of their hands so that they're not tempted to spend it. Indeed, one of the weaknesses of the informal sector is that it provides few reliable opportunities to invest financially, so villagers and slum dwellers with cash surpluses that they don't want to turn into goods may well choose to place them with a neighbor who will be willing to pay a return on the capital.

IN GROUPS

Other devices involve multiple contracts within a group of people. The simplest we can call *saving-up clubs.* In these, members agree to save cash more or less regularly until a specified date (often an expensive religious festival), whereupon the fund is released and returned to the depositors in time to buy food, presents, or whatever else the occasion demands. In these clubs the deposits remain the exclusive property of the depositor, and the group is used as a force for *discipline.* It is much easier to save regularly and to delay taking savings back until the time for doing so has come if everyone else is doing so. You feel shamed if you don't follow suit. It is much easier, for example, than saving at home.

But while the fund is building up, why not let some of the participants borrow it on a short-term basis? If this is done, then we have a savings-and-loan club, now usually referred to in the literature as an *ASCA* (accumulating savings and credit association). This is a truly group-based device, since it consists of a set of agreements among all the participants that allows some of them to save down while at the same time all of them are saving up and earning interest. Because ASCAs offer so many options, it is not surprising that the ASCA idea has evolved over time into elegant and sometimes big and powerful formal institutions, of which successful *credit unions* are the best example.

Poor people can run successful ASCAs, but they also get into trouble with them, because they need a certain amount of record keeping, hard for the illiterate poor to do. Indeed, credit unions mostly serve the educated upper poor or the middle classes. The need for the bookkeeping arises from the fact that different members of the ASCA behave in different ways. Some borrow and some don't, and those who borrow may borrow different amounts of money on different dates for different periods. If they pay interest on their loans, as is the case in many ASCAs, the amounts have to be individually calculated and then shared out fairly among the group as a whole.

A device that pooled savings but did away with these complexities might be easier to manage. This is what the *ROSCA* (rotating savings and credit association) does. Poor people may be more intensively and more successfully involved in ROSCAs than in ASCAs. In a ROSCA everyone in the group deposits the same amount of money at the same interval; each time, the whole amount is given to one member. When there have been as many distributions as there are members, the ROSCA ends. Everyone has put in and taken out the same amount. For example, ten of us each put $10 a week on the table, and each week for ten weeks one of us walks away with $100.

ROSCAs are easy to manage, and very cheap—no fees, no interest charges. But what's the point? What's the point of my putting $100 in and taking $100 out? Where's my benefit? And how can that benefit outweigh the time and trouble of coming to the meeting and the risk that some other member may cheat me by running away as soon as he has received his lump sum? For the hundreds of thousands of ROSCAs that are operating around the world at any one time, the point is, of course, the opportunity to save small amounts and turn these into a usefully large lump sum. The very fact that a ROSCA does nothing other than this is the strongest evidence of just how important saving is for the countless poor users of ROSCAs.

Are these informal saving devices handling only trivial amounts of money? Certainly not. The evidence is that huge amounts of money are transacted in this way every day in the world's slums and villages, because these devices are a vital part of life for the poor households that use them.[2]

We will look briefly at the results from one recent piece of research.[3] In Bangladesh, in India, and in South Africa, a number of households in villages and slums, almost all poor but with a few middle-income, non-poor households deliberately included, were carefully tracked for a year to discover the type and value of their financial transactions, that is, their savings and withdrawings and borrowings and lendings and repayments (hence the novelty of the study). The aim was to get a systematic view of the patterns of use of financial services and devices over a full year. Results from the study show that their use is intensive and in aggregate of high value.

There were forty-two households in the Bangladesh study (half rural, half urban), and among them in the year they used twenty-seven different types of informal services and devices, like the ones reviewed in the previous section. Some devices were used by almost all households—saving at home, of course, but also interest-free lending and borrowing. Other heavily used devices included private interest-bearing loans, money guarding, saving-up clubs, and ASCAs.

On average, each household began a fresh use of one or other of these devices twenty-six times during the year, an average of one every two weeks. The amounts of cash flowing through these systems was anything but trivial. On average, each household handled US$713 in the year; that is, US$713 in cash flowed out into savings or as repayments on loans or flowed in as retrievals of saving or as loans. This sum is about 40 percent of annual per household income in Bangladesh,[4] or perhaps 75 percent of average annual income for poor households. In other words, these households were pushing or pulling three-quarters of their income through the informal money market. In South Africa the informal-sector devices handled an average of US$2,252 from each poor household over the course of the year— three-fifths of its income.

No one was doing it for fun. As the study went along, the views of the participating households were recorded. Almost all expressed a dislike for engaging in such transactions but claimed that there is no way to manage without them, a point we suggested earlier in our dry analysis of the financial consequences of poverty. The dislike arises largely from the *unreliability* and *uncertainty* that bedevils informal financial devices. It wasn't that they were cheated—there were few reports of that—but that they never knew if and when you would be able to transact. People may or may not lend to you, and if they do, they may or may not lend enough. The neighbor may not return your savings when you need it. The ROSCA may work—or it may fail and leave you scrambling to get your cash back. Coping with all these disadvantages requires constant hard work and carries the danger of social friction—quarreling, name calling, reputation sullying.[5]

Despite this, the market is huge. Using these forty-two households as a guide, and calculating the population of Bangladesh at 115 million, of whom 60 percent are poor, the market in informal finance in Bangladesh may be as large at US$10.4 billion annually.[6]

In Bangladesh alone, then, an undeveloped market worth an estimated US$10.4 billion a year is crying out for more reliable operators—a market of poor people, for whom MFIs are the specialist providers. What a prospect for the MFIs!

THE MFIS

Poor people use MFIs in increasing numbers. How do MFI services compare with the informal systems we have been reviewing? Since MFI work is becoming more and more diverse, let us answer that question by confining ourselves to the classic and still largest schemes expressly designed for poor people, schemes based on the principles popularized by the Grameen Bank and by Village Banking. Compared to the majority of other MFIs, these schemes bring services closer to poor people's doorsteps and require smaller payments. Studies find that, compared to other MFIs, they often reach a larger portion of poorer clients. Such schemes offer poor people, usually organized into groups, loans that are repaid in a series of small (often weekly) repayments over a period of up to a year. In other words, they offer a saving-down service remarkably similar to that of the slum moneylenders that we met a few pages back. They allow their members to compress up to a year's worth of weekly savings into a single large lump sum taken as an advance.

Such schemes are hugely and deservedly popular. MFI loans score in three important ways over those of slum moneylenders: they are much cheaper, they tend to give bigger (and rising) advances, and perhaps most crucial, they are (usually) much more *reliable*. As with deposit collectors and slum moneylenders, once you get into the rhythm of saving $2 every week and getting back a useful $100 every year, it is in your best interest, and that of the MFI, to go on doing it cycle after cycle. It is a wonderfully convenient, disciplined, and reliable way to package tiny savings into usefully large sums.

THE VIRTUES OF COMPULSION

In addition to offering saving-down or loan services, the classic microfinance schemes usually require people to do some saving up in order to join and take a loan. Typically, MFI members in schemes of this sort deposit a small fixed saving amount at each weekly meeting.[7] An average member may take a loan from the MFI of, say, $100 within a few weeks of joining the scheme, after which the borrower must carry to each weekly meeting perhaps $2 in loan repayments, 25 cents in loan interest payments, and only 10 cents in savings deposits. These compulsory deposits cannot be retrieved when the member wishes. In some schemes they can be drawn down in part under certain conditions; in others they are locked in until the member leaves the scheme (with all loans fully repaid).

As an adjunct to the loans, this system has made good sense for MFIs. It has provided some real security against loans that are otherwise secured only by the solidarity of the group. Security of this sort is increasingly welcome as MFIs struggle to maintain the quality of their loan portfolios in the face of growing MFI competition. The security arises from the fact that although the weekly savings deposit is very small, compulsion and illiquidity work together so that after some years an individual member's savings balance becomes large relative to the value of the member's current loan. The aggregate value of such small compulsory savings can in time grow to become an important part of the MFI's loan fund. In some of the older schemes, for example, the compulsory savings holdings are as much as one-third or even one-half of loan outstanding balances.

From the point of view of the typical MFI member, these compulsory savings may be regarded simply as part of the price of borrowing.[8] Many poor people in schemes I have visited in South and Southeast Asia and East Africa have told me that. It is borne out by their tendency to merge the savings in with the loan repayments and see both together as their weekly "bill" for the loans. Nevertheless, when members do finally leave the MFI, they are often very pleased to find that their compulsory savings have, over time, built up to a substantial and very useful sum. This remains true even if one of the commonest uses for these savings is to pay down the last MFI loan. So, compulsory savings serve MFIs well and are not unacceptable to their clients.

THE CASE FOR VOLUNTARY SAVINGS

But this book makes the case for voluntary savings services. Voluntary savings services are those in which the customer is not obliged to save as part of a contract for some other financial service, such as a loan. The client exercises choice over whether or not to save, and, when a variety of savings schemes are offered, over the timing and amount of savings and withdrawals. Voluntary savings services include but are not the same as "open access" savings (where customers can gain access to their savings whenever they like), since savers may deliberately choose savings instruments that tie up their savings for a period of time. This "illiquidity preference" we have met already; it drives the bargain that poor people make with deposit collectors and money guards and lies behind the solemn undertakings made to each other by members of savings-up clubs.

But why should MFIs offer voluntary savings services to poor people? The strongest of many reasons is because there is a strong demand for them. Finding a way to meet this demand will allow MFIs to greatly expand their business with the poor.

As it happens, the villages and slums where the IDPM research was carried out are areas of intensive coverage by Bangladeshi MFIs, including several of the biggest and most widely known. This gives us an opportunity to make direct comparisons between the informal devices and the MFIs.

In terms of reaching the households, these MFIs have already done well. Like the informal services and devices, the MFIs offer *proximity;* they go to the villages and do their banking work within walking distance of the homes of their customers, and their customers like it. No fewer than thirty out of the forty-two households contained MFI members.[9] This puts MFIs up there with saving at home, informal lending, money guards, and ASCAs as among the most familiar systems.[10] Of these thirty MFI households, all were using the MFI compulsory savings system, and twenty-three took or were holding loans during the research year.

The MFIs are also doing well in terms of reliability—a key area, as we have seen. Although there were some complaints that MFIs promised loans that they didn't deliver, many respondents remarked that MFIs are generally consistent and reliable in their behavior, relative to other partners. This was rewarded with consistent behavior toward the MFIs on the part of the MFI members, many of whom were making their weekly MFI payments regularly while at the same time making excuses to other financial partners. So far so good.

But the MFI's share of business was a minority one. Measured as a share of the value of transactions, MFIs were found to have handled just under 14 percent of all the transaction value recorded in the study, or just over 19 percent of the transaction values of the thirty respondent households with MFI membership. An average of US$249 flowed in the year between the MFIs and each of their thirty members, whereas, as we have seen, each household was, on average, conducting US$740 of transactions in the year in the informal sector *in addition* to anything they were doing with the MFIs (the average transaction value for all forty-two households including the formal and semi-formal sectors was US$918).

In terms of their share of all arrangements, MFIs had an even lower profile. Of all the financial contracts reported in the study, MFIs handled 10 percent. Their share among upper poor and poor households was even lower, at 7 percent—and this in an area where MFIs compete heavily.[11]

Why should this be so? Why should poor households choose to do more business each year in the informal market, a market they find distastefully unreliable, when they have access to the much more reliable MFIs? The answers that the households gave to this question can be easily summarized—what the MFIs offer, good though it is, meets only a part of the households' financial needs.

Of the twenty-three poor and very poor households in the study,[12] sixteen enjoyed MFI membership, while seven didn't. All those who hadn't joined MFIs gave the same basic reason for not joining: the fixed weekly or monthly payments over a yearlong period would be either impossible or very difficult to meet. The same comments came from several households who had joined MFIs; three of them managed their MFI loans exclusively by "on-lending" them to others who had the capacity to meet the strict repayment schedules. The same ambivalence that we noticed in the informal sector when we compared professional and casual moneylenders is true of MFIs: to those who have the capacity to make them, regular, equal payments helpfully offer a disciplined way to save up or pay down loans, but for others less well placed they stand in the way of using the service at all.[13]

Thus the *frequency*, the *amounts*, and the *terms* of the services offered by MFIs are the keys to understanding why they have captured only a small part of the business among the poor and very poor. The IDPM findings suggest, for example, that 96 percent of all financial deals entered into by the poor and very poor were worth less than US$100, while the average value of the MFI loans explored in the study was US$131. More than half of all deals struck by poor and very poor people were for less than US$10. Overwhelmingly, deals in the informal sector are short-term; typically, small sums are deposited or lent or borrowed and then returned within a month or two. And the poorer the household, the more likely it is that the deals will have highly flexible payment terms. For example, only one-third of all transactions made by poor and very poor households were made within systems that required regular equal payments, and of that one-third almost 75 percent is accounted for by their relations with MFIs.

To do more business with the poor, MFIs will have to find ways to capture more of their savings, whether they are saving up or saving down. To do so, they will have to broaden their range of products and match the convenience of the informal sector. They will have to make it easier for the poor to save with MFIs by accepting savings more frequently, in a greater range of values, and in values that vary over time. They will have to allow poor clients to turn savings into the sums they need more frequently and in a greater range of values (including small sums) than at present. And they will have to offer secure and profitable investment opportunities for their lump sums once they have been built up. Some of this can be done by more and better loan products, such as short-term emergency loans, overdrafts, and lines of credit. But much of it will have to be done with some form or other of voluntary savings account.

Can MFIs do this? Should they? Can it be done safely? Can it be done in ways that promise more profits or more sustainable access to loanable funds? Or are savings services for the poor inherently uneconomical for professional service providers like MFIs? In looking for models, should MFIs turn to the rich tradition of formal banking and find out how the Units of the Bank Rakyat Indonesia captured so many millions of dollars of poor peoples' savings, or how Peru's Caja Municipales and Kenya's Equity Bank—to take just two more recent examples— have learned how to understand the savings needs of their poorer clients? Perhaps the credit union system, rooted as it is in informal practices, offers good guidance; look, for example, at how the Caisses Villageoises d'Epargne et de Crédit Autogérées are developing systems for remote rural members in the Pays Dogon district of Mali. Can voluntary savings services easily be introduced alongside traditional MFI lending practices—as many followers of Village Banking and of Grameen methodology (including Grameen itself, with Grameen II) are now trying to do on at least three continents? Or should we step out on new paths, as *Safe*Save has in the urban context of the slums of Dhaka with its combination of daily collection services and highly flexible savings and loan products?

Whatever is tried, what advice can be given on how to go about it? How should practitioners research, design, and deliver products, market them, expand them, manage their costs, and make them safe? These are some of the fascinating issues that are explored in this book.

Notes

[1] The late Fritz Bouman (who coined the terms *ROSCA* and *ASCA*) was a pioneer observer of how poor people manage their money. References to his work and that of many others researching the money management behavior of poor people worldwide can be found at www.gdrc.org.

[2] Informal finance is also responsible for a large share of international and interregional financial flows, in the form of the remittances that migrant workers send home from abroad or from centers of employment in their own countries, often through informal channels. In many countries, such as Mexico, the volume of these flows far exceeds the transactions carried out through MFIs (Dale Adams, in correspondence with the editor). Such remittance money is further evidence that the poor save instinctively, given the opportunity to do so.

[3] The research was done in 2000 as part of the Finance and Development project executed by IDPM (Institute for Development Policy and Management at the University

of Manchester, UK) for DFID ([UK] Department for International Development). Dr. David Hulme of IDPM managed the research from Manchester, and Stuart Rutherford supervised its execution in Bangladesh. Orlanda Ruthven and Sushil Kumar supervised a parallel study in India the same year. Further description can be found on the IDPM website at www.man.ac.uk/idpm. The South Africa Financial Diaries research was directed by Daryl Collins at SALDRU (Southern Africa Labour and Development Research Unit) at the University of Cape Town from 2003 to 2004 (see the www.cssr.uct.ac.za website).

⁴ This assumes per capita income at US$380 and average household size of five.

⁵ Informal finance has other weaknesses, some of which—such as the shortage of reliable opportunities to make long-term financial investments—are noted elsewhere in this chapter. Dale Adams, in correspondence with the author and editor, notes other key weaknesses: high transaction costs in some schemes, lack of safety for deposits, and the indivisibility of some forms of saving (especially saving in kind). For more on the risks of informal savings, especially in Africa, see the *MicroSave* website (www.microsave.org).

⁶ Both the Indian and South African studies arrived at similar broad conclusions: the financial life of the poor is rich and complex but rarely ideal.

⁷ In some schemes a part of the loan (often 5 percent) is deducted at source and saved in the name of the member or the group.

⁸ Standard MFI accounting practice recommends that compulsory savings be factored into the calculation of the interest rate on loans.

⁹ One Dhaka slum woman had managed to join seven MFIs.

¹⁰ MFIs, however, are not the most *used*, since, as we shall see, the number and value of transactions made with MFIs in the year was much lower than those made using many of the informal devices.

¹¹ Similarly, the South Africa and India studies found that the households in the study, particularly the poorer ones, transact much more heavily in the informal sector than with formal and semi-formal institutions. In South Africa the poor households were using informal devices for two-thirds of their financial transactions.

¹² There were six non-poor, thirteen upper poor, and twenty-three poor or very poor households in the study.

¹³ Similarly, poor South African households noted that they like informal devices because they are flexible when problems arise. Furthermore, banked funds, although safe, are too far away when emergencies arise.

2

Prerequisites
for Intermediating Savings

Katharine McKee

The first chapter of this book presented compelling reasons for providing voluntary savings services. This chapter addresses one fundamental question: what conditions must an institution meet in order to offer these services? Mobilizing small deposits requires more stringent standards than managing small loans for one reason, above all else: while credit funds come from investors, lenders, donors, or MFIs, deposits belong to the poor. This alone compels institutions to consider mobilizing deposits only if their capacity and governance are clearly up to the task.

For credit-only institutions, mobilizing deposits should be approached with great caution. To be profitable, mobilized deposits must usually be lent out, a process called financial intermediation. Managing financial intermediation is typically much more complex than managing credit (or savings) alone. Keeping assets well matched with liabilities is a complex balancing act—and losing this balance puts the institution's operating funds and equity at risk. To add to this challenge, liquid deposit products—products that allow withdrawals at any time—typically involve less predictable transactions than credit. This unpredictability heightens the risk of fraud, mismanagement, and illiquidity.

Furthermore, mobilizing small liquid deposits can be more costly than managing large ones. Services that are not financially viable can undermine an institution's viability. To reiterate, when it comes to savings, unprofitable services, mismanagement, fraud, and illiquidity are extremely serious; they put the savings of the poor at risk.

The author is grateful for the valuable feedback from John Berry, Annica Jansen, and Tulasi Prasad Uprety.

Only some institutions have the capacity, governance, and cost structure directly to provide liquid savings services. This chapter outlines the conditions that must be met in order to offer a new savings service. It then suggests some alternatives by which institutions that do not meet these conditions might still see that their clients have a means to save.

2.1 PRECONDITIONS FOR INTERMEDIATING NEW SAVINGS SERVICE—THE FOUR CIRCLES

A senior manager or board member must ask not whether savings services are important but "should *my* institution undertake a new savings service?" The answer to this question will hinge on the answers to several other questions: Does the new service fit with and add value with respect to our mission? Will it improve our financial performance, strengthen our competitive position, or diversify our risk (through more diverse clients, assets, and liabilities)? Will we be able to manage the new demands on our staff, systems, and financial statements? In all cases an institution that wants to intermediate deposits should meet four minimum conditions.

The preconditions for a yes decision might be visualized as four concentric circles (see Figure 2–1). The inner circle represents client demand—will the services that the institution can offer attract a sufficient volume of deposits? The answer to this question will depend, in part, on whether potential clients trust the institution enough to deposit their savings with it. Managers and board members should proceed only if effective demand is adequate.

The second circle represents the supply side—does the institution have the financial soundness, cost structure, and capacity to successfully manage the new product(s)? *Can* it do so responsibly and well? For the security of both depositors and provider, the institution should be at or close to profitability, and should have stringent credit management, a realistic business plan for ongoing viability, strong systems, sufficient physical security, and management and staff that can manage the new product.

The third circle represents effective governance. Does the institution have an effective board or other governance body that exercises reasonable oversight of the institution, ensures sufficient discipline, and serves as a check on management? *Should* the institution offer savings to its members or the general public? At a minimum the institution should have a board that is sufficiently knowledgeable, sufficiently engaged, and has sufficient powers to be able and willing to step in if management is putting either savers' deposits or the institution's viability at risk. Regardless of the type of institution, the board must serve as the principal safeguard against malfeasance and mismanagement.

Beyond these three circles are other external checks and environmental factors that can increase the likelihood the institution will operate as a disciplined provider of savings services. Ideally, any provider of savings services would be subject

Figure 2–1. Preconditions for Intermediating Savings

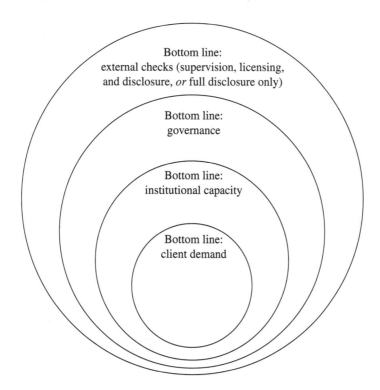

Bottom line:
external checks (supervision, licensing,
and disclosure, *or* full disclosure only)

Bottom line:
governance

Bottom line:
institutional capacity

Bottom line:
client demand

to capable external supervision or, at a minimum, a rigorous licensing process. *However, although supervision and licensing are desirable, their absence should not necessarily prevent an MFI from offering savings services.* The bottom line here is, if it is not supervised by the government, an MFI should protect consumers through plain-language financial disclosures. Thus, the fourth circle requires either supervision and licensing or full disclosure on an ongoing basis.

These four circles represent essential conditions for successfully introducing a new voluntary savings service. They must be high hurdles, with a bias against a quick yes decision based more on wishful thinking than reality. For an MFI, determining whether it can manage savings operations and whether its governance is sufficiently strong will be easier and cost less than conducting market research to see whether there is sufficient effective demand. Therefore, the MFI will consider the second and third circles before it considers the first. The chapter will now examine the circles in the order that the MFI would: internal capacity, governance, client demand, and external checks.

2.2 THE FIRST QUESTION—THE INSTITUTION'S CAPACITY

The first question an MFI needs to answer is, can the institution intermediate savings securely and profitably? This section will examine in detail the capacity that is required to intermediate deposits. First and foremost, it will look at questions of financial viability.

2.2.1. Financial Viability, Now and in the Future

An institution should only offer voluntary savings services if it is at or very close to profitability. Otherwise, the risks to the depositors are unjustifiable. Before adding on savings services, institutions should already be sustainable.

Why should financial viability be a precondition for offering savings services? Above all, financially viable operations provide a minimal but essential assurance that operating costs will not come from clients' deposits. Second, financial viability establishes that the institution will bring a basic competence and efficiency to its operations. An institution is less likely to place poor households' savings at risk if it can competently extend and collect loans on at least a break-even basis.

An institution that intermediates savings must possess and maintain adequate capital to provide a cushion against unanticipated losses, thereby protecting the depositor and the institution. Achieving sustainability enables an institution to build up capital. Adequate reserving against loan losses protects capital. Maintaining overall institutional profitability helps ensure capital adequacy on a going-forward basis. As further protection of capital adequacy, some MFIs may have access to additional capital when needed from investors, liquidity facilities, or other sources.

If deposits are to finance the loan portfolio, rigorous credit management is essential. The most prevalent reason that financial institutions fail is that they cannot collect on the loans they extend. High rates of delinquency quickly spiral into defaults that consume reserves, retained earnings, and other capital. When loan capital comes from donors or banks, the effects for the institution can be devastating enough. When loan capital comes from the deposits of the poor, it is unconscionable. Credit-only institutions should only intermediate deposits if they have a demonstrated history of stringent credit management. The savings of the poor should not be put at risk due to poor portfolio management. Of course, viability and effective portfolio management do not assure that a credit-only MFI will continue to be profitable once it mobilizes deposits.

New savings services must not threaten the institution's future financial viability. This should be demonstrated through realistic, conservative business planning. Savings services need not necessarily cover their own full costs. In many cases credit services cover indirect costs while savings add value in other ways:

by increasing the volume of loanable resources, attracting clients that will generate profits through their use of other services, or helping the institution meet its mission. In any case management and the board should:

- *Be explicit about what level of costs they expect the new savings services to cover by when.* To establish these expectations, management should develop a realistic business plan and contingency plans should assumptions prove too optimistic. Reserves, capital, and operating funds should be sufficient to cover initial operating losses and losses due to catastrophic events. Sources of cross subsidy should be adequate and reliable.
- *Project profitability based on a cost of capital that includes the full administrative, financial, and reserves costs of savings net of fees revenues (from, for example, transaction fees).* Savings operations usually require additional staff, training, and security as well as an upfront investment in market research, product development, physical infrastructure, and new systems development.
- *Have a reasonably secure place to invest its mobilized deposits at a rate that enables the MFI to recover its financial and administrative costs.* Typically, this place is the loan portfolio. However, in competitive environments where subsidized loan capital is abundant, using deposits to fund the portfolio can undermine profitability. Similarly, in many environments MFIs will find that they attract significantly more deposits than they need for loans. This poses a serious challenge to cost recovery that must be addressed up front: prudent investments outside of microfinance such as government treasury bills or fixed deposits in a commercial bank are unlikely to provide a high enough rate of return to recover the high costs of mobilizing small deposits.

The MFI's management and board also must assure that its internal controls, liquidity management, and asset liability management are strong enough that uncontrolled risks do not undermine profitability.

2.2.2 Management Systems

Once an institution starts to intermediate deposits, managing liquidity and balancing assets with liabilities become imperative and demanding. Implementing strong internal controls and instituting a strong internal control environment are also critical. Not doing these tasks well puts deposits and the institution at risk.

Sound management of liquidity and of the asset liability mix is crucial for any institution that aims to intermediate deposits. Either the institution should offer products and terms that nearly eliminate interest rate and liquidity risk, such as short-term loans and fixed deposits with matched terms, or it should have the staff skills, policies, and management systems to manage both properly. For the latter cases this book recommends that, at the very minimum, institutions effectively use the following tools: trend analysis of six basic financial ratios; short-term cash flow forecasting; cash flow budgeting; and analysis of the gap, the net interest margin (NIM), and core deposits (see Chapters 12 and 13).

Ideally, the institution should have a backup source for liquidity, that is, a bank or other liquidity pool that can help it manage external shocks, in particular, co-variant risk in the loan portfolio.[1] However, particularly for small institutions operating in more remote areas, this often is not possible.

To protect depositors and themselves against the risks of fraud, error, and negligence, MFIs must institute a strong internal control environment. Internal controls and internal audits are essential but not sufficient. They will be effective only if they are reinforced by the MFI's culture, policies and procedures, information systems, and training and supervision of staff. Clients' deposits will be secure only if an MFI prioritizes this security as an integral part of its operations (see Chapter 11). This is a function of management and staff.

2.2.3 Management and Staff

The capacity of the institution's personnel is a critical aspect of "getting to yes" on savings mobilization. Does the financial institution have (or can it add) adequate management and other staff to design and launch successful small savings operations? Management must effectively lead the process of analyzing whether to introduce savings or a new savings product, designing and testing the product(s), and developing a business strategy for its delivery. Management must also have the skills to reorient existing staff or recruit and train new staff to interact with clients in new ways. For a credit-only institution, introducing voluntary savings typically requires more and more capable managers and, for large institutions, new and different types of staff (for example, marketing staff, tellers, and internal auditors to ensure effective new internal controls).

Management must also be able to motivate the board and staff to make the significant changes required to provide the new services responsibly and profitably. These changes are not only structural and organizational—they are cultural as well. The best-designed products may fail if clients do not feel comfortable and respected when they deposit and withdraw their savings.

The perception of target clients also drives a final aspect of management capacity. Target clients will only entrust the institution with their hard-earned cash if they perceive its managers to be capable and honest. Clients must also trust that their deposits will be physically safe.

2.2.4 Physical Capacity

The final component of this second circle—institutional capacity—concerns the physical infrastructure required for responsible deposit-taking. Institutions that mobilize deposits must have the physical facilities and security to afford adequate protection and inspire the trust of clients. Institutions that provide office-based services also must have offices that can accommodate large numbers of clients. These clients will make large numbers of transactions. Relative to managing only credit operations, a management information system (MIS) that can handle savings operations often must be able to process an exponentially larger number of transactions. Any institution that intermediates voluntary savings needs an information system, manual or computerized, that provides information that is sufficient, accurate, timely, and transparent. Seeing that this infrastructure is in place is ultimately the responsibility of the board or other governing body.

2.3 THE SECOND QUESTION—EFFECTIVE GOVERNANCE

The second critical precondition is that an appropriate governing body or bodies be in place to oversee the MFI's management. In effect, it should be the board that makes the final judgment as to whether the other preconditions—client demand and institutional capacity—have been met. The governing body must carefully question and analyze the case management makes for moving forward with new savings services. And it is the board that must ensure that the savings activities are implemented in such a way that neither the institution's viability nor the clients' deposits are compromised. The board should be raising and answering questions like these: Are adequate management resources, staff, facilities, systems, and controls in place? How will the board monitor performance of the deposit-taking activities? What are the danger signals that will trigger board intervention to resolve problems while there is still time?

While the board is internal to the MFI, if it is effective, it should perform a critical check on management that is analogous to the discipline imposed from the outside by a regulatory body. Above all, the board should have adequate capacity to analyze the financial statements and audits, review financial projections, and assess financial performance in a thorough and critical fashion. In reality, however, many MFIs, especially those without outside ownership or supervision, are staff-driven—strong management can too easily persuade the board to its viewpoint.

While well-informed, effective governance is essential, ensuring that this condition is met can be problematic. Key stakeholders such as licensing authorities or important donors, or non-prudential measures such as minimum requirements for MFI board members, might make it more likely that the effectiveness of MFI governance is adequately assessed. In any case effective governance and management oversight is a minimum precondition for MFIs to offer voluntary savings. Only if effective management and governance are clearly in place should an MFI consider the demand for savings services.

Some, including most banking regulators, would argue that only for-profit institutions should be permitted to intermediate savings from the public. They would cite two key advantages of for-profits. First, owners may be able to provide additional capital in the form of equity if necessary. Second, as owners with a direct financial interest in the institution's performance, they may have stronger incentives to be proactive in governance.

However, sad experience suggests that for-profit ownership is no guarantee of solvency. Furthermore, credit unions and other non-profit, member-owned institutions around the world have demonstrated their ability to intermediate savings successfully. Well-managed non-profits in some settings also have proven capable of effective governance and intermediation despite the absence of owners. For these reasons the author believes that non-profit organizations should be considered as candidates for offering deposit services if the preconditions described in this chapter have been met. Such an approach offers a pragmatic way to balance the goals of access and protection.

2.4 THE THIRD QUESTION—CLIENT DEMAND

The most fundamental question that managers and boards must ask is this: Is there effective demand? Sensing that existing or prospective clients want services is not enough. Institutions must be reasonably sure that savers will actually step forward and deposit their money at the terms that the institution offers.

Whether prospective clients demand a new product will depend on how they evaluate it relative to their alternatives, which frequently are informal, including gold bangles, building materials, cattle, or other in-kind options. Careful analysis of the prospective product's competition is essential. Will new products fill important gaps in the client's financial landscape? Will the proposed product strike the balance among product features, security, convenience, and price better than competing products?

There are two approaches to answering these bottom-line-demand questions. The first is to find out by offering the product. If loan officers report that clients need a way to save for school fees, managers can develop a school-fee product, backup systems, and training; print up the brochures; and start marketing. Sometimes the institution will guess well and will attract the volume of deposits it wants without many adjustments. In most cases simply offering a product without much up-front analysis is likely to waste money, staff time, and the institution's credibility. Doing so might even compromise the institution's mission or financial soundness.

The more cost-effective approach is to research the market before launching the new product to determine whether there is demand and for which types of products and features (see Chapters 6 and 7). Market research need not cost a lot or consume a great deal of time. In fact, an MFI that does its homework will likely spare itself a great deal of time, expense, and customer ill will. If market research is inconclusive, management may want to conduct a small pilot test and market the product on a limited scale.

Finally, in addition to sufficient institutional capacity, governance, and demand, an MFI should be subject to some external check on its operations.

2.5 EXTERNAL CHECKS

A number of external checks can further protect depositors. These include well-informed creditors or donors that pay attention to the MFI's performance; external audits and ratings; industry performance standards and transparency initiatives; and accreditation, examination, and other self-regulatory mechanisms such as those provided by credit union federations. Licensed, supervised MFIs benefit from more formal checks—the licensing process, prudential and non-prudential norms, and the examination process. Finally, depositors can be protected by deposit insurance or by government ownership or by its implicit backing of institutions, such as state banks, that it will not allow to fail.

All of these factors can help make depositors' savings more secure. Most of them also increase the chance of success, from a business perspective. However, requiring any or all of these external checks—particularly supervision by financial regulators—as a *condition* for an MFI to offer saving services risks placing reasonably safe and convenient savings services beyond the reach of those who need them most.

2.5.1 Should Unregulated MFIs Intermediate Savings?

Microfinance experts hotly debate whether unregulated microfinance institutions should intermediate savings. Two extremely important values are in conflict. On the one hand, many experts argue that intermediation should only be undertaken by institutions that are licensed and well supervised. How can we even consider allowing unregulated MFIs to put at risk the hard-won savings of those who can least afford to lose them? The specter of very poor households losing their life savings when a microfinance NGO fails deeply concerns central bankers, donors, and practitioners alike. This is the principle of *security* or depositor protection.

The principle that often conflicts with protecting savers is optimizing poor people's *access* to relatively safe and convenient savings services. After all, in most countries families in rural areas could be waiting a very long time before a licensed, well-supervised bank sets up shop nearby. The typical government requirements to open new bank branches—for example, that they employ guards, include enclosed spaces with secure doors, and be staffed to provide internal controls such as dual-signature systems—make it difficult for a commercial bank to operate profitably in many rural areas. And once the bank branch arrives, will it offer services appropriate to the realities of poorer households? Or, will its requirements, such as minimum account balances, exclude many members of the community?

The tradeoff between the principles of security and access is tough for two reasons. First, effective government supervision (which could help ensure security from outside the MFI) is a scarce resource. Advocates who prioritize security over access argue that regulatory authorities should only license institutions to intermediate deposits, to the extent that the authorities have the capacity to supervise them on an ongoing basis. In most countries, however, regulatory authorities simply do not have the capacity and, in some cases, the commitment to add the supervision of MFIs to their existing responsibilities. Second, internal security measures—such as guards, vaults, and more intensive staffing—are costly. "Appropriate" levels of depositor protection may place services out of the reach of poor households, especially in less densely populated places.

Yet if lack of regulatory capacity restricts access of poor households to savings services, are their interests really being protected? Mounting evidence documents that keeping savings in kind or with informal providers exposes the poor to considerable risks—risks of loss, theft, fraud, and pressures from family and friends to dip into cash or liquid assets around the house.[2] Many clients would prefer to keep at least some of their savings accessible in the credit-only MFIs from which they borrow. Realistically, what alternatives do most poor people have for reasonably safe and appropriate savings services? For tens of millions of poor households around the world, insisting that only licensed, adequately regulated financial institutions be permitted to intermediate savings dooms them to lack of access to savings services and to de facto reliance on poorer substitutes.

Furthermore, government regulation and supervision of depository institutions is no surefire guarantee that savers' accounts will be safe. Failure of even large government-backed banks resulting in the loss of tens of thousands of small savings accounts has been distressingly common in recent years. Regulation can provide a false sense of security if actual oversight is lax or stretched beyond capacity.

2.5.2 Balancing Security and Access: Full Disclosure

So, how can these dueling principles of depositor protection and access be optimized? Ideally, banking laws and regulations should be adjusted to permit well-managed microfinance NGOs—those that meet the preconditions discussed earlier—to become licensed, supervised financial institutions empowered to offer deposits to the general public. In this ideal scenario there would be enough well-trained examiners, who understand what makes microfinance tick, to oversee MFIs sensibly and appropriately.

Until this ideal become a reality, however, one must consider whether strong microfinance NGOs should be able to intermediate savings *if* they fully disclose to the public that they are not regulated and explain in plain language their key financial ratios and conditions. Where capable supervision is not an option, government banking authorities should implement a licensing process that identifies which MFIs are strong enough to mobilize and intermediate deposits—which meet stringent criteria for financial performance, systems, security, and management. The Bangladeshi experience is one in which unregulated MFIs intermediated savings from members, broadly defined, for several decades without dire results. In addition to meeting any licensing criteria, an MFI should disclose its financial conditions according to a format prescribed by the international community or a financial regulator.

Plain-language disclosures should describe the MFI's financial condition, state that the institution is unregulated and that depositors should expect no recourse if it fails, clarify the effective lending and deposit rates, list the board members, and provide other such information that would assist prospective depositors to judge the safety and soundness of the MFI and the value-for-money of its savings services. Plain-language disclosure enhances depositor protection without foreclosing access. The disclosures alert and enable depositors to consider for themselves whether the institution has sufficient internal capacity and is strongly governed.

2.5.3 Legality

From the MFI's perspective, a crucial question is whether offering deposit services to the public is legal. Both the law and the extent to which it is enforced vary tremendously from country to country. Some countries specifically permit non-bank MFIs to mobilize and intermediate deposits from the public, while other countries expressly forbid this. In many countries, though, the law is silent, conflicting, or ambiguous. Where the law is unclear, regulators often have been willing to look the other way and permit well-managed, well-capitalized MFIs to offer savings services. Managers and boards must determine whether mobilizing and intermediating deposits is legal and, if this is unclear, whether the legal risks of intermediation are small enough to consider proceeding. Policymakers should also consider whether additional safeguards (for example, requirements that owners and managers of financial institutions register when starting up a new institution) might be in order to protect depositors against pyramid schemes and other unscrupulous operators.

Of course, the security of deposits will be affected not only by external checks but by other factors that are external to the MFI as well.

2.6 WHAT ABOUT A STABLE AND POSITIVE ENABLING ENVIRONMENT?

Some microfinance experts discourage savings mobilization in countries plagued by high or highly erratic inflation, conflict, or political instability. They are concerned that these environments put depositors' savings at risk. They also worry that uncontrolled inflation, government restrictions on interest rates or reserves, or widely available subsidized credit may make it difficult for a sustainable institution to provide clients with a positive real return on their savings. These concerns are realistic. Great caution should be taken in considering initiating the launch of savings service in high-inflation environments.

At the same time, not providing services can deprive those most in need of savings of a vehicle for diversifying their risk. Despite the risks and low returns posed by these difficult environments, many clients may still prefer to save in an institution rather than informally, and they should be provided that choice. Even in hyper-inflationary environments, a significant number of poor people may want to be able to save both in kind and in cash.[3] Therefore, for the MFI, these questions of risk and returns should still take the form of the questions above: Given the circumstances, is there still effective demand? In light of this unfavorable economic or regulatory or political environment, can the institution continue to provide these services and maintain its viability?

2.7 WHAT THESE PRECONDITIONS MEAN FOR DIFFERENT TYPES OF INSTITUTIONS

In summary, the preconditions for offering new savings services are as follows: (1) adequate client demand; (2) adequate institutional capacity (financial sustainability, credit management, staffing, systems, and facilities); and (3) effective governance that provides an ongoing check on management (see Box 2–1). Taken together, these preconditions guard against the most important client risk—loss of savings. They are meant to prevent theft, fraud, mismanagement, depletion of the institution's capital base, and liquidity crises, any of which can leave the institution unable to honor depositors' claims. These preconditions also protect the institution against the many risks *it* faces in introducing new savings services (see Box 2–2).

How do these preconditions vary for different types of institutions? They don't. Any institution that proposes to intermediate voluntary savings should meet these preconditions. The ongoing debate over regulation and licensing of deposit-taking institutions draws numerous important distinctions among types of institutions and whom they serve: members only versus the general public, borrowers versus non-borrowers, and large institutions versus small institutions. From the perspective of the MFIs, however, these distinctions melt away before a basic bottom line—deposits should be safe.

While the preconditions apply to any institution considering mobilizing deposits, which preconditions are most challenging and how they are met will vary considerably for different types of institutions. Some institutions simply may not have the capacity, culture, or cost structure to mobilize small deposits themselves. Others may need to offer quite simple savings services so that their staff can keep deposits secure. The following section suggests some options for institutions that cannot easily meet the preconditions discussed above.

Box 2–1. Summary Checklist of Prerequisites for Intermediating Deposits

Legality: Is it legal? If this is unclear, are the authorities willing to waive or adjust legal or regulatory requirements? If the institution is not supervised, is it prepared to implement full disclosure on an ongoing basis?

Current profitability: Has the institution reached sustainability?

Credit management: Does it have a demonstrated history of stringent credit management and results to match?

Liquidity and asset liability management: Does the institution have the skills, policies, and systems needed for proper liquidity and asset liability management? Alternatively, do the proposed product terms nearly eliminate interest rate and liquidity risk?

Internal controls: Are internal controls sufficient? Are they reinforced by the MFI's culture, policies and procedures, information systems, and training and supervision of staff? Is security prioritized as an integral part of operations?

Human resources: Does the MFI have (or can it add) adequate management and other staff to design and launch successful small savings operations? Does management have the skills to reorient existing staff or recruit and train new staff to interact with clients in new ways, inspire confidence, and, for credit-only institutions, handle the more complex management involved in mobilizing and intermediating deposits? Do managers have the trust of the target clients?

Facilities: Will the physical facilities afford adequate protection, accommodate clients, and inspire their trust? Can the information system handle the expected number and type of transactions associated with the new service? Does the information system, whether manual or computerized, provide information that is sufficient, accurate, timely, and transparent?

Governance: Does the institution have an effective board or other governance body that exercises reasonable oversight, ensures sufficient discipline, and serves as a check on management? Is it sufficiently knowledgeable, sufficiently engaged, and does it have sufficient powers to be able and willing to step in if management is putting either savers' deposits or the institution's viability at risk?

Demand*: Is there effective demand for the proposed product? Will it strike the balance among product features, security, convenience, and price better than competing products?

Future profitability*: Does it have a realistic business plan that demonstrates its ongoing profitability? Is the plan explicit about what costs the new service is expected to cover by when? Are projections based on a cost of capital that includes the administrative, financial, and reserves costs of savings? Does it include sufficient reserves, capital, and operating funds to cover initial operating losses and losses due to catastrophic events without using client deposits? Does it have a profitable place to invest excess savings?

---

* These prerequisites are listed last because assessing them requires staff time and, often, cash outlays. A microfinance institution should first do a simple internal assessment to see if it meets the other preconditions.

Box 2–2. Mobilizing Deposits:
Risky Business for a Microfinance Institution

An MFI that mobilizes deposits assumes many risks. Any of the following can happen:

- Demand is inadequate, leading to wasted time and money and potentially significant financial loss. The investment in the new product and staff, improved technology, and marketing materials is unproductive.
- The product does not work well for the clients, leading to dropout. Credibility with clients and the community erodes.
- The product costs too much to deliver. Rather than providing a low-cost source of expansion capital, it cuts into operating margins and financial performance.
- The institution is diverted from its core competencies. The new savings program demands a lot of senior staff time, organizational energy, and capital—and the credit program suffers as a result.
- The institution gets in trouble with legal, regulatory, or tax authorities, costing it considerable time and bother and risking its reputation and even closure.
- The institution's donors or investors are disappointed and withdraw support.

Although the stakes are less dramatic for a depository institution that introduces new savings services targeted to poorer clients, offering these services still poses risks to its operational effectiveness, financial performance, and reputation.

2.8 GETTING TO YES: OTHER OPTIONS

What if, after careful analysis, an institution does not meet the preconditions discussed above? What if an MFI does not have the internal capacity or governance needed to intermediate liquid deposits? Or, what if going down market to serve smaller depositors does not appear to be viable? As several authors in this volume point out, there are other options. First, an MFI might offer products that staff with very little education can manage soundly. It might, for example,

- offer only credit and savings products with short matched terms (see Box 12–2), or
- couple an illiquid savings product that requires regular fixed payments with access to flexible emergency loans (see Box 8–7).

Used by self-help groups and small cooperatives, these strategies greatly reduce the demands of liquidity and asset liability management and internal controls.

Where institutional capacity or governance is not sufficiently strong, another option is to provide access to services without actually intermediating deposits.

For example,

- Rather than providing financial services directly, an NGO might undertake the easier task of promoting small cooperatives or self-help groups to provide simple financial services to themselves. It might also link these groups to a formal financial institution that could provide them with credit and a secure place to save.
- A credit-only MFI can partner with a regulated depository that gives the MFI's clients a means to save. This can benefit both the clients and the quality of the MFI's loan portfolio.
- An MFI might collect deposits but not lend them out. However, this presumes that the MFI has a secure place to invest deposits that will yield a high enough return to cover the high costs of mobilizing small deposits.

These strategies free institutions of some of the most rigorous demands of intermediation.

Formal financial institutions may need to overcome a different constraint, a high cost structure that makes it difficult for them to collect small deposits. Commercial banks that cannot afford to serve small depositors as individuals might partner with an NGO or a credit-only MFI that promotes or serves groups. By organizing clients into groups, these NGOs or MFIs can lower the commercial institution's administrative costs.

2.9 CONCLUSION

The chief obstacles to secure and viable financial intermediation are likely to be different for different types of institutions. For credit-only MFIs, institutional capacity and governance may well be stumbling blocks. Their questions may be, can we develop the staff, systems, management, and board capacity to intermediate savings securely? If not, can we find other ways to provide our target market with access to the benefits of savings services? For savings institutions considering a move down market, the greatest questions will often be costs and culture. Can we serve significantly more expensive clients profitably? Can we lower our cost structure enough? Do we have, or can we create, the institutional drive and culture, from directors to collectors, to reach poorer customers?

Given the potential value of well-designed savings services to the many millions of poor households without access, the answers to these questions have great importance for development stakeholders worldwide. Practitioners, policymakers, investors, and donors must work together to improve the calculations—to the benefit of the poor.

Notes

[1] Covariant risk refers to a risk that can be higher because it varies in the same way for a given portfolio. A portfolio of loans from a single geographic region is subject to a high covariant risk because they are vulnerable to the same local natural disasters or epidemics.

[2] Graham A. N. Wright and Leonard Mutesasira, "Relative Risk to the Savings of Poor People" (2000), in *Regulation: The Conventional View v. Poor People's Reality* (Nairobi: *MicroSave*, n.d.); and Matthew Titus, "Costs in Microfinance: What Do Urban SHGs Tell Us," in *Beyond Micro-Credit: Putting Development Back into Micro-Finance*, ed. Thomas Fisher and M. S. Sriram (London: Oxfam, 2002).

[3] Sergio Antezana, contribution to "Virtual Conference on Savings Operations for Very Small or Remote Depositors," May 2002.

3

The Keys to Cost Recovery

David C. Richardson
and Madeline Hirschland

Whether mobilizing small deposits is financially feasible has been hotly debated. Some microfinance experts have claimed that high costs and slim margins make it impossible to capture small deposits and cover costs. These claims notwithstanding, credit unions, also known as financial cooperatives, have been covering their costs while providing microsavings services for over 150 years. A 2002 survey by the World Council of Credit Unions (WOCCU) solicited savings deposit information from eighty-five credit unions in Guatemala, Ecuador, Bolivia, Romania, and the Philippines. Of their 2.4 million depositors, 2.3 million—94 percent—had an average balance of only US$33 (see Table 3–1). This distribution of deposits is typical of credit unions in other countries as well. With few exceptions these credit unions are financially self-sustainable; they do not receive external funding. Although mobilizing deposits is newer to other types of microfinance institutions (MFIs), they too have been able to mobilize small deposits and recover costs. Table 3–2 presents data from a number of MFIs that are doing precisely that.[1]

The debate is no more. Mobilizing small deposits can be not only feasible but profitable—the question now is how. Credit unions have discovered that there are two keys to viable savings mobilization: attracting an adequate volume of deposits and managing operating costs. If an MFI cannot cover the costs of mobilizing deposits, either its administrative expense ratio is unnecessarily high or it has not mobilized an adequate volume of deposits.

Managing administrative costs while achieving volume is particularly challenging for two types of institutions that serve small depositors: those serving

The authors express their gratitude to Mohammed Azim Hossain for his helpful comments.

43

Table 3–1. Number and Size of Accounts of Eighty-five
WOCCU-affiliated Credit Unions

Range (US$)	# of Accounts	% of Accounts	% of Volume	Average (US$)
0–300	2,300,414	94	26	33
301–1000	98,473	4	19	544
>1000	44,365	2	55	3,614
Totals	2,443,252	100	100	118

less densely populated areas and those that do not have the option to mobilize large deposits also. For these institutions recovering costs requires innovations in delivery systems and staffing that have implications for every aspect of operations from products to marketing, pricing, and management systems.

This chapter provides an overview to cost recovery. It discusses key principles and strategies for:

- attracting a sufficient volume of deposits,
- managing the costs of any microsavings operation, and
- managing costs when serving mostly small or rural depositors.

As translating these principles into practice is the subject of much of the rest of the book, the chapter refers the reader to chapters that provide more detailed guidance wherever possible.

3.1 ACHIEVING ADEQUATE VOLUME

Developing a volume of savings that is large enough to be viable is a long-term proposition. A savings product is viable if its total costs per unit mobilized are less than the costs of alternative sources of funds that have similar terms.[2] A key to lowering unit costs is to spread the fixed costs portion of these costs over a larger volume of deposits. In other words, for a savings product to be viable, an MFI usually must mobilize a large volume of deposits. However, unlike credit-led institutions, a deposit-oriented institution must seek out and persuade savers to deposit their money. To succeed, it must gain savers' trust. This takes time.

In WOCCU's experience, most credit unions take at least five years to achieve a volume large enough to recover full costs.[3] Similarly, many MFIs find that they must serve only their core clientele for several years before they can convince the broader public that the MFI is a safe place to save. Indeed, in Table 3–2 it is the older institutions' deposits (BAAC, BRI, and Banco Caja Social) that have the largest volumes of deposits and the lowest administrative costs. Each holds at least US$431 million in deposits, has mobilized deposits for at least a decade, and has an administrative cost ratio of less than 3 percent.[4]

Developing trust, however, is not sufficient to mobilize a sufficient volume of deposits. Credit unions have discovered that the following principles are also necessary to attract sizeable sums from large numbers of savers.

3.1.1 Target Wealthier Net Savers as Well as Net Borrowers

Most MFIs erroneously assume that their borrowers can provide the volume of savings they need for lending. In fact, to mobilize deposits successfully, an MFI must expand its target group from only "net borrowers," people who borrow more than they save, to include a completely different group of clients, people who save larger amounts and typically do not hold a loan. These "net savers" provide the bulk of the resources needed to be self-sustaining. Financial markets typically have many more net savers than net borrowers. WOCCU finds that the ratio of savers to borrowers in an excellent program is often five to one. Furthermore, most net borrowers are poor while larger net savers tend to be better off.

Attracting this wealthier clientele can require significant changes in everything from product mix to marketing, office structure, and corporate culture (see Chapters 4, 7, and 10). These changes can be worth the effort. In the study discussed above, 56 percent of the deposit volume of the eighty-five credit unions came from just 2 percent of the savings accounts. These net savers were not from the poorest market segment; on average, they held US$3,614 in deposits. Does this mean that MFIs should not provide savings services to poorer people, who typically are net borrowers? To the contrary, in this example depositors with an average account size of only US$33 accounted for 26 percent of the volume of deposits (and 94 percent of savers). By also attracting wealthier clients, however, MFIs can obtain a large enough volume of deposits to make their savings operations viable and thereby enable themselves to serve the poor (see Box 3–2).

3.1.2 Physical Presence

An MFI's physical image directly affects clients' confidence and trust, which, in turn, affects how much they deposit. How much they deposit will also be influenced by how far they must travel to do so. Managers of MFIs that offer office-based services should therefore focus on three aspects of their institutions' physical presence:

Location: Branches should be in safe neighborhoods near substantial commercial activity such as a market or religious institution. To attract deposits from the public, nothing can substitute for a safe and convenient location.

Physical appearance: Each branch should look professional. The lobby and service areas should have enough space, lighting, and privacy.

Security systems: The security systems should inspire trust. They might include alarms, strong boxes, and armed guards.

Table 3–2. Approximate Administrative Costs of Saving Services[1]

Note: Because different costing techniques were used, the cost figures should be seen as representative rather than precise. Some are for individual services for small or remote depositors while others are for overall savings operations. They should not be used to compare institutions.		

Institution[2] **(year of data collection)**	**Service(s) Costed**	**Admin. Cost Ratio**
Office-based Services		
Bank for Agriculture and Agricultural Cooperatives (1998): • US$3.3 billion in deposits; 7.0 million accounts • Focus on savings since mid-1980s • 520 deposit accounts per employee	**Liquid passbook:** Avg. balance: < than US$150 (7% PC GNI)	2.9%
Bank Rakyat Indonesia Unit System (1996): • US$2.9 billion in deposits; 16.1 million accounts • Focus on savings since 1986 • 690 deposit accounts per employee	**All**: Liquid, semi-liquid, and time deposits. Avg. balance: US$182 (17% of PC GNI)	2.2%
Banco Caja Social (1996) • US$431 million in deposits; 1.2 million accounts • Mobilizing savings since 1911 • 450 deposit accounts per employee	**Liquid passbook:** Avg. balance: US$235 (11% PC GNI) **Time deposit:** Avg. balance: US$3,413 (335% PC GNI)	<1%[3] .07%
Workers Bank (1998) • US$9.5 million in postal savings deposits; 76,600 accounts. • Created in 1973: took over government postal savings bank • Staff double as postal staff	**Contractual:** Avg. balance: US$183 (8% PC GNI)	7.9%

Institution (year of data collection)	Service(s) Costed	Admin. Cost Ratio
Cooperative Bank of Benguet (2002) • US$1.3 million in deposits; 9,487 accounts • Established with savings services in 1992 • 344 deposit accounts per employee	**Liquid passbook:** Avg. balance: US$94 (9% PC GNI) **Time deposit:** Avg. balance: US$1,584 (155% PC GNI)	6.5% 3.7%

Field-based Services

ASA (2000) • $25.3 million total (2002: $25.8 million mandatory; $17.4 million liquid or time deposits); 1.2 million accounts • Mandatory savings since 1989; voluntary since 1997 • 232 deposit accounts per employee	**All:** Contractual, voluntary, and mandatory-voluntary passbook. Avg. balance: US$26 (7% PC GNI). (In 2002: avg. mandatory: US$12; avg. liquid/time deposits: ~US$8)	8.6% 0% marginal cost for liquid passbook service
VYCCU (2001) • US$184,000 in deposits; 4,125 accounts. • Mobilizing savings since 1991; from the public since 1997 • ~375 deposit accounts per employee	**Lockbox, monthly mobile collection:** Avg. balance: US$23 (10% PC GNI[4]) **Remote mand-vol:**[5] Avg. balance: US$17 (7% PC GNI)	5% 17%

[1] The data for this table are from the following sources: Delbert Fitchett, "Bank for Agriculture and Agricultural Cooperatives (BAAC), Thailand," 75–105; Klaus Maurer, "Bank Rakyat Indonesia," 107–44; Sylvia Wisniwski, "Banco Caja Social," 177–214; Renée Chao-Béroff, "Caisses Villageoises d'Épargne et de Crédit Autogérées (CVECA), Mali," 215–51, all in *Challenges of Microsavings Mobilization—Concepts and Views from the Field,* ed. Laura Elser, Alfred Hannig, and Sylvia Wisniwski (Eschborn, Germany: GTZ, n.d.); John Owens, "The Partner Savings Plan of the Workers' Bank, Jamaica: Lessons in Microsavings from ROSCAs," in *Promising Practices in Rural Finance,* ed. Mark D. Wenner, Javier Alvarado, and Francisco Galarza (Washington, DC: Inter-American Development Bank, 2003), 309–25; Gerry Lab-oyan, managing director of the Cooperative Bank of Benguet, based on a costing exercise conducted by the bank in 2002; Graham A. N. Wright, Robert Peck Christen, and Imran Matin, "ASA's Culture, Competition, and Choice: Introducing Savings Services into a MicroCredit Institution" (Nairobi: MicroSave, 2000); ASA's 2002 financial statements; Mohammed Azim Hossain, ASA's head of finance and MIS, email interchange with Madeline Hirschland, 2003; and VYCCU's financial statements and a costing study conducted by Madeline Hirschland in 2001.

[2] These are different types of institutions: BAAC and BRI are government-owned banks with national coverage; Banco Caja Social is a commercial bank with social roots and national coverage; Workers Bank (now Jamaica National Microcredit Company Limited) is a commercial bank with social roots that offers services through 247 post offices; Cooperative Bank of Benguet is a cooperative rural bank; ASA is an NGO with national coverage; and VYCCU is a rural community-based cooperative.

[3] These figures do not include new or small inactive accounts, both of which cost more.

[4] This high figure is misleading. The per capita GNI figure, US$236, is for all of Nepal, including large, largely non-monetized hill regions where incomes are much lower than in the plains where VYCCU operates.

[5] Offered by an agent based in a remote area, these accounts represent only 2 percent of VYCCU's total number of deposit accounts.

Box 3–1. Attracting Large as Well as Small Deposits: Risks, Reasons, and Requirements

Attracting large and institutional deposits carries real risks as well as benefits. Because large depositors have more savings options, their deposits are likely to be more volatile and will thereby increase liquidity and interest rate risk (see Chapters 12 and 13). At the same time, an MFI will only attract deposits that are significantly more volatile than other deposits if it sets its interest rates substantially above market rates.

Serving large and institutional depositors can also shift the MFI's focus away from the poor. Large depositors have more savings options and may demand more or different services than smaller ones. Their higher profitability, volatility, and typically louder voices may motivate management to focus on this higher-income clientele. Furthermore, better-educated staff that are able to relate to better-off clients probably are not as good at relating to the poor. Large and institutional depositors may also require upgraded branches; the cost of these branches and staff can force management to focus even more on attracting larger deposits.

On the other hand, serving large as well as small depositors can lower concentration risk while increasing the volume of loanable funds and profitability. Conversely, excluding clients who are no longer poor undermines profitability, because attracting and serving a new customer costs many times more than serving an established one. Furthermore, poor or nearly poor clients whose situation has improved also need and deserve services.

Above all, the alternative to cross subsidization may be to exclude the very poor altogether or to offer them lower quality services. If an MFI serves only small depositors, it may need to establish a minimum account balance, charge fees to cover its costs, or offer more rigid services that it can provide at less cost. These restrictions are likely to exclude some of the poor altogether.

Therefore, management should consider how far up market the MFI can go without losing its focus on the poor and how it can attract large and institutional deposits. To attract large depositors, an MFI may have to offer more services, some of which may appeal primarily to better-off clients. To maintain a focus on the poor, the MFI's leaders will need to reflect this priority through their actions, the MFI's mission, and its institutional culture, policies, incentive systems, hiring process, and services that meet the needs of the very poor.

Adapted from "Savings Operations for Very Small or Remote Depositors: Summary of Proceedings 29th April–17th May 2002" (2002).

The location and small physical size of many credit-only institutions' premises would limit their ability to mobilize large volumes of deposits.

3.1.3 Product Diversity

An MFI will be able to attract a large volume of deposits only if it offers products that people want (see Chapter 7). Most successful credit unions offer a range of savings products that target different market niches such as:

Passbook savings or demand deposit accounts for people seeking liquidity;

Savings clubs, also known as *contractual products*, for people who want to accumulate small amounts of savings to meet a specific need at a specific point in time, such as school fees or festival or wedding expenses;

Term deposits for people who want to deposit a single lump sum and are willing to sacrifice liquidity in order to receive a higher yield; and

Retirement and *children's savings accounts* for people who seek a long-term, high-yielding account to help provide for their or their children's future and to teach their children to save.

Most people have fairly common and predictable needs over the course of their life. Offering a range of "life cycle" products that meet these needs can attract and keep people saving with an institution throughout their lifetime. This is important, because satisfied clients and low dropout rates are keys to maintaining a high volume of deposits.

3.1.4 Total Employee Involvement in Marketing

Credit unions have found that one of their most powerful marketing resources is their work force (see Chapter 10). Credit unions typically make every employee, from accountants to loan officers, responsible for bringing in a certain number of savers, and volume of savings. Empowering everyone with this responsibility establishes a corporate culture permeated by the drive to market products, attract new savers, and pull in more deposits.

This culture can be reinforced by a well-designed incentive system supported by appropriate information (see Chapter 15). Where branches can borrow internal funds for lending, branches can be motivated to mobilize deposits if they are set up as profit centers, if they are accountable for their results, and if the price set for these internal funds is higher than the cost to the branch of mobilizing deposits (see Box 3–2).

Motivating employees to market products will only work if they know how to do so. Training staff—particularly field staff—in how and where to promote products is essential (see Box 10–4). An institution-wide focus on marketing—

Box 3–2. Achieving Volume: Lessons from the BRI Unit System

In 1989 the BRI unit system had $534 million in deposits. By 1996 it had US$4 billion. What did the BRI do to mobilize deposits on such a massive scale?

First, from 1982 to 1986 BRI undertook extensive market research and pilot testing to assure that its products and promotion met the demand of its market. It ultimately offered four savings products to meet the bulk of the market's demand: a liquid passbook account with a lottery; a semi-liquid passbook account that allowed two withdrawals monthly; a term deposit for three, six, nine, twelve, or twenty-four months; and a current account for institutions facing certain legal restrictions.

Management reasoned that for staff members to be motivated to mobilize deposits broadly, they must be *responsible for*, *aware of*, and *affected by* their performance.

- So that branch staff could be held accountable for branch results, the BRI began to account for its branches as profit centers.
- So that staff were aware of their performance, the MIS provides staff with key, timely, and transparent indicators of productivity and profitability.
- So that staff would benefit from the branch's good performance, BRI established a staff incentive system based on these indicators that rewarded profitability.
- So that mobilizing deposits was more profitable than borrowing funds, management set the cost for internal loans from within the BRI—known as the *internal transfer price*—0.5 percent higher than the highest interest rate for deposits. For the incentive system to work, mobilizing deposits had to be more profitable than obtaining other funds for lending.

With these elements in place, the more deposits a branch mobilized, the greater its profitability and the higher the pay its staff received. These elements were reinforced by a new culture of service and productivity that emanated from the senior levels; comprehensive retraining of staff in the new products, systems, and service orientation; and intensive supervision—one supervisor for four units.

The final key to massive growth was to provide staff with a methodology and detailed training for how and where to mobilize deposits. In 1987 the BRI addressed this final challenge by initiating its Systematic Approach to Savings Mobilization (see Box 10–4).

See Marguerite Robinson, *The Microfinance Revolution*, vol. 2, *Lessons from Indonesia* (Washington, DC: World Bank), 262–304.

instituted through expectations, incentives, and training—can significantly increase the volume of savings deposits.

3.1.5 Effective Liquidity Management

Mobilizing a significant volume of deposits is useful only if these assets generate revenues. While an MFI must have access to enough cash to meet its expenses and the demand for withdrawals, holding too large a volume of deposits as liquid non-earning assets will undermine its profitability. The process of maintaining this balance—having enough but not too much liquidity—is called liquidity management and is essential to cost recovery. Liquidity management is the subject of Chapter 12.

In summary, to recover the full costs of offering savings services, an MFI must mobilize a large volume of deposits. An MFI can do this by employing five strategies:

- Searching for net savers to expand the savings deposit portfolio rapidly,
- Developing a physical image that conveys security and a convenient location,
- Offering a mix of savings products that meet significant market demand,
- Motivating and enabling all employees to market savings products effectively, and
- Managing liquidity effectively.

3.2 MANAGING OPERATING COSTS

Operating costs can be broken down into three categories: financial costs, direct administrative costs, and indirect administrative costs. Managing these costs properly is an important principle of self-sustainability.

3.2.1 Financial Costs

Interest rates on deposits not only affect an MFI's costs —the higher the rate, the higher its financial costs—but they also play a critical role in attracting deposits. Setting interest rates too low or administrative fees too high can seriously undermine volume and, in turn, profitability. How to set interest rates and fees is discussed in Chapter 9. However, the following guidelines can help strike the balance between attracting a large volume of deposits and managing financial costs:

If an MFI is just starting to mobilize savings, offer interest rates that are higher than those of the competition. While this will result in higher financial costs, the more attractive rate will entice people to save with the MFI.

Offer interest rates that are at least 1 percent higher than those of the bank. People usually see banks as safer places to save than credit unions or MFIs. A higher interest rate is needed simply to make up for this difference in perceived security.

Pay a positive real rate of return. Paying a rate that is higher than inflation is costly and not essential in many markets, but it is likely to attract a significantly higher volume of deposits.

Do not pay interest for accounts under a minimum amount. The smallest accounts typically cost more than the revenues that they generate. Furthermore, calculating and paying interest increases transaction costs.

Offer some "value added" features in place of some interest. A ticket for a lottery with an attractive prize, a free life-insurance policy that pays out a sum equal to the savings balance if the person dies, or valued household items may attract a higher volume of deposits than an interest rate increase of a similar value.

3.2.2 Direct Administrative Costs

Direct administrative costs are those costs that can be directly linked to savings mobilization activities. Chief among these are the costs of staff and marketing. Since these "out of pocket" outlays of cash result directly from savings mobilization, management should expect to recover them first. Managing costs is critical to cost recovery, and this section suggests some important strategies for doing so.

Without enough deposits, however, an MFI may find it impossible to recover the costs of mobilizing savings, even with all of the strategies below. If an MFI cannot recover its direct administrative expenses, it should reconsider how to achieve an adequate volume of deposits. While costs can be managed and minimized, there is no substitute for volume, which is the most painless way to achieve operating efficiency. Furthermore, mobilizing a sufficient volume of deposits only from small savings accounts may not be realistic. It may also be necessary to mobilize large deposits.

Average Costing

If an MFI allocates all the costs of a deposit account to that account—a concept called *marginal costing*—it may conclude that mobilizing small deposits is not economical. If, instead, it averages the costs of all of its savings accounts and spreads those costs across its entire volume of savings deposits—*average costing*—then it will find that mobilizing small deposits is more feasible. From a financial perspective, serving small depositors can make sense if an MFI considers the average costs of its savings program as a whole, including all its products and account sizes. Cross subsidization, from large to small accounts and from more lucrative to more costly savings products, can be the key to serving large numbers of small depositors while remaining financially self-sufficient.

The institutions in Table 3–2 illustrate how serving larger depositors lowers administrative costs. Administrative cost ratios are lower for institutions with higher average balances relative to per capita GNI. The institutions or services with administrative cost ratios of less than 6 percent have average balances of at least 15 percent of per capita GNI. With one exception, the ratios of more than 5 percent are associated with average balances of 13 percent or less.

At the same time, for some institutions, mobilizing large deposits is not an option. If they operate in a competitive market where subsidized loan funds are widely available at a lower cost than mobilized deposits, they may lack a sufficiently profitable place to invest a large volume of deposits. Investing deposits in their loan portfolio may actually undermine their profitability. In other cases institutions cannot legally mobilize deposits from outside their membership. Still others may not be able to compete against banks that are perceived as more secure but that do not serve the MFI's lower-income markets. Even where it is possible, competition can make it difficult to earn a sufficient profit from investing large deposits to recover the costs of mobilizing small ones (see Box 9–2).

Managing costs rigorously can offset the lack of larger accounts. Indeed, the institutions featured in Table 3–2 have found ways to offer savings services with administrative cost ratios as high as 8.6 percent while remaining financially sustainable.[5] Accounts with the highest administrative costs—such as small passbook accounts—may be offset by other products such as loans, in the case of ASA, or time deposits, in the case of the Cooperative Bank of Benguet.

At the same time, many institutions find that small, stand-alone, demand-deposit accounts—if these accounts are not offset by larger accounts and are not tightly integrated with other products—simply are not viable. For these institutions, demand-deposit accounts may be offered by using some of the innovations discussed in Section 3.3 below.

Human Resources

Salaries and benefits, typically the largest administrative cost, can be managed by:

> *Paying market rates:* Paying people fairly and rewarding their positive performance is important. Paying them more than market rates, however, is neither necessary nor wise. Unfortunately, MFIs that receive donor subsidies often inflate salaries. Once high salaries are in place, the MFI can change them only by hiring new staff. MFIs should be extremely careful not to overpay staff.

> *Hiring at the minimum education level needed:* MFIs also can control personnel costs by carefully matching the requirements of a job to the people hired. Mobilizing savings involves three main jobs: marketers, tellers, and security

guards. Most of the responsibilities linked to these positions require, at most, a high school education, while many of the skills needed can be learned on the job. In fact, the most important qualification for these jobs is honesty, which has nothing to do with education or job experience. Therefore, MFIs can save significantly on personnel costs by hiring people from the same socioeconomic levels as the clients.

Staffing leanly: Credit unions that are just starting up savings operations should keep their staff structure small. A minimal branch structure would include just one marketing person, one teller, and one security guard.

Designing staff incentive systems so that they do not inflate salaries: Finally, staff incentive systems should be designed with care. Particularly in microcredit operations, incentive systems often have raised the level of compensation and/ or the expectations of the employees beyond what the MFI can reasonably afford to pay staff who primarily mobilize savings (see Chapter 15).

Marketing

The main marketing expenses of savings mobilization are advertising and sales promotions. Advertising can be very expensive and must be managed with great care (see Chapter 10). The following strategies can help:

Match the type of advertising to the market niche: Two groups of people use savings services: poorer people who do not have significant resources to save and richer people who do. Cost effectiveness demands different marketing strategies for the two. Mass marketing through flyers, radio, TV and newspaper ads, and word of mouth can make large numbers of poorer people aware of the savings services. Mass marketing tends to be less effective for richer people, for whom personal visits work much better. Although much more costly per person reached, personal visits are a great way to convince wealthier people of the services' quality and safety. Personal marketing to poorer people with meager resources is not cost effective.

Set the advertising budget as a percentage of the deposit base: Linking the advertising budget to the size of the deposit base is a good way to monitor and adjust advertising expenses. Most MFIs with a small deposit base have few resources for advertising. As deposits grow, they can invest in more costly forms of advertising.

Conduct promotional activities throughout the year: Cultural events and national holidays provide excellent opportunities to promote savings using prizes and raffles. Because many people enjoy the chance to win something and respond favorably to different incentives to save, these activities can be very cost-effective ways to get people to save.

3.2.3 Indirect Administrative Costs

Indirect administrative costs can be broken down into four areas: human resources, administration, depreciation, and protection. Quantifying these costs is difficult because they must be allocated among a number of activities such as lending, mobilizing deposits, and marketing. (Techniques for allocating costs are detailed in Chapter 14.) The important question is not whether the allocation is completely accurate but whether these costs can be fully recovered with the MFI's operating revenues. This is because the indirect costs most likely are already being covered through other activities. For example, lending activities probably already generate revenues that completely cover the costs of accounting, MIS administration, and the executive director's department.

Savings mobilization contributes to indirect cost recovery by increasing the MFI's loanable resources. In so doing, savings mobilization spreads the fixed indirect administrative costs over a larger lending volume and thereby decreases the indirect administrative expense rate for the MFI's lending activities. Furthermore, convenient savings services build clients' goodwill and assets that can bolster loan repayment.

To minimize indirect administrative costs, successful credit unions have learned to:

Focus savings activities in the main office before opening branch offices. Tempted by the prospect of quickly penetrating the market, some MFIs start mobilizing saving by rapidly opening branch offices. This strategy is ill advised. Each branch office dramatically increases fixed costs. Starting with the market around the central office is safer and more cost effective because the fixed costs are already covered by the lending operations. An MFI should only expand to other markets after the variable costs of the central market operations are covered.

For smaller institutions, use a manual information system. A computerized system may not be necessary. Many successful credit unions with up to US$5 million in deposits and up to five thousand savers use only a manual system backed up by strong internal controls. For smaller institutions, purchasing a computer and software for tracking deposits makes sense only if donations are available for this purpose.

Review the salaries and benefits of executives. The high salary and benefit levels of executive managers can burden an entire institution with a high indirect overhead rate. A credit union's total administrative expense ratio[6] should not exceed 10 percent. If an MFI's administrative expense ratio exceeds 10 percent, the salaries and benefits of the executive management team should be divided by the average total assets to see how much those expenses contribute to the ratio.

3.3 COVERING COSTS WHILE SERVING SOLELY SMALL DEPOSITORS OR RURAL AREAS

When it comes to small depositors, proximity is crucial. Offering services that are close enough to attract depositors while still covering costs can be challenging. In less populated low-income areas either the operating costs of an office must be very low or services must be delivered in other ways. In either case, minimizing staff costs will be imperative. Lower-cost strategies may also be essential for MFIs that cannot attract large deposits. This section describes a number of delivery and staffing options that can enable these two types of institutions—those providing convenient services in rural areas and those that cannot cross subsidize services—to serve small depositors while recovering costs.

As Table 3–2 illustrates, providing proximity by offering services in the field tends to lower the number of clients handled by each staff person and increase administrative cost ratios. Of the services featured in Table 3–2, those offered by staff who travel to clients (ASAs and VYCCUs) are the most costly. The institutions with the lowest administrative costs have branch-based services and the largest number of accounts per employee.

3.3.1 Low-cost Delivery Systems for Rural Areas

As described in detail in Chapter 8, delivery systems that minimize costs while serving rural areas include:

Simple offices: Part-time, one-room offices can be established close to where people live, work, or congregate. Such an office might be a suboffice of a large MFI that wants to serve more rural areas without a costly, full-fledged branch. Alternatively, the same type of setup might be home to an autonomous community-based financial institution. The latter are one of the only ways to serve remote areas where, for cost reasons, large MFIs and financial institutions do not operate. In either case one or two staff working a few hours daily or a day a week might cover costs while serving a few hundred clients (see Boxes 8–2, 8–3, and 5–3).

Mobile collection: Where there is no office, instead of incurring the costs of establishing and staffing one, MFIs can deploy commissioned agents or salaried employees to collect deposits. Traveling by foot, bicycle, or other vehicle, collectors typically visit either daily or weekly. However, credit unions find that mobile collection significantly increases their administrative costs (see Boxes 8–4 and 8–5).

Clients as mobile collectors: An MFI can provide services that are convenient for most people while lowering its transaction costs by allowing individual clients to make deposits for other individuals or on behalf of a group. In remote areas this may be the only way that an MFI can deliver convenient, viable services. This system shifts the costs of field-based collection from the MFI to a client. Usually, the product must be extremely simple, with uniform required deposits for all.

Lockboxes: An MFI can sharply cut its own costs while providing a client with maximum convenience through the use of a lockbox, a small, locked box with a slot. Clients can deposit small variable amounts at any time at home or in their work place, but funds can be "withdrawn" only by using a key held by the MFI. The MFI incurs costs only when it collects or accepts the contents of the box.

"Piggybacking" services onto other delivery systems: Serving clients where they are already transacting business can make it affordable to offer services that are convenient. And, using existing buildings, management systems and staff can sharply cut costs. MFIs offer savings services within another financial service, alongside a nonfinancial service, or through other institutions. For example, (1) a bank that cannot afford to manage small, stand-alone deposits may be able automatically to withhold a savings deposit each time it processes a laborer's paycheck as part of a payroll service for her employer; (2) for Nepali farmers who live several hours walk from their dairy cooperative, being able to save when they sell their milk is very convenient—convenience that the cooperative could not afford to provide in any other way; and (3) in many countries deposit services are offered through post offices; for rural residents who travel to post offices, these services are very convenient.

Self-managed groups: A self-help group approach transfers costly management functions to groups that collect and manage their own savings. The institution organizes, trains, and supervises the groups, who meet very close to their homes. Deposits are usually regular, fixed, and inaccessible, and are lent to group members or are stored in a bank that may provide the group with a loan (see Box 8–7).

E-technologies: From hand-held personal digital assistants to smart cards, point of service devices, ATMs, and phone and Internet banking, e-technologies lower transaction costs. Some MFIs use them to serve more rural areas and offer products with flexible payments that suit the poor. Others have dropped them because ongoing implementation costs are much higher than with their prior systems. Most e-technologies require access to reliable, affordable power and data communications; a strong MIS and information-technology team; and suppliers who can offer and support software, hardware, security, and communications at a reasonable price.

MFIs that strive to be sustainable typically expect their operations to cover the costs of growth—of reaching new clients—as well as the costs of existing operations. In the case of small, self-managed organizations such as self-help groups or cooperatives, growth comes from establishing new groups rather than from significantly growing existing ones. Institutions that promote this type of organization typically do not expect to cover their own costs over time but, rather, expect to invest a limited amount of funds to develop small sustainable organizations. Experience from a number of institutions suggests that the cost per member for establishing such an organization ranges around US$11 to US$140 (see Table 3–3).

All these options provide convenience at a low cost by lowering staff costs.

3.3.2 Managing Staff Costs

The delivery systems above lower staff costs by employing one or more of the following strategies:

Combining functions into a single position: Many institutions deploy a single staff person rather than a team to handle cash and transactions. But, combining these functions increases the risks of fraud and mismanagement. MFIs that do so should manage these risks through additional internal controls (see Section 11.3.2).

Separating functions to lower educational requirements: In some cases having different staff members handle different functions can lower the education needed for one of the positions. For example, separating the loan officer and collector positions may make sense because assessing individual loans may require several more years of schooling than collecting deposits. Similarly, less educated staff might collect deposits and issue receipts while more educated staff might update the records.[7]

For institutions with many branches: Decentralizing operations is a key to minimizing the cost of managers' travel time, which can be substantial in rural areas. It is crucial that this strategy be accompanied by strong internal controls. To decentralize, management should provide branches with detailed guidance and training in all aspects of operations.

For small, single-branch institutions, such as cooperatives with a few hundred members, sharing external support services: Training, auditing, and developing marketing materials can cost a lot. Outsourcing, networking, or drawing on a central facility can spread these costs over many units (see Box 8–3).[8]

Relying on volunteers or staff from other institutions: Self-help groups and many small cooperatives rely heavily on volunteers (see Box 8–4). Using volunteers does impose tradeoffs; for example, it requires intensive training and simpler services. Where services are "piggybacked" on the delivery system for another service or institution, using its staff can cut costs dramatically, particularly if the staff is under-utilized. Developing staff accountability can be challenging.

Table 3–3. Cost of Establishing Small, Self-Managed Organizations

Program (year of data collection)	Type of Organization	Outreach/Age of Program	Years for Group to Become Sustainable	Cost per Member
Kupfuma Ishungu Project, Zimbabwe (2002)	Self-help groups (~6 members per group)	14,000 in 4 years	~1 year	US$67 (15% PC GNI)
DEPROSC cooperatives, Nepal (2002)	Savings and credit (cooperatives, ~140 members in each)	15,000 in 3 years	3 to 5 years	US$12–20 (5% to 8% PC GNI)
CVECAs, Mali (1997)	Member-owned village banks (~410 members per bank)	21,500 in 10 years	11 years, including federations and technical assistance	US$140 (48% PC GNI)
NABARD, India (2003)	Self-help groups (~20 members per group)	7.8 million in 10 years	3 years, after which negligible ongoing support is needed	~US$11 (2% PC GNI)

This table indicates a range of costs. It should not be used to compare programs, as these differ significantly in terms of the range of services offered and the environments in which they operate. The data are from the following sources: Hugh Allen, "End of Term Evaluation of Kupfuma Ishungu Rural Microfinance Project (RMFP), Zimbabwe" (CARE, 2002); Prahlad Mali, "Savings Operations for Very Small or Remote Depositors: Summary of Proceedings 20th April–17th May 2002" (2002); Renée Chao-Béroff, in Laura Elser, Alfred Hannig, and Sylvia Wisniwski, "Comparative Analysis of Savings Mobilization Strategies," in *Challenges of Microsavings Mobilization—Concepts and Views from the Field*, ed. Alfred Hannig and Sylvia Wisniwski (Eschborn, Germany: GTZ, n.d.); Girija Srinivasan, "Savings Operations" (May 2002); and Girija Srinivasan, email with Madeline Hirschland, February 2003.

Employing clients and local people: Excellent clients or informal financial operators—such as ROSCA organizers—can make strong, low-cost field staff; they tend to be local, have little education, and start with a good understanding of the operations. For example, strong self-help group leaders can be paid to create and monitor groups at a fraction of the cost of professional staff. Especially in rural areas, employing local staff saves the costs of travel time and transport.

Limiting hours and days of operation: Small cooperatives, satellite offices, self-help groups, and mobile collection units may offer services on a weekly or less frequent basis or, in some cases, for just an hour or two each day.

Expecting accuracy: Inexact record keeping can skyrocket staff costs. Following up on errors can consume large amounts of staff time. Furthermore, where errors abound and management is distracted by following up on them, staff can more easily hide fraud. Strong internal controls, simple standardized policies and procedures, a culture of intolerance for errors, and staff incentives that promote mistake-free work are important means to control staff costs.

Keeping operations simple: In most cases managing costs requires using volunteers or paid staff with very little education. To employ this type of staff, every aspect of the MFI's products and systems must be simple and standardized—easy to understand and easy to manage. Simple products and policies allow for simpler and less costly accounting, monitoring, auditing, and information dissemination, and can prevent fraud (Box 8–2). Whether computerized or manual, a simple, streamlined MIS is crucial to employing less educated staff or volunteers and using their time well.

Investing in training and supervision: Relying on volunteers or staff with little education does impose some costs; if operations are staffed in this way, comprehensive training and ongoing supervision are imperative. Depending on the products offered, staff and volunteers need to be trained in how to update records, calculate interest, manage liquidity, and implement internal controls.

These staffing and delivery options are examined and illustrated in detail in Chapter 8.

3.4 CONCLUSION

Recovering the costs of mobilizing small deposits is challenging, particularly in rural areas or where mobilizing large deposits is not possible. In fact, the challenge of cost recovery conditions every aspect of savings operations. In particular, the need to control staff costs requires simplicity and innovation in everything from product design to service delivery, systems for financial management, and internal controls. How this can be achieved is the subject of much of the rest of this book.

This chapter presented the keys to sustainable deposit mobilization. There are only two: achieving volume and controlling costs. Everything else is a subset. Credit unions have used the strategies presented in this chapter to deliver savings services while recovering costs. By employing the strategies, an MFI that wants to serve the poor will most likely be able to achieve what credit unions have: outreach, scale, and efficiency.

Notes

[1] Cost data for savings mobilization is still rare in microfinance. The institutions in this table represent a range of institutional types that offer savings services for which costing exercises have been undertaken.

[2] The total costs of a savings product are its financial and administrative costs minus its income from transaction, ledger, and other fees received for savings services. To compare the total costs of a savings product to the total costs of alternative sources of funds, the costs of the savings product should include the implicit "cost" of holding savings in reserve. While all funds received from an alternative source can be invested, some percentage of savings must be held in reserves. (See Section 14.6 for step-by-step guidance on how to assess the viability of a savings product.) An MFI recovers the costs of mobilizing deposits through fees and by investing the deposits, typically in the MFI's loan portfolio.

[3] Because it takes time to develop trust and because of the need to develop products, systems, and staff, administrative costs are higher early on. How an institution covers these high initial costs depends on its situation. Larger institutions may be able to use revenues from other products or raise interest rates. Small, member-owned institutions may rely on volunteer management until they can afford to pay staff (see Box 8–2). For other institutions, these costs are appropriate places for donor subsidy.

[4] ASA, the fourth mature large-volume institution, has a high cost ratio due to other factors discussed below.

[5] Because VYCCU's remote product represents just 2 percent of VYCCU's total number of accounts, it should be considered an outlier. With this product, cross subsidies enable an office-based institution to deepen its outreach on a very small scale.

[6] The administrative expense ratio is defined as all administrative expenses (such as salaries, benefits, supplies, utilities, and depreciation) divided by the average total assets.

[7] "Savings Operations for Very Small or Remote Depositors: Summary of Proceedings 29th April–17th May 2002" (2002).

[8] Laura Elser, Alfred Hannig, and Sylvia Wisniwski, "Comparative Analysis of Savings Mobilization Strategies," in *Challenges of Microsavings Mobilization—Concepts and Views from the Field,* ed. Alfred Hannig and Sylvia Wisniwski (Eschborn, Germany: GTZ, n.d.), 288.

4

Developing or Strengthening Savings Operations

What's Involved

*Mohammed Azim Hossain, Gerry Lab-oyan,
Kathryn Larcombe, and Khem Raj Sapkota*

Most of this book looks at specific aspects of savings mobilization, from products to pricing, promotion, and management systems. But what about the bigger picture? What must a microfinance institution do to start seriously mobilizing deposits?

Experienced practitioners agree: the changes an institution must undertake go well beyond simply offering a new product. In a successful deposit-taking institution, depositors and deposit transactions typically far outnumber borrowers and loan transactions. Successfully mobilizing deposits requires changes in staff attitudes, skills, and functions; new management systems; and even a new organizational structure, staff, and office. In other words, mobilizing deposits is transforming.[1] To succeed with it, the most senior managers must be open and completely committed to changes at every level of the organization and must be personally involved in the change efforts. Without this, the savings initiative will go very slowly or will affect the organization only minimally.

This chapter looks first at the steps involved in developing or strengthening voluntary savings operations. It then examines the most common challenges. These challenges vary by type of institution. For example, for a new microfinance institution (MFI) or one that has just transformed into a bank, becoming known and trusted is a huge and critical task. Not so for a large state bank—which may grapple most with how to reorient large numbers of staff. The chapter illuminates

The authors offer their sincere appreciation to Aris Alip and David Cracknell for their valuable feedback.

these differences with cases from a range of institutions: new and established, small and large, weak in savings and new to it, shifting from compulsory savings and from member-only savings, autonomous and state-supported. It ends by examining the smaller challenges that face institutions that choose to serve only their borrowers.

4.1 STEPS TO DEVELOP
OR STRENGTHEN SAVINGS OPERATIONS

While the challenges of developing savings operations vary, the steps needed are basically the same. For many institutions they start not with savings but with credit.

4.1.1 Establishing Financial Discipline

An institution should mobilize deposits only if it can keep them secure; stringent credit management and internal controls, sound liquidity and asset liability management, and sustainable operations are essential. For institutions that could meet these criteria but do not, developing savings starts with strengthening management. So, for example, the World Council of Credit Unions (WOCCU), an industry leader in supporting savings operations, starts its savings work with its partners by helping them to meet rigorous financial standards (see Box 4–1).

WOCCU expects credit unions to protect savings by establishing "the core disciplines of delinquency control, loan loss provisions, liquidity reserves, control of non-earning assets, profitability and capital reserving." A key to achieving these standards is measurement. WOCCU measures financial discipline with its PEARLS financial-performance ratios. The system defines forty-four financial ratios that are used to track financial discipline in six key areas. For each ratio WOCCU has set a value that indicates that a credit union has achieved an appropriate level of financial discipline. Of course, WOCCU helps credit unions and other MFIs institute the credit management and other policies, methodologies, and practices necessary to achieve these ratios.[2]

4.1.2 Phases of Implementation

Only when its credit and financial management are solid should an MFI develop savings operations. First, the new initiative will need a motor—a strong champion from the board of directors and the commitment of senior management. Second, skillful planning of the organizational transformation process and even reorganizing the institution will be critical. An institution will usually need to upgrade and, in many cases, relocate its branches. It must then research the market; design the service and management systems to support it; and test and refine these. Finally, it will be ready for large-scale implementation. The entire process

Box 4–1. Strengthening Operations in a Small Institution: Moderna Credit Union

When the Moderna credit union in Nicaragua turned twenty-five years old, it had 504 members and just forty-four depositors. Only 4 percent of its loan portfolio was funded by savings. The credit union suffered from high delinquency and had no loan loss provisions, credit policies, or marketing or business plans. Just four years later Moderna had 2,400 members including 1,370 savers and—above all—professional commercial operations. With technical assistance from WOCCU, Moderna strengthened its savings operations in two stages, with method and discipline.

Developing financial discipline. To assure the security of deposits, WOCCU first worked with Moderna to achieve WOCCU's standard targets for costs, liquidity, capital adequacy, cash holdings, delinquency, provisioning, and non-earning assets. Moderna:

- Developed a business plan and regularly reported to WOCCU on its performance;
- Reconciled its accounting and instituted a new transparent accounting system;
- Instituted rigorous risk-based lending policies, delinquency analysis, and collection;
- Improved its liquidity management and established adequate reserves; and
- Adopted new policies and procedures for internal controls and savings.

Only after meeting these standards did Moderna turn its focus to mobilizing deposits.

Marketing: Image, Products, and Promotion. During the second stage WOCCU helped Moderna develop a market-oriented image and products. WOCCU trained and assisted Moderna's staff with market research, product development, customer service, marketing, and savings management. It also funded improvements in Moderna's physical facility. Moderna developed a trustworthy image in numerous ways. It remodeled its building to make it more attractive, welcoming, and secure; introduced professional-quality forms and stationery; and trained its employees to be friendly and professional. After conducting market research for the first time, Moderna introduced seven savings products with attractive features and rates. It also increased its competitiveness by offering more convenient hours, developing a more efficient MIS, and marketing itself as a safe institution that provides valuable services. It marketed its products with raffles, radio spots, banners, posters, and fliers, and started to recruit members by visiting markets, businesses, and organizations.

Moderna also enhanced its image by becoming part of a national certified credit union brand organized by WOCCU. The brand conveys that its members are trustworthy, efficient, and professional. For Moderna, this image reflected reality: by 2001, Moderna could boast well-defined policies and procedures, professional documents, friendly attentive service, shorter waits, fewer errors, and convenient quality services.

Summary of José Benito Miranda Díaz, "Nicaragua: Putting the Framework into Place," in *Striking the Balance in Microfinance: A Practical Guide to Mobilizing Savings*, ed. Brian Branch and Janette Klaehn (Washington, DC: PACT Publications, 2002), 185–211.

can take several years depending on the service, managers' commitment, and the institution's size and management capacity.

1. Developing a committed core of managers. Developing successful savings operations will require the support of every part of the institution. Developing a nucleus of the head of the MFI and senior managers highly committed to savings is critical. This group should be ready to change the organization's policies and structure. Their openness will help them find the right policies for the new initiative. The core group must also be able to introduce savings to the rest of the staff. Identifying the core group, training its members and exposing them to institutions that are successfully mobilizing deposits is an important first step in developing savings operations. Support from outsiders with expertise in savings can be extremely helpful and, in many cases, crucial (see Box 4–2).

2. Planning and reorganization. In most organizations the institutional transformation process needed to develop these operations is a major undertaking that benefits from project management skills; careful planning and control are essential.[3] Implementing savings often requires hiring additional managers and restructuring the institution. This can include developing operations and marketing functions.[4]

3. Upgrading premises. To inspire trust, meet government regulations, and provide convenient access, many institutions must seriously upgrade or even relocate their branches. Microcredit institutions may need to add a waiting room, back office, counters, and a safe or strong room. Some institutions will need to refurbish their buildings to make them inviting and efficient, while others will need to relocate altogether to a more trafficked and safe location. This can be extremely expensive. These costs should be anticipated and built into the institution's budget.

4. Researching the market. Market research is the key to developing viable services that meet client demand. Many institutions know only their current market: low-income borrowers. To offer a stand-alone liquid service that is viable, they will need to understand and attract a much larger and usually better-off market. This can require offering additional services.

5. Designing the product(s) and delivery. A well-designed service can attract enormous demand. Of course, its design should be driven not only by market demand but also by the MFI's management capacity and the need to cover costs. For many institutions, the costs of mobilizing deposits turn out to be higher than expected, and recovering costs is a major challenge (see Box 4–3). Forecasting costs and setting an appropriate interest rate are crucial steps in designing the service (see Appendix 4.1 and Chapter 9).

Box 4–2. Adding Savings to Credit:
Tchuma, Mozambique

Tchuma was founded in 1999 with the plan that it would mobilize deposits only after its credit operations were running well and it had established itself in the market. So, in 2002, when it had forty-five hundred active clients and a portfolio of about US$750,000, Tchuma began developing savings operations. The principal motivation was to fund its loan portfolio and provide a service that clients said they wanted.

A partnership with the Fundació Un Sol Món, the development body set up by the Caixa Catalunya, a Spanish savings bank, provided an experienced banker as a consultant for a year. During the first eight months the consultant analyzed Tchuma and its procedures and, with a team drawn from all its key operational areas, researched the market and developed the products—a simple passbook savings account and a contractual product with higher interest for higher balances. The team also developed financial projections, procedures, and training material. In all of this the consultant's expertise was crucial.

Developing the product was relatively easy; delivering it was more difficult. Tchuma's existing premises needed remodeling, so management tested the first product in a new branch. Because its software supplier could not complete a new savings module until six months after the pilot was to be launched, Tchuma opted for a temporary MIS solution—and over a year later was still using it. This delayed the rollout of the first product by nine months and the launch of the second savings product for over a year. Tchuma learned from hard experience the pivotal importance of a solid, well-integrated MIS.

Launching the new product required a change of attitude by all staff and significant management time. Yet, at the same time as it was initiating savings, Tchuma was as busy as usual: changing its credit methodology and management structure, opening two new branches, and considering initiating operations in other provinces. Of all these undertakings, only the launch of the savings product could be postponed. In short, giving the pilot the attention it warranted was difficult. Even Tchuma's donors were much more interested in its portfolio performance than in its savings operations. After all, credit brings in money, while savings operations are, at least initially, simply a drain on resources. Despite the difficulties, within a year of launching its new savings services in one branch, Tchuma had 1,213 savings accounts that held some US$17,500, an average of US$14 per depositor. These results were still below the level Tchuma had desired, however.

---

6. Preparing for pilot testing.[5] Even for a pilot test, an MFI will need the initial management systems, trained staff, and promotion to support the new product:

Management systems. Compared to credit, the less predictable cash flows from liquid savings services make it harder to prevent fraud, manage liquidity, and balance assets and liabilities. Most MFIs need to institute a more rigorous internal control environment and comprehensive new internal controls before

Box 4–3. Expanding Services to the Public: VYCCU Savings and Credit Cooperative Ltd.

VYCCU, a cooperative in the plains of Nepal, was six years old and had about one thousand members when it obtained a limited banking license that allowed it to mobilize liquid savings from the public. VYCCU sought a license in part because it wanted to mobilize enough savings to meet its members' demand for loans. Becoming a regulated institution and mobilizing deposits from the public required many changes and posed several challenges.

In order to mobilize savings from the public, VYCCU had to:

- *Educate its members:* Ensure that members understood the initiative by providing them with reading materials, training, and exposure visits to other institutions.
- *Develop skills:* Train staff and governing members in how to keep new accounts, manage more complex liquidity, and prepare new reports.
- *Upgrade the office:* Expand from one to three rooms by adding a back office and waiting room, improving security, and purchasing furniture and office equipment.
- *Understand and fulfill regulations:* Understand banking systems and the policies of the Central Bank; coordinate operations with government offices.
- *Plan for financial sustainability:* Develop a three-year plan for how future transactions would enable VYCCU to cover all expenses and losses.
- *Design new products:* Design different schemes to collect more savings and provide more flexible loans.
- *Upgrade and formalize management systems:* Revise the accounting system, formalize policies and procedures, and develop the capacity to generate reports.

The biggest challenges were staff and cost recovery. VYCCU needed the skills of a chartered accountant to handle the more complex liquidity management and reporting requirements. At the same time, meeting new legal requirements and serving the public increased VYCCU's costs and reduced its operating margin: VYCCU had to upgrade its office and pay for technical assistance for two years; maintain a higher rate of reserves; lower its lending rates to comply with government regulations and compete in the market; hire two new counter staff and three new security guards; and pay for more stationery, travel, and communications. Its more commercial look meant that VYCCU received fewer subsidies at the same time that members expected more services. To cover its higher costs, VYCCU had to attract larger depositors away from more secure and better-capitalized for-profit institutions that offered a wider range of services. The changes also meant that VYCCU's volunteer board had to put in longer hours.

Despite these challenges, mobilizing deposits from the public enabled VYCCU to meet its goals. Within a few years of receiving its limited banking license, VYCCU was serving four times as many depositors, meeting its members' demand for credit, offering more products, and serving a larger area. And, it continued to cover its full costs with operating revenues.

offering services on even a pilot basis. New or improved liquidity management, asset liability management, and information systems will also be crucial. For some institutions these changes are not complex; managers may simply need to figure out what is required and review and adjust the present systems. However, "knowing what you don't know" is difficult. Outside experts can be crucial to identifying and developing the systems needed.[6]

Human resources. The new operations are likely to require a new organizational culture, attitudes, skills, and staff. That, in turn, requires retraining existing staff and, over time, large-scale training of new staff as well as changes in incentives and the mission (see Section 4.2.2).

Promotional strategy. Actively developing the awareness, trust, and interest of the target market will be crucial for many institutions—those that are new, that operate in competitive environments, that are not perceived as highly professional, or that aim to break into higher-income markets (see Box 4–4). Other institutions may find that word-of-mouth advertising is sufficient, especially if they are offering simple, demand-driven products (see Section 4.2.3).

7. Pilot testing.[7] A pilot project should test how the product is received in the market, how well new operating procedures and management systems work, and the product's effect on staff workloads, financial viability, liquidity, and systems. Pilot testing is crucial to successful commercial rollout. Management should carefully consider how the pilot site is selected and should expect that a pilot test will take six to twelve months.[8] The test should generate the information needed to solve potential problems before the product is offered branch wide.[9]

8. Evaluating the pilot and changing the design. Based on the results of the pilot, management may need to change the product design to better meet demand and control costs, more realistically project usage and costs in order to reset interest rates appropriately, revise the management systems and training that will support the product, and develop or refine the marketing strategy. Where the pilot test reveals the need for major changes, and in large institutions, management may want to run a second pilot before offering the product institution wide.[10]

9. Preparing for institution-wide implementation. Based on the pilot test the institution should develop a business plan for rolling out the new services. It should address the logistics of expansion. In addition, offering the product on a large scale will require a significant investment in training and systems development. Although the initial systems will have been designed before the pilot test, the test will probably expose major areas for further development and revision.[11]

Developing systems is an ongoing process. In particular, if the MIS is computerized, continuing revisions may require substantial time from a professional information-technology team. Similarly, managers can mistakenly develop a new

Box 4–4. Starting Up with Savings: Cooperative Bank of Benguet, the Philippines

The Cooperative Bank of Benguet (CBB), a rural bank in the Philippines, started offering savings services from the moment it opened its doors in 1992. As a new institution, CBB found its greatest challenges were establishing the track record and reputation needed to attract depositors, developing an MIS to record a growing volume of accounts and transactions, managing liquidity when depositors were testing whether they could really withdraw their savings, and controlling the risk of fraud.

CBB's first step in developing savings services was to *define its target savings market:* small savers. Management decided to start by attracting rural and remote savers. These were seen as more stable because they are sheltered from external shocks, more predictable because their cash flow is seasonal, and cheaper to serve because rural people transact less frequently. Serving rural savers also seemed to be a good way for a new player in the market to attract small urban depositors; that is, by developing a good business image with rural and remote savers, CBB could attract their urban relatives and friends. While it was building its volume of rural small savers to a viable level, CBB also chose for cost reasons to offer competitive savings products to medium and large savers in the areas near its head office.

CBB then *designed its savings products.* CBB did not engage in protracted market research. Rather, it surveyed products already in the market and the preferences of potential clients quickly. It sought information to make a few specific decisions: minimum balance and account sizes, minimum size to earn interest, interest rates, liquidity, and policies regarding dormancy, pre-termination, and account rollover. These short studies yielded the information CBB needed to design its two products, a liquid passbook and time deposits.

Next CBB set out to *attract small savers.* In order to establish a track record and reputation, CBB focused on breaking even quickly. It also defined "trust and confidentiality" as the core image it would strive to convey throughout its operations and marketing. CBB designed and tested a variety of savings promotions to draw in customers. It also sought to gain community goodwill by locating branches at trafficked points in rural and remote areas and by offering savings products as part of a package of microfinance services.

CBB *managed its chief operational challenges* by setting a relatively high level of cash reserves, acquiring locally proven software and a larger and faster computer, and instituting numerous internal controls to minimize and detect fraud.

CBB quickly succeeded both in establishing itself and in serving small depositors. In twelve years CBB mobilized over US$1.2 million in more than ninety-four hundred accounts. Although rural banks in the Philippines normally break even in two to three years, CBB turned a profit within just one year. Furthermore, 91 percent of its accounts hold an average of just US$28. At the same time CBB has also attracted larger, less costly accounts: 63 percent of CBB's volume of deposits is held in accounts of over US$1,200.

internal-control system and think that the job is complete; in fact, continually revisiting and improving on these as new risks become apparent is crucial.

Some institutions start by mobilizing deposits only from their borrowers. After testing and strengthening their products and systems, they start mobilizing deposits from the general public. This sequencing limits the number of new accounts and enables the MFI to test and refine its systems with a customer base that is familiar and predisposed.

4.2 MAJOR CHALLENGES

People who are interested in developing or strengthening savings operations often focus on products. Relative to other challenges, "getting the product right" is fairly straightforward. Building client trust, developing staff and systems to support the product, and recovering costs can be much tougher. Four of these bigger challenges—recovering costs, developing sufficient internal controls, managing liquidity, and balancing assets and liabilities—are considered in detail in other chapters. This section discusses three challenges that are not discussed elsewhere in the book: developing staff, building client trust, and managing information.

4.2.1 Developing Staffing and Staff

Staffing for savings will depend on the volume of transactions supported by the branch, the number of branches, and the range of financial products it offers. Section 8.1 describes the efficient branch staffing model used by the BRI unit system. In most cases an institution should anticipate the following changes in staffing when it moves into savings mobilization.

Counter staff: To manage the greater volume of transactions, more cashiers will be needed to staff the counter. These staff must know how to manage transactions and handle cash and controls. In a large branch a customer-service person may be appropriate. In any case, all front-line staff must be ready and able to promote savings products in addition to their existing workload. They must consider it their job to attract customers, inspire trust, convey goodwill, and meet customer needs. In many cases they also must be able to relate to a wider range of clients than they did in the past. In recruiting and training staff, these qualities should be front and center.

Branch financial manager: This role is pivotal and may be new. If the branch already has a fully employed financial manager, the branch manager will need to consider carefully how to reshuffle tasks in order to enable this person to shoulder significantly more work and more varied work. Closing the books daily can be demanding, and the greater variety of less predictable transactions requires more attention to detecting irregularities, enforcing controls, and monitoring liquidity. This person must be the safe pair of hands that follows procedures to the letter and the eyes that constantly watch for irregularities. The financial manager must be prepared to be the first in the office in the morning and the last to leave at night, and must rarely fall ill.

Branch manager: Although not a new position, the branch manager will have to handle numerous new responsibilities: managing formerly unknown risks, motivating staff, and looking at such vital issues as managing queues in the branch. The branch manager must be able to oversee more complex and demanding liquidity and asset liability management, internal controls, information systems, and reporting requirements.

Head office: Depending on the size of the institution, the head office may also require additional financial managers, information-technology staff, internal auditors, and marketing staff. In particular, it is vital that the head office develop a counterpart to the branch financial managers; this person should be able to advise, supervise, and if necessary, cover for the branch financial manager. Headquarters support staff who are not directly involved in savings will need to understand its demands in order to define procedures that are simple and adequate to support branch operations.

Because of costs, many smaller institutions start by working primarily or solely with the staff they have. For example, marketing is a crucial and, in many cases, new function. At least initially, however, many institutions form their marketing team from existing staff, use consultants to develop their marketing expertise and expect their front-line staff to promote their products. Tchuma in Mozambique made the difficult decision to shorten its banking hours in order to manage the additional workload associated with mobilizing deposits with its existing staff.

Human Resource Management: Training

Savings-oriented human resource management is crucial to developing successful savings operations. Management must consciously develop a savings mobilization culture and mechanisms for accountability. If the existing institutional culture, staff incentives, and evaluation system reward only strong credit performance, management must change these to prioritize savings. The leaders of BRI's unit system paved the way for massive savings mobilization by establishing a culture of accountability, profitability, and responsiveness to the market that it reinforced through incentives and training (see Box 3–2).[12]

Training is the lifeblood of change. Furthermore, the demand for well-designed savings services can grow very quickly. It is crucial to have the capacity to recruit and train large numbers of staff before offering the new service institution wide. Many institutions provide senior managers and staff with initial and ongoing training in the importance and mechanics of managing deposits. This should include training in policies and procedures, management systems, marketing, and customer service. Initially, the value of savings transactions is very small relative to the value of credit transactions. This can lead staff to pay insufficient attention to this side of the business. Allowing the branches to deviate from procedures at this early stage on the grounds that the values involved are small will create bad habits that will be difficult to correct later on. In this context, training conveys the importance management places on savings. Furthermore, with savings, the focus on meeting the customer's needs must permeate the institution. Training will be a key to achieving this, as will changes in incentives and recruitment (see Box 4–5).

The task of training counter staff, in particular, is enormous. Training even one cashier can require almost constant supervision for several weeks and, even during the pilot phase, a number of cashiers are needed to allow for breaks, leaves, promotions, and terminations. Furthermore, cross training cashiers and other counter staff so that they can stand in for one another and for other administrative staff can be very useful. Even during the pilot phase, new cashiers must be trained almost constantly. Projecting and providing for this and other training needs—and assuming rapid growth—is critical to developing sound savings operations.

Developing Commitment

Before taking on additional staff, however, management will first need to assure itself—through the pilot test and cost-benefit analysis—that the new service will be worthwhile. Therefore, the new workload will initially have to be handled by people who probably think that they are already working to their limit. Convincing credit officers to promote the new product and temporarily to take on new roles—often as cashiers—can be particularly challenging (see Section 4.3.2).

Many institutions find that one of the biggest obstacles to developing sound savings operations is staff resistance. With an established organization that is already focused on its existing activities, "creating space" to introduce a completely new activity that requires completely different ways of working can be quite difficult. Managers may have a hard time focusing their attention on savings. Branch staff may not want to promote flexible services with non-standard payments that require more careful record keeping and controls. They also may perceive credit to be more critical to their institution's viability.

MFIs can overcome staff resistance and develop their commitment in numerous ways:

Exposure to others' experience: Visits to other formal financial institutions, within and outside the country, and reading materials can help board members and senior managers develop a shared vision of large-scale savings mobilization, its benefits, and the changes it requires.

Mission and compelling rationale: A key to changing the institutional culture is to change the institution's mission to incorporate savings as well as credit.

Box 4–5. From Mandatory to Commercial Voluntary Savings: Banco Caja Social, Colombia

In the early 1990s Banco Caja Social converted from being a *caja de ahorros* into a commercial bank. This conversion and the permanent demands of a highly competitive market brought major changes and challenges to the institution. Soon after, regulatory changes in Colombia required the bank to terminate a ten-year-old, successful product that provided loans linked to mandatory savings. Although Banco Caja Social was already offering voluntary deposit services (time deposits represented up to 40 percent of its deposit volume), the mandatory savings product still had represented a significant part of its savings portfolio and had accounted for more than 80 percent of its savings accounts. Nevertheless, within a few years the bank was financing nearly its entire loan portfolio with US$392 million in voluntary deposits. Its experience shifting into commercial voluntary savings is instructive.

Replacing the mandatory savings product with voluntary savings products for the commercial market demanded efforts from the bank staff and sales force. Several management decisions enabled Banco Caja Social to succeed:

- *Recruitment and training:* Using psychological and socioeconomic indicators, Banco Caja Social began to recruit and train staff not only on their banking skills but also on their abilities to establish long-term relationships with the clients. The bank also began to invest a lot in training its sales force to promote savings services.
- *Incentive system:* An incentive scheme was developed to reward performance, introducing the concept of variable salaries that depend on achieving goals. Client feedback is used to assess the quality of customer service (see Box 15–3).
- *Market research:* Banco Caja Social invested heavily in market research. A special department designs and conducts qualitative and quantitative research to understand how the target market perceives the bank's products. Moreover, each savings product has a product manager charged with evaluating and improving its quality. Banco Caja Social's executives credit much of its products' success to market research.
- *New product development:* Market research drives the design, testing, and marketing of its products. Banco Caja Social has learned that clients demand a broader array of terms, prices, liquidity, and access than it can feasibly offer. By constantly monitoring client demand and satisfaction, the bank ensures that it is providing products with the attributes most in demand by its market.
- *Marketing and promotion:* Banco Caja Social conducts and frequently updates targeted promotional campaigns to strengthen its position in the market. Banco Caja Social distinguishes its products by giving them names that are simple, descriptive, and memorable, such as "Progress" and "Day by Day."

—Hillary Miller Wise

The advocates for savings mobilization should be ready to explain over and over in simple, clear, and compelling terms why this change is important (see Box 4–6). For many credit-based MFIs, the value of savings as a reliable source of loan capital is initially more compelling than its value to clients.[13]

Role modeling and commitment at the senior levels: Seeing senior management take on new roles and show their commitment to the new savings operations can convince staff at lower levels that the changes are serious.

Transparent, participatory product development process: Bringing managers and staff from across the institution into the process of researching the market and developing the product can be instrumental in obtaining their and their colleagues' commitment to the changes required.[14]

Pilot project: A successful pilot project can convince skeptics that the poor can save. The results of the project can be used in training to convince staff of the value of the changes they are being asked to implement.

Internal communication: Ongoing internal communication about progress through meetings, memos, or newsletters can reinforce management's prioritization of savings mobilization.

In these ways, and with training and incentives, everyone from senior managers to branch staff must be persuaded that from now on "things are going to be different."

4.2.2 Managing Information

An institution's MIS strongly affects its efficiency and can make the difference between savings operations that are viable and those that are not. Adding or strengthening savings operations often requires a new banking information system that can handle a huge volume of new transactions, balance accounts more frequently, and meet the audit and reporting requirements of the regulators.

Computerization at the branch level can contribute greatly to efficiency and can make it easier to offer products with irregular payments. Kenya's Equity Bank found that introducing a computerized MIS enabled it to cut clients' transaction time by 70 percent. By enabling Equity to serve many more customers, Equity's banking information system has been a critical factor in its ability to grow at a rate of more than 60 percent per year (to more than 354,000 customers by July 2003).[15]

At the same time, computerization is not always essential. For example, although the BRI did eventually computerize its units, computerization was not necessary for them to be viable.[16] Indeed, using a manual MIS at the branch level, ASA offers a somewhat flexible savings service to over one million clients and recovers its costs. Because it serves clients in the field, it does not need a computerized MIS to increase its capacity to serve customers in the branch. The volume

Box 4–6. Strengthening Savings in a State Bank: Product and Promotion at BAAC, Thailand

BAAC is a government-owned bank that was established to deliver agricultural credit. Since 1990, the German development institution GTZ has worked with BAAC to help it become financially self-reliant while providing a range of financial services including savings. By 1995, BAAC had succeeded in attracting 4.1 million deposit accounts with an average balance of US$136. Yet some senior managers wanted to reach many more small savers and obtain a larger and more stable deposit base. To this end, in 1995, BAAC developed *Om Sap Thawi Choke* (OSTC) or "*Save and Get a Chance*," a liquid passbook product with a minimum opening balance of just over US$1 and a lottery. By the end of 2002 BAAC held more than 2.3 million OSTC accounts that represented nearly a quarter of its 9.5 million deposit accounts and 10 percent of its volume of deposits. The key to this growth was a well-designed product and careful attention to developing staff commitment.

With the support of GTZ, BAAC moved from developing the OSTC product to offering it in nearly six hundred branches in just two years. Together, GTZ and BAAC's Savings Promotion Division set a time frame for developing, testing, refining, and rolling out the new product. During the initial six months, BAAC and GTZ designed the product and marketing strategy—without market research. They also brought headquarters, regional, and branch managers together in workshops and working groups to refine the product. This paved the way for its acceptance. By keeping the process transparent and having as many staff as possible participate, the division secured staff commitment for field testing.

Over the next year the division tested, evaluated, and refined the product, first on a small pilot basis and then on a large scale. During this process, the division—ever ready to explain the product's benefits—earned management's commitment to OSTC. It also developed the procedures to support the new product and prepared training curricula to instruct branch staff in how to offer and manage it. During the final six months the division conducted workshops nationwide for all branch managers and two additional staff per branch. They also assisted most branches to implement the product, providing materials such as the pilot-test results, legal support when the product was criticized as gambling, and lottery machines.

Initially, senior managers and branch staff doubted that low-income earners would be able and willing to save with BAAC. These doubts gave way when senior managers visited similar Indonesian and German institutions that serve low-income clients and when BAAC's pilot tests dramatically showed Thais' demand for savings products. Ongoing communication and a participatory development process convinced branch staff and others that mobilizing deposits, in general, and OSTC, in particular, were good choices. The introduction of OSTC succeeded because the dynamic forces of the bank together with GTZ persisted in explaining the value of the new product, which was underscored by the striking success of the pilot test. In fact, after two years, every BAAC branch was eager to offer the OSTC.

—Marie-Luise Haberberger, GTZ

of transactions per day can be a factor in deciding when to install savings software. As a rule of thumb, when a branch is handling one hundred or more transactions per day, savings software might make sense. Otherwise, additional personnel might be needed.

Finding the right software, migrating to it, and customizing it can be one of the most significant and ongoing challenges of developing or strengthening savings operations.[17] It requires real expertise and is often costly and time consuming. When choosing software, managers should be sure that they choose or develop specifications for software with the following features:

Security features such as access-level control, protection by passwords, and an audit trail. For example, if the amount that the cashier can disburse without higher authority is limited, the MIS ideally will require an additional authorization code or will highlight in the daily report transactions that require that authority.

Capacity to handle an ever-increasing volume of transactions and data and different savings products, cash, and check deposits. The system should be flexible enough to allow the modification of existing products and the introduction of new ones.

Potential for integration into accounting software. Management should carefully assess whether the savings and the accounting software can be linked so that transactions at the branch level are correctly assigned and transfers between branch and head office are adequately recorded.

Capacity to generate data on cash flow. In the pilot phase the MIS should be able to generate information that can inform future projections, such as the amount of cash that should be held at various levels—with the cashier, in the safe, and in a liquid account at the bank. Only experience and a good information system to track that experience will enable managers to define the amounts that appropriately balance security and returns with liquidity—having enough cash to meet customer demand during the day.

Back-up and auto recovery capability.

Managers should also consider the question of transactions at branches other than where the account is held. A simpler (and cheaper) MIS will only permit transactions (deposits and withdrawals) at the branch where the account is held, but clients, especially in urban areas, typically expect to be served in any branch. The only real solution to this—having the system online—can be immensely expensive. Transactions off-system, while offering a more flexible service, are an invitation to fraud. Prohibiting off-system transactions entirely is the safest route, but in areas prone to power cuts, this can diminish customer service.

Whether computerized or not, what information should the MIS provide? To meet central bank regulations an MIS must be able to report balances accurately to show that the institution is meeting prudential and reserve requirements. Management reporting can be more complicated. Managers should either find a well-tested product or think very hard about what they want to know. For example, knowing the number of accounts and overall average account balances is crucial, but should individual account balance information be month end (which is easier to obtain) or a monthly average (which is more useful)?

Managers should consider the various types of information needed. These will include information related to the performance of the savings product—for example, new accounts this month and number of accounts by size of balance—and to the calculation of incentive payments to staff (see Chapter 15). They will also include information useful for understanding its markets, such as the number of male and female account holders and whether they are depositors only, borrowers only, or both. Gathering input from all the parties that use the information system will be crucial to assuring that it meets their needs.

4.2.3 Inspiring Clients' Trust

People will deposit their savings with an institution only if they perceive it to be secure, reliable, trustworthy, and professional. Therefore, institutions that seek to develop or strengthen savings operations must carefully and methodically develop such an image. To start, managers should clearly articulate how the institution is currently perceived in the market, how they would like it to be perceived, and what they must do to get there. This understanding should come from market research into potential clients' demand and perceptions of the institution and its competition (see Chapter 6).

Management must deliberately and consistently communicate and promote the image it seeks through every aspect of its operations (see Chapter 10). For many institutions, this type of market orientation can represent a significant and important change in institutional culture, particularly for microcredit institutions (see Box 4–7).

To build and strengthen its positive reputation, an institution should have the following:

Excellent customer service. Above all, service that is professional, efficient, friendly, and responsive is vital. Managers must recruit staff with this in mind. Front-line staff should be expected to work quickly; to know and clearly communicate product rules, policies, and procedures; to dress and act professionally; and to treat customers with respect. Training, performance evaluations, and staff incentive schemes should clearly convey and reinforce these expectations. Management should monitor customer service through devices such as customer focus-group discussions, surveys, and "mystery shoppers" (individuals paid to test and report on customer service).

Box 4–7. Strengthening Savings at Postal Savings Banks: Tanzania Postal Bank

As parastatal financial institutions, postal savings banks are expected to offer a full range of savings services nationwide—most often through a dedicated branch network and through post offices operating under agency agreements. While the banks are expected to provide widely accessible, low-cost savings facilities to low-income groups, they are not subject to market demands regarding hiring and firing, performance standards, and profitability. It is not surprising that when compared to commercial institutions, their customer service is often poorer.

There are structural issues too. Having to work through a network of agencies, most of which perform very few transactions, makes it difficult for postal savings banks to move away from manual passbook accounts and to provide consistent levels of customer service. Furthermore, liquidity constraints at post offices mean that agency withdrawal limits are typically very low.

Since 2001, Tanzania Postal Bank (TPB) has found itself in an increasingly competitive market for low-income depositors, particularly from a revitalized and considerably larger National Microfinance Bank. Manual passbook–based accounts and lengthy queues in its banking halls put TPB at a disadvantage.

Together with *MicroSave,* TPB developed and tested a computerized savings account called the Domicile Quick Account (DQA), which significantly increased TPB's speed of service. Although the account was limited to the branch in which the customer opened it, DQAs proved popular with many TPB customers.

DQAs began to change the image of TPB among low-income depositors, but alone the account was not enough to make the bank truly competitive. TPB also needed to modernize its image and to upgrade its service. Decisions were made to:

- Move operations in major towns from post office premises to dedicated branches. While in post offices TPB could not completely control its image with customers or how the banking hall was arranged.
- Gradually rebrand its branch network by upgrading its branch infrastructure, presenting a much clearer, more professional, and consistent image.
- Upgrade its computerized MIS to enable customers to make transactions at any online branch. TPB's network will extend to all of its own branches, though not to the post office agencies.
- Improve its marketing and customer service. A marketing manager was hired from a leading commercial bank. He introduced clear, consistent, marketing material and improved customer communications. While increasing service levels on the manual passbook–based account is difficult, TPB expects that service will improve as more customers convert to online DQA accounts.

TPB still battles against a parastatal institutional culture and background. Despite this, DQAs have made significant progress: as of August 2004, 73,423 DQA accounts with deposits of US$11.6 million represented approximately one-quarter of TPB's total deposit liabilities. In terms of value of transactions, DQA has become TPB's most significant type of account. TPB anticipates further progress once all branches are networked using its new banking system.

—David Cracknell

Market-driven services. Product terms should reflect market demand, and services should be available in convenient locations at convenient hours without long waits.

Governance: An institution that is governed by people who are known, respected, and knowledgeable, and that regularly provides transparent information will inspire the trust of savers. So will supervision and inspection by outsiders.

Professional management: Management should promote managers whom clients will perceive as strong, risk conscious, and trustworthy. Strong internal controls, well-defined and transparent services, and easy access to funds will also inspire trust.

Secure, attractive, and professional appearance: Branches should project a positive image through everything from their physical layout to their colors, signs, and lighting. Consistently designed branches can powerfully reinforce the institution's image or brand (see Section 10.1).[18]

Carefully designed promotion: From advertising to publicity, promotion should consistently convey key messages related to the institution's image. Institutions can develop an image that exudes safety and can become a familiar presence by forging relationships with authorities and community leaders and by sponsoring or otherwise being involved with community events.[19]

4.3 SERVING ONLY BORROWERS:
MOVING FROM MANDATORY INTO VOLUNTARY SAVINGS

Many unregulated microcredit institutions cannot legally mobilize deposits from the public but can do so from their borrowers or members. For institutions that plan to serve their borrowers or members only, how do the steps and challenges above differ?

Although these institutions need not change as completely as other microcredit institutions, the steps described above are the same with a few important exceptions. First, the volume of savings from solely low-income borrowers is unlikely to justify the hiring of new branch staff: credit officers will likely have to double as savings collectors. Second, relocating or upgrading branches to serve the same clientele may be unnecessary, especially if clients are served in the field rather than in the branch. Third, the intent of market research may not be to understand new market segments; instead, management will want to know how much a new product will attract new funds and how much it will draw demand away from the MFI's other products.

For institutions that plan to serve only their borrowers, the greatest challenges are likely to be managing costs, gaining staff commitment, upgrading liquidity management, and controlling for fraud. However, these challenges look somewhat different than they do for institutions that plan to serve the general public (see Box 4–8).

Box 4–8. Shifting from Compulsory to Voluntary Services for Borrowers: ASA

ASA is an extremely efficient, sustainable microcredit NGO with over 2.2 million borrowers and a repayment rate exceeding 99 percent. Because ASA is not regulated, it is unable to mobilize savings from non-members. Furthermore, mobilizing savings from non-members would not be cost effective; with subsidized funds widely available to fund its loan portfolio, ASA lacks a profitable place to invest deposits. Nevertheless, in 1997 ASA decided to improve its services to borrowers by augmenting its mandatory savings with voluntary savings services.

ASA moved into voluntary savings quickly. Within one year it designed and tested four products; adjusted its MIS, liquidity management, and internal controls; hired fourteen new auditors; introduced products to the branches via memos from headquarters; and rolled out the products institution wide.

To manage the voluntary savings, ASA hired more regional managers, reorganized its central office to better monitor branches, and increased zonal managers' visits to clients to verify transactions (see Box 11–2). But more records, more complex liquidity planning, and recording and auditing irregular payments all required more of branch staff. ASA offset their increased workloads with greater efficiencies (see Box 8–6). After closely analyzing its existing MIS, it adopted simpler records and made other adjustments. It also improved staff skills through ongoing on-the-job training made possible by its tight supervisory structure. Finally, it managed unexpected liquidity crunches with a number of short-term measures and then amended its liquidity management systems to prevent similar crises in the future (see Box 12–6).

Staff resistance was a greater impediment. In theory, ASA's new mandatory-voluntary product allowed borrowers to deposit as much over the mandatory minimum as they chose and to withdraw all but 10 percent of their loan size. In fact, many staff did not see the value in accepting irregular deposits. Focused on their lending and repayment targets, and aware that ASA already covered its costs from its lending operations, these staff simply instructed their clients to save twice the mandatory minimum each week. Perhaps with incentives and training, more staff might have accepted flexible deposits.

With several of the products, demand was not what ASA anticipated. For example, with its hybrid mandatory-voluntary product, clients' high level of withdrawals left ASA with a lower average account balance than it had had with its purely compulsory product. ASA's low-income clients, who already shouldered weekly loan payments, may not have had additional cash to accumulate weekly. In order to manage these unexpectedly small and active accounts on a viable basis, ASA tightly integrated them into its existing credit delivery system and dropped its social education during group meetings (see Box 8–6).

In contrast, ASA's liquid product for members' relatives and friends, while very popular, turned out not to be financially viable. In eighteen months, with only word-of-mouth marketing and no effort to change its image or culture, ASA held more than a half million of these accounts. Like the hybrid product, the accounts were small with a high volume of transactions. But unlike the hybrid, they could not be folded into existing mandatory transactions; they cost a lot to administer. To be viable, the product also needed large deposits. The same was true for ASA's time-deposit product. With a five-year maturity and a US$20 minimum, the product was not attractive to low-income clients. More market research might have saved ASA the time and cost of offering these two products, both of which ASA eventually dropped.

4.3.1 Covering Costs

Microcredit institutions that introduce a liquid savings service only to their low-income borrowers often find that the costs are prohibitive. After making loan payments, many low-income borrowers have few additional funds to invest and may be primarily interested in using a savings account for liquidity. This is especially the case for institutions that have a mandatory savings requirement; when they shift to voluntary savings, the institutions can find that withdrawals as well as deposits increase significantly. Net savings grow only slightly, if at all, while the number of transactions and related work climb. This hikes costs without growing revenues.

One way to make a liquid service viable when serving solely low-income borrowers is to "piggyback" it onto the loan delivery system. In particular, institutions with a mandatory savings requirement can fairly easily transform this into a mandatory-voluntary product that allows for deposits and withdrawals in excess of the mandatory amount. This can be viable if the two services use precisely the same delivery system and records, with each member holding a single mandatory-voluntary account. The MIS should be highly efficient, and low or no interest can be paid on liquid or small accounts (see Box 4–8). A cost study of two Nepali institutions offering a mandatory-voluntary product found its administrative cost ratios to be just 1.5–3.2 percent, even though the cost ratios for the voluntary transactions alone were 8–9 percent.[20] In ASA, the costs for the product as a whole were high, over 8 percent, but the marginal cost of the voluntary service was negligible.

4.3.2 Reorienting Staff

Mobilizing voluntary savings with the same staff who do credit is difficult. Credit officers see credit as their primary business, recognize that they must be able to cover costs with loan interest or service charges, and therefore prioritize loan recovery over all else. Because achieving loan targets is tough, they may lack the motivation to also mobilize savings. Credit staff may not see savings mobilization as critical to their job or to their institution's success. Training and changing financial and nonfinancial incentives are essential to bringing credit staff on board.

4.3.3 Liquidity Management

Institutions that shift from mandatory to voluntary savings services for their borrowers face some particular liquidity challenges. Initially, the volume of savings is likely to drop as clients test whether they can actually withdraw their savings. This drop tends to last for less than a year. Some institutions have discouraged these withdrawals by explaining to clients that this can hurt the institution. Others have managed this initial testing by introducing the change in phases across the institution. In any case, management should anticipate that accounts may be very active and that the ongoing average account balance may be lower than it would have been with mandatory savings, especially if clients are poor and savings and loan payments are made at the same time.

4.3.4 Internal Controls

Many institutions that provide voluntary services to only their borrowers use individual staff who serve clients outside of the branch in their communities. This coupled with the shift to irregular payments can invite fraud. Institutions should manage these risks by instituting some of the specific controls outlined in Section 11.4.

4.4 CONCLUSION

Moving into savings is "transforming." It requires institutions to meet financial standards and to take sequenced steps to prepare for, develop, and implement the new services. Any MFI that moves into savings operations will have to address a number of challenges:

- inspiring clients' trust;
- developing staff commitment, attitudes, and skills;
- developing sufficient management information capacity;
- managing liquidity and balancing assets and liabilities;
- adhering to minimum internal control standards; and
- recovering costs.

These challenges of developing or strengthening savings operations can be met only if the board and senior management are seriously committed.

APPENDIX 4.1 SAVINGS PROJECTIONS WORKSHEET

This worksheet[21] is designed to help managers project the income, expenses, and profitability of savings products. The worksheet requires managers to do two things. For the *estimated variables* in Table 4–1, managers must estimate values based on market research and their knowledge of the MFI's operations. For the *calculated variables*, managers must calculate the values using the formulas in the table. The worksheet results will only be as good as the data put into it. Managers should modify the worksheet and update the data regularly to reflect the MFI's reality and information gained from pilot tests. Due to space limitations the worksheet includes just one year. To be useful, managers should extend this sample worksheet to include quarterly data for three to five years.[22]

The worksheet is adapted from a more complete *MicroSave* computerized spreadsheet that is part of the *Savings Pilot-Test Toolkit*. Readers are encouraged to download it from the *MicroSave* website. A computerized spreadsheet enables managers to conduct sensitivity analyses and to examine the key factors that will determine the success or failure of a proposed savings product.

Notes on Worksheet

> *In all cases estimates should only included marginal costs, that is, the additional costs associated with the new savings service (for example, not total rent but only new rent).*

Line 1. Items that have been fully depreciated should be subtracted from the numerator.
Line 3. Most MFIs that have not offered savings services before will need more space. Whether and how much additional space is needed will depend on the number of new staff.
Line 5. This cost has two components. The first is the up-front cost of planning and pilot testing—this component requires a quarterly *estimate* of the amount and value of head office time required. The second component is the staff cost of ongoing monitoring which will be *calculated* based on the number of savings transactions.
Line 18. Ideally, the percentage of indirect expenses the MFI allocates to the new savings product will be based on a rigorous costing analysis of existing products (see Chapter 15).
Line 25. Total cash income less total cash expenses. This differs from total net income: the total costs of fixed asset acquisition are charged directly to the quarter in which the expense was incurred, and the depreciation charge is not included as an expense.
Line 31. Based on the average of total net savings from current and previous quarters.
Line 32. If all accounts earn interest, this figure should be 100 percent. If there is a minimum interest-earning balance, the figure will be lower but will increase as the average account balance grows.
Line 38. There must be just enough staff so that the number of staff hours available per week equals or exceeds the number of hours spent on transactions per week.
Cells a, b, c, and g correspond to the final quarters of lines 28, 29, 30, and 38, respectively.
Cells m, n, o, and q through gg are self-explanatory.
Cell p refers to the percentage of savings not set aside as reserves.

Abbreviations:

acct	account	curr	current	pre	previous
admin	administrative	exp	expense	qtr	quarter
avg	average	hrs	hours	wk	week
				ttl	total

Unless otherwise stated, *cell* refers to the current period.

Table 4–1. Savings Projection Worksheet Explanation of Variables

Line or Cell	Estimated Variables: Basis or Definition
2. Computer maintenance	Anticipated quarterly computer maintenance expense.
3. Rent—if new space required	Quarterly rent for additional office space related to new product.
6. Training	For staff efforts related to new product.
7. Marketing	Based on market position of new product.
8. Other	Other fixed direct expenses associated with new product.
16. Other	Other variable direct expenses associated with new product.
22. Other	Additional income associated with new product.
26. New accounts in period	How many new accounts will be opened each quarter.
32. % of volume earning inter.	Percentage of volume of savings held in accounts that earn interest.
39. Equipment, furniture, etc.	Should include equipment, furniture, fittings, etc.
p. % savings avail. to invest	Investable savings—the portion of savings not set aside as reserves.

Line or Cell	Calculated Variables: Formulas
1. Depreciation (equip. etc.)	(cell 40 / cell v) / 4 quarters
4. Remuneration of add'l. staff	cell 38 * cell x * 3 months
5. Head office/monitoring	(cost of planning and managing pilot test) + ([cell 33 + cell 34] * cell y)
9. Total fixed direct expense	sum of cells 1 to 8
10. Interest	([cell 30 previous qtr. + cell 30 current qtr.] / 2) * cell 45 * (cell z / 4)
11. Account opening docum.	cell 26 * cell aa
12. Deposit documentation	cell 33 * cell bb
13. Withdrawal documentation	cell 34 * cell cc
14. Daily closing docum.	No. of working days per month * 3 months * cell dd
15. Account closing docum.	cell 27 * cell ee
17. Total variable direct	Sum of cells 10 to 16
18. Indirect expenses	(cell 9 + cell 17) * cell ff
19. Total expenses	cell 9 + cell 17 + cell 18
20. Interest	cell 31 previous quarter * cell gg/4
21. Account opening fees	cell 26 * cell hh
23. Total income	cell 20 + cell 21 +cell 22
24. Total net income	cell 23 – cell 19
25. Total net cash flow	(cell 24 – cell 39) + cell 1
27. Accounts closed	cell 28 previous quarter * cell n
28. Net no. of accounts	(cell 28 previous quarter + cell 26 current quarter) – cell 27 current quarter
29. Average balance / account	Estimate for first quarter. All other quarters: cell 29 prev qrtr. * ([1 + cell o] /4)
30. Total net savings	cell 28 * cell 29
31. Avg. investable savings	cell p * ([cell 30 previous quarter + cell 30 current quarter] / 2)
33. Number of deposits	cell 28 * cell q
34. Number of withdrawals	cell 28 * cell r

Line or Cell	Calculated Variables: Formulas
35. Weekly hours: deposits	([cell s * cell 33] / 60 minutes per hour) / 13 weeks per quarter
36. Weekly hrs: withdrawals	([cell t * cell 34] / 60 minutes per hour) / 13 weeks per quarter
37. Weekly hours: total	cell 35 + cell 36
38. Number of staff	cell 37 / cell u. Round up to nearest whole number.
40. Cumulative equip etc.	line 40 previous quarter + line 39 current quarter
d. Average total deposits	(0 + sum cells 30 for each quarter) / 5
e. Total admin. expense	([sum of cell 9 all qtrs.] + [sum of cell 17 all qtrs.]) – sum cell 10 all quarters
f. Total financial expense	(sum of cell 10 for each quarter) – (sum of cell 21 for each quarter)
h. Income / expenses	(sum cells 23 all qtrs. – sum cells 21 all quarters) / (cell e + cell f)
i. Income / direct expense	(sum cell 23 all qtrs. – sum cell 21 all qtrs.) / ([cell e – sum cell 18 all qtrs.] + cell f)
j. Financ. exp. / avg. ttl. savings	cell f / cell d
k. Admin. exp. / avg. ttl. savings	cell e / cell d
l. Direct exp. / avg. ttl. savings	(cell e – sum cell 18 all qtrs.]) / cell d
m. Number of accounts / staff	cell a / cell g

Table 4–2. Savings Projection Worksheet

Income and Expenses Associated with New Product
(in 1000s)

Months	0–3	4–6	7–9	10–12
EXPENSES				
1. Depreciation (equip. etc.)	16	32	32	48
2. Computer maintenance	5	10	10	15
3. Rent (if required)	0	0	0	0
4. Remuneration of additional staff	75	150	150	225
5. Head office/manager monitoring	25	24	22	20
6. Training	110	10	0	30
7. Marketing	50	25	15	10
8. Other	0	0	0	0
9. Total fixed direct expenses	281	251	229	348
10. Interest	5	15	23	32
11. Account opening documentation	135	100	90	80
12. Deposit documentation	10	17	24	29
13. Withdrawal documentation	15	26	36	44
14. Daily closing documentation	10	10	10	10
15. Account closing documentation	0	1	1	2
16. Other	0	0	0	0
17. Total variable direct expenses	176	169	184	197

Summary of Year One Results

a. Number of accounts	1,940
b. Average balance per acct	8,376
c. Total savings (1000s)	16,246
d. Average total savings (1000s)	8,614
e. Total admin expenses (1000s)	1,759
f. Total financial expenses (1000s)	331
(total interest expenses—fee income)	
g. Total number of staff	3

Key Ratios

h. Total income/total expenses	31%
i. Total income /total direct expenses	40%
j. Financial expenses/avg total savings	3.8%
k. Admin expenses/avg total savings	20.4%
l. Direct admin expenses/avg total savings	15.1%
m. Number of accounts/staff person	647

Other Variables for Calculations
Accts, transactions, and staff variables

n. Accounts closed in quarter	2.5%

	0–3	4–6	7–9	10–12
18. Indirect Expenses	114	105	103	136
19. Total Expenses	570	525	516	680
INCOME				
20. Interest	47	132	204	272
21. Account opening fees	135	100	90	80
22. Other	0	0	0	0
23. Total income	182	232	294	352
24. Total net income	(388)	(293)	(222)	(328)
25. Total net cash flow	(565)	(453)	(190)	(473)

Projected Inputs to Income and Expenses

Months:	0–3	4–6	7–9	10–12
Accounts				
26. New accounts in period	675	500	450	400
27. Accounts closed in period	17	29	39	
28. Net number of accounts	675	1,158	1,579	1,940
29. Average balance per account	7,500	7,781	8,073	8,376
30. Total net savings (1000s)	5,062	9,012	12,749	16,246
31. Avg investable savings (1000s)	1,898	5,278	8,160	10,873
32. % of volume that earns interest	32%	33%	34%	35%

(as % of total accounts previous quarter)	15%
o. Annual increase in savings balances	75%
p. % of savings available to invest	2.5
q. No. of deposits per account / month	2.5
r. No. of withdrawals per account / month	2.0
s. Staff time per deposit (minutes)	3.0
t. Staff time per withdrawal (minutes)	41
u. Working hours per week	
Expense variables	
v. No. of years over which equipment etc. is depreciated	3
x. Remuneration per additional staff person per month (1000s)	25
y. Head office/manager monitoring cost (per transaction)	0.50
z. Interest rate on savings accounts (with balances over the minimum)	2.5%
aa. Account opening documentation*	200
bb. Deposit documentation**	2.0
cc. Withdrawal documentation**	3.0

Transactions and staff

33. Number of deposits per quarter	5,063	8,686	11,844	14,548
34. No. of withdrawals per quarter	5,063	8,686	11,844	14,548
35. Staff hours on deposits / week	13.0	22.3	30.4	37.3
36. Staff hours on withdrawals / week	19.5	33.4	45.6	56.0
37. Total staff hours / week	32.5	55.7	75.9	93.3
38. Number of staff	1	2	2	3

Setup costs: capital assets (1000s)

39. Equipment, furniture, etc.	193	193	0	193
40. Cumulative equip., furn., etc.	193	385	385	578

dd. Daily closing documentation***	150
ee. Account closing documentation*	50
ff. Indirect exp (as % of total direct exp)	25%

Income Variables

gg. Interest earned on investments	10%
hh. Account opening fee	200

* cost per account opened or closed

** cost per transaction

*** cost per day

Notes

[1] Marguerite Robinson, a pioneer in the area of microsavings, has emphasized for years the wholesale changes that must accompany the mobilization of small deposits. For example, see Marguerite S. Robinson, "Introducing Savings Mobilization in Microfinance Programs: When and How?" CGAP Focus Note 8 (1995), in *Are You Really Ready? The Potential Pitfalls of Savings Mobilisation* (Nairobi, Kenya: MicroSave, n.d.), 2.

[2] See Brian Branch and Janette Klaehn, "The Keys to Striking the Balance: An Introduction to Savings Mobilization," in *Striking the Balance in Microfinance: A Practical Guide to Mobilizing Savings*, ed. Brian Branch and Janette Klaehn (Washington, DC: PACT Publications, 2002), 11–13.

[3] David Cracknell, email interchange with Madeline Hirschland, August 2004.

[4] Ibid.

[5] For important practical detail, see *MicroSave*'s pilot testing toolkit at the *MicroSave* website (www.MicroSave.org).

[6] Cracknell, email interchange.

[7] See *MicroSave's* pilot testing toolkit.

[8] Michael McCord, Graham A. N. Wright, and David Cracknell, "A Toolkit for Planning, Conducting, and Monitoring Pilot Tests: Savings Products" (Nairobi: *MicroSave,* 2004), 12, 21.

[9] Marguerite Robinson, *The Microfinance Revolution,* vol. 1, *Sustainable Finance for the Poor* (Washington, DC: World Bank, 2001), 261.

[10] Graham A. N. Wright, "Beyond Basic Credit and Savings: Developing New Financial Service Products for the Poor" (Kampala: *MicroSave*-Africa, 1998), 8–11. See also Klaus Maurer, "Bank Rakyat Indonesia," in *Challenges of Microsavings Mobilization— Concepts and Views from the Field,* ed. Alfred Hannig and Sylvia Wisniwski (Eschborn, Germany: GTZ, n.d.), 14; and Sylvia Wisniwski, "Microsavings Compared to Other Sources of Funds," in Hannig and Wisniwski, *Challenges,* 13.

[11] Robinson, *Microfinance Revolution*, 1:261; and Marguerite Robinson, *Microfinance Revolution*, vol. 2, *Lessons from Indonesia* (Washington, DC: World Bank, 2002), 270– 79.

[12] Robinson, *Microfinance Revolution*, 2:262–304.

[13] Cracknell, email interchange.

[14] Ibid.

[15] Ibid.

[16] Robinson, *Microfinance Revolution*, 2:313.

[17] Cracknell, email interchange. Also, different institutions require different software.

[18] Graham A. N. Wright et al., "Strategic Marketing for Microfinance Institutions" (Nairobi: *MicroSave,* 2003), 17.

[19] Laura Elser, Alfred Hannig, and Sylvia Wisniwski, "Comparative Analysis of Savings Mobilization Strategies," in Hannig and Wisniwski, *Challenges,* 282–83; Jim Jerving, *Financial Management for Credit Union Managers and Directors* (Madison, WI: WOCCU, 1989), 71; Maurer, "Bank Rakyat Indonesia," 118–19; and Ulrich Wehnert, "Rural Bank of Panabo (RB), Philippines (Case Study)," in Hannig and Wisniwski, *Challenges,* 155, 168–70.

[20] Gokul Pyakurel, "Time Cost Study on Savings Mobilization Implemented by Seven Microfinance Institutions in Nepal" (Kathmandu: Centre for Self-Help Development, 2004).

[21] All credit for the worksheet goes to *MicroSave;* shortcomings in its adaptation are the fault of the editor.

[22] Managers should also adjust several other items: If capital assets—such as computers and furniture—take different numbers of years to depreciate, they should be tracked separately. If the MFI charges other types of fees for savings products (such as transaction fees), each fee should be included as a separate line item. If the MFI pays different interest rates for different sizes of deposits, each category should be tracked separately.

5

Managing to Go Down Market

Regulated Financial Institutions and the Move into Microsavings

Robert Peck Christen, N. Srinivasan,
and Rodger Voorhies

When it comes to offering microfinance services, regulated financial institutions—from commercial and public banks to finance companies and credit unions—typically have striking advantages: expertise in managing financial services, supervision to help ensure that deposits are safe, a volume and diversity of clients that reduces covariant risk, and, often, a secure image in the market. They also may have branches in rural areas. Commercial bank-based microcredit has proven profitable: in Latin America, commercial banks now account for 25 percent of all microlending, and commercial institutions are significantly increasing their provision of microcredit elsewhere as well.[1] But, what about savings?

Numerous not-for-profit institutions—in particular, savings banks, state banks, rural banks, and credit unions—already serve large numbers of small depositors in towns and cities in the course of their regular operations. In addition, a handful of regulated institutions have deliberately expanded their services "down market" on a large and profitable scale. For example, after several years of trying different services and delivery systems, Standard Bank of South Africa developed a new delivery channel—staffed ATMs—that profitably serves a lower-income market. This channel now accounts for over half of its seven million depositors; a 2003 report suggests net annual revenues per account of about US$4.44 and a cost-to-revenue ratio of about 60 percent.[2]

Similarly, the Bank Rakyat Indonesia (BRI) developed its unit system to serve smaller and more rural clients than its conventional branches. In 2003 the BRI's

The authors are grateful for valuable feedback received from Carlos Cuevas and Kathleen Stack.

approximately four thousand units held US$5.3 billion in deposits. Representing just over one-third of the bank's deposit volume, these low-cost funds contributed to the fact that the units brought in nearly half of BRI's 2003 profits.[3] The Atwima Kwanwoma Rural Bank of Ghana also has reached a lower-end market by developing a distinct delivery channel—a mobile collection service. In just three years the service grew to represent one-sixth of the bank's deposits and one-quarter of its deposit accounts. Even banks that enter these markets on a much smaller scale, like Hatton National Bank in Sri Lanka, can reap significant public-relations benefits and meet corporate social responsibilities by serving these less advantaged groups. In short, depending on how it is done, expanding services to smaller and more rural depositors can provide regulated institutions with a bigger and more diverse market, a positive public image, profits, and a substantial source of stable funds for lending.

Yet, despite these potential benefits, few regulated institutions have chosen to expand their savings services down market. And, relative to the demand for savings services, the supply from purely commercial institutions—especially in rural areas—is tiny. Why is this?

For regulated financial institutions, there are three major obstacles to expanding savings services to smaller and more rural depositors: costs, controls, and culture. Covering the high administrative costs of mobilizing small deposits will be possible only if these deposits can be invested in high-yielding, risk-adjusted assets. For most institutions this means that mobilizing small deposits can be financially viable only if they also engage in microcredit.[4] That small depositors often will accept transaction fees and no or negative real interest rates can also help. But even with low financial costs and a high rate of return, it can be difficult to recover the administrative costs of serving small depositors within a conventional bank branch.

To serve small rural depositors, most mainstream financial institutions must develop distinct delivery channels, channels similar to the ones described above that cut administrative costs while bringing services close enough to clients to be useful. Yet, lower-cost delivery channels can pose a significant challenge: how to maintain standards of control and accountability. At the same time, although the corporate culture of many regulated institutions—particularly private banks—is not oriented toward serving the poor, using different delivery channels and staff can at least partially overcome this obstacle.

Once the benefits of serving lower-end and rural markets exceed the costs, institutions will promote these services naturally. But getting to this point takes time and resources. Figuring out how to overcome the obstacles of costs, controls, and culture requires serious senior-level commitment. Therein lies the greatest challenge—but also the key—to mobilizing small deposits. The history of microfinance makes it clear that when they have the will, institutions find secure and cost-effective ways to serve the poor.

This chapter discusses what it takes for regulated financial institutions successfully to move down market with savings—to mobilize deposits from lower-income or more rural markets than they already do. It begins by taking a closer look at the challenges of going down market for these institutions. It then describes the means to overcome these challenges:

- delivery options that cut costs while bringing services close to clients;
- other operational changes that are needed, such as products, staffing, and MIS;
- appropriate organizational structures for managing microfinance operations; and
- regulatory changes that might be helpful or necessary.

Finally, it discusses the crux of the issue: the commitment an institution must have to move successfully into these markets.

5.1 A CLOSER LOOK AT THE CHALLENGES

What makes serving small and rural depositors challenging for regulated financial institutions? Most mainstream institutions have the professional staff, physical infrastructure, array of services, and management systems needed to attract large depositors, keep their deposits safe, and meet government regulations. These requirements imply a cost structure that can make managing large numbers of small accounts difficult. An attractive, secure, and air-conditioned banking hall, well-educated tellers, security guards, and computerized systems come at a cost—and covering this cost requires relatively high loan and savings balances.

For example, a transaction in the banking hall of Opportunity International Bank of Malawi (OIBM) costs the institution US$1.35. Yet, 86 percent of Malawians live on less than US$1 a day. Not surprisingly, a small market survey of even moderately poor urban Malawians found an average preferred deposit size of less than US$3 (see Box 5–1).

Cross subsidization can only go so far. Any banking hall has a limit to the number of daily transactions it can handle. The average size of the accounts to which transactions are associated must be large enough to allow for complete cost recovery. From this perspective each small borrower or depositor transaction may displace the transaction of a larger client. In most cases an institution set up to attract better-off clients simply cannot afford to serve large numbers of smaller depositors in its banking hall.

To reach poorer clientele, regulated institutions often need lower-cost delivery channels, channels that rely on a cheaper physical infrastructure, fewer staff hours, and/or less educated staff who can be paid less. However, lowering staff and infrastructure costs can change the nature of internal control and security. While some electronic technologies can even increase controls while lowering transaction costs, serving depositors from a small, thinly staffed office or with a mobile collector is inherently less secure than doing so from a substantial building with

Box 5–1. The Challenges of Going Down Market: OIBM, Malawi

OIBM was established in 2003 as a microfinance bank in a country in which an estimated 8 percent of the population has access to financial services from a bank and 86 percent of the population earns less than a dollar a day. Recognizing that OIBM's viability would depend on its ability to attract both poor and better-off clients, its senior management built an attractive modern building in a commercial center, hired managers from the banking sector, and established both a corporate and a microfinance division. To minimize back-office expenses, OIBM provides each customer with a complimentary biometric smart card that costs the bank US$5.

OIBM is located in the city of Lilongwe, a few miles from the central market and two to ten miles from numerous poorer areas that it aims to serve on the outskirts of the city. Microcredit officers motorcycle or take buses to organize and serve groups of poor borrowers in these areas. Senior management recognized that in order to reach smaller depositors, particularly in rural areas, it needed to develop separate delivery channels both because of the demand of its target market and because of its own cost requirements.

On the clients' side, a quick market study found that fewer than one-quarter of respondents in poorer outskirts of the city were willing to make the trip to OIBM's branch to deposit their funds. Nearly three-quarters were willing to travel just three miles or less. On the other hand, 43 percent of respondents were interested in saving with a mobile collector, 30 percent in saving in a lockbox, and 18 percent—possibly a relatively poor segment of those surveyed—in saving with a group. Clearly, OIBM needed a way to bring services closer to this target market.

In fact, OIBM's own cost analysis suggested that delivering services outside of the branch would meet its needs. In the survey noted above, nearly two-thirds of those willing to save reported that they would save US$2.50 a week or less (and nearly one-third stated that they would save no more than half this amount). At the same time, each transaction in OIBM's banking hall cost the bank about US$1.35. Management also analyzed the number of clients that the banking hall could serve, the average number of transactions per client and the volume of deposits needed to break even. It found that even if it could attract smaller depositors to the branch, it could not afford to serve them there. Management worried that the number of small depositors and their small transaction sizes would prevent OIBM from developing the volume of deposits needed to recover the costs of operating the banking hall. In fact, the average account balance for small accounts has grown steadily even among the 40 percent of depositors who opened their accounts with the minimum balance of US$4.50. These accounts have also proven stable and reliable.

OIBM's management explored the feasibility and costs of several options—mobile ATMs, satellite offices, and mobile vans—before deciding to test two satellite offices staffed one-half-day per week by mobile staff. Using forty-foot shipping containers, these modular "branches" provide limited savings and lending services right in poor communities. They can be built for about 25 percent of the costs of a regular branch. Since customers do not have to pay taxi and bus fees to travel into town, these branches have different fee and service charges. If they prove feasible, OIBM hopes to establish eight more satellite offices to serve rural communities near the main roads outside of Lilongwe on weekly market days.

a vault. It is this change that can make it so difficult for mainstream financial institutions to employ alternative delivery channels.

Serving the poor can also be difficult culturally. Professional staff who are well suited to serving better-off clients may have a hard time relating to the poor—and the poor may not use a service if they feel unwelcome. Furthermore, better-off clients may be unwilling to wait in lines next to or behind poor depositors, who may slow down tellers by transacting in many small coins. Commercial institutions often carefully cultivate a professional image that appeals to better-off customers. This image may be difficult to maintain when also serving poorer clientele. While public or socially oriented institutions may be able to bridge this divide more easily, the cultural challenge—particularly finding staff that can attract both poorer and better-off clients—should never be underestimated.

On the demand side, a major obstacle is often proximity. For many small and rural depositors, the bank branch is too far away. While better-off clients may travel regularly to a commercial center where a branch is located, poorer and more rural clients are less likely to. To be valuable to these savers, services may have to be available close to their homes or work. In the OIBM market study cited above, 70 percent of respondents were willing to travel only three miles or less to make a deposit. The Atwima Kwanwoma Rural Bank more than doubled its volume of deposits by providing a doorstep service (see Box 5–2). When it comes to savings, distance and ease in making transactions matter.

5–2 DELIVERY SYSTEMS:
THE KEY TO MANAGING COSTS, CULTURE, AND PROXIMITY

Delivery channels that serve poor individuals outside of conventional branches are the key to managing costs, culture, and proximity. In many environments even a banker committed to serving the rural poor would find it difficult to manage large numbers of small transactions cost effectively. However, appropriate delivery technology coupled with suitable product design and streamlined procedures can drastically reduce transaction costs and/or increase average account balances to a viable level. Chapter 8 describes in detail a number of delivery innovations that do this while bringing services physically closer to clients. Many of these are being used by regulated financial institutions to go down market. For example:

- Standard Bank of South Africa uses *staffed ATMs* to serve a lower-end market previously unserved by South African commercial financial institutions.
- Hatton National Bank in Sri Lanka developed a system of *small offices* staffed by a mobile collector and administrative assistant to serve rural areas.

Box 5–2. Mobile Collection: Atwima Kwanwoma Rural Bank

Established in 1983, Atwima Kwanwoma is the largest of Ghana's rural banks. A public bank with four branches and a head office, Atwima Kwanwoma serves the area within twenty miles of its central office. In 1999 the bank introduced two new products—a traditional *susu* product and a group-guaranteed savings-and-loan product—with which it hoped to increase its volume of deposits and improve its market position. In 2001 the bank also starting deploying mobile units to bring services to villages in its service area. The results were dramatic. By 2002 the bank's deposits had grown from US$639,000 to US$3.7 million; the number of accounts had doubled to 44,423. Half of the new depositors and over one-fifth of the new deposits were accounted for by the *susu* product.

The *susu* product was designed to attract savers such as traders and artisans who would deposit a fixed amount daily or weekly—if they could do so at their "doorstep." The product is familiar and convenient. Unlike deposits for the bank's other products, which require a visit to the branch, the *susu* deposits are made with mobile bankers during a daily or weekly visit to customers' work places. Withdrawals can be made at the bank, or literate customers can withdraw from the mobile banker by using a withdrawal check. Clients must deposit a minimum of US$0.55 per day (or US$2.75 per week). The actual average deposit size is about US$2.20. The product is nearly identical to products offered by informal *susu* collectors but promises more security, greater access to credit, and no service fee. Mobile bankers deposit customers' fixed daily or weekly deposits in the bank at the end of each day. The customer can withdraw these savings at the end of the month or, after three months, can use them as collateral for a loan or convert them into an interest-bearing account. The new product required many changes in operations:

Staffing: New staff included a product and service development manager responsible for all the new services, a *susu* coordinator, and fifty mobile bankers who have the esteem of the community and twelve years of schooling (three to five years less than the bank's regular tellers).

Promotion: The bank promoted the product over the radio and met with local village leaders to ask them to promote it as well. Staff also visited churches, displayed posters, deposited handbills in all local post office boxes, and distributed free key holders to new clients.

Internal controls: Early on, a lack of proper internal controls resulted in fraud by mobile collectors. When these were fired, the bank found it difficult to locate all their customers. Therefore, management created two new positions: stand-by mobile bankers, who periodically accompany the mobile bankers and take their place when they are ill or resign; and monitoring clerks, whose job is to check office records against client passbooks.

Incentive scheme: Because the mobile bankers needed a lot of motivation, the bank pays a commission in addition to salaries to mobile bankers who mobilize more than a target volume of deposits (and whose clients do not withdraw too frequently). Some of the mobile bankers are paid purely by commission.

The scheme was launched without pilot testing. As it grew, unanticipated issues arose. First, the MIS did not seem sufficient. Mobile bankers serve at least five hundred depositors and must work overtime to post all transactions in the manual system. Second, the mobile bankers forward a lot of problems to management, possibly because some policies were not defined or communicated clearly.

Godfried Odame-Asare, interview and email exchange with Madeline Hirschland, April 2003 and October 2004.

- The Equity Bank of Kenya deploys *mobile vans* to serve tea farmers in prosperous but hard-to-reach rural areas.
- Numerous commercial and rural banks in Ghana and India *serve informal deposit collectors and/or informal savings and credit groups.*
- Commercial and rural banks in Ghana also *hire or commission their own mobile collectors* to extend their outreach to poorer market segments.
- Credit unions in West Africa, Madagascar, the Philippines, and Ecuador *organize and serve groups* of poor rural women who lack the resources or mobility to participate in the credit union as individuals.
- In Brazil, retail chains with point-of-service devices allow customers from participating banks to withdraw funds. The banks pay a commission for each transaction for the opportunity to *piggyback* on this existing financial infrastructure.

For commercial institutions, this last approach, piggybacking the delivery of savings services onto other financial transactions or delivery systems, may at present be the most promising for lowering costs. For example, Bank do Nordeste in Brazil found that it was able to cut the cost of a transaction at the teller window by a factor of ten, down to US$0.25, by serving clients in post offices rather than in their own banking halls. Banks have also experimented with piggybacking deposits for a contractual product on top of other transactions such as loan payments, school fee payments, or payroll deposits.

Similarly, outsourcing—having informal-sector deposit collectors, informal savings groups, or savings groups promoted by non-profits manage transactions with individual depositors—can also help with costs, controls, and culture. These third parties aggregate small individual transactions into larger ones, thereby lowering the financial institution's transaction costs and increasing its average account balances. By outsourcing transactions, the financial institution can pass on the responsibility for control and accountability to a third party. And, unlike many commercial institutions, non-profits and informal service providers are used to working with poor or rural clients.[5]

However, both piggybacking and outsourcing can encounter significant principal-agent issues. Coming to a mutually beneficial commission or fee agreement and assuring that the agent provides a high enough quality service can be difficult.

Finally, electronic technologies, in particular mobile phone technologies, could greatly expand services to rural areas and smaller depositors by drastically reducing administrative costs. These technologies hold great promise if they can gain acceptance in these markets, overcome security issues, and manage cash at some point in the transaction.

Some of these delivery mechanisms—such as serving informal groups or deploying mobile collectors—may seem beyond the purview of conventional institutions. In this context, Ghana's financial landscape is worth noting. In Ghana, where informal savings collectors and groups are common, a wide range of commercial and rural banks deploy collectors. These banks see this as an acceptable form of banking. For banks in other places, the stumbling blocks vis-à-vis these delivery mechanisms may be not only controls—which Ghanaian banks manage—but also culture.

In any case, all these delivery options lower administrative costs by lowering staff costs, which are the single largest driver of total administrative costs. They reduce the amount of staff time needed and/or they make it possible to use staff with lower levels of education.

5.3 OTHER OPERATIONAL CHANGES TO SERVE LOWER-END MARKETS

Most institutions that aim to expand their services to lower-end markets will need to modify their operations in several other ways as well.

Staff profiles: While front-line microsavings staff may need less schooling than conventional banking staff, they must be friendly, inspire trust, and understand and respect poor and rural customers. OIBM finds that training front-line staff to maintain the culture of respect to the poor is a huge issue; the attitude of its staff has a major impact in attracting savings and requires constant attention.

Products: The keys to serving the poor are low- or no-minimum-balance requirements and liquidity, at least in the form of a loan. If staff and clients have little education, then an institution should offer only a few simple products that together offer both liquidity and illiquidity and meet as much demand as possible.[6] Cost recovery can be improved by limiting the number of free transactions, offering contractual products that accumulate funds, and instituting product features that motivate higher balances (see Chapter 7).

Pricing: Because of the scarcity of services, small and rural depositors usually are not highly price sensitive. Therefore, high costs can be partially offset by paying low or negative real interest rates and by charging administrative fees, particularly for small accounts and rural transactions (see Chapter 9).

Promotion: From language to colors, media, messages, and music, appropriate advertising for lower-end markets often differs significantly from advertising for upper-end and urban markets. In many uncompetitive lower-end markets, word of mouth is a very effective—and cheap—means of promotion. For example, ever since OIBM opened with a series of short radio dramas about the importance of savings, it has been able to grow based solely on word of mouth. In other lower-end markets, however, promoting the value of saving will be essential in order to stimulate demand (see Chapter 10).

Internal controls: Several of the delivery mechanisms described above call for individual staff members to manage transactions from start to finish and/or require staff to carry cash outside of the office. This can increase the risks of fraud, mismanagement, and theft. Institutions manage these risks by instituting additional controls that are described in Section 11.4.

Management information systems: As discussed in Section 3.3.2, record keeping must be simple and easy to understand in order to control costs and be usable by people with little education. In many environments manual systems are appropriate at the branch level.

Staff incentives: Very small account balances make high levels of productivity crucial. For this reason staff members must be held immediately accountable for their performance in terms of growth in clients, savings and loan volumes, loan repayment, and branch profitability. Institutions use a variety of mechanisms to institute a sense of accountability: financial and nonfinancial incentives, promotions, and the sanctioning of non-performers (see Chapter 15). All require that staff members receive good information on job expectations and how their own performance measures up.

Generally, small savings and credit—microfinance—operations are much more labor intensive than mainstream financial operations; they involve larger numbers of transactions, more staff, and higher client loads. Therefore, the capacity to process vast amounts of information quickly and the decentralization of operational decisions are crucial. In all these ways mobilizing small and rural deposits differs from conventional savings mobilization. Managing these differences requires careful attention to how these microfinance operations are organized within the institution.

5.4 ORGANIZATIONAL STRUCTURE

Because microfinance operations differ from conventional financial operations, it is critical that they operate with a high degree of autonomy and transparency. Microfinance operations can be organized in a number of ways: as a fully integrated *product line,* possibly with its own staffing; as a *separate division or department* within the institution; or as a *subsidiary.* Although we do not have enough information yet to know under what circumstances certain structures are better than others, we can make a few observations.

An integrated product line, division, or department can benefit substantially from the institution's physical infrastructure, management, reputation, and administrative support. If they are responsive to the requirements of microfinance, the human resource, auditing, technology support, and research-and-development teams can add a lot to the microfinance operations. Simply having senior management regularly review pricing in light of the volatility and risk of deposits can be a key to avoiding financial crises. Integration also provides both the microfinance operations and the financial institution with a more diversified investment portfolio.

Either type of integration—product line or division—can backfire, however, if the microfinance operations receive too much subsidy; if microfinance operations undercut rather than contribute to profitability, the institution will be unlikely to promote costly services on a large scale. Hatton National Bank may be a case in point. Hatton's microfinance services are tightly integrated into branch operations: its staff and pricing are not differentiated, and the program is implicitly subsidized by the bank's other operations. While the program is highly regarded, it accounts for less than 1 percent of the bank's total volume of deposits (see Box 5–3).

An integrated microfinance operation also may not have enough autonomy to establish a culture and make decisions crucial to its success. Microfinance operations may be impaired by the institution's senior managers who do not understand its requirements and standards. They may make inappropriate decisions regarding staffing, products, pricing, and management systems and may hold staff to inappropriate standards or restrictions. These decisions can make it difficult to reach the intended markets and to recover costs.

Both these risks—that microfinance operations will receive too much subsidy and undermine profitability and that they will not have enough autonomy—are higher if the operations are fully integrated as a product line rather than managed as a separate division or department. Managing microfinance operations in a separate division or department may be crucial where the culture of serving lower-income markets, the use of incentive systems and low-wage staff, and the infrastructure and management systems required differ significantly from those employed for the rest of the institution's operations. These differences may be more pronounced with credit than with savings. In fact, in some cases institutions may appropriately choose to use a fully integrated product line to go down market with savings while employing a separate division or department to manage their down-market credit.

When microfinance operations are managed through a subsidiary, the risk of uninformed senior-management decisions is nearly eliminated. A subsidiary can find it easier to establish accountability and a cost-conscious culture that is oriented toward the poor. It will have the authority to assure that staff, systems, and operations are cost effective and appropriate for the micro market. Furthermore, a subsidiary may still benefit from the parent institution's supervision and may be able to use the institution as a liquidity pool.

However, when the microfinance services are not integrated, they often are marginalized by top management. Similarly, subsidiaries often do not receive the senior-management attention that they need and may be cut off from information and structural opportunities available to the parent institution. A subsidiary will derive much less benefit from the parent institution's reputation and brand identity. Furthermore, as a regulated institution, recovering costs while serving only low-end markets will be a challenge. Finally, unlike a product line or a separate division, a subsidiary may not have the legal authority to mobilize deposits, or these deposits may not be covered by deposit insurance. Thus, while it may make

Box 5–3. Commercial Downscaling: Hatton National Bank

In 1989 Hatton National Bank, a commercial bank in Sri Lanka, initiated its Gami Pubuduwa scheme (GPS) to extend its credit and savings services deeper into rural markets. By 2004 the GPS had established units in 79 of its 140 branches and in twenty-four villages. These units had mobilized US$8.7 million in seventy thousand deposit accounts for an average account balance of US$124, 13 percent of per capita GNI. GPS's success can be attributed to its organizational structure, staffing, tailored services, and use of cross subsidies.

Organizational structure: GPS is an integral part of the bank's regular operations. Branch staff keep separate GPS ledgers for monitoring purposes. However, successful GPS clients graduate to Hatton National Bank's small industry financing program, GPS staff can pursue a clear career path within the bank, and GPS units are administered by the branch managers. At the head office the GPS is managed by the Development Banking Division, which is headed by a senior bank executive.

Staffing: The bank carefully selects and specially trains experienced staff from the bank's mainstream operations for the GPS work. Staff must have the same qualifications as a clerical worker in a regular branch, including twelve years of schooling. Assigned to the region from which they come, these village banking advisers or "barefoot bankers" understand local customs, economic activities, and leadership hierarchies. Their job is twofold: to promote the bank's services in rural areas, and to gather information on businesses suitable for Hatton National Bank financing. Village banking advisers figure large in the village; they participate in social, religious, and cultural activities and make a point of mixing with clients and other villagers.

Services: The bank targets the upper poor and vulnerable non-poor by slightly modifying its regular deposit services; it reduced its minimum opening and interest-earning balances, simplified records and reports to account holders, and made depositing easier. Meetings with depositors are scheduled at village centers such as schools and temples and in the course of the village banking adviser's fifteen to twenty daily credit-management visits. In contrast, withdrawals must be made at the bank branch, ATMs, or customer-service centers. The village banking adviser serves people who live or work within about twelve miles of the branch.

Cross subsidies: The GPS and individual GPS units were able to become operationally self-sufficient in three years because Hatton National Bank's regular bank operations provide cross subsidies. Hatton National Bank assigns a disproportionately high share of its indirect costs to the branches rather than charging these to the GPS units. The branches also bear all but the marginal costs of the branch-based units. Hatton National Bank has not pursued the chief means by which the high costs of small accounts are lowered. First, Hatton National Bank offers the same interest rates to GPS clients as to its other clients; in fact, it allows these clients to earn interest with a lower balance. Second, it does not use less educated, lower-cost staff to serve GPS clients. On the other hand, GPS provides Hatton with a competitive market platform and penetration in rural markets, for which direct and indirect benefits to the bank are difficult to estimate.

Joselito S. Gallardo, Bikki K. Randhawa, and Orlando J. Sacay, "A Commercial Bank's Microfinance Program: The Case of Hatton National Bank in Sri Lanka," World Bank Discussion Paper No. 369 (Washington, DC: World Bank, 1997); and Gamini Yapa, managing director, email interchange with Madeline Hirschland, October 2004.

sense to offer credit services through a subsidiary, offering deposit services through a subsidiary may not be possible.

Might certain situations be better served by one or another organizational structure? A fully integrated product line may be the simplest and most cost-effective organizational structure for institutions

- that are simply extending their existing services to rural markets, such as with Equity Bank's mobile vans (see Box 8–4). Using a new technology to expand to more rural markets does not require the same cultural and operational changes as employing less educated staff to offer simpler products to lower-income markets.
- that outsource by linking up with informal-sector providers or with groups organized by NGOs. For example, NABARD (National Bank for Agriculture and Rural Development) uses the fully integrated product line model to influence commercial banks to serve informal groups and deposit collectors.
- with strong social missions for whom the culture of serving the poor will not be foreign. This may be the case for Atwima Kwanwoma Rural Bank, which employs deposit collectors to serve local entrepreneurs.

Conversely, a division or subsidiary structure may best serve purely commercial institutions and others for which microfinance markets differ significantly from their existing market. If these institutions fully integrated microfinance services as a new product line, establishing an appropriate culture, making appropriate decisions, and controlling costs might be difficult. For these institutions a division or subsidiary structure may still allow for supervision by senior management and other benefits from the institution while also providing for a separate microfinance budget and cost structure.

In both Standard Bank and BRI, microfinance operations are housed in a separate division and represent a large and profitable part of their portfolio. Indeed, Standard Bank started with a subsidiary and shifted to a division model because the latter was more profitable (see Box 5–4).

5.5 GOVERNMENT REGULATIONS AND SUPPORT

In order to mobilize small and rural deposits and recover costs, regulated financial institutions may need to change their operations in ways that existing government regulations do not permit. For example, regulations may require that branches meet physical infrastructure and minimum capital requirements that are not cost effective for small satellite offices. They might also prohibit deposits to be mobilized outside of a branch, by commissioned agents, or from groups. On the lending side, collateral requirements and interest rate ceilings may make it impossible

Box 5–4. Reaching Down and Scaling Up through Technology: SB, South Africa

SB, South Africa's largest retail bank, had tried for years to cover costs while serving low-income urban markets through its regular branches. In 1994 it developed a separate ATM delivery system and product to serve this market. Although SB first offered this service through a subsidiary, E Bank, it soon merged E Bank into itself and renamed the service E Plan. By 2003 over half of SB's seven million customers were E Plan holders. The high costs of holding a small E Plan account, the location of the ATMs, and the technology itself place E Plan out of reach of many of the poor. Nevertheless, E Plan has broken new ground; it covers costs while serving a larger lower-income market than South African banks ever have before.

The service: Located on busy streets or in shopping centers, SB's inviting ATM kiosks are open long hours and are staffed by two to four assistants. Each kiosk serves eight thousand to ten thousand clients. The E Plan ATMs offer a single liquid-savings product with a minimum balance of about US$7.25 and interest and other benefits for balances over US$38. The ATM card serves as a debit or cash withdrawal card at many shops with point of sales devices. Clients pay a monthly fee of US$0.59 and US$0.65 per ATM transaction. The E Plan ATMs use graphics and simple menus in English or Afrikaans. Service-oriented assistants who speak the local language help customers who need it. SB encourages E Plan holders to transact with the ATMs by charging six times more (US$3.60) for a branch transaction. That 10 percent of E Plan transactions still occur over the counter suggests that some clients do not understand or trust the ATMs. In late 2004 SB and three other banks collaborated to better serve the unbanked by introducing the *Mzansi* account: there is no monthly fee, the first deposit or electronic transfer each month is free, and the transaction fee is the same no matter which bank's ATM is used.

From organizational structure: By 1996 E Bank had a half million customers, but its twelve outlets had not attracted enough of SB's low-balance clientele to be cost effective; perhaps clients did not trust the new brand and delivery system. In response, SB merged E Bank into itself as a division and reframed it as SB's main mass-market product. SB then shifted 570,000 low-balance clients from its more costly branch-based delivery system to E Plan. This cut costs and created economies of scale for SB, while the new clients benefited from E Plan's lower interest-earning balance.

For former E Bank clients the merger was mixed. They could now use SB's twenty-six hundred other ATM outlets—if they could manage the more complex screen without assistance. They were also subject to SB's more complicated banking processes. The new E Plan staff often did not relate as well to lower-income clients as the E Bank attendants had. While the merger gave clients access to SB's other products, these interested few of E Plan's low-income clients. And, SB's larger customers endured longer waits when E Plan clients sometimes overloaded SB's regular ATMs.

Costs and the poor: E Plan enables SB to serve the lower-income market more cheaply. Building an E-Centre costs SB about US$100,000, about 40 percent of

Continued on page 106

Continued from page 105

what a branch office costs. Because E Plan assistants deal with automated transactions, they require less education and training and lower salaries than branch cashiers. Nevertheless, low average balances mean that SB must rely on fees rather than interest margins to cover its costs. Thus SB encourages clients to make at least four transactions a month—at a total monthly cost to the client of US$3.50. This can be prohibitive for the 50 percent of South Africans who live on less than US$3 a day.

Jo Ann Paulson and James McAndrews, "Financial Services for the Urban Poor: South Africa's E Plan" (Washington, DC: World Bank, 1999); and Stubblefield Lobenhofer, Bredenkamp, and Stegman, "Standard Bank of South Africa's E Plan."

to serve the poor and recover costs. Furthermore, reporting requirements may be unrealistic with respect to small transactions.

Numerous institutions have been able to convince their country's regulatory body to relax these restrictions for their microfinance operations. They have accomplished this by developing a strong relationship with regulators, responding quickly to regulators' legitimate concerns, and educating them about the requirements and value of sustainable microfinance. Having regulators visit a well-functioning program and see, firsthand, its mechanics and potential to serve marginalized populations can help a lot, as can board members who have senior-level corporate experience and a history of working with regulators. Indeed, in a number of countries commercial microfinance has gone well beyond bending regulations; government support has enabled microfinance to be implemented on a national scale.

Governments can motivate banks to move into microfinance through investments in physical infrastructure, financial incentives, guidance and training, and policy requirements. For example, the governments of China and Indonesia subsidized national infrastructures of small state bank offices that have provided the base for much wider microsavings mobilization than is found in most of the developing world. In Indonesia low capitalization requirements have also helped enable small autonomous offices to flourish in rural areas. And in India hundreds of banks serve millions of low-income women as a result of a three-pronged strategy by NABARD. To develop a national initiative, this apex-level development organization combines advocacy at federal, state, and institutional levels; financial incentives to formal financial institutions; and training in NABARD's chosen microfinance technology—self-help groups. Raising the program to the level of a national priority has given it the thrust it needs with bankers and other partners (see Box 5–5).

5.6 COMMITMENT

Moving down market with savings requires strong senior-level commitment. If the commitment is there, solutions to the challenges of mobilizing small deposits

Box 5–5. Going National, Reaching Seven Million Rural Poor: NABARD, India

Since 1993 NABARD has motivated 35,300 managers of over 560 banks to provide financial services to 16.7 million of India's rural poor through self-help groups. Most of these clients had not previously been served by banks. The self-help groups have accumulated over US$300 million in banked savings or about US$20 per member. NABARD has developed these groups with the support of more than three thousand NGOs and other institutions at an estimated cost of US$10.50 per member. Many of the banks now offer the self-help group services as normal products at market rates of interest.

In India, banks are present even in remote areas. NABARD's greatest challenge was to convince the managers of these banks that the poor can save and that serving them can be financially viable. This required a financial technology, self-help groups, that could generate a large volume of deposits at low cost. Self-help groups consist of no more than twenty members who regularly save a fixed amount while pursuing a development agenda. By aggregating their individual savings into a single deposit, self-help groups minimize the bank's transactions costs and generate an attractive volume of deposits. Through self-help groups the bank can serve small rural depositors while paying them a market rate of interest. In using the technology NABARD learned that starting small, testing models, and encouraging local experimentation were crucial. Allowing local partners, banks, and self-help groups to figure out the most efficient ways to manage is a key to controlling costs, promoting local ownership, and helping to ensure sustainability. NABARD itself plays three roles in developing the program:

Advocacy: Expanding the program to a massive scale required extraordinary marketing. NABARD's message was simple: serving self-help groups is a profitable business proposition that fulfills banks' social objectives and obligations. The scope of the task, however, was enormous. NABARD had to convey this to banks, state and local governments, NGOs, academic institutions, training institutions, planners, and policymakers powerfully enough to convince them to undertake the program. NABARD initiated contact through meetings, workshops, conferences, lobbying, and publications. Seeing is believing, however. Arranging for exposure visits for individuals to see self-help groups and the banks serving them in action became NABARD's most effective tool for conveying the program's mechanics and potential. NABARD succeeded, in part, by raising the program to the level of a national priority. It influenced the government of India to highlight the program in its annual budget and to report on yearly progress. This ensured that all those involved gave it the priority it deserved and that organizations that were involved were competent.

Capacity Building: NABARD also trained banks and built a trained and committed corps of people to promote self-help groups. This corps consisted of bankers, government functionaries, NGO staff, and others (like teachers and postal workers). Within six months to two years these trained personnel mobilize groups, convince a bank that groups are worthy customers, and guide the groups to manage their affairs.

Continued on page 108

Continued from page 107

NGOs do this well. With training, commitment, and a feel for rural communities, bankers, government functionaries, social workers, teachers, and health workers also proved to be effective. NABARD developed its corps of promoters through its training and by arranging exposure visits.

Financing: NABARD supports the program with grants for building capacity, forming groups, and advocacy; and refinancing to encourage banks to lend to self-help groups. NABARD uses financial incentives to attract banks until they are convinced that the technology is sound.

---

will follow. Securing this commitment often requires convincing bankers of a few things: that the poor can save and are creditworthy; that they can afford market interest rates; and that, despite the small size of their deposits and loans, per volume transaction costs need not be high. In short, banking with the poor can be profitable.

To commit to moving down market, bankers must see that there is a suitable cost-effective way to serve small depositors. An exposure visit to a tightly managed microfinance program can enable them to appreciate quickly how it can be done and the issues involved. Training in the principles of best practice microfinance can fill in the details. Above all, understanding the potential of microfinance to diversify risk, expand markets, increase profits, and create a positive public image is crucial. Once the commitment to innovating to reach the poor is there, translating it into the institution's corporate objectives is essential.

In the process of convincing bankers to go down market, there is a clear role for subsidy, if it is time limited. External funds might be provided for training, systems development, and/or investments in physical infrastructure such as mobile vans or satellite offices. Before banks are convinced that their microfinance operations can be financially viable, refinancing at a subsidized rate or support for a guarantee fund might also be appropriate. But these supports should be for a short term with a clearly planned exit time table. If the microfinance operations are to succeed, the institution should be strongly committed to the program early on.

How does one know whether the commitment is sufficient? Some good indicators are that senior managers promote best practice principles of microfinance, that they assign strong senior managers and their own financial resources to the task, and that they are patient enough to learn how to make the business work locally.

Strong Local Champions Who Accept Best Practice Principles of Microfinance

Successful microfinance programs demand a lot of themselves. They commit themselves to full cost recovery and the policies that will get them there. These include pricing to recover high operating costs, performance-based incentives schemes that enforce accountability and enhance productivity, quick and convenient services that generate a large enough volume of savings and credit to be viable, and high standards for loan-portfolio quality and profitability.

If the microfinance initiative is to succeed, those who champion it—its *prime movers*—must demonstrate by word and action that they understand and embrace these principles of best practice microfinance. They must thoroughly understand how the principles translate into successful microfinance operations and must be able to explain this convincingly to authorities and staff alike. Prime movers who have the credibility and power to protect the program from unsound practices will be local, not international. If they are not the authority overseeing the institution, then they should have the power to influence its policies, human resource management, and organizational structure.

Senior-level Commitment That Is Deep and Long

Whether or not they are the prime movers behind the initiative, the very top director and management in the organization must be deeply committed to exploring microfinance. If they are not the prime movers, then they need not understand best practices completely, but they should then enable the prime movers to decide matters pertaining to the microfinance program. Strongly committed board members and top managers will engage enthusiastically in discussions of the ways in which the bank will need to be modified to accommodate microfinance and will actively seek solutions to the problems related to the organization of microfinance. If they actively engage early on, they will probably be supportive as the program unfolds. If they are too busy to get involved and do not prioritize the program at the outset, however, then they probably will not later ensure that problems that inevitably arise are solved efficiently.

Real Management Resources

Microfinance is extremely management intense. Successfully installing it in a commercial institution takes substantial, high-level management resources. It requires a cadre of a half a dozen committed and talented managers, at least one or two of whom are senior or have the unconditional support of the most senior managers in the bank and at least one or two who are very effective human resource managers.

To succeed, a bank needs to include these staff in its microfinance program from the outset. Otherwise, when they are needed, the necessary groundwork, systems, and staff will not be in place to ensure an effective rollout. While such heavy management commitment does not seem to be needed initially, the greater the up-front commitment, the steeper the subsequent growth curve. Banks that do not commit these resources up front grow at their own peril later. As they roll the program out bank wide, they may well find that their systems and management are not sufficient to handle the challenges of growth; they did not internalize what was needed bank wide to take the program to scale.

Patience to Be a Learning Organization

Successful microfinance organizations learn most of what is critical to their success through trial and error, not through consulting services. Banking organizations must understand that microfinance is substantially distinct from mainstream finance in most operational areas. Before they launch their microfinance products branch wide, they will need to spend one to three years and significant resources designing, experimenting, testing, adjusting, and retesting the services and systems. It takes eighteen months to two years to know whether the products, policies, and procedures are sound and whether staff discipline is sufficient to take the service to scale. In particular, the institution should not take the program to scale until it has weathered its first delinquency crisis.

Banks must be able to learn from best practices elsewhere in the world, while at the same time adapting savings and lending methodologies, MIS, and promotional strategies to local circumstances and their own comparative advantage in their chosen market. They must move past simply replicating products and systems developed in other countries to develop their own expertise and specialized operations. This requires patience and, above all, constructive engagement with the target market through pilot exercises before commercial rollout. To the extent that a bank fulfills these criteria, success is quite possible. To the extent that it does not, installing microfinance becomes more expensive and less certain.

Impatience has heavy consequences. Measured in numbers of transactions, microfinance is a high-volume business that requires agility and efficiency. When banks that are overly enthusiastic about early successes rush systems and procedures into use, they often see these systems later collapse under the weight of seemingly minor problems.

Some institutions will find these new markets more profitable than others. Banks with large branch-office networks located in poorer neighborhoods may already reach poorer clients with pension payments, money transfers, and public-housing loans. For these banks, microsavings and micro and small business lending are natural cost-effective complements to their existing financial activities. Similarly, state and postal savings banks may benefit from large existing branch networks. Institutions with lower cost structures, such as rural banks and cooperatives, may also move into these markets more easily (see Box 5–6). Because of their higher cost structure and, often, middle- and upper-class retail niche, commercial banks typically go down market by serving better-off rural markets or the nearly poor who are unbanked. State banks, rural banks, private banks with a social mission, and cooperatives may have cultures, missions, and an existing client base that make it easier to commit to savings operations for the poor.

Box 5–6. Extending Credit Union Services to Poor Rural Women

Freedom from Hunger (FFH) has worked with twenty-two credit unions or credit union federations in Ecuador, Africa, and the Philippines to extend their financial services beyond urban and peri-urban areas to serve self-managed groups of poor rural women. These credit unions hold over US$1.8 million in savings from 151,000 of these women, an average of US$12 per person. After searching for suitable regulated partners, FFH initiated its down-scaling strategy in 1993 with the Credit Union Federation of Burkina Faso. Success in Burkina and FFH's other down-scaling successes paved the way for similar success in Ecuador.

Within six months of being introduced to the strategy, the Ecuadorian credit unions had promoted women's groups. The groups were receiving loans from the credit union, on-lending them to their members, and making regular deposits—part voluntary and liquid and part mandatory—that are withdrawable when the loan is repaid. To get to this point FFH first oriented and secured the commitment of the credit unions' boards. It then helped the credit unions assess the market and establish new credit and savings policies, hire and train extension staff to promote groups and deliver services, develop transport and logistical support, establish supervision systems, and integrate the field-based monitoring into existing operations and systems.

For the Ecuadorian credit unions, serving clients in their communities rather than at branch offices was novel. This decentralization required changes and posed challenges:

Pricing: Because serving far-flung, low-balance clients costs more, interest rates and commissions had to be higher than for other loan products. For credit unions that prided themselves on their low interest rates, this was tough. At the same time, loan interest rates could not exceed the central bank's ceiling. This forced the credit unions to be efficient.

Staffing: The credit unions had to hire, train, and motivate a new category of staff to deliver services in rural communities. Appropriate salaries and incentives for these staff had to be established and integrated into the personnel system.

Organizational structure: To ensure accountability and sound management, clear lines of authority and communication were needed from the outset. Rural loan officers are attached to specific branches and are supervised by coordinators for the product.

Policies: The credit unions had to determine the membership status of the association members and, often, change their policies to allow group deposit accounts. The credit unions allowed one representative from each association to vote at annual meetings.

Internal controls: New systems of control had to be developed to verify transactions that take place outside the branch with the associations and rural loan officers.

After a year of rural operations two Ecuadorian credit unions are covering about half of their new costs while serving 160 groups—over fourteen hundred rural women. The groups have saved US$65,104—and the new operations have contributed to the credit unions' growth, income, and profitability; improved their competitiveness; and deepened their market penetration.

—Kathleen Stack

5.8 CONCLUSION

For many regulated financial institutions, going down market with savings involves developing lower-cost delivery channels and also going down market with credit. This is the case for all eight of the institutions whose strategies for extending savings services to poorer or more rural clients have been discussed in this chapter. With the possible exception of e-banking, lower-cost delivery channels, in turn, often require control innovations. In most cases going down market also demands a different type of staff, a different product mix, differential pricing, different promotional strategies, and different incentive and MIS. To manage these distinct operations institutions may need to establish a separate organizational structure—a division or even a subsidiary. And, in most cases, success with these many changes will depend on whether management has reoriented itself and its staff toward serving the poor.

Pioneering institutions are already leading the way. Their key is not any particular delivery innovation or organizational structure. Their key is commitment. Commitment is demonstrated by the resources an institution brings to the table. Banks that are committed to the microfinance enterprise assign promising young managers to take charge of it, provide it with substantial office space and a budget, create a board level–oversight committee, pay for training visits to successful programs in other countries, and ensure high-quality relations with its primary movers. These institutions incorporate best practice principles and experiences into their internal dialogue and discussions. Finally, banks that are serious about microfinance are not only committed and engaged early on, but also are patient with the necessary learning curve before a full-scale launch of the program.

Small and rural clients are a distinct business opportunity. These clients can be served on a commercial basis if banks are willing to customize their services and delivery channels. All sorts of commercial entities serve a variety of market segments with different prices and qualities according to customer demand. If banks similarly learn to customize cost-effective services for low-end clients, they can find a large and profitable market.

Notes

[1] Robert Peck Christen, Richard Rosenberg, and Veena Jayadeva, "Financial Institutions with a 'Double Bottom Line': Implications for the Future of Microfinance." CGAP Occasional Paper No. 8 (Washington, DC: CGAP, 2004), 1, 5.

[2] Jennifer Stubblefield Lobenhofer, Caryn Bredenkamp, and Michael A. Stegman, "Standard Bank of South Africa's E Plan: Harnessing ATM Technology to Expand Banking Services" (Chapel Hill, NC: Center for Community Capitalism, 2003), 14.

[3] From BRI via Klaas Kuiper, email posting to DevFinance Network, January 2005; BRI website via W. Heimann, email interchange, January 2005.

[4] For some institutions, however, the high cost of provisioning for high-risk loans makes microcredit a less viable investment option than other high-yielding earning assets. Furthermore, if government reserve requirements are too high, finding an investment option with a yield high enough to recover costs can be very difficult even when employing the strategies suggested in this chapter. As stated in Chapter 2, an institution should not mobilize deposits unless it can invest them in a reasonably secure place at a rate that enables it to recover its costs.

[5] Much appreciation is due to Ernest Aryeetey for his insights on issues of outsourcing and the informal sector.

[6] Marguerite Robinson, *The Microfinance Revolution*, vol. 1, *Sustainable Finance for the Poor* (Washington, DC: The World Bank, 2001), 258–60.

PART II

SERVICES

Meeting Demand While Covering Costs

6

Developing Products Based
on Market Research

Graham A. N. Wright

Microfinance is one of the few remaining "product-driven" businesses in the world. Most other industries long ago moved from producing something and then trying to sell it to a "market-driven" approach whereby they first identify customers' needs and then design products to meet them. In fact, unless they have a monopoly, commercial entities that simply market a product without referring to what customers want soon go out of business.

Nevertheless, many microfinance institutions (MFIs) still neglect to develop client-responsive, market-driven products. Instead, they attempt to replicate models and products from other places irrespective of the local economy and culture. These MFIs mistakenly assume that the unmet financial service needs of microfinance clients worldwide are homogenous. For example, the prevailing wisdom holds that poor people—everywhere—need three basic savings products: a fully liquid current account, a partially liquid passbook account, and an illiquid fixed or term deposit. In reality, this product mix often is not appropriate (see Box 6–1).

Many MFIs fail to consider the unmet needs of their potential clients because they believe that MFIs are the only source of financial services for poor people. These MFIs reason that the poor will value whatever service an MFI provides. This is rarely the case. Long before any formal financial-service provider started, poor people had developed their own methods for storing money.

In fact, the informal sector is often far more appealing to clients because of the range of services it offers, the speed and flexibility with which these are provided,

The author is grateful to Kathryn Larcombe and Stuart Rutherford for their valuable comments.

Box 6–1. ASA's Discovery

After conducting limited market research, the Bangladeshi NGO ASA began to offer the following products:

1. A current account
2. A contractual savings account with monthly installments
3. A fixed-deposit account

This product mix was not ideal. The fixed-deposit and contractual products were not well matched to client demand. There was almost no demand for the fixed-deposit account. Although there was demand for the contractual product, many clients preferred weekly installments. On the other hand, the current account suited clients well but did not meet ASA's requirements. Although the accounts were heavily used, they yielded a low level of net savings deposits that ASA could use for on-lending. Most ASA clients' cash income was already encumbered by loan commitments and compulsory savings requirements, and thus the potential for mobilizing large amounts of savings from this group was limited.

To mobilize large amounts of savings, ASA would have had to diversify its client base by understanding and responding to the needs of people from a much broader range of socioeconomic strata than they had typically served with their micro-loan products. In many Bangladeshi villages, for example, remittances from relatives working abroad are an important source of cash income and thus potential savings. More extensive market research could have saved ASA the time and energy it put into reorganizing its systems and rolling out these products.

Graham A. N. Wright, Robert Peck Christen, and Imran Matin, "ASA's Culture, Competition, and Choice: Introducing Savings Services into a MicroCredit Institution" (Nairobi: *MicroSave*, 2000).

---

and their proximity (see Box 6–2).[1] If they do not understand their competition in the informal sector, MFIs may have a hard time attracting and retaining poor clients.

In this context, it is no surprise that many MFIs worldwide suffer chronic problems with clients leaving their programs. In East Africa client dropout rate ranges between 25 percent and 60 percent per year. Such high desertion rates represent a substantial barrier to achieving operational sustainability. When an organization is losing over one-quarter of its clients every year, it is running hard to stand still. Analysis of the reasons for dropouts almost invariably points to inappropriately designed products that fail to meet clients' needs. In East Africa many clients are driven out by the requirement that they hold a loan at all times while what they need—but are not offered—are savings services.[2] A mismatch between client need and product design is bad for clients and MFIs alike.

The key to overcoming this mismatch is market research. Market research is an activity designed to understand the MFI's operating environment and to identify the needs of its clients and potential clients. Market research is usually conducted

---

Box 6–2. Diversified and Informal: Prudence

Although Prudence is a client of an MFI, the bulk of her savings transactions take place in the informal sector. Like many women in Tanzania, Prudence belongs to more than one ROSCA or *kibati*. Her first ROSCA involves four people and requires a daily contribution of US$0.29 per person. The daily contribution goes to one person for a whole month in rotation. The monthly aggregate "prize" is US$26.57. Her second ROSCA consists of four people and requires a US$2.90 weekly contribution per person resulting in US$11.57 "prize" per week. "I like the first one better because it forces me to put aside that amount every day," she says.

In addition, Prudence belongs to an ASCA, known as a *kibindo*, organized within her forty-member MFI solidarity group. The weekly contribution to Prudence's *kibindo* is just over a dollar. *Kibindo* members take loans for a variety of reasons from meeting emergency and consumption needs to responding to business opportunities or simply paying the MFI's weekly loan installment. The *kibindo* fund is distributed among the members just before Christmas each year—last year Prudence received US$109. "It allowed our family to really enjoy the festive season."

Prudence also belongs to an informal insurance group organized along ethnic lines in order to cover funeral-related expenses. Prudence's group has about one hundred members. Every member contributes US$14.29 per month and is then assured of financing in the event of a funeral or a celebration within the member's immediate family. "It is very important to get a decent burial in my tribe," she says. "This means taking the body to our land of origin. I joined the group so that in case of an emergency, I have a source of money and people to help me."

Prudence also has a small secret fund of cash (typically around US$3 to US$5) that she keeps in her house to meet emergencies requiring a rapid response. For longer-term savings Prudence has a cow that is looked after by her brother back in her home village some 150 miles from Dar-es-Salaam. "I have to think about when I am older and this is a start."

---

with a view to responding to those needs and opportunities by improving current marketing, promotion, and outreach activities; refining existing products or developing new products; and re-engineering delivery systems.

This chapter examines each element of the process by which an MFI might use market research to develop or refine a product (see Figure 6–1):

- Defining the questions,
- Choosing the tools,
- Using the results to develop a product concept,
- Refining the concept into a prototype, and
- Testing the prototype.

While many MFIs carry out these steps simultaneously, this approach significantly increases the risks associated with the product development process.[3] It is therefore preferable to carry out these steps in a largely sequential manner.

Figure 6–1. Market Research within the Development Process

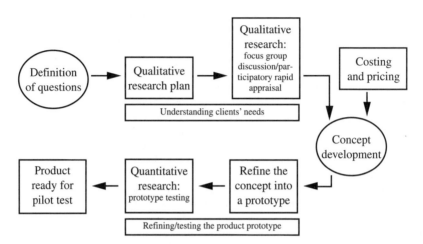

6.1 RESEARCH QUESTIONS

Market research is undertaken to answer specific questions about clients or potential clients. What questions to ask will depend on the maturity of an MFI's program.[4]

An MFI that is just venturing into developing savings services will need to undertake the most extensive research. Its fundamental question will be, in the proposed service area, what product(s) are required and what are the best systems to deliver them. To this end it will want to understand, on the one hand, clients' financial needs, and on the other, what formal and informal financial services are currently meeting these needs. To learn about this "financial landscape," a start-up program will want to answer questions such as:

- How do poor people manage their savings deposits? Are there savings banks, deposit takers, insurance salesmen, or savings clubs that the poor can access? If not, how do they save, and how convenient do they find the available forms of savings?
- Can the poor temporarily turn their assets into cash? Are there pawnbrokers or are there schemes that allow them to mortgage land or other major assets safely? If such devices exist, are they exploitative or enabling?
- Can poor people make provision for known life-cycle expenses? Can they provide for daughters' marriages, their own old age and funeral, and for their heirs? Are there clubs, general savings services, insurance

companies, or government or employer-run schemes that satisfy these needs?

- Can poor people secure themselves against emergencies? What happens when the breadwinner is ill, or when a flood or drought occurs? Does the government have schemes that reach the poor in these circumstances? If not, what local provision can people make?
- What are the socio-cultural or historical issues that my MFI will face? For example, are there instances of collapsed financial service organisations? Do women save in different ways than men?[5]

An MFI that has already determined its initial savings product and delivery system will face a more limited set of questions about its precise target market. Questions might include: Whom do I expect to serve? Will this market buy my products? How should I promote my services to them? What rate of interest should I pay under what conditions? What fees should I charge?

An MFI that is already offering services will want to answer questions about its ability to attract and retain clients. It will want to know whether its customers are satisfied and whether they perceive it as a good safe place to save, why it is losing clients, why it is not gaining more clients, and what is determining its rate of growth and profitability. Related to all these concerns will be an interest in knowing about its competition.

Finally, an MFI that is well established and operates in a competitive market will want ongoing information on the market it serves and its competitiveness. Questions that will be of interest include: Whom do I really want to reach? What products are most marketable? How can I improve my products—what do clients dislike about them? What new products can I introduce? How do I stay a step ahead of the competition? How am I differentiated in the market, and how does the market perceive this position? How do I become the most profitable institution possible? In this and all cases, the questions that an MFI aims to answer will drive what type of market research it undertakes.

6.2 RESEARCH OPTIONS AND TOOLS

Once the MFI has defined its research questions, it will need to determine what types of market research to use to answer them. Market research takes many forms, some of which are more demanding and informative than others. When an MFI is developing its products, it will want to use several of the more demanding tools, in particular participatory rapid appraisal, focus-group discussions, and competition analysis. After this start-up phase, MFIs that strive to offer client-driven services will continue to collect information by employing less demanding tools such as dropout questionnaires, the review of routine monitoring reports, and structured discussions about clients at staff meetings. They will use this ongoing information to alert them to issues that require more in-depth research activities (see Table 6–1).

Table 6–1. Options for Market Research

	Information available within the MFI	Information available from outside the MFI

Primary (information generated just for the research)	Ongoing activities:
	• Feedback from front-line staff through structured, client-focused discussion at staff meetings
	• Focus group discussions with staff
	• Simple questions on loan application or account opening forms
	Suggestion boxes in branches
	Dropout questionnaires
		Periodic activities:
		• Focus-group discussions with clients, potential clients, and dropouts
		• PRA exercises including:
		   • Seasonality analysis
		   • Financial sector trend analysis
		   • Product attribute ranking
		   • Relative preference ranking
		   • Life-cycle needs analysis
		   • Cash mobility mapping
		   • Wealth ranking
		• Customer consultative groups
		• Three- to six-question mini-surveys
		• Competition analysis of informal and formal sectors (see Appendix 6.1)

Secondary (information that already exists)	Ongoing activities: • Analysis of MFI's own financial and management information • Review of monitoring and evaluation reports	Ongoing review of: • Competition analysis (formal sector) • Industry data from national and international networks, industry publications, and websites • Public information on legal and environmental issues

More intensive market research typically relies on two types of information: *external* to the MFI, that is, it comes from non-clients, clients who have dropped out, or other institutions; and *primary*, that is, it is not otherwise available and is generated for the purpose of the research. It is essential to look at non-clients drawn from the appropriate market segment, since these are the potential clients of the future. Tools to elicit this information include:

Focus-group discussions: A focus group is typically composed of six to eight participants from a similar background brought together to discuss a series of related and tightly focused issues, for example, why clients leave the program or how and where the target market is currently saving. A skilled moderator facilitates each session using a carefully designed discussion guide.[6]

Participatory rapid appraisal (PRA) exercises: Under the *MicroSave* approach, PRA exercises are conducted within focus groups and use a variety of physical tools such as matrices, cards, and maps to guide the discussion. For example, as a first step participants might prepare cards, writing on each card one attribute or component of a product (for example, the interest rate, the maturity, the weekly meeting, the application fee). This helps the moderator understand how clients perceive the product. Then, as a second step the participants might rank these product attribute cards in order of their importance to clients making a decision on whether to use the product or not.[7]

Customer consultative groups: Customer consultative groups comprise eight to twelve of the MFI's experienced clients who are paid a small stipend to participate every quarter in focus-group discussions with senior staff. With MFIs that offer group-based services, these clients are usually group leaders. Consultative groups must be developed carefully and persistently, but they eventually yield important insights and information. Some MFIs also use this approach with their front-line staff and hold quarterly "front-line staff consultative groups." These groups provide a longitudinal overview of the MFI's operations and how they are perceived by its clients. In addition, the ongoing discussions over time allow the development of excellent rapport and trust, enabling the MFI to examine sensitive issues with greater ease.

Competition analysis: Competition analyses provide an at-a-glance view of the formal- and informal-sector competition that the MFI faces in the market. This allows the MFI to assess the relative strengths and weakness of its products and to develop and refine strategies for marketing them. Checking the competition analysis with clients and potential clients is important because how potential and actual clients perceive products can differ significantly from the actual terms of these products (for a sample matrix, see Appendix 6.1).

Except in large MFIs, these activities usually are carried out on a periodic rather than ongoing basis. They will be conducted when new products are being developed, every few years, or in response to signals from monitoring of operations. For example, a surge in dropouts noted in a monitoring report might signal management to conduct focus-group discussions with client dropouts. Periodic market research can be conducted "in house" by the staff of the MFI or can be contracted out to a professional market-research company. The benefits and drawbacks of these alternatives are summarized in Table 6–2.

Ongoing market research usually relies on information from:

Table 6–2. Strategies for Conducting Market Research:
In-house or Contracted Out

	In-house	**Contract out**
Advantages	• Allows the people who understand and care about the results to run the process • Provides unique learning opportunities to senior management • Provides important experience to MFI staff. Involving MFI staff is likely to enable them to more deeply and readily understand the results • MFI staff are more likely to draw appropriate conclusions from the results than outsiders	• Should provide maximum professionalism • Should save the MFI staff time • Will result in analyzed data and a report ready for presentation

Disadvantages	• Requires special skills to
	  • moderate focus group discussions
	  • develop/administer questionnaires
	  • analyze data effectively
	• Significantly diverts staff from other duties
	• Staff have biases regarding the clients
		• Most market research companies have little/no understanding of the sector within which MFIs operate
		• MFIs are often "low value" clients relative to larger businesses and thus may be neglected or given poor service by the market research company
		• If the market research company is good, it will probably be expensive

Internal sources, that is, sources from the MFI's existing operations. These sources would include current clients, information systems, and staff. For example, internal information could come from simple questions that are incorporated into an account opening form.

Secondary sources, that is, information that already exists. Sources of secondary information include the MFI's monitoring and evaluation reports and industry publications.

This type of research is conducted by the MFI's staff and provides it with continual feedback. This ongoing, low-level market research alerts the MFI to the need to conduct more in-depth primary research.

Similarly, the primary research effort is often driven by ongoing monitoring systems that track key indicators linked to the strategic goals or institutional/ product risk analysis of the organization.[8] For example, if dropout rates rise above a certain level, the MFI may conduct market research to understand the reasons why; the research focuses on causes of client exit. The indicators should be an integral and functional part of the management information system.[9]

6.3 DEVELOPING THE PRODUCT CONCEPT

Once the initial market research is complete a product-development team will use the results to develop the product concept. Involving a good mix of people in this process will maximize the range of perspectives and understanding of the issues. Ideally, a team of six to ten people will include staff from

- the "front line," that is, field agents and branch managers who deal with clients daily;
- Finance, who can project costs to enable the MFI to set interest rates and fees appropriately;
- Information technology, because changes to the management information systems are an important consideration;
- Marketing, especially those directly involved with the initial market research; and
- Operations, who will understand the overall implications of the product changes for the MFI.

To develop the product concept, the team should define eight aspects of the product—the "eight P's":

Product design: the product features such as the opening and minimum balances, amounts that can be deposited, when and how often withdrawals can be made and whether notice is required or other conditions apply, and how frequently interest is paid (see Chapter 7).

Price: the interest rates paid for different size accounts; the frequency and basis for calculating interest; and withdrawal, statement, and ledger fees (see Chapter 10).

Promotion: advertising, public relations, direct marketing, publicity, and all aspects of sales communication (see Chapter 9).

Place: the distribution or delivery system by which the product is made available where and when it is wanted. Options include branches, suboffices, mobile bankers, lockboxes, working with informal-sector providers, and delivering services through or by groups (see Chapter 8).

Positioning: how the MFI defines its distinct competitive position in the mind of the target customer. Distinguishing features might be low transaction costs, high interest rates, flexible deposits, quick access in case of emergencies, security of deposits, or professional service. Positioning refers to how potential clients perceive the product and the institution relative to its competition (see Chapter 9).

Physical appearance: the presentation of the product, such as how the branch looks, whether it is tidy and newly painted or decaying, and the appearance of brochures, posters, and passbooks.

People: how the clients are treated by the people involved with delivering the product—in other words, the staff of the MFI. It also includes recruitment, internal communications, performance monitoring, and training. To get the best performance from staff, MFIs need to recruit the right staff and then invest in training on customer service, products, the MFIs' processes and procedures.

Process: how the transaction is processed and documented, including the wait involved and the forms to be filled.

The best product concepts often emerge from a two-step process. First, the team examines the results of the market research and brainstorms a range of product ideas. Or it may do just the opposite—brainstorm and then conduct market research to validate those preliminary ideas. This latter approach is often of higher risk because the research team is approaching the market research with a particular theory or premise and may, as a result, fail to see important opportunities or, indeed, pitfalls. In either case, the second step should be to examine these ideas more analytically using a product concept design matrix (see Appendix 6.2). A crucial element of product concept development is projecting costs and developing pricing options. This should be done on the basis of a systematic analysis of the MFI's cost structure (see Appendix 4.1).

6.4 REFINING THE PRODUCT CONCEPT INTO A PROTOTYPE

The next step in developing a product is to test and revise the product concept to reflect clients' preferences and language. This is accomplished through a series of mini-focus-group discussions. A member of the market research team explains the product concept to a small group of clients and seeks its reactions. The team uses these reactions to further refine the concept before presenting it to the next focus group. This process continues until the product concept has been polished into a prototype that is:

- clear and simple to understand,
- expressed in clients' language, and
- priced in a way that clients will find most acceptable.

The product prototype communicates the concept's benefits in a way that consumers will readily grasp. It is a simple, unambiguous description of the product.

Table 6–3 shows an example of the type of results that the concept refinement process often yields.

Table 6–3. From Concept to Prototype:
The Smart Student's Savings Scheme

Product concept	Mini-focus-group reaction	Product prototype
The Savings for Kids scheme offers savings services for schoolchildren and draws them into the MFI bank as new customers.	• Don't call us kids! We're smarter than that. • We prefer to save at home in a box. • We don't like going to banks. • We want to know how much savings we have once in a while.	• The Smart Student's Savings scheme gives students the chance to save in the MFI bank for their own important needs. • Students' savings are collected weekly at school assembly. • Statements are issued quarterly.
The Savings for Kids account offers: • minimum balance of US$7 • unlimited access • 2.5% interest on accounts > US$68	• Increase the opening balance—our parents pay this anyway! • Interest is not important. A chance to win a prize in a lottery would be preferable.	The Smart Student's Savings account offers: • minimum balance of US$14 • unlimited access • a quarterly lottery for savers with more than US$34 in their accounts. Great prizes: bikes, cell phones, and cash!

Most MFIs fail to conduct this small but important step, and many have suffered the consequences. In some cases, staff members struggle to communicate products that are actually quite simple. In others, MFIs market an excessively complex product. They then find themselves with angry clients who misunderstood its terms, or they lose potential clients who pass the product up because they cannot understand it. As a rule of thumb, if a product's terms cannot be described in five to seven concise sentences, they are too complex.

6.5 TESTING THE PROTOTYPE

Once the MFI has developed the product prototype, it will want to determine:

- the proportion of target customers who find the idea appealing,
- who is most likely to buy the product, and who is least likely,
- how the product is used, and how it affects demand for the MFI's other products,
- clients' positive and negative reactions,
- how the product is perceived, particularly relative to the competition,
- if the appeal of the prototype is limited, why that is, and
- the product's impact on the MFI's staff, operations, and finances.

Typically, the MFI will use a pilot test of the product to gather this information. In some cases, however, a pilot test might pose a high risk to the MFI or would cost a great deal of time and effort, for example, to re-engineer information systems. In these cases the MFI may first conduct quantitative research to find out the level of appeal of the prototype.

Called a prototype test, this quantitative research provides a final check on the marketability of the prototype before investing in a pilot test. A prototype test uses a survey instrument that describes the product and asks respondents if they would buy the product and why or why not. This information allows the MFI further to refine the prototype or its marketing so that the product is targeted more specifically to the most appropriate market.[10]

A well-conducted pilot test will find out this information with a higher degree of certainty than a prototype test. Because a prototype test asks potential clients, "Would you buy this product," it generates information on theoretical demand. In contrast, a pilot test provides data on actual demand. Furthermore, pilot testing a product provides a more comprehensive overview of the issues and opportunities that the MFI may face as it rolls out the product. Thus, if the risks and costs are low, the MFI might want to move straight into pilot testing. Moving directly to pilot testing is more likely to be appropriate for small or medium MFIs that are able to react quickly to its results. Regardless of whether an MFI does a prototype test or pilot test, full analysis of the issues raised by the test may require staff to go back to the market-research techniques outlined above to adjust the product further.

It is essential that MFIs pilot testing a new product clearly communicate that the product is under testing and that it is being made available as a "special offer."

In some cases the pilot test may indicate that the product is inappropriate for the clients or unprofitable for the institution. In these circumstances it is important to ensure that:

- the MFI has the monitoring and evaluation systems in place to identify and analyze the problem;
- the MFI withdraws or amends the product;
- the product's terms and conditions are honored for the clients that took it under the pilot test; and
- the reasons for withdrawing the product are clearly communicated to the clients.

6.6 HOW MUCH WILL ALL THIS COST?

The cost of the market-research process will depend on the nature and scope of the research program. (See Appendix 6.3 for a sample research plan.) Research focused on refining one medium-sized MFI's products to reduce dropouts will cost less than "open-field" research designed to scope out business opportunities in a new area or to develop new products. Furthermore, the cost of the pilot test will depend on its duration and the number of issues that it generates. Table 6–4 provides a rough guide to how long the process of market research should take, from inception to having a prototype ready for pilot testing. The time line will vary from MFI to MFI depending on the skills of their staff and the quality of their management systems.

Table 6–4. Time Required for Development
of Market-driven Products

Procedure	Estimated person-days to complete		
	Simple product refinement	Simple product development	Complex product development
Planning/mobilization	2	3	5
Market research, including analysis/report writing	25	30	50
Costing and pricing[1]	2	5	7
Concept development	2	2	3
Refine to prototype	1	2	3
Quantitative prototype testing			35
Total person-days	**32**	**42**	**103**

Pilot testing is not included because the time it takes varies immensely depending on the nature of the product, the success of the pilot, and other factors.
[1] This assumes that the MFI's MIS is already set up to analyze costs by product.

Table 6–5. Competition Market Matrix Worksheet

	Our MFI	1) MicroBank Ltd.	2) Community cooperative	3) Informal groups	4) Mobile collectors
Product Terms					
Opening balance	US$7	US$68	US$3	US$1–10	US$0.70–7
Minimum balance	US$7	US$68	US$3	None	None
Requirements	National ID	2 referrals	US$7 share capital	None	None
Deposits	At weekly meetings	At all times (ATM)	During office hours	Weekly or monthly	Daily
Withdrawals (monthly)	Up to 3 at meetings	Any number at all times	Up to 2	By rotation	Month-end
Price					
Interest rate	2% for > US$68	5% for > US$340	None	None	None
Opening fees	US$2	US$6.80	US$.68	None	None
Ledger fees	None	US$2 per month	US$1.40 per quarter	None	None
Deposit fees	None	None	None	None	None
Withdrawal fees	US$.34	None	None	None	3% monthly
Closing fees	US$2	US$6.80	US$2	None	None
Promotion					
Dissemination	At group meetings	None	At annual meeting	Word of mouth	Word of mouth
Advertising	1 annual campaign	Radio/newspapers	Notices in branch	None	None

	Weekly groups in Thika, Nairobi (3 sites), Meru	ATM at branch in Nairobi only	Weekly groups in Nairobi (3 sites)	Branch in Thika	Any community
Place					
Positioning					
Slogan/vision	Flexible services for you	The solid bank	Cooperate for progress	None	None
Corporate image	New, fast, responsive	Professional; poor not welcome	Slow but very cheap	Not applicable	At the doorstep
Product image	For business-people; earns interest	For the rich: high fees and interest, quick service	Save only to get loans: fees "eat your money"	Our own bank—but trust your partners	Very convenient—if collector is good
Physical Evidence	Clean, new, professional	ATM, large, impressive	Shabby	No paper work	Simple
People	Warm, professional	Disdainful of poor	Members are welcome	Trusted friends	Friendly
Process	Quick but only weekly	High-tech, efficient	Slow but friendly	Efficient, inflexible	Quick, convenient

APPENDIX 6.2. CONCEPT DESIGN MATRIX

Table 6–6. Concept Design Matrix Worksheet

Client	Competition	Our MFI
Core Product: The reason *why* the customer pays money—a benefit (e.g., financial return, security) or the need it fulfills (e.g., liquidity, livelihood).		
What is the unmet need or want?	How is this need or want being met by others (consider all sectors)?	How are we addressing this need or want now, if at all (e.g., a product, training, referrals)?
Actual Product: The specific features that characterize *what* the customer is buying, including the product design (terms, interest rates, eligibility requirements) and package (length and clarity of the application, color of the passbook). These are three of the "Eight P's"—Product design, Price, and Physical appearance.		
What terms/conditions do the clients want?	What actual products compete with the product concept?	How does the new product relate to others offered by our MFI?
Augmented Product: How the customer receives the product—the way it is delivered and serviced (turn-around time, hours of operation, waiting-room facilities, and customer service in terms of friendliness, accessibility, staff knowledge). These are six of the "Eight P's"—Promotion, Place, Positioning, Physical appearance, People, Process.		
What preferences, characteristics, and priorities of clients should help determine our communication strategy? Are clients: • literate • geographically concentrated • in same business • mobile • other	How do competitors sell their actual products (e.g., marketing, incentives)? What are their augmented products? How are they and their product(s) perceived in the market? What can we learn from this?	How does our MFI sell its current products? What are our augmented products? How are we and our products perceived in the market by clients and non-clients?

Based on Monica Brand, "New Product Development for Microfinance," Bamako 2000 Innovations in Microfinance Technical Note No. 1 (Washington, DC: USAID, 2000), 2, 9–10; and Monica Brand, "New Product Development for Microfinance: Design, Testing, and Launch," Microenterprise Best Practices Technical Note No. 1 (Bethesda, MD: Development Alternatives, 1998), 28–32.

APPENDIX 6.3. SAMPLE RESEARCH PLAN

I. Research Issue

MFIA is experiencing low demand for its year-old contractual deposit product. Initial review of secondary data suggests that this is related to the length of the maturities, the size of the required minimum payment, and the hours that services are available. MFIA wishes to understand the details behind the reasons for low demand with a view to refining its current savings products (both urban and rural).

II. Research Plan

A.   *Four to Six PRA Sessions on Each of the Following:*
   1. *Product attribute ranking:* To understand which elements of MFIA's system/ product really matter to clients and potential clients and which do not. To allow triangulation with the information from the focus-group discussions below.
   2. *Defining and ranking the reasons for low demand:* To allow MFIA to get a clear understanding of the chief reasons underlying low demand. To allow triangulation with the information from the focus-group discussions below.
   3. *Wealth ranking and dropout:* To allow MFIA to analyze the nature of de-positors and non-depositors, specifically whether they are predominantly at either end of the socioeconomic spectrum of the potential market. Are those who use the product primarily poorer or richer? What about those who don't use it? For what reasons?

B.   *Two to Four PRA Sessions on Each of the Following:*
   1. *Financial-sector trend analysis:* To provide the background setting and to allow MFIA to understand the competitive environment in which it is oper-ating and changes in it over time.
   2. *Seasonality analysis (if the results of the focus-group discussions suggest this is important):* To look for seasonal-driven issues that are driving de-mand. To allow triangulation with the information from the focus-group discussions below. (Below is a discussion guide on demand for the six to eight focus-group discussions. This may require changing in the light of the results of the PRA work.)

III. Discussion Guide for Focus Groups on Low Demand for Contractual Product

A.   *Welcome*

Thank you for coming. We are grateful for your time. We are from an organiza-tion called *MicroSave. MicroSave* is a research organization that looks at financial services for people who do not have access to banks. We try to ensure that the clients' voices and ideas are heard by organizations like MFIA that provide financial services to poor people. We are holding these discussion groups to try to understand why clients are not using MFIA's contractual deposit services. We would very much like to record these discussions to help us remember them and so that we do not miss any of the issues and ideas you give us. The details of these discussions will not be shared with MFIA, and your names will be kept confidential, so please feel free to express your opinions about the products openly. As a first step we should introduce ourselves. You start, and we will follow. My colleague here will prepare name tags.

B.   *Warm-up Questions*
1. Please tell us if you are a customer of MFIA. If so, for how long?
2. What business do you run?
3. What makes people like you decide to use MFIA's deposit services? (If the response is interesting, follow up with this probe question: Were your expectations met?)
4. What makes people decide not to use MFIA's deposit services?

C.   *General Questions*
1. For what purposes would you use the contractual savings account? (Follow up with this probe question: Why would you make contractual deposits?)
2. Does the MFIA product meet your needs? If not, why not? (Follow up with these probe questions: Are you using the MFIA product? Is the product offered by MFIA appropriate for your needs?)

D.   *Impact on Savings Demand Questions*
1. What are the main reasons for clients not using MFIA's savings services? (Follow up with this probe question: For what reasons do people in your community not use the MFIA's savings services? *Note:* Ensure that the reasons are probed carefully to discover underlying reasons.[11])
2. Have you seen a change in the number of people using the contractual savings products in the last year? If so, why? (Follow up with these probe questions: Is the number of people using MFIA's contractual savings services increasing or decreasing? Why is this happening?)
3. What should MFIA do to improve its savings program? (Follow up with this probe comment: Please make recommendations on how MFIA might revise its savings program to better suit your needs.)
4. What procedures or systems would you like to see change in MFIA? (Follow up with this probe question: If you were the manager of MFIA, which rules would you change so that more people would use the contractual savings product?)

5. In what other ways could MFIA have better met your needs? (Follow up with this probe comment: Describe other ways that MFIA might attract its depositors and keep them as loyal clients of the organization.)
6. Closure: Thank you for your answers. The discussion has been very helpful and informative. We are very grateful for the information you have provided. Do you have any questions or suggestions for us?

Notes

[1] Dale W. Adams and Delbert Fitchett, eds., *Informal Finance in Low-Income Countries* (Boulder, CO: Westview Press, 1992).

[2] Graham A. N. Wright, *MicroFinance Systems: Designing Quality Financial Services for the Poor* (London: Zed Books, 2000); and David Hulme, "Client Exits (Drop Outs) from East African Micro-Finance Institutions" (Nairobi: *MicroSave*, 1999).

[3] For a detailed examination of these risks and how they can be managed, see Lynn Pikholz and Pamela Champagne, "Toolkit for Institutional and Product Development Risk Analysis" (Nairobi: *MicroSave* and ShoreBank Advisory Services, 2002).

[4] William Grant, "Marketing in Microfinance Institutions: The State of the Practice" (Washington, DC: USAID Microenterprise Best Practices, 1999), 27–29.

[5] Stuart Rutherford, "A Critical Typology of Financial Services for the Poor," ActionAid Working Paper No. 1 (London: ActionAid/Oxfam, 1996), 7–8.

[6] For more on focus groups, see Richard A. Krueger and Mary Casey, *Focus Groups: A Practical Guide for Applied Research* (Thousand Oaks, CA: Sage Publishing, 2000); and Graham A. N. Wright et al., "Focus Group Discussions and Participatory Rapid Appraisal for MicroFinance—A Toolkit" (Nairobi: *MicroSave*, 2001).

[7] For more on PRA, see Wright et al., "Focus Group Discussions."

[8] See Lynn Pikholz and Pamela Champagne, "Implementing Risk Management at MicroSave's Partner Microfinance Institutions," *MicroSave* Briefing Note No. 34 (Nairobi: *MicroSave*, n.d.), 1–2.

[9] For more practical guidance on how to conduct market research, see "Market Research for MicroFinance Toolkit" (Nairobi: *MicroSave* and Research International, 2001).

[10] For more on prototype testing, see "Prototype Testing Using Quantitative Techniques" (Kampala: *MicroSave* and Research International, 1999).

[11] Typically clients will say, "I cannot make the payments." The *reasons* for this need to be explored and understood. Was the payment size too high or too frequent or for too long a time? Was the office or its hours of operation inconvenient? Or did the client have to leave his or her employment temporarily in order to care for sick household members?

7

Savings Products

Madeline Hirschland

The previous chapter discussed the product development process. This chapter turns to the products themselves. Microfinance practitioners are increasingly focusing on designing products that are driven by demand. Understanding market demand is crucial. As we shall see, however, savings products are rather straightforward. There are three basic types. When serving small depositors, the biggest product-related challenge is usually not to design a new product that is unique to a specific market but to find an overlap between what people want and what the microfinance institution (MFI) can manage cost effectively. An MFI's challenge is to offer just a few products that meet as much of the target market's demand as possible—and are managerially feasible and financially viable. As this chapter illustrates, numerous MFIs have risen to the challenge.

This chapter looks first at how low-income people want to save, the types of products that meet their demand, and what these products cost and require of managements. It then discusses *product mix*—the set of products an MFI might offer. Finally, it considers how all this might differ for institutions that serve only small depositors.

7.1 WHAT DO SAVERS WANT?

Most people want to save in a number of ways. This is because they save from a variety of sources. For example, a single household might save from the annual harvest, from a monthly remittance sent by a relative abroad, from uneven daily profits from hawking, and by withholding a handful of rice from the family's meals. As a result, this single household might want to save a single lump sum

Many thanks to Fawzia Abu Hijleh, Kathryn Larcombe, Leonard Mutesasira, Stuart Rutherford, and Mark Staehle for their valuable feedback on this chapter. Any shortcomings are, of course, my own.

annually, smaller amounts weekly or monthly, and very small amounts irregularly.

People also want to withdraw in a variety of ways, because they save for a variety of purposes. The household in the previous paragraph might need its savings to purchase the goods it hawks, buy a plot of land that is suddenly available, cover emergency medical expenses, pay quarterly school fees, get by during the "hungry season," finance a haj pilgrimage, and provide for old age. Thus, it wants to save for days, months, and years. For expected events it wants its funds safely out of reach—*illiquid*—until the appointed time. But for unexpected needs, unrestricted access is imperative.

People also may not want to save at all. They may simply need a financial institution in order to receive transfer payments—such as remittances, salary, or pension payments—that they want to use immediately or to save in some other form.

One preference holds regardless of the source and use of savings: people usually do not want others to know whether and how much they deposit or receive as a payment. Therefore, they usually prefer an individual account to a group one. An individual account also gives them more flexibility to transact at the times and in the amounts that they want.

In sum, people typically want savings that are liquid and savings that are illiquid; the option to deposit small amounts regularly and irregularly and large amounts once in a long while; and the opportunity to save for the short, medium, and long term. Which of these demands are their highest priorities and which are unmet will vary from market to market. Whatever the demand, it can usually be met with a few simple products.

7.2 TYPES OF PRODUCTS

Savings products come in three basic types: demand deposits, contractual products, and time deposits.

Demand deposit products allow savers to deposit and withdraw what they want when they want with no advance commitment. Depositors must simply maintain the minimum required balance. Demand-deposit accounts can also be used to receive transfer payments. Demand-deposit transactions may be made using passbooks, ATM cards, or checks. *Passbook accounts* use only passbooks; *savings* or *regular savings* accounts use ATM cards or passbooks; and *current accounts* use checks as well as ATMs. In many countries only certain types of institutions are permitted to offer current accounts. Current accounts are likely to be considerably more volatile than regular savings. *Semi-liquid* products restrict the number of withdrawals per month; *liquid* products do not.

In most under-served markets, more savers—particularly small savers—want demand-deposit accounts more than any other product (see Table 7–1). The poor find them particularly useful because they do not require a regular income flow and because they permit withdrawals, which are crucial for emergency needs. Perhaps for this reason, savers typically prefer liquid accounts, even though most may actually withdraw infrequently.

For the MFI, demand deposits tend to provide a large, stable volume of funds but are costly and demanding to manage. Their low financial costs are overshadowed by high administrative costs (see Table 3–4). Because demand-deposit products especially attract the poor and allow withdrawals, average account balances are usually lower than for any other product (see Table 7–1), while the number of transactions can be much higher. For example, while BURO, Tangail's volume of demand deposits grew by 7 percent in the year 2000, withdrawals during the year equaled 225 percent of the year-end volume.[1] The unpredictable sizes and timing of passbook transactions necessitate more rigorous internal control and liquidity management than is needed for the other product types.

With *contractual savings*, also known as accumulated fixed-term deposits or programmed savings, clients commit to depositing a fixed amount of their choosing regularly for a specified period of time. After the maturity date they can withdraw the entire amount plus interest. Early withdrawal is prohibited or penalized.

Table 7–1. Proportions of Demand and Time-deposits in Some Mixed Outreach Institutions

	Demand deposits		
	% of accounts	% of volume	Avg. balance (US$)
Banco Caja Social	96	65	232
Centenary Rural Dev. Bank	99	95	186
Financiera Calpia	75	27	41
Prodem FFP	92	26	271
Rural Bank of Panabo	95	54	249
	Time deposits		
Banco Caja Social	4	35	3,407
Centenary Rural Dev. Bank	1	5	1,055
Financiera Calpia	25	73	2,788
Prodem FFP	8	74	7,612
Rural Bank of Panabo	5	46	4,348

Data for Financiera Calpia from Sergio Navajas and Claudio Gonzalez-Vega, "Innovative Approaches to Rural Lending: Financiera Calpia in El Salvador" (Columbus: Ohio State Univ., 2000), 10; Prodem from Eduardo Bazoberry, "The Bolivian Experience of the Prodem Private Financial Fund S.A." paper for Paving the Way Forward for Rural Finance (Washington, DC: WOCCU, 2003), 3. All other data from Alfred Hannig and Sylvia Wisniwski, "Mobilizing Microsavings: The Experience of Seven Deposit-Taking Institutions," draft paper (Eschborn, Germany: GTZ/UNDP, 1996), 18.

Contractual products help depositors to accumulate funds to meet specific expected needs, such as expenses associated with school, a festival, a new business, an equipment purchase, or a new house. They also can enable depositors to capture a portion of a regular fixed payment such as salary or pension payment that can be automatically deposited into the account. In some cases clients shape a generic contract to meet their needs by choosing between a range of terms offered by the MFI, for example, weekly or monthly payments in any increment of US$1 with a three-month, six-month, or twelve-month term. In other cases the MFI tries to attract depositors by setting the product's name and maturity to match a specific need. For example, with a Christmas account clients save a fixed amount monthly for eleven months and withdraw these funds with interest before Christmas.

Poor people often like contractual products. The products provide the discipline to save for future needs and, because they resemble familiar informal schemes, the poor understand them easily. Although fixed payments can exclude those whose income is unreliable, payment schedules can be softened (see section 7.5). Nevertheless, contractual products may meet little demand among the poor if their incomes are already committed to loans or businesses that require regular payments.

For the MFI, a contractual product has many advantages. Compared to a passbook product, it typically has a more predictable cash flow and larger account balances. It also can be a simple means to foster goodwill and inspire clients to save; offering a range of contractual products can be as easy as changing a product's name and maturity, yet can make clients feel that the MFI is attuned to their needs. Contractual products also generate information on clients' capacity to repay a loan.

With a *time deposit,* also known as a fixed deposit, a client makes a single deposit that cannot be withdrawn for a specified period of time. The MFI offers a range of possible terms and usually pays a higher interest rate than on its passbook or contractual products.

Time deposits can meet substantial demand among farmers, non-poor savers, and people who occasionally receive remittances. Unless the minimum deposit is small and the terms are short, time deposits may not meet much demand among other poorer clients. Although poor farmers may want to deposit a large sum at harvest time, some institutions that serve primarily day laborers and microentrepreneurs have found that their time deposits attract virtually no funds.

For MFIs that serve a mixed-income market, time deposits can provide a significant source of relatively low-cost funds—often the largest source, particularly if an MFI can attract large and institutional depositors (see Table 7–1). This is because time deposits tend to be larger than other types of deposits and involve fewer transactions. However, time deposits that attract larger depositors or are offered in competitive markets can be volatile, which can be difficult for less sophisticated institutions to manage. In the Philippines this has led many rural banks to limit time deposits to no more than 25 percent of their savings portfolio.[2]

Table 7–2 summarizes how these product types look to the depositor and the MFI.

Table 7–2. Voluntary Product Types from the Client's and MFI's Perspectives

| | Client | | MFI | | |
	Value	Costs	Management	Design Decisions
Demand deposits	Unexpected needs or opportunities; smooth consumption; store excess cash; receive transfer payments • low or no interest • does not require regular income	• large number of accounts, small average balance • least profitable: low financial costs; high administrative costs • stable; current accounts are more volatile	• heavy demands on staff, MIS, and internal controls • constant liquidity management	• minimum opening deposit • deposit sizes allowed (minimum and increments) • number of deposits allowed monthly • advanced notice required for withdrawals? (how much for what amount?)
Contractual savings	Expected needs; discipline • higher interest • usually requires regular income	• longer-term funds • larger average balances • more profitable: lower administrative costs, higher financial costs (typically) • may be volatile	• fewer administrative requirements • cash flow nearly predictable	• deposit amounts and frequencies • possible terms • option to pay late or withdraw early? (consequences?) • payout: lump sum or stream of payments?
Time deposits	Expected needs; store long-term surplus; transfer payments • highest interest • requires large deposits • inaccessible	• longer-term funds • largest average balances (fewer accounts) • most profitable: lowest administrative costs, highest financial costs • most volatile	• requires little management; two transactions per account • volatility means that ALM is important	• deposit amounts • options for term • option to withdraw early? (consequences?) • payout: lump sum or stream of payments

7.3 VARIATIONS

MFIs can vary the three product types in numerous ways in order to attract specific market segments.[3]

- Instead of paying out a single large sum, a time deposit or contractual product can provide a stream of smaller payments (for example, for old age or tuition).
- Payouts can be triggered by an event—such as a wedding—rather than a term.
- To enable farmers to sell their harvest at advantageous prices, deposits and withdrawals can be made in kind, as with a grain bank.
- How deposits are invested can be restricted.
- Payouts can go to a third party, such as a relative living in another region, the university to which tuition is due, or a supplier who provides the MFI's depositors with a discount on the item for which the deposits were made.[4]
- Savings can be linked to loans. For example, achieving a certain volume or term can trigger a loan that, along with the saved funds, enables the client to purchase the item for which he or she saved.

Managers' marketing ingenuity should be bounded only by the three criteria noted above—demand, manageability, and viability—and by a fourth, simplicity. Simplicity is essential. Products must be easy for staff to explain and easy for customers to grasp. A simple product also lowers costs by easing information management, liquidity management, promotion, and supervision.

Popular variations on the three basic product types include:

Pension savings: Many institutions attract middle-aged depositors by offering a pension product that combines the variable deposits of a passbook with the fixed term of a contractual product. Typically, savers deposit irregular amounts and withdraw the entire sum or an annuity only after a period of five or ten years, when they reach a certain age, or upon their retirement. For the MFI these accounts can generate a large volume of long-term stable funds (see Box 7–1).

Youth savings: These accounts aim to develop an early loyalty to the institution while accustoming young people to saving. Similar to a pension account, variable deposits are accessible when the child reaches maturity. Some MFIs allow withdrawals at any time but find that youth rarely withdraw their funds. Youth accounts attract a small volume of stable, long-term funds. Because deposits are small, administrative costs are high despite the low level of withdrawals.

Payroll savings: MFIs handle the payroll for an entire business or government institution by establishing a regular savings account for each employee into which the MFI automatically deposits salary payments. By linking a savings service with a cash management/transaction-based service, such an agreement gives the MFI a competitive advantage with the organization's employees and can help provide employees with the discipline to save.

Remittance products: Some MFIs that have developed the commercial part-nerships and legal status to accept remittances offer products that make it easy and secure for clients to save these remittances. In so doing, these MFIs boost their revenues and volume of deposits. Banco Solidario in Ecuador provides remittance recipients with a smart card that enables senders to ensure that their money is used as they want, for example, that it accumulates in a savings account to buy a home.[5]

Box 7–1. The Demand for Pension Savings: Grameen Bank's Pension Product

Of all the novelties of Grameen II—the new collection of products that have re-placed the classic version of Grameen in all its branches—the new savings products are among the most popular. Members like the new weekly savings, which accepts voluntary in addition to compulsory deposits and allows almost unlimited withdrawals on demand. But pride of place goes to Grameen Pension Savings, a contractual-savings scheme with monthly deposits and a five-year or ten-year term.

Grameen's pension scheme requires all borrowers with loans greater than US$130 to contribute US$0.80 monthly. For a ten-year term Grameen pays interest at 12 percent a year so that deposits almost double by the end of the term. At the end of the term savers will be able to take the accumulated deposits and interest as a lump sum or as monthly income. The savings scheme is so attractive that many borrowers save multiples of the required minimum monthly or open more than one account. They are popular among members with loans of less than US$130. Indeed, some clients see payments into the scheme as a better use of available resources than paying down Grameen loans, and many remark, "Grameen should have done this years ago." In the first thirty-two months Grameen mobilized pension deposits totaling US$37.2 million.

Grameen's scheme is in fact a version of the Deposit Pension Scheme (DPS), a commercial bank product that, for years, has been extraordinarily popular with Bangladesh's middle classes. But in the early years of microfinance in Bangladesh, no one thought that such a product would be attractive to the poor.

As the average age of Grameen members continues to rise, more and more may prefer to divert their spare cash from loan repayments into long-term savings. Bangladesh may discover that, after all, the poor are not so different, that their appe-tite for the DPS is every bit as strong as among the middle classes.

—Stuart Rutherford

Each of these products helps provide the depositor with the discipline to save: either by setting aside savings automatically or by encouraging or requiring the depositor not to use the funds until a specific time when they will be needed. Of course, product features that encourage higher levels of savings are also good for the MFI.

What about Compulsory Savings?

Many MFIs that focus on the poor require them to deposit an amount equal to a fraction of their loan amount. Similarly, many cooperatives that do not rely on collateral require that all their members buy a share and deposit a fixed amount monthly. Compulsory savings, also known as mandatory or forced savings, can take many forms, some better for clients than others. In most cases it is a mixed bag.

Compulsory savings can play a vital role for poor people. By taking the place of collateral, it enables the MFI to serve people who otherwise would not qualify for a loan; lack of collateral is one reason that banks do not lend to the poor. Compulsory savings can also provide the discipline, physical security, and illiquidity that enable people to accumulate assets for the future.

Even for people who appreciate a regular illiquid means to save, however, compulsory savings has drawbacks. The fixed-deposit amount and timing of withdrawals are unlikely to match their needs. Even if an emergency loan is available, clients may resent paying interest on it when they cannot withdraw their savings. Yet, to access their savings, they may have to terminate their membership, thereby ending their access to a loan. Borrowers in group-guaranteed schemes may strongly dislike having their savings vulnerable to the defaults of group members. And for clients who would prefer to use their funds, compulsory savings amounts to an increase in the effective interest rate on their loan.

For MFIs, compulsory savings is a significant stable source of funding for the loan portfolio. And, because it involves fewer transactions and does not require significant reserves, it costs less than regular savings. However, especially where savings requirements are tied to the loan product, the result can be dissatisfied customers, loan plateaus, and client desertion. To avoid losing access to more savings, clients may stop taking bigger loans. And if terminating membership is the only way to withdraw savings, when a need for savings arises, members may drop out. In short, MFIs would do well by themselves and their clients to improve on compulsory savings.

One option is to replace compulsory savings with a contractual product, which can attract a similarly large volume of stable funds (see Table 7–3). Loan repayment can then be motivated by character assessment, peer pressure, and/or access to a follow-on loan.[6] If this is not possible, management can at least add value to compulsory savings by:

Table 7–3. Comparison of Contractual and Compulsory Savings

	Contractual savings	**Compulsory savings**
Access	• Determined in advance by client • Earlier access prohibited or penalized	• At end of loan cycle, determined by MFI, or upon terminating membership • Emergency loan may be available
Amount	• Set by client • According to ability and desire to save	• Set by institution • Related to loan amount
Payment period	• Regular • Determined by client	• Regular • Determined by MFI
Management issues	• Predictable cash flow per account but unpredictable number of accounts	• Highly predictable cash flow • No marketing required

- Transforming compulsory savings into a compulsory-voluntary product that enables clients to save and withdraw savings in excess of the required minimum (see Section 4.3);
- Where compulsory savings is tied to a loan, calling it a "compensating balance" or "loan security fund" and allowing it to be withdrawn once the loan is repaid;
- Using compulsory savings as collateral for the individual but not for the group;
- Requiring small equal payments made at the same time as loan payments instead of a large up-front payment; and
- Paying an interest rate comparable to the rate paid for a similar voluntary product.

Whether or not an MFI requires clients to save, it will need to consider carefully the mix of savings products that it offers.

7.4 PRODUCT MIX

With all these options, how should an MFI decide which set of products to offer? While market research will suggest a range of products and terms, in most cases offering all of these is managerially impossible. For most institutions, the trick is to offer just a few products with which clients can meet many of their needs. This section provides guidance for choosing this mix.

The Key: Providing Liquidity and Illiquidity

Above all, the product mix should provide both liquid and illiquid options. Such a mix has three advantages: it can meet the bulk of customer demand, balance higher-cost stable (liquid) funds with lower-cost volatile (illiquid) ones, and attract sufficient volume to fund the loan portfolio. To deliver a manageable mix that includes both liquid and illiquid options, most successful microsavings institutions employ one of two strategies.

Many successful microfinance operations provide just two or three generic and flexible savings products that clients can use for a range of purposes. For example, most of the institutions in Table 7–4 that serve a mixed-income clientele simply offer time deposits with a range of terms and two liquid passbook accounts. In fact, the acclaimed BRI Unit system has attracted 25.9 million deposit accounts with just three products: a liquid passbook account for the public, a similar account for institutions, and an illiquid time deposit product with terms of one to twenty-four months.[7]

Other institutions, in particular credit unions, aim to attract depositors of all ages by offering a few well-chosen "life cycle" products. Cooperatives like Moderna credit union in Table 7–4 succeed by offering some mix of the six products advised by the WOCCU: a regular savings account, a youth account, an institutional account (a liquid account with a high minimum balance and transaction fees), a pension account, time deposits, and contractual products named and designed to meet specific local demands.

Can an Institution Mobilize Both Compulsory and Voluntary Savings?

Many institutions, especially credit unions, mobilize large volumes of voluntary deposits as well as mandatory ones. For example, in Guinea, the Yete-Mali cooperative's required collateral savings represent just 5 percent of total deposits. The rest are voluntary.[8] In fact, many institutions allow clients to make a voluntary deposit along with—and into the same account as—their mandatory minimum (see Box 8–6). Depositors make good use of this service. For example, both ASA's and the VYCCU's accounts allow members to save as much as they wish. In 2002, ASA's clients held, on average, 66 percent more in their deposit account than the compulsory requirement—and had withdrawn about one-third of this excess over the course of the year. In a three-month period VYCCU members saved, on average, 78 percent more than required. Furthermore, these mandatory-voluntary deposits represent just one-quarter of VYCCU's total deposits—the rest are completely voluntary.

Of course, customers will hardly deposit voluntarily if they believe that their savings might be taken to cover others' defaulted loans. Furthermore, credit officers who are accustomed to collecting required payments may be reluctant to promote voluntary savings. With appropriate policies, incentives, and training, however, offering a mix of products that includes both compulsory and voluntary savings can be successful.

How Far to Stretch: Large and Institutional Depositors

Attracting large individual and institutional depositors is a key to developing a large and viable volume of deposits. For example, in 1997 two-thirds of the accounts in the Union Progresista Amatitlaneca (UPA) credit union in Guatemala held US$17 or less, with an average balance of just US$4. Yet the 4 percent of UPA's accounts that held US$877 or more accounted for 76 percent of its total volume of deposits and helped pull the average account size up to $169.[9] Likewise, institutional accounts at the Bank for Agriculture and Agricultural Cooperatives (BAAC) in Thailand raised its average account balance from US$315 to US$563, while constituting only 1 percent of BAAC's deposit accounts.[10] Most of the volume of deposits mobilized by ACCION's affiliated financial institutions in Latin America comes from larger time deposits.[11]

At the same time, offering specialized products to attract large and institutional deposits also carries risks. These include mission drift, higher costs, greater liquidity, and interest-rate risk (see Box 3–1).[12] For example, Opportunity International Bank of Malawi (OIBM), a new microfinance bank, recognizes that it must attract large depositors in order to cover its overhead costs and mobilize a high enough volume of accounts to fund its loan portfolio. To attract these depositors, the bank invested in an attractive, air-conditioned office, and it staffs a department solely devoted to attracting corporate clients. The Corporate Department found that many of its potential clients expect OIBM to offer additional services, such as a foreign-exchange service, that are primarily relevant to upper-end markets. Offering foreign-exchange services would require the bank to hire specialized staff with more education and higher salary requirements than other staff. Whether these investments would be offset by benefits or would alter the bank's focus on small depositors are big questions.[13]

With this in mind, to what extent should an MFI offer products specifically to attract large and institutional depositors? The answer will depend on the nature of the market and the institution. Could the institution successfully compete for these market segments? What additional products, staff, and infrastructure would it take to attract these depositors? Would these investments be likely to pay off? Can the institution recover costs without attracting these markets? When considering whether to develop products to target large and institutional depositors, managers should be fully aware of potential benefits and costs.

Table 7–4. Savings Product Mix in Eight MFIs (figures in US$)

	Demand deposit	Time deposit	Contractual / other
Mixed outreach institutions (serve small and large depositors, urban, and possibly rural areas)			
BRI unit system 25.9 million accounts Avg. balance: $100	Individuals: $1 minimum Institutions: $11 minimum	$111 minimum	
Nyesigiso cooperatives 18,184 accounts Avg. balance: $10	Passbook: No minimum Payroll: No minimum	$95 minimum	Compulsory: for rural women's groups
Prodem FFP 120,000 accounts Avg. balance: $949	Single branch: $3 minimum Any branch or ATM: $7 minimum	$100 minimum	
Moderna credit union 1370 accounts Avg. balance: $163	Passbook: $10 minimum for US$ account; $7 for local currency account Youth: $0.35 minimum Children: $0.35 minimum Institutional: Semi-liquid. $70 minimum	"Salary": deposit harvest proceeds and receive fixed monthly payments	Christmas contract. Planned expense contracts (e.g., vehicle): When 70% of expense is saved, remainder is available as a loan.

	Demand deposit	Time deposit	Contractual / other
Teba Bank 503,748 accounts Avg. balance: $371	Payroll account Regular with checks & ATM option: $6 minimum ATM: No minimum	$146 minimum	
Caja Municipal de Arequipa 18,561 accounts Avg. balance: $600	Passbook: $15 minimum Current-like: $15 minimum	$61 minimum	Government-mandated pension account
Institutions that serve relatively small or remote depositors only			
BURO, Tangail 24,446 accounts Avg. balance: $19	Passbook: $0.20 minimum		Pension contract: weekly for 5 years. With 3 missed payments, converts to passbook account
Bhumiraj cooperative 185 accounts (72% of house- holds in service area) Avg. balance: $7.50	Passbook: for large and institutional depositors only		Compulsory: Uniform, monthly. Can be withdrawn after 5 years Youth: Irregular deposits
MMD self-help groups ~185,000 members Avg. balance: ~$9			Compulsory: uniform, weekly. Group decides when to disburse

	Demand deposit	Time deposit	Contractual / other
SafeSave cooperative 10,000 accounts Avg. balance: $20	Passbook: No minimum unless client holds a loan.		

The data in this table comes from the following sources: Bank Rakyat Indonesia: Zakaria Zaharia, email interchange with author, 2003; and Klaas Kuiper, email posting to DevFinance Network, January 2005; Nyesigiso: Marisol Quirion, email interchange with the author and "Savings in Nyesigiso" (2003); Boubacar Diallo, email interchange with author, December 2004; and Filles Goldstein and Issa Barro in collaboration with Dominique Gentil, *The Role and Impact of Savings Mobilization in West Africa: A Study of the Informal and Intermediary Financial Sectors*, vol. 2, *Presentation of the Microfinance Systems Visited* (Nairobi: *MicroSave*, 1999), 63–64; Prodem: Roberto Hernandez and Yerina Mujica, "What Works: Prodem FFP's Multilingual Smart ATMs for Microfinance" (Washington, DC: World Resources Institute, 2003), 8, 14; and Eduardo Bazoberry, phone conversation with author, December 2004; Moderna Credit Union: "Nicaragua: Putting the Framework into Place," in *Striking the Balance in Microfinance: A Practical Guide to Mobilizing Savings*, ed. Brian Branch and Janette Klaehn (Washington, DC: PACT Publications, 2002), 195–98; Teba Bank: Jennifer Hoffmann, email interchange with author, May 2004; and www.teba.co.za; Cajas Municipal de Arequipa: Jill Burnett, Carlos Cuevas, and Julia Paxton, "Peru: The Cajas Municipales de Ahorro y Creditos" (Washington, DC: Sustainable Banking with the Poor, World Bank, 1999), 24–25; BURO Tangail: Stuart Rutherford with S. K. Sinha and Shyra Aktar, "BURO, Tangail Product Development Review" (Dhaka: DFID UK, 2001); and BURO Tangail 2002 Annual Report; Bhumiraj Cooperative: Records of Treasurer, Ganesh Tamrakar, discussed during site visit by author, July 2001; Mata Masu Dubara: Hugh Allen, "CARE International's Village Savings and Loan Programs in Africa: Microfinance for the Rural Poor that Works" (Atlanta: CARE, 2002), 15–18; SafeSave: Stuart Rutherford and Mark Staehle, email interchange with author.

7.5 PRODUCTS FOR SMALL AND RURAL DEPOSITORS

How do products and product preferences differ for the poor? While the poor have the same saving needs as others, their incomes tend to be small, irregular, and vulnerable to many day-to-day demands. Therefore, they need to be able to deposit frequently in amounts that are small and variable (see Box 7–2). Being

---

Box 7–2. *Frequency, Variability, Reliability: The* Safe*Save Experience*

Because their incomes are tiny, irregular, and unreliable, poor and very poor people repeatedly must turn to savings or loans to finance even the most basic expenditures. So they tend to have complicated and frustrating financial lives, constantly manipulating a jumble of devices and services, mostly informal. *Safe*Save's founders observed the huge potential market among the upper poor and poor for money-management services that emphasize three key qualities—frequency, variability, and reliability. It is a market that most MFIs have yet to explore.

- *Frequency* is important. Give a rickshaw driver in Dhaka the chance to save once a month, and he may save twenty cents: give him the chance to save on a daily basis, and his monthly savings may rise to five dollars.
- *Variability* is important because the poor have uneven irregular and unreliable cash flows. Fixed weekly deposits, especially over a long period such as a year, can be impossible for the poor to manage. Similarly, a fixed withdrawal schedule is very hard for poor people to reconcile with their unpredictable spending needs.
- *Reliability* is rare in finance for the poor. A reliable financial partner is little more than a dream for most poor people.

Pursuing frequency, variability, and reliability led *Safe*Save to experiment with unconventional, costly, or risky procedures. Frequency, for example, led to daily doorstep collection, which is costly unless done by low-paid, local staff, and full of internal control risk. Variability called for savings and loans without fixed terms and payment schedules, causing liquidity-management headaches and augmenting the internal control risk. For *Safe*Save, confronting these costs and risks has spurred imaginative new ideas. Internal control failure, for example, has led to measures such as investing in hand-held computers and training field staff to use them that would have been unimaginable when *Safe*Save started.

For *Safe*Save, success will mean demonstrating that the operating sustainability it reached in 2004 can be maintained over the long run, despite downward pressure on microcredit interest rates (*Safe*Save charges an annual effective rate of 36 percent). This will depend upon whether or not *Safe*Save continues to attract and retain poor and very poor clients who are willing to pay for the cost of the service.

—Stuart Rutherford

able to access funds in case of an emergency may also be essential. *For the poor, a product that requires a regular fixed deposit or a non-negligible initial payment or that does not provide access to funds may simply be irrelevant.* At the same time, the poor may greatly value the discipline provided by the *opportunity* to save frequently and *incentives* not to withdraw.

Designing products for small and rural depositors is challenging. Small balances, long distances, and product features that respond to the needs of the poor cost more. Yet, managing costs typically means using lower-cost staff and manual information systems that make complicated liquidity management unfeasible. Finally, poor and rural savers may be put off or excluded by formal banking products and procedures. As described below, products for small and rural depositors meet these challenges in numerous ways.

Viable Account Balances

People who earn a dollar a day may have trouble opening an account with a minimum balance requirement of even five dollars. If they can open an account, their average deposit size may be less than thirty cents. On top of this, the product features most valued by the poor increase costs further. Providing opportunities to transact frequently requires more staff time. Accepting deposits of variable sizes demands more rigorous internal controls. And, allowing withdrawals at any time requires greater liquidity management. In short, institutions that serve solely small depositors must navigate a narrow strait between covering their own costs and making their products accessible to the poor.

Not surprisingly, the most pressing product-design challenge is how to attract account balances that are viable while providing the liquidity the poor demand to manage emergencies. A product that is designed well can help increase account balances by giving clients the option to withdraw their funds while motivating them not to. Some product features strongly motivate higher levels of savings. Other products simply prohibit withdrawals but provide loans as an alternative source of liquidity. For example,

Tying interest rates and lottery tickets to account size: At Banco Caja Social the larger the clients' account size, the higher their interest rate and the better their chances to win a lottery. For example, the bank's youth product pays no interest on account balances of US$40 or less, 1.5 percent for accounts holding between US$40 and US$3,000, and 3.5 percent for larger accounts. Banco Caja Social also holds lotteries for its regular savers. They receive one ticket for every US$100 in their account.[14] (See Box 10–3 on lotteries and Section 13.3 on tiered interest rates.)

Linking insurance to account size: The Sangrur Central Cooperative increased deposits by linking regular savings with accident and death insurance. To receive the insurance for free, passbook savers had to maintain a balance of at least US$24. The bank pays the premiums directly to the insurance company.[15]

Awarding benefits based on the minimum monthly balance: Many institutions pay interest or allocate lottery tickets based on the minimum rather than the average monthly balance. This motivates depositors not to withdraw funds without good reason and makes it easier to calculate interest due.

Providing emergency loans, tying loan size to savings amount: At Equity Bank, Jijenge contractual account holders save regular fixed amounts that they can withdraw before the agreed-upon time only by paying a high fee. However, the account also provides access to an emergency loan equal to as much as 90 percent of savings. Jijenge provides a disciplined way to accumulate and protect savings; it discourages withdrawals through a fee while providing "access" in the form of a loan. Clients choose the size of their fixed payment, its frequency (weekly or monthly), and the term of their account (one to five years).[16]

In general, contractual products attract larger average balances than passbook accounts. At the same time, they can exclude the poor because they are illiquid—which can be mitigated through access to emergency loans—and because they require fixed regular payments. An MFI can soften these payments in several ways. It can extend the contract term to allow for missed payments; it can permit withdrawals for emergencies by converting the product to a no-interest passbook account; or, as in a pension or youth product, it can have a maturity date but allow variable-sized payments at irregular times. While these modifications make the MFI's cash flow less predictable, they also make serving the poor more feasible for the MFI by generating higher balances than the same clientele might have with passbook accounts.

Product design can help solve the cost-recovery challenge inherent in serving only small or rural depositors. But product design alone is not enough. Many institutions find that offering a stand-alone liquid savings product to only small or remote depositors is not financially viable. The critical issue for cutting costs—how services are delivered—is discussed in the next chapter. One crucial piece of the answer is to use lower-cost staff. This means offering more manageable products.

Manageable Products

To control costs, institutions that serve solely small or rural depositors often use manual information systems and staff with little schooling. Furthermore, some of these more rural MFIs may not have a backup source of liquidity. These institutions must offer products that are easy to manage. In particular, their products must not require complex liquidity management. Institutions simplify liquidity management in a number of ways:

Features that limit unexpected demands for funds: The Small Farmer Cooperatives in Nepal use product rules to limit unexpected demands for funds. Some cooperatives require a week's notice to withdraw funds over a certain amount. Others pay a much lower rate of interest for accounts that allow large or frequent withdrawals without such notice. Many limit the amount that they guarantee a client can withdraw without notice. When they can accommodate larger requests, they levy a 2 percent fee for the amount in excess of the limit.[17]

Short-term high-interest time deposits that discourage regular savings: With an annual inflation rate of 10 percent, the Village Savings and Credit Associations (VISACAs) in Gambia paid no interest on passbook savings accounts and 20 percent on time deposits with terms as short as three months. Not surprisingly, its passbook savings accounts attracted only 11 percent of its deposit accounts. The remaining accounts were accounted for by highly predictable time deposits, the terms of which are carefully matched with loans. By not lending out the passbook savings deposits, the VISACAs eliminate the need for complex liquidity management.[18] (However, paying an overly high interest rate on time deposits risks attracting more rate-sensitive volatile deposits that are more difficult to manage.)

Offering only compulsory savings and emergency loans: In many remote areas the only feasible delivery mechanism to serve small depositors may be self-managed groups or simple cooperatives. Usually managed by volunteers with a few years of schooling, these organizations typically provide one simple savings product—illiquid monthly deposits that are the same amount for all members—coupled with emergency loans. The result is simple, predictable cash flows.

Products and Procedures for the Informal Sector

Many small and rural savers work in and save in the informal sector and have no formal means of identification. To attract these people products must be simple and familiar, paperwork should be minimal, and alternative forms of identification are imperative.

Easing identification requirements: Prodem convinced the Bolivian government to allow savers to open accounts with birth certificates rather than identification cards. Centenary Rural Development Bank requires only a letter from a local religious or clan leader.[19] While smart cards that include electronic fingerprints can replace other formal forms of identification, these cards can be prohibitively expensive for small accounts. Indeed, Prodem uses these cards for clients who are willing to pay a higher annual fee for the opportunity to transact business at multiple branches. For other clients, Prodem and many other institutions use just a passbook with a photo.

Mimicking the informal sector: Workers Bank of Jamaica found that a product with features similar to local informal schemes attracted the low-income market more effectively than the bank's more traditional products. The bank designed a contractual product that resembled local informal savings schemes know as partners.[20] Within three years the bank held US $3.36 million in over seventeen thousand accounts. The Partner Savings Plan offered the familiar name and discipline of the informal schemes but with greater security, interest, and the ability to choose the deposit amount and withdrawal date.[21]

Replicating the informal sector: In many parts of Ghana the poor save with informal collectors who typically provide a one-month contractual product with daily doorstep collection. At the end of the month they return all but one daily deposit; they retain that deposit as payment for their service. In Northern Ghana, where there are no such informal schemes, ActionAid works with communities to select collectors and then trains them to provide precisely the same product.[22]

Product Mix When Serving Small or Rural Depositors

The need to limit costs sharply and to simplify management will also affect an MFI's product mix. MFIs that serve solely small or remote depositors may wish to consider the following options:

Offer a single liquid product: Backed up by computers, *Safe*Save—whose collectors have only a primary-school education—offers a single liquid-savings product that encourages longer-term deposits through its interest-rate structure. Similarly, after having found a stand-alone liquid product to be too costly and a five-year contractual product to be in little demand, ASA now offers just one savings product, a combined voluntary-mandatory account that clients like and ASA can afford.[23]

Offer a contractual product rather than fixed deposits: If only two products are offered, a regular savings product and a contractual (rather than a time-deposit) product often best suit low-income depositors who are not farmers.[24]

Offer a single illiquid product and loans: Self-help groups and many small, young cooperatives offer only an illiquid mandatory product. All members, whether they hold a loan or not, deposit the same fixed amount monthly. Liquidity is provided in the form of an emergency loan facility.[25] Interestingly, the Nyesigiso federation of cooperatives offers passbook savings and time deposits in its town-based branches but just one easier-to-manage compulsory product and loans to groups in rural area.

"Grow" into a broader product mix: As they develop their management capacity, even very small cooperatives might offer a few easy-to-manage voluntary products in addition to mandatory savings. In a remote area of Nepal the Bhumiraj cooperative employs one part-time staff person who has ten years of schooling. Originally the cooperative offered only credit and compulsory savings, US$0.33 a month that could be withdrawn in five years. With training and one year's experience, it began offering youth accounts that allow variable deposits of at least US$0.13 and have fixed terms of many years and also

liquid accounts for a handful of larger depositors, primarily small shopkeepers. These two products increased the cooperative's total deposits by over 26 percent (see Box 8–2).[26]

7.6 CONCLUSION

Most people could make use of a wide variety of customized products. For MFIs, the trick is to offer a few simple products that meet as much of this demand as possible and are manageable and financially feasible. Above all, these products should offer an attractive mix of ready access and motivation for longer-term savings.

Serving small depositors entails particular challenges. The features that poor people want the most—access to their funds and the opportunity to deposit frequently in amounts that are small and irregular—raise operating costs. Covering these costs is especially difficult for MFIs that serve solely small or rural depositors. As this chapter has illustrated, MFIs are overcoming these challenges. Their products are excellent examples of customer-responsive innovation arising from genuine commitment to reaching the poor.

Notes

[1] Stuart Rutherford with S. K. Sinha and Shyra Aktar, "BURO, Tangail Product Development Review" (Dhaka: DFID, 2001), 5.

[2] John Owens, posting to DevFinance Network, April 2000.

[3] These variations primarily involve the form, amount, and timing of deposits and withdrawals. Returns and how they are offered—for example, in the form of a lottery—are discussed in Chapters 9 and 10.

[4] José Benito Miranda Díaz, "Nicaragua: Putting the Framework into Place," in *Striking the Balance in Microfinance: A Practical Guide to Mobilizing Savings*, ed. Brian Branch and Janette Klaehn (Washington, DC: PACT Publications, 2002), 195–98.

[5] Don Terry, interview in "Emerging Link: Remittances and Microfinance," *Microenterprise Americas* (2002), 29.

[6] Craig Churchill, Madeline Hirschland, and Judith Painter, *New Directions in Poverty Finance: Village Banking Revisited* (Washington, DC: SEEP Network, 2002), 95.

[7] Klaus Maurer, "Bank Rakyat Indonesia," in *Challenges of Microsavings Mobilization—Concepts and Views from the Field,* ed. Alfred Hannig and Sylvia Wisniwski (Eschborn, Germany: GTZ, n.d.), 116–18.

[8] Filles Goldstein and Issa Barro, in collaboration with Dominique Gentil, "The Role and Impact of Savings Mobilization in West Africa: A Study of the Informal and Intermediary Financial Sectors," *Presentation of the Microfinance Systems Visited* (Nairobi: MicroSave, 1999), 2:56.

[9] Gloria Almeyda and Brian Branch, "The Case of Union Popular and Union Progresista Amatitlaneca (UPA) Credit Unions" (Washington, DC: SBP/World Bank, 1999), 35.

[10] Delbert Fitchett, "Bank for Agriculture and Agricultural Cooperatives, Thailand (Case Study)," in Hannig and Wisniwski, *Challenges,* 89.

[11] Lynne Curran, "Financing microfinance loan portfolios," *Small Enterprise Development Journal* 16, no. 1 (2005).

[12] Large and institutional accounts tend to be more volatile. For example, VYCCU offers two products that attract solely large and institutional accounts. Without these products its average monthly growth rate ranged from 0 percent to 9 percent. With them, the rate varied nearly twice as much, from 5 percent to 12 percent.

[13] Madeline Hirschland, conversations with managers, August 2003.

[14] Sylvia Wisniwski, "Banco Caja Social, Colombia," in Hannig and Wisniwski, *Challenges,* 189.

[15] Pillarisetti Satish, "Rediscovering Rural Finance by Retooling the Existing Institutions," paper presented at "Paving the Way Forward for Rural Finance: An International Conference on Best Practices in Rural Financial Institutions," Washington DC, June 2003; Satish, conversation with author, June 2003.

[16] Graham Wright, "Designing Savings: Equity Building Society's Jijenge Savings Account," *MicroBanking Bulletin*, no. 9 (July 2003): 29–32.

[17] Stefan Staschen, "Financial Technology of Small Farmer Co-operatives Ltd. (SFCLs): Products and Innovations," Rural Finance Nepal Working Paper No. 2 (Kathmandu: Rural Finance Nepal, 2001), 12, 33–37.

[18] Douglas Graham, Carlos Cuevas, and Korotoumou Ouattara, "Financial Innovation and Donor Intervention in Africa: The Village Savings and Credit Association (VISACAs) in the Gambia," Economics and Sociology Occasional paper No. 2067 (Columbus: Ohio State Univ. Rural Finance Program, 1993), 3–4, 7.

[19] Richard Nalela, "Centenary Rural Development Bank," paper presented at "Paving the Way Forward for Rural Finance" conference, 9.

[20] A local market study had found that nearly two-thirds of all surveyed households participated in these informal schemes and that nearly 60 percent of them joined in order to save.

[21] John Owens, "The Partner Savings Plan of the Workers' Bank, Jamaica: Lessons in Microsavings from ROSCAs," in *Promising Practices in Rural Finance*, ed. Mark D. Wenner, Javier Alvarado, and Francisco Galarza (Washington, DC: Inter-American Development Bank, 2003), 312–15.

[22] Kwame Addei Agyei, conversation with the author, 2001.

[23] Mostaq Ahmmed, "ASA Experience," paper presented at "Paving the Way Forward for Rural Finance" conference, 7–8.

[24] Time-deposit products can be important to farmers, who often seek to save the proceeds from harvests or the sale of livestock—infrequent large amounts—to invest at a later time.

[25] Hugh Allen, "CARE International's Village Savings and Loan Programmes in Africa: Microfinance for the Rural Poor that Works" (Atlanta: CARE, 2002), 15–18.

[26] Bhumiraj cooperative's records, July 2001.

8

Beyond Full-service Branches

Other Delivery Options

Madeline Hirschland

Many poor people use semi-formal and formal services for only a small fraction of their financial transactions. Mostly, they rely on informal options—from ROSCAs to clay pots—even when these savings devices are less lucrative, flexible, or secure. One reason is that informal options tend to be available near their doorsteps at hours they can manage. Rarely are formal and semi-formal services so convenient.

For the poor, convenience is critical. Many clients will deposit their money only if they can do so quickly. For frequent small deposits, a service that requires an hour's walk or a long wait may have little value (see Box 8–1). When it comes to withdrawing funds, the issue is not distance—which can help clients have the

---

Box 8–1. Convenience Matters

In 1998 the agricultural bank of Thailand, BAAC, found that the distance to branches located in sub-district towns discouraged many of its rural customers from making small deposits. In response, BAAC pilot tested the use of vehicles that collected savings at village markets, temples, and other frequented places. After six months the average balance in the vehicle accounts was four times the average balance in the branch accounts. Despite their more limited hours, the mobile units' proximity made them much more attractive to clients.

GTZ, *Marketing for Microfinance Depositories: A Toolkit* (Washington, DC: PACT Publications, 2000), 52.

The author is very grateful for the valuable feedback provided by Sergio Antezana, Ken Appentang-Mensah, David Cracknell, Nav Raj Simkhada, and J. D. Von Pischke.

discipline not to withdraw—but access. Clients will keep emergency funds on deposit only if they know they can withdraw them or obtain a loan when they need to. If they have to wait a week to access funds, they may not deposit in the first place.

For MFIs, providing convenience can be costly; this challenge is magnified when serving small depositors, whose invested deposits generate less revenues, and depositors in rural areas, where mobilizing deposits requires more time and travel. Delivering services that are both affordable and convenient can be the toughest challenge of serving small and rural depositors. Happily, numerous institutions have risen to the task. They have:

- Established low-cost offices near their clientele;
- Deployed mobile units or collectors to expand and deepen outreach;
- "Piggybacked" savings services onto other existing delivery systems;
- Served groups rather than individuals, or allowed some clients to deposit for others;
- Promoted groups of depositors to manage their own savings close to home;
- Distributed lockboxes that aggregate deposits made at home at any time; and
- Used e-technologies that lower costs for MFIs and clients.

This chapter aims to help readers understand which of these options for serving small and rural depositors might best fit the environment in which they work. It describes, illustrates, and assesses each option and summarizes which are most appropriate in different contexts. For comparative purposes, it starts by examining an efficient branch-based delivery model.

8.1 EFFICIENT BRANCHES

BRI units have long set a gold standard for efficiency. With five to twelve staff members, units serve an average of forty-five hundred savers and seven hundred borrowers. With an average deposit size of US$100 (14 percent of per capita GNI) the administrative cost ratio for mobilizing deposits is approximately 2 percent. The units are not necessarily close to depositors; they serve an approximately twenty-mile radius that includes an average of sixteen to eighteen villages.[1] Serving this size area enables the units to generate enough volume to recover costs. In 2003 each unit and smaller village post mobilized on average US$683,000.[2]

The staffing for a small BRI unit includes a manager; a teller, who handles both cashiering and accounting; a credit officer; an administrative officer; and a guard. Units employ an additional credit officer for every 400 borrowers and an additional teller for every 150 to 200 daily transactions (150 in non-automated units, 200 in automated ones.) Except for the guard, unit staff must have a high-school education and computer and accounting skills.[3] This staffing is almost the same as that recommended by WOCCU for a small full-service branch.[4]

While locating full-service branches fairly far apart and/or in towns may be necessary to recover their costs, villagers may be unwilling to travel that far to deposit a small amount. Compared to the size of the deposit, the time or bus fare needed may be too high. For this reason both BRI and WOCCU have found that using smaller offices staffed by three or fewer people is a cost-effective way to serve more rural areas.

8.2 SIMPLE OFFICES

Because lower-cost offices can be sustained by smaller volumes of business, small offices can be located closer to one another or in more rural areas—closer to more clients. Relative to a full-service branch, simpler offices cover costs by limiting service hours, using a bare-bones structure, and employing as few as one part-time staff member. This type of office might be a satellite office of a larger institution, or it might be a small autonomous cooperative.

MFIs usually establish *satellite offices* to expand outreach to less densely populated or poorer areas without incurring the overhead expenses of a full-fledged branch. For example, Opportunity International Bank of Malawi has established small satellite branches in poor urban communities for just 25 percent of the cost of a conventional branch (see Box 5–1). Furthermore, if offices are open only one day a week, one or two full-time employees might staff several offices. Satellite operations are usually integrated with those of the nearest branch, which also supervises them (see Box 5–3). Relative to autonomous cooperatives, satellite offices may benefit from more professional management, supervision by the MFI, and access to a liquidity pool. However, they are unlikely to be able to serve remote areas.

Probably more than any other option discussed in this chapter, *small autonomous cooperatives* can, from a cost-recovery point of view, viably serve remote, sparsely populated areas. This is because they do not incur the high transport and staff costs involved in traveling to and from a distant central office. Remote cooperatives usually cover their full operating costs from the outset by relying on a volunteer board or management committee to handle many functions until they can afford to pay a bookkeeper. Because their board and staff typically have little schooling, small young cooperatives usually offer only a few products that are not managerially demanding, such as compulsory savings and loans. Over time, some grow and offer voluntary savings services and longer hours.[5]

The total cost of the external support needed to establish a small cooperative or village bank and guide it to the point of self-sustainability varies. For the Nepali cooperatives described in Box 8–2, the total investment in institutional development divided by the number of members ranged from US$12 to US$20 over the course of about three years. For the Malian village banks described in Box 8–3,

---

Box 8–2. Autonomous Cooperatives: A Model for Remote Areas in Nepal

More than half of Nepalis live in hill regions where the high costs of service delivery prevent MFIs from operating. The NGO DEPROSC supports Grameen-style MFIs in the plains, but in the hills DEPROSC promotes autonomous cooperatives such as the Bhumiraj Savings and Credit Cooperative Society Ltd.

From the nearest town the Bhumiraj cooperative is a rough half-hour drive and a half-hour walk on a mountain path. Until recently, the cooperative operated out of the home of the treasurer, who has ten years of school and works there two hours a day, six days a week. In 2001 Bhumiraj's 152 members represented 72 percent of the households in its steep, one-third square mile service area.

Bhumiraj is one of 106 hills cooperatives supported by the Canadian cooperative support organization CECI. All are profitable; board members handle transactions until they can afford to pay a bookkeeper. Initially, bookkeepers are paid US$4 a month. Cooperatives with more products, at least 400 members, and longer hours pay about US$75. The cooperatives serve an average of 140 members and become self-reliant in three to five years. During this period the promoting NGO mobilizes the groups, trains the members, provides technical support and monitors their work. Its total cost per cooperative from inception to the point that the cooperative no longer receives technical support (about three years later) is US$1,700 to US$3,000—or US$12 to US$21 per member. If a cooperative cannot meet members' demand for credit, CECI helps it access a loan from an external source. CECI and DEPROSC do not provide loan capital or operating expenses.

—Prahlad Mali

---

the cost was approximately US$140 per member over the course of up to eleven years.

Remote autonomous cooperatives have limitations. Because they serve a single market and lack access to a ready source of excess liquidity, their portfolios are not diversified and they are subject to high covariant and liquidity risk. The share requirements, mandatory savings, and membership fees that are typical of small

---

Box 8–3. Serving the Sparsely Populated Sahel: CVECAs

CVECAs are autonomous village banks that serve a low-income, sparsely populated region of Mali where the illiteracy rate is over 95 percent. The banks provide high-interest time deposits (most of their accounts) and a no-interest passbook service. In 1998 nearly 10 percent of the region's adults were active members, an average of 231 per bank; over two-thirds of the accounts had a balance of less than US$50. Although the French donor CIDR paid for investment costs, training, and supervi-

Continued on page 163

Continued from page 162

sion, the CVECAs recovered all their other expenses from the outset. Over the course of eleven years CIDR invested about US$140 per client; when CIDR terminated its support, the CVECAs were covering the costs of a federation and technical support. In a region with a poor, sparse, and illiterate population and high travel costs, how was this accomplished?

Decentralization with significant training: As much as possible, CVECAs rely on local labor and resources. Travel is limited to obtaining biannual refinancing and external auditors. Local volunteers and staff with little education require extensive training. For example, up to four committee members are taught numeracy so that they can produce a simple operating report, check the bank's records, and assemble its annual financial statement.

Use of volunteers: The bank's volunteer management committee oversees bank operations, promotes services, analyzes and approves loan requests, and recovers loans. Typically illiterate, the committee's seven to thirteen members receive a small year-end payment in recognition of their services.

Part-time staff and profit-based salaries: Each CVECA has two employees who work one day a week. Most are literate in the local language or Arabic and have attended primary school. These staff members manage financial transactions, keep all records, maintain internal controls, prepare the budget and financial statements, and monitor performance. They are paid about one-third of the bank's profits; at first this is next to nothing but can rise to the level received by an administrator in Mali, US$3 a day.

Simple operations: Records and systems are very simple but provide sufficient controls to keep funds secure. To simplify liquidity management and avoid having a costly external liquidity pool, passbook deposits are not lent out and time deposits are simply reprocessed as loans with a shorter maturity.

Low-cost structures for technical support: A regional federation of banks monitors its members, creates new banks, initiates and supervises the quarterly peer auditing required for refinancing, and contracts for refinancing with the agricultural development bank. With no paid staff, the federation's costs include only building maintenance, biannual meeting expenses, and support for troubled banks. The banks and federations contract for auditing services, management training, and assistance in preparing refinancing documentation from a private provider. They pay only for the actual service rendered, not for a costly in-house technical support structure that the network would not use in full.

The CVECAs' initial governance structure proved inadequate. After CIDR's involvement ended, CVECA managers who wanted to mobilize more deposits and earn more began to solicit deposits and extend loans to wealthier outsiders attracted by the CVECAs' high rate of return. The managers lacked the skills and authority to manage these deposits, and loans and repayment rates plunged. CIDR has gotten reinvolved to strengthen the CVECAs' governance and management.[1]

—Renée Chao-Béroff

[1] Cerise, "CVECA Mali," *Theme: Gouvernance en Microfinance, Deuxime Partie, Les Etude de cas Cerise* (Cerise, 2002); and Dramane Mariko, email interchange with editor.

cooperatives may be prohibitive for the very poor. Above all, management committees that are not business-minded may concentrate loans among themselves or may make loans that are unsound, as happened with the CVECAs. This can contribute to high rates of default and, in extreme cases, bankruptcy. This risk can be lessened through strong bylaws, sufficient internal controls, a simple, transparent MIS, and a sound credit methodology. Furthermore, the management committee should consist of business-oriented community members who oversee daily operations. Being part of a larger organization or having some form of ongoing external supervision is also essential to hold them accountable.

8.3 MOBILE COLLECTION

Mobile collection is another way to enhance convenience. For some clients, a mobile service reduces travel time; for others, it brings services close enough to be useful. Even though lower transaction costs for clients mean higher costs—and more security and control headaches—for MFIs, many MFIs find mobile collection to be worthwhile because it can attract more deposits.

- The state agricultural bank of Thailand, Atwima Kwanwoma Rural Bank in Ghana, and Kenya's Equity Bank mobilize deposits using teams in vehicles. An Equity vehicle serves up to eighteen centers that are four to forty miles from the branches (see Box 8–4).
- Traveling alone, by bicycle or by foot, collectors in Bangladesh handle variable-size deposits, loan repayments, and small withdrawals. *Safe*Save collectors visit individuals daily. ASA and BURO, Tangail credit agents mobilize deposits during their weekly borrower-group meetings.
- Numerous commercial banks and not-for-profits in India, Ghana, and Nepal use individual collectors to offer contractual products (see Box 5–2). VSSU, an Indian NGO, uses solely collectors and contractual products; it serves eight thousand clients, turns a profit without subsidy, and funds its entire portfolio with savings.
- Before the Bank Dagang Bali collapsed due to improper lending, its branches employed three teams of collectors. The first served nearby areas by foot, the second served more distant clients by motorcycle, and the third served the most distant by car. The teams often collected many deposits at once by visiting government institutions or factories on payday.

Mobile schemes can fail due to high costs or fraud. For example, the commercial Himalaya Finance and Savings Company (HFSC) used collectors on bicycles to provide a contractual product. HFSC was serving fifty-four thousand clients when the service was ended abruptly due to large-scale collector fraud. Numerous institutions that have found mobile services to be very popular have had to drop them because of their high costs.

Box 8–4. Serving Rural Kenyans: Equity Bank's Mobile Units

Equity Bank initiated mobile banking services in 1999 in order to serve small and microentrepreneurs and small farmers in densely populated rural areas. Often lacking accessible roads, electricity, and low-cost transport services, these areas are not served by commercial banks. By 2004, mobile Equity units were serving 28,720 clients at forty locations. During the unit's one or two visits each week, customers could avail themselves of Equity's full line of financial services, including demand and time deposits, inter-branch transfers, loans, account statements, and financial advice. Customers pay US$0.64 per transaction for this service, which is often less than the cost of transport to the nearest branch. With a minimum account size of US$5.28, customers' average savings balance in 2003 was US$53.

Equity delivers its mobile services from centers that consist of a rental satellite structure and a specially equipped vehicle. Toyota Land Cruisers have been designed as complete banking units with a check reader, card scanner, receipt printer, and special teller windows in the side of the vehicle. They are fully secured with bullet-proof panels and a device to track the car in case of theft. Solar panels and rechargeable batteries power the laptop and the other equipment. When the vehicle arrives, customers line up outside.

Each center is attached administratively to one of Equity's branches. Each branch supports up to eight centers, which are, on average, twelve and one-half miles from the parent branch and serve up to 13 percent of the branch's total number of clients. While in use, the center is guarded by two armed police officers and staffed by a credit officer, a mobile officer, and two or more cashiers, depending on seasonal demand. Mobile operations are handled as part of branch operations and are subject to branch financial management and controls. One mobile unit serves up to eighteen centers, which can be attached to different branches.

Originally, mobile unit computers connected with branches only once per day. Now, units maintain both voice and data communication with the parent branch throughout the day. Branch managers monitor the mobile unit for cash—replenishment is needed only on rare occasions—and security. Connectivity permitting, transaction data is transmitted from the unit to the branch hourly using data-enabled mobile phone lines.

The cost effectiveness of the mobile is not yet known, but several benefits are clear. Customers benefit from greatly reduced transaction costs. This benefit translates into increased customer satisfaction: Equity has gained an excellent reputation. The units also relieve congestion in the bank branches, which would otherwise serve an average of ten thousand customers during end-of-month peaks.

Gerhard Coetzee, Kamau Kabbucho, and Andrew Njema, "Taking Banking Services to the People: Equity's Mobile Banking Unit" (Nairobi: *MicroSave*, 2003); David Cracknell, email interchange with author, April 2004; and Alex Muhia, email interchange with author, January 2005.

The costs, potential for fraud and geographic and income outreach of mobile services vary a lot according to whether collection is done by mobile units or by individuals who travel by foot or bike.

Mobile Units

Similar to simple offices, mobile units bring services to places people congregate in rural centers—marketplaces, villages, or religious centers—that could not support a full-fledged branch. These places must be within a reasonable drive of the parent branch. Four-wheel vehicles usually visit a service site once a week, on market days when possible. They are managed as part of branch operations and may offer the same services (see Box 8–4).

The chief challenges of mobile units are costs and security. Even spread over several locations, the cost of buying, outfitting, and maintaining a unit can be high, particularly if the vehicle must cover rough terrain and withstand attacks by armed thieves. Costs are also increased by armed guards, staff travel time, and data-transfer technology. To be viable, units need to attract a large volume of business; they are not a likely means to serve remote areas or rural areas that are largely poor. Indeed, whether and where they can cover costs and how the costs compare to those of offices with limited hours should be carefully considered.

Individual Collectors

While mobile units may expand outreach to new areas, individual collectors usually deepen outreach within an existing service area by serving small depositors who might not use a branch that is a bus ride or long walk away. Collectors visit clients close to their homes or work places, or, to lower costs, they can collect in a place clients frequent, such as a market or meeting site. They normally visit daily, weekly, or at the client's convenience. Some MFIs hire collectors as salaried employees; others pay them on a commission basis. Collectors typically handle one passbook product and/or a contractual product. In some cases they also accept loan payments. Depending on the population density and whether they also handle loans, collectors may visit sixty to two hundred clients daily (see Box 8–5). Collectors are often used in commercial areas in cities and towns or reasonably densely populated rural areas. Bicycles can be a cost-effective way to extend their reach.

Individual collection faces two related challenges: recovering costs and preventing fraud. MFIs deploy collectors individually rather than in teams in order to control costs. This increases the risk of fraud, however, which must be offset with internal controls (see Section 11.4.2).[6] MFIs also control costs by hiring less educated staff. Where salaries are relatively high, another option can be to pay collectors on commission. Even with these measures, covering the costs of mobile collection is challenging and requires a constant search for greater efficiency. Administrative cost ratios for individual collection vary tremendously,

Box 8–5. Doorstep Collection in the Slums of Dhaka: *Safe*Save

Registered as a cooperative in 1997,[1] *Safe*Save provides flexible financial services to about ten thousand residents of densely populated slum areas in Dhaka, Bangladesh. Services are provided by individual *Safe*Save collectors who visit clients' homes or shops six days a week (branches are not set up for over-the-counter operations, although loans are disbursed in the branch). When the collector visits, clients may save or withdraw as much or as little as they like, as well as make loan payments. *Safe*Save has encountered plenty of demand for its services and many compliments from clients who appreciate the convenience of the service. Its greatest challenge is profitability. Although *Safe*Save's operational sustainability is about 110 percent, margins are tight, and downward pressure on loan interest rates could force it to redesign its service (perhaps losing its focus on the poor) or turn to subsidy.

*Safe*Save's average account balance is just US$20, while its average deposit amount is only US$0.35. Its deposit accounts are highly liquid; per year, the cash flow through them is at least ten times the net growth in average balances. Not surprisingly, *Safe*Save's administrative expense ratio is very high. But daily doorstep services cost only about US$10 per client per year and about US$0.10 per transaction. Within about eighteen months a *Safe*Save branch begins to generate a surplus.

To maintain profitability, *Safe*Save rigidly controls its costs, particularly its staff costs. It does this by hiring staff who are needier and less formally educated, and paying them well. As *Safe*Save's clients are poor, this approach also results in better service. While branch managers and their assistants typically have a college education, the collector's job requires no more than five to ten years of schooling. Products are intuitive, while simple, clear procedures give collectors no discretion over services. Although collectors must be trusted and have excellent people skills, they only need to be able to write and perform simple arithmetic to record transactions (either on paper or on hand-held computers, with which *Safe*Save has been experimenting successfully). This makes it possible to hire branch employees at an average monthly wage of about US$60, around twice the per capita GNI.

But staff costs are only the beginning. A typical *Safe*Save branch rents its premises for less than US$100 per month, including utilities. Given the density of Dhaka's slums, the area served by a branch is a little over half a mile in diameter, and most work is done by foot. Travel and promotion cost only about US$5 per month per branch.

There is one cost, however, on which *Safe*Save does not skimp: a computerized MIS. A good MIS is indispensable for managing and analyzing a large number of unpredictable transactions (*Safe*Save records more than one million transactions per year for only ten thousand clients). Without it, internal control would not be possible, and the institution's reliability and customer service would come into doubt. A good MIS is also vital to calculating staff performance incentives, which have been critical to maximizing portfolio yield and keeping costs low.

A final key to *Safe*Save's cost recovery is that it integrates relatively high-priced credit (although never mandatory) with relatively low-yielding savings. *Safe*Save charges 36 percent effective annual interest for loans and offers 6 percent effective annual interest for savings balances over US$16. So far, as long as they get a reliable, convenient service, clients accept this pricing arrangement.

—Stuart Rutherford and Mark Staehle

[1] Legally a cooperative, *Safe*Save functions like an NGO. Its owner-members are academics and professionals, rather than clients.

from under 6 percent in one institution to over 60 percent in another, depending on many factors, including average account size, the distance collectors travel to depositors, how frequently depositors are visited, the salary levels of staff, and the effectiveness of internal controls. In some cases banks use mobile services initially to create a deposit base, after which they phase these services out because of their high costs.

Many MFIs manage with less educated collectors by offering products with predictable cash flows, such as contractual products. This simplifies record keeping and makes it easier for supervisors to detect fraud. However, regular fixed payments can exclude many of the poor. Some MFIs are experimenting with personal digital assistants (PDAs) or smart cards that may make it easier and less time-consuming to manage irregular payments (see Section 8.8). They will see whether small accounts can justify the costs of these technologies and whether they can manage the higher risk of fraud. *Safe*Save's initial experiment with PDAs found that the direct costs associated with PDAs were about twice those of a manual system, but that the benefits in work flow efficiency and internal control offset those higher direct costs. That cost-benefit analysis is ongoing, but the system gradually is being expanded at *Safe*Save's (rather than donors') expense.[7]

8.4 "PIGGYBACKING" ON AN EXISTING DELIVERY SYSTEM

Where feasible, one way to recover costs while providing a convenient service can be to use the delivery system for another service. This can be done in numerous ways. For example,

Piggybacking on a non-financial service: In the hills of Nepal some small dairy farmers can deposit and withdraw savings when they sell their milk to their Small Farmers Savings and Credit Cooperative (SFCL). For the farmers, this is highly convenient and adds value to the up to two-hour walk to the SFCL. For the SFCLs, extending services nearer to their members' homes would be prohibitively costly.

Piggybacking on a financial service: During their weekly credit group meetings, ASA borrowers can make a voluntary liquid savings deposit or withdrawal as they deposit their compulsory savings. For ASA and its clients, the marginal cost of the voluntary transaction is virtually nil (see Box 8–6). In contrast, many institutions that serve similarly poor clients find that offering them a stand-alone, demand-deposit service is not viable.

Delivering alongside another's delivery system: In the city of La Paz, Bolivia, the regulated financial institution FIE mobilizes deposits from the borrowers of the NGO Pro Mujer after the weekly meetings of Pro Mujer's borrower groups. These groups could not manage the large volume of savings they had mobilized from themselves and, as an unregulated institution, neither could

Box 8–6. Using an Existing Delivery System: ASA's Mandatory-Voluntary Product

A profitable NGO, ASA provides its over two million low-income members with an individual loan-and-mandatory-savings product. Since 1997 ASA has also provided about 360,000 clients with a voluntary liquid-savings service. The service takes the form of a mandatory-voluntary product delivered during weekly group meetings near clients' homes.

During the meeting, when credit officers collect required savings payments, clients may deposit any amount equal to or higher than the mandatory US$0.17. They also are free to withdraw up to US$9 in savings as long as they leave 10 percent of their loan amount in their savings account. Larger and emergency withdrawals can be made at the branch, located within five miles of members' homes. On average, ASA's hybrid accounts hold US$20, about US$8 of which is liquid. (These figures are for all ASA's members. For 1.7 million of these, their group sets the size of their voluntary payment, although they can still withdraw savings in excess of 10 percent of their loan amount.) On average, clients withdraw about one-third of this amount over the course of a year.

For ASA, attracting large deposits to offset the high costs of smaller ones is not an option. In ASA's competitive environment, subsidized loan funds are widely available, and high-yielding investment opportunities are not. ASA cannot afford to mobilize a large volume of low-yielding deposits. Furthermore, as an NGO, ASA is prohibited from mobilizing deposits from non-members by the Bangladeshi government. For all these reasons ASA has had to cover the cost of managing small liquid accounts without cross-subsidizing them.

ASA's marginal operating costs for the voluntary service are virtually nil; branch staffing and operating expenses did not change when the voluntary service was added. Furthermore, staffing and costs are identical for branches that offer the product and those that do not. The costs of the new service were negligible because ASA tightly integrated it into existing streamlined operations and became even more efficient:

- *Record keeping:* The voluntary-mandatory transaction replaced the mandatory one. To offset the more complex record keeping, ASA made its already-streamlined MIS more efficient, thereby reducing the number of forms credit officers must complete.
- *Liquidity management:* Because projecting liquidity needs with the new service demanded more of the branch manager's time, ASA delegated part of the task to credit officers for whom ASA developed a simple manual projection tool.
- *Internal controls:* Because variable savings payments made it easier for credit officers to commit fraud, branch managers verified savings passbooks against field records more frequently, every two months. To minimize the time this takes, branch managers do it during their surprise audit visits to groups and collect and check all the passbooks at one time.

Mohammed Azim Hossain, head of finance and MIS at ASA, conversation with author; Graham A. N. Wright, Robert Peck Christen, and Imran Matin, "ASA's Culture, Competition and Choice: Introducing Savings Services into a MicroCredit Institution" (Nairobi: *MicroSave,* 2000).

Pro Mujer. Under the current arrangement, Pro Mujer promotes FIE's savings products during its group meetings, while FIE agrees not to compete for Pro Mujer's borrowers.[8]

Delivering through another's delivery system: Jamaica National Microcredit Company Limited offers savings services through Jamaica's 247 post offices as well as in its own branches. A social pillar in most Jamaican towns, the post offices give the bank a platform for serving rural markets. Postmasters supervise the postal clerks. The bank pays the offices a 3 percent commission on transactions but has not been able to control the quality of administration and service. Providing excellent quality deposit services through the post offices has always been difficult, because the bank must rely on government postal workers rather than being able to place its own employees at the post office window. Services might also be piggybacked onto other institutions such as retail chains or petrol stations with smart-card readers or lottery outlets.

Piggybacking savings services onto the delivery system for another services offers several advantages. For clients, depositing or withdrawing when they transact other business saves time. Conversely, especially for MFIs in remote areas, serving clients where they already gather can be crucial to cost recovery. Using existing buildings, management systems, and staff also costs the MFI less, particularly if these had been under-utilized. To realize these cost savings the MFI, like ASA, must integrate the savings service efficiently. Piggybacking can also speed outreach, especially if the other system already has many users, and can attract higher-income customers that can diversify the MFI's risk and increase its revenues.[9] Using the delivery system for an existing service may not be the best way to reach new clients, especially poorer or more rural markets. However, outreach can be extended by combining piggybacking with other delivery options (discussed in Section 8.9).

At the same time, piggybacking poses distinct challenges that may be hard to overcome. Piggybacking requires managers and staff to be committed to changing staffing, training, incentive schemes, and management systems and to achieving high levels of productivity.[10] Making these changes in a delivery system over which one does not have control can be very hard—as the Jamaican National Microcredit Company has found with the Jamaican postal system. Furthermore, not-for-profits like farmers' cooperatives and government post offices may be subject to political interference or may lack a culture that promotes rigorous management, growth, responsiveness to clients, and innovation.

8.5 ALLOWING ONE CLIENT TO MAKE DEPOSITS FOR OTHERS

MFIs can make services more convenient and lower their own costs by allowing individuals to deposit for other individuals or groups. MFIs do this in many ways:

In the URAC-UDEC program in Mexico, a volunteer treasurer chosen by the group collects deposits weekly from individual members and takes them to the institution. URAC-UDEC reduces the potential for fraud by requiring members to withdraw in person at the office and by checking all passbooks against office records every six months. The minimum deposit is US$0.22. Of the program's 12,700 members, just over half have balances below US$11.26, and only about one-third have balances over US$22.52. This URAC-UDEC system can extend services into rural areas because affordable transportation is accessible locally, which is not the case in many rural markets.[11]

Like many cooperatives, the VISACAs in the Gambia allow groups to join as if they were individual members. Traditional groups have represented 4 percent of the VISACAs' membership.[12] Similarly, the BISCOL Cooperative allows groups with at least ten members to join the cooperative. Each group collects an equal amount of monthly savings from each of its members at a meeting within about half a mile of their homes. Then a representative of the group deposits this amount with a staff person at a designated time and collection site within four miles of their homes. This strategy keeps BISCOL's costs low; staff need not visit each group, nor must they train the groups in record keeping.

*Safe*Save clients often make deposits or loan repayments for other *Safe*Save clients (although the account holder must be present for withdrawals and loans). The arrangement between clients is informal and can change from day to day.[13]

The efforts required by the institutions above vary. In some cases the cooperative or MFI trains the groups to keep records of members' individual transactions. In other cases the institution opens an account in the name of a group rather than an individual. In still other cases the institution does not deal with groups at all; it serves one person.

The advantage of all these systems is that they can lower costs to the MFI while making transactions more convenient for many clients. The disadvantage is that entrusting savings to another community member can leave clients vulnerable to fraud. When the institution trains clients, this risk can be reduced by instructing them in the use of proper internal controls.

8.6 SELF-HELP GROUPS

A good option for rural areas is self-help groups (SHGs). SHGs provide limited but highly convenient services to large numbers of small, rural depositors and are easily promoted by NGOs that have no expertise in financial intermediation. The NGOs usually do not recover the costs of promoting these groups.[14] However, the SHGs are financially self-sufficient. Often, their members are small depositors who are not served by other formal or semi-formal institutions.

Found everywhere, but especially in South Asia, SHGs provide their members with a mandatory illiquid savings service coupled with access to loans.[15] Composed of between five and twenty members, each group meets monthly or weekly close to members' homes. At each meeting all members save the same amount. The group then lends these savings to members, store them in a lockbox, or deposit them in a group bank account in order to leverage a group loan. If an emergency strikes, members often can access a loan quickly from their group's emergency fund, a feature that they value highly.

Because the SHG approach is so simple, it has tremendous potential for scale. Unsophisticated NGOs can rapidly promote large numbers of groups even if the members are illiterate. The NGO simply trains them and provides limited supervision. In India, NABARD, the government rural-development bank, has grown its SHG program to serve over seven million clients in ten years at an estimated cost of US$10.50 per member (see Box 5–5). In Niger, the CARE Mata Masu Dubara savings groups serve over 160,000 members; a similar program in Zimbabwe grew to serve 14,000 rural women in four years at a cost of US$24 per member; and in Mexico, savings groups promoted with support from the Department of Agriculture serve over 12,800 women (see Box 8–7).

The disadvantages of a self-managed model are limited services (because semi-literate volunteers cannot readily manage flexible payments and interest calculations), high covariant risk, and vulnerability to fraud. These risks can be reduced through linkages to a bank or, in some cases, to a federation. Linkages can also enable groups to offer more flexible services by giving them access to a liquidity pool, loans for on-lending, or the services of a bookkeeper paid for by the group. However, expecting SHGs to be linked to a bank or federation may make the approach less suitable for areas that are distant from these institutions. In either case, groups often exclude poorer people who may not be able to manage fixed regular payments and whom other members may not wish to include. Organizations that seek to include poorer people may find it best to start by serving them and then expanding coverage to others.

The institutional sustainability of SHGs can be challenging. Experience suggests the following keys to success: groups start out homogenous and harmonious; a clear vision on the part of the promoting institution and groups; simple, well-understood policies; a basic record-keeping system; and strong training in internal controls, bookkeeping, and democratic management.[16]

Organizations that promote SHGs normally do not expect to cover their costs with operating revenues. Rather, they see their costs as an investment in a financial and social infrastructure for markets not served by other formal and semi-formal institutions. SHGs often aim to generate social value well beyond the impact of their financial services. Developing and collectively managing their own savings can increase women's self-esteem, and groups can become mutual support networks that also serve as bases for literacy training, anti-drug campaigns, or other mutual support activities that may be highly valued by members, in particular women.

Box 8–7. SHGs: CARE's *Kupfuma Inshungu Program*

The Kupfuma Inshungu Program operates in sparsely populated, rural Zimbabwe. In just four years it promoted 2,221 groups that provide simple financial services to over fourteen thousand members—including about two-thirds of the women in the villages it serves. About one-fifth of these are net savers. The total cumulative cost to the program has been just US$24 per member.

There are two keys to this achievement. First, the program trains and supervises only groups. It does not engage in financial intermediation. Second, the groups operate very simply. Five to fifteen members collect and lend out their own savings during monthly meetings. They all save the same fixed amount. The groups do not manage withdrawals or ever-growing liabilities. Instead, they disband at a predetermined time of their own choosing, after which they form again. All members withdraw their savings with interest and then join again if they choose. In this way, the program—though not itself sustainable—develops sustainable groups that deliver valued services.

Self-management: The groups are self-selected and self-managed. They develop their own bylaws and elect officers and money counters annually. They also decide on interest rates, their monthly savings amount—typically between US$0.15 and US$0.60 per member—the order in which they will fill members' loan proposals, and the length of each operating cycle. At the end of the cycle the group can set a new contribution level or decide to suspend its activities until a better time. Because all funds are disbursed regularly, the accounting is simple and the risks inherent in managing large sums are avoided.

Group sustainability: The groups also are largely sustainable. Of the 40 percent that have graduated to receiving only two staff visits a year, 95 percent remain in operation. The groups appear to be cohesive, highly motivated, and confident. They have written regulations, well-crafted and well-maintained accounting systems, strong officers, and attentive supportive members. They can pay a high rate on their savings because they incur virtually no expenses.

Costs: The Kupfuma Inshungu Program generates no operating revenues with which to cover the investment cost of promoting groups. These costs are low, however, and management may soon reduce them further. By clustering groups for training and field officer visits, each officer handles an average of eighty-five groups that include about 550 members (a ratio international comparisons suggest may be too high). At least twenty-four groups, however, have formed without any outside promotion. These groups have requested training from existing groups, who usually agree to do this for free. The program may formalize this development. It would train existing group leaders to train new groups, which would pay the trainers for this service.

The Kupfuma Inshungu Program's services and delivery system suit members. Transactions take place quickly in the village at convenient times. Transparent self-management provides security. Members can save without borrowing, groups withdraw according to their seasonal needs, and loans are available for individual emergencies. And their savings generate positive real returns.

—Alfred Hamadziripi

Some material is from Hugh Allen, Jestias Rushwaya, and Peter Koegler, "End of Term Evaluation of Kupfuma Ishungu Rural Microfinance Project (RMFP), Zimbabwe" (CARE, 2002).

8.7 LOCKBOXES

Money can be deposited through a lockbox slot at any time but can be retrieved only by using the key. Typically, clients keep the box in their shop or home; an MFI staff member holds the key. Some MFIs employ a mobile collector to collect money held in lockboxes on a biweekly or monthly basis, while others expect clients to take their box to the office at their convenience. Withdrawals normally can be made only at the office.

For small depositors, lockboxes offer the ultimate in convenience. Lockbox holders can easily deposit any small amount whenever they please. Because a lockbox accepts irregular deposits and does not require travel to an office, it can extend services to poor people with irregular incomes or restricted mobility and people who live or work within the branch's service area but far from the office.

For the MFI, introducing lockboxes can increase deposits while cutting costs. Because it is so convenient, clients often will deposit as much or more than they would if they had to walk to a bank or wait for a collector, even a daily collector. For the MFI the box aggregates frequent small deposits into less frequent larger ones. For example, the Rural Bank of Talisayan in the Philippines introduced lockboxes when it found that its daily mobile collection service was too costly. The boxes are made of waxed cardboard that is brightly decorated with the name of the bank and saving slogans. Mobile agents open them biweekly or monthly and count and record the contents in the presence of the client. Using lockboxes reduced the bank's transactions per client dramatically—from twenty-two to two per month—while the savings per client increased. Rural banks in the Philippines have found that maintaining a high level of saving in lockboxes requires ongoing promotion.[17]

Saving in a lockbox may be more secure than saving under a mattress but less secure than saving in an MFI account. Small and portable, a lockbox can easily be stolen. Although its contents are confidential and clients can only withdraw at the office, its visibility can make savings vulnerable to the demands of friends and family. The MFI should train lockbox holders to guard against fraud by counting the contents of the box when it is emptied and checking to see that the collector records the amount properly.

Relative to small account balances, the monetary value of the lockbox itself can be significant. Some MFIs require lockbox account holders to make a deposit for the box that is refunded once they terminate their account. Others expect clients to buy the box outright. Still others split the cost with the client.[18]

8.8 E-BANKING, FROM HAND-HELDS TO ATMS

E-banking can lower transaction costs relative to the costs of transactions in the banking hall.[19] It also provides equal or greater security, efficiency, and accuracy.[20]

For these reasons e-banking has the potential to expand services to more rural areas and to smaller depositors who require products with flexible payments. Some MFIs that have developed e-technologies have found that the investment costs are justified by lower operating costs and higher volumes. Others have dropped these technologies because, although transactions cost less, implementation continues to cost much more than with their existing system.

One key to success may be assuring that the new technology adds value for clients and the financial institution rather than merely replicating an existing product. For the financial institution, the volume of business needed to offset the costs of the new technology usually must come from the wide variety of services that e-technologies can support, such as handling bill payments, government pension payments, and remittances. Second, for many smaller and medium-sized institutions, going it alone is not feasible or cost effective; it can be essential to partner with banks or a network of institutions that have already managed e-banking's many challenges.

E-banking is demanding. Financial institutions should consider such technologies only if they or their partner has access to reliable, affordable power and data communications; a strong MIS and information-technology team; and suppliers who can offer and support software, hardware, security, and communications at a reasonable price. Moving into an e-technology usually costs more than anticipated. These new technologies may require new government regulations. Where this is not the case, obtaining licenses and complying with government banking and card-company regulations can be time-consuming. Developing a smooth interface with existing in-house information systems and, where applicable, interoperability with external banking and payment systems, can be a huge task. Then, too, the new technology will require market research, marketing, incentives, training materials, and training to assure that it is appropriate, easy to use, and acceptable to customers. A network of financial institutions can help in shouldering some of the many demands of e-banking such as developing comprehensive, appropriate security and risk-management systems, and establishing and managing numerous partnerships with everyone from software providers to merchants that have POS devices and regulators. Getting illiterate or semi-literate customers to accept these technologies may be a major challenge for institutions that seek to serve small and rural depositors.

What technologies are feasible and appropriate depends on many factors: the target market, e-banking infrastructure, technical capacity in-house and externally, availability of affordable hardware and software, power and communications infrastructure, and the legal and regulatory environment. So far, electronic technologies have enabled institutions to extend their outreach to lower-income and peri-urban markets, although comprehensive e-banking solutions for poor and rural depositors are not yet in place. As costs fall and technology, knowledge, and shared solutions develop, e-banking is likely to become an increasingly powerful means to extend outreach, at least to rural areas. For now, the e-technologies that

MFIs most frequently use to reduce costs and increase productivity are PDAs and smart cards.

PDAs

PDAs are hand-held computers that can be used by even minimally educated staff to record transactions and do calculations. PDAs usually import and export data into the MIS through a daily physical connection to the computer system; wireless communication is possible but not necessary. To use PDAs, an MFI should have high-speed access to MIS data. At present, developing PDA software and integrating it into an existing MIS costs US$20,000 to US$80,000; maintaining the software costs US$3,000 to US$10,000 per year; and the PDAs themselves cost US$100 to US$200 each.[21]

PDAs provide MFIs with many benefits. By eliminating the need to enter data into manual records before entering it into the computerized MIS, PDAs increase the productivity and efficiency of staff and reduce the need for paper records. PDAs also increase the accuracy of records and improve internal controls. Furthermore, the ability to provide clients with immediate account information can improve customer satisfaction. On the credit side, PDAs can help standardize and speed up the loan-approval process and improve loan monitoring and repayment.

These benefits may be offset by the cost of PDAs. However, where labor costs are relatively high and MFIs track a large quantity of data, PDAs can reduce operating costs, particularly when improved client retention and reduced fraud are considered. For a number of well-respected MFIs, however, the technology did not yield the savings expected, and integration between their PDA software and MIS proved costly and challenging. Nevertheless, for many MFIs, PDAs may be the most beneficial and feasible entry point into e-banking.

Smart Cards

When used in savings, a smart card serves as an electronic identification card and passbook. A chip inside the plastic card stores the cardholder's name, account number, identification code, account balance, and recent transaction data. Some MFIs use a digital fingerprint for identification so that they can easily serve customers who are illiterate or who have no formal identification. In addition to using the cards for cash transactions, customers can store funds on their cards electronically. This "loaded" value can be withdrawn at any of the MFI's branches or ATMs,[22] and, if the MFI participates in a smart-card network, the card can be used to pay for purchases or retrieve cash at any member retail outlet or ATM.

Smart cards can be used in conjunction with a staffed card-reading device in the branch that verifies identification; with a staffed POS device in, for example, a retail shop, that verifies identification and records transactions; and with unstaffed ATMs in a town or city, which also verify identification and record transactions.

Card-reading devices currently cost between US$100 and US$200 while POSs cost at least US$350. (ATMs are discussed below.)

The primary issues with smart cards are their cost and the MFI's ability to manage and maintain the technology that goes with them. Smart cards cost from US$2 to US$10 each. Although the rapid development of technology may change this, MFI-only cards still typically cost less than network cards. A cheaper though less secure alternative to a smart card is a *mag card,* a magnetic-stripe card, which does not contain a computer chip but serves as identification. Mag cards cost significantly less than smart cards, about US$0.25 to US$0.50 at present. Because they require continual online connection, however, they have less potential to serve rural areas with poor or costly telecommunications.

Many MFIs pass these costs on to customers. For depositors who find the cost too high, MFIs sometimes provide a lower-cost passbook account that does not include a smart card. For SKS in India, the initial development cost for a system with smart cards and PDAs was more than US$125,000. Although SKS's illiterate clients and loan officers had no problem adopting the technology, SKS dropped it because the costs outweighed the benefits.

Cash and ATMs

Cash machines and ATMs can be very attractive to the segment of depositors who appreciate being able to withdraw funds from multiple locations at any hour. These unstaffed machines handle transactions using a smart card or mag card. Cash machines cost less and simply dispense cash, while ATMs cost more and have more features.[23] MFIs that develop their own network of machines must buy, install, network, restock, maintain, and guard them and will incur communications charges. Where banks share an ATM and POS infrastructure, however, an MFI can expand its outreach and may be able to lower its costs by securing access to this *switch* network. To participate, the MFI will have to meet more onerous fiduciary requirements, issue cards, install devices that are inter-operable with this network, and pay fees for participation, usage, and service. For example, to enable its customers to use a network of 1,000 ATMs, Banco Ademi paid an initial entry fee of US$10,000 and pays an annual membership fee of US$2,400. Each transaction costs the customer US$0.20. Implementing the ATM technology cost Banco Ademi less than US$70,000. In comparison, a single ATM now costs between about US$10,000 and US$35,000.[24]

Cash machines and ATMs provide less value to small depositors who transact in only one location. The cost of establishing and maintaining machines in close proximity to one another is prohibitive. Furthermore, low-income depositors who want to deposit frequent small amounts of cash may be reluctant to deposit this cash into a machine, fearing that they will have no recourse if their funds are recorded incorrectly. An ATM may also not be able to accept tattered paper currency and, because accepting more denominations increases the cost of the machine, an

MFI may not be able to afford ATMs that accept cash deposits or small denominations. For example, ATMs have lowered Prodem's transaction costs and attracted a large number of new depositors; at the same time, the machines are located adjacent to its branches, do not accept deposits, and are available only to customers who pay a US$7 annual fee for a smart card (see Box 8–8).

Mobile Phone and Internet Banking

Transactions through Internet kiosks or mobile phones can replace checks or a physical trip to the bank or ATM. With Internet banking customers authorize payments and transfers from their account on line. Where banking regulations allow, Internet kiosks can also allow customers to make deposits and withdrawals. To support Internet banking the financial institution has to provide each client with an Internet account, develop a website in the local language, and address security issues.[25] Clients need to be able to access and navigate the website. Mobile phones can also be used to authorize transfers and payments. Where mobile phones are common and prepaid phone cards are easily purchased, authorizing a deposit from the card by phone may hold tremendous potential for lowering transaction costs for both customers and MFIs. With mobile phones, as with Internet banking, customers must be able to navigate the technology, which typically involves choosing from menus of options.

These e-technologies can cost much less than card-based banking; the financial institution does not pay for the communication infrastructure, connectivity, cards, software, or hardware. The challenge with these and other electronic technologies is to make them usable and acceptable to poor semi-literate and illiterate clients. Once this challenge is met, then, as the costs of e-technologies fall, e-banking will gain the potential to reach increasingly smaller and more rural depositors in environments with the necessary power, communications, and information-technology infrastructure.

8.9 COMBINING OR OFFERING PARALLEL DELIVERY SYSTEMS

The delivery systems discussed above accomplish different things: some extend services to rural areas, others extend them to small depositors in existing service areas, and a few lower the MFI's per-client transaction costs. Many institutions combine them. For example,

- Because the convenience of mobile collection comes at a high cost, many institutions combine it with other cost-savings delivery systems such as lockboxes (rural banks in the Philippines) or piggybacking on the loan delivery system (ASA in Bangladesh).
- Some institutions establish basic offices to expand outreach to rural areas and then use these as a base for another delivery system—such as lockboxes,

Box 8–8. Prodem FFP's Intelligent ATMs

In just three years, Prodem FFP, a Bolivian nonbank financial institution, moved from serving fourteen hundred depositors to serving over thirty-eight thousand, many of whom are illiterate, rural, and do not speak Spanish. Its volume of deposits sky-rocketed from US$280,000 in 2001 to US$10.38 million in 2003. Prodem attributes this growth to using smart cards that rely on fingerprint identification and "intelligent" ATMs.

Because each card's chip holds the customer's name, account number, and digital fingerprint, card holders can transact at any Prodem branch or ATM without transaction slips or formal identification. Depositors insert their card and place their thumb on an electronic fingerprint reader. A voice then welcomes them in their native tongue—Aymara, Quechua, or Spanish—and guides them through the transaction by prompting them to touch colored icons on the screen.

The cards are also suited to rural branches. By storing the customer's balance and last five transactions, the card's chip makes an online connection to headquarters unnecessary. In rural Bolivia online connectivity would be both infeasible and unaffordable. Prodem estimates that it would increase costs by US$70,000 per year. Instead, staff download transaction data from the ATM and transmit it to headquarters daily.

Prodem's ATM technology has lowered its overall cost of funds. Indeed, its estimated cost of funds from savings is just 2.45 percent, even though it operates primarily in rural areas. Because they lower staff and overhead costs, transactions through ATMs cost less than in the branch. Prodem invested about US$600,000 for its first twenty ATMs, software development, and smart cards. To recover the investment, each ATM must generate US$70,000 in additional deposits per year for three years.

Prodem offers two types of savings accounts: a smart card account that has a US$7 annual fee and minimum balance, and a passbook account with a US$3 annual fee and minimum balance. While smart-card holders can transact at any branch and can withdraw (a minimum of US$12) from any ATM, passbook holders can transact only at their home branch.[1] For small depositors who do not travel, a passbook with a photo serves nearly as well as a smart card and is more affordable.[2] For customers who handle larger amounts of cash, want quick 24-hour access or transact business in more than one location, the smart card offers tremendous convenience and security. Indeed, it is many customers' only option for a deposit account that they can use away from home and eliminates the risk of fraud from lost or stolen documents or forgery. It is little wonder that smart cards and intelligent ATMs have quickly made Prodem Bolivia's market leader in rural savings mobilization.

---

[1] For cost reasons, Prodem's ATMs were designed to handle just two types of bills, US$20 and 100 bolivianos (BOB), equivalent to about US$12.72). For this reason, they do not accept deposits, and withdrawals must be made in multiples of US$20 or 100 BOB.

[2] Sixty-one percent of Bolivians work in the informal sector, where they earn an average of US$960 per year. For them, the US$4 savings for the passbook account represents, on average, more than one day's income.

Box 8–8 is based on Eduardo Bazoberry, "The Bolivian Experience of the Prodem Private Financial Fund S.A.," paper presented at "Paving the Way Forward for Rural Finance: An International Conference on Best Practices in Rural Financial Institutions," Washington, DC, June 2003, 1–9; Bazoberry, conversations with the author, June 2003 and Fall 2004; Roberto Hernandez and Yerina Mujica, "What Works: Prodem FFP's Multilingual Smart ATMs for Microfinance" (Washington, DC: World Resources Institute, 2003); and Samuel Silva, "Quantum Leap: Microcredit Boosted by Technology," *Microenterprise Americas* (2002): 33.

groups, or individual collectors—to penetrate that market even deeper. Hatton National Bank, a commercial bank in Sri Lanka, extends its services to rural areas with satellite offices that then serve as a base for mobile "barefoot bankers" (see Box 5–3).

- The URCPN federation of cooperatives in Burkina Faso uses three parallel delivery systems to serve different market segments: full-fledged branches; satellite offices; and self-managed, village-based groups.[26]

8.10 CONCLUSION: SECURITY, LIQUIDITY, AND ACCESS?

Full-service branches can provide secure liquid services, but, for many potential clients, access to these services is too far from their homes or businesses to be useful. For financial institutions as well, full-service branches may not be an affordable means to serve small or rural depositors. In many rural contexts the choice is not between offering voluntary savings services from a conventional branch or other less secure or flexible alternatives but between the latter and no semi-formal or formal services at all.

Which of these alternative delivery systems is best in a particular environment will depend on many factors: population density; wealth; roads; electricity and communications infrastructure; other available formal, semi-formal, and informal services; and the education level of potential staff. In remote areas, small autonomous cooperatives or SHGs may be the answer. In better-off or more populated rural areas, mobile vans and satellite offices may provide higher-quality services; combined with individual collectors, these may also bring services close enough to be valuable to the poor. Where feasible, e-technologies may provide high-quality services while lowering transaction costs for client and MFIs alike. Table 8–1 (in Appendix 8.1) summarizes which of the options discussed above make sense, for now, in different environments.

How far e-technologies can expand the reach of full-service financial institutions is not yet known. Their costs are falling. Furthermore, from mobile-phone banking in the Philippines to "intelligent" ATMs in Bolivia, MFIs are working to make these technologies more acceptable to people who may not be literate but have money to save. In the future these technologies may be able to provide to small and rural depositors services that are accessible, liquid, and secure.

The cases in this chapter shed some light on what institutions are achieving now. The tables in Appendix 8.1 summarize key aspects of six of the institutions described earlier. Of the six, two—the BRI units and Prodem—provide services from or next to full-service branches in towns or cities. In comparison to the other four, these institutions share a number of characteristics: they provide longer banking hours and offer a fuller product range that includes time deposits. They also attract accounts with a higher average balance (in terms of per capita GNI)[27] and have lower administrative cost ratios.[28] They maintain these lower cost ratios even though their front-line staff are better educated and receive higher salaries (relative to per capita GNI) and even though, in the case of Prodem, the client load is not particularly high. Relative to those of the other institutions, their operations are more fully staffed, with credit and savings handled separately. Except for administrative cost ratios (for which data is rarely available), these observations are typical of successful branch-based savings operations.

The other four institutions bring services to clients where they live or work. To control the potentially high costs of doing so, they employ volunteers or staff with somewhat less education who offer—in three of the four cases—a single savings product as well as loans during very limited hours. None of the institutions collects deposits using multiple staff in a secure physical infrastructure— and several have neither safeguard. These characteristics are typical of institutions that provide community-based services.

In short, in order to manage costs, institutions that bring services close to small and rural depositors usually accept tradeoffs between providing this proximity and other qualities that these markets also value highly. *They also compensate for these tradeoffs.* They may have limited hours but provide some way to withdraw funds if needed; offer illiquid services but provide access to emergency loans; or employ mobile collectors but offset the increased risk with additional controls. In short, these delivery options adroitly balance convenience, security, and liquidity. In so doing, they bring services within reach of small rural depositors.

Table 8–1. Extending Outreach: Matching Markets with Delivery Systems

Market	Delivery options	Outreach to the poor	Challenges
Sparsely populated rural areas with minimal infrastructure (electricity, telephone, roads)	• Autonomous cooperatives • Autonomous SHGs • Piggybacking if other institutions / services are available • Lockboxes *Less remote areas:* • Serving one individual on behalf of others combined with mobile collection	*Cooperatives, SHGs, and serving individuals on behalf of a group* may exclude the poor by requiring regular fixed payments. *Piggybacking* may exclude poor by serving only users of the primary service.	• Liquidity management • High covariant risk *Piggybacking:* principal/agent issues.
Villages and rural areas with limited infrastructure	Same as above plus: • Mobile units • Mobile phone banking • Mobile collection	*Mobile units:* High cost may necessitate fees or other features that select out the poor. *Mobile phones:* Usage depends on availability and acceptance.	Same as above except: *Mobile units & phones* are usually linked to larger institutions with lower covariant risk & more capacity to manage liquidity; *Mobile units and collection:* high costs.

Towns and rural markets with more developed infrastructure	Same as above plus: • Full-service branch if area is better off & densely populated • Satellite offices Depending on communications infrastructure & laws: • Smart cards & POS devices • Internet banking • ATMs	**Full-service branches** may not be able to afford to serve poor. **Internet banking, ATMs and POS devices:** Usefulness depends on acceptance, whether they handle deposits as well as withdrawals, and accessibility—cost, distance, and skills needed to use them.	**E-technologies (ATM, POS, internet banking):** Reliable power and available support services **Lockboxes:** security
Urban slum communities and urban markets	• Piggybacking • Satellite offices • Mobile collectors • Serving one individual on behalf of others • Lockboxes • Smart cards & POS devices • Internet banking • Mobile phone	Same as above, namely: **Piggybacking** may exclude poor by serving only users of the primary service. **Serving individuals on behalf of a group** may exclude the poor by requiring regular fixed payments. **Mobile phones and POS devices** depend on availability and acceptance. **POS devices** are useful if they accept deposits as well as withdrawals.	**Piggybacking:** principal/agent issues **Mobile collection:** risk of fraud, costs, security **E-technologies (ATM, POS, internet banking):** Reliable power and available support services **Lockboxes:** security

Table 8–2. Delivery Systems, Cost Factors, and Costs

Institution / delivery system	# of accounts / depositors	Average balance (% of per capita GNI)	Client load	Salaries (% of per capita GNI)	Costs
BRI Units[i] Full-service units in sub-district towns	25.9 million accounts	US$100 (14%)	1,300 accounts (1,233 deposit accounts) per staff	US$2,400 to 8,000 (348% to 1159%)	Administrative cost ratio: 2.2%
ASA[ii] Collectors piggyback on existing credit groups near clients' homes	360,000 savers	US$20 (6%) ~US$8 is liquid[iii]	880 accounts (459 deposit accounts) per credit officer	US$520 to $1,655 (144% to 460%)	Administrative cost ratios:[iv] Full cost of all savings: 8.6% Marginal cost of voluntary savings: 0%
CVECAs[v] Small autonomous cooperatives in villages	3,419 accounts	US$ 102 (39%)	115 active clients per staff (part-time)	up to ~US$156 per year (60%)	Investment per client: US$140. (Cooperatives recover all costs; promoting institution does not recover costs.)
Kupfuma Inshungu[vi] Self-managed groups in villages	14,000 savers	US$1 to 3: does not accumulate from cycle to cycle (<1%)	550 depositors per staff	at least US$2,300 per year (479%)	Investment per client: US$24 (Groups recover all costs; promoting institution does not recover costs.)

Prodem's[vii] ATMs & full-service branches in commercial centers	38,000 accounts	US$271 (30%)	231 clients (155 depositors) per staff person (not including guards & maintenance staff)	Not available	Administrative cost ratio for all savings: 2.5%
SafeSave[viii] Individual collectors at clients' homes or workplaces	10,000 savers	US$ 20 (5%)	~170 depositors per collector, or 120 per total staff	$US400 (100%) to 1,500 (375%); collectors earn $600 (150%) to 900 (225%)	Administrative cost ratio for all savings and credit services: 32%

[i] Zaharia Zakaria, email interchange with author, 2003.

[ii] Mohammed Azim Hossain and Dr. Mostaq Ahmmed, email interchange with author; "ASA at a Glance," 2002; and ASA website, 2002.

[iii] Figures are for all 2.1 million depositors: for 1.7 million of these, their group sets the size of their voluntary deposit.

[iv] Figures for 2000. Branch operating costs before and after adding the voluntary service were identical. Graham A. N. Wright, Robert Peck Christen, and Imran Matin, "ASA's Culture, Competition and Choice: Introducing Savings Services into a MicroCredit Institution" (Nairobi: *MicroSave*, 2000); and Mohammed Azim Hossain, conversation with author, August 2001.

[v] Renée Chao-Béroff, "Caisses Villageoises d'Épargne et de Crédit Autogérées (CVECA), Mali," in *Challenges of Microsavings Mobilization—Concepts and Views from the Field*, ed. Hannig and Wisniwski (Eschborn: GTZ, 1999).

[vi] Hugh Allen, Jestias Rushwaya, and Peter Koegler, "End of Term Evaluation of Kupfuma Ishungu Rural Microfinance Project (RMFP), Zimbabwe" (CARE, 2002); Alfred Hamadziripi, conversation and email with author, May 2003.

[vii] Eduardo Bazoberry, "The Bolivian Experience of the Prodem Private Financial Fund S.A.," paper presented at Paving the Way Forward for Rural Finance: An International Conference on Best Practices in Rural Financial Institutions, Washington DC (June 2003), 2–3; Eduardo Bazoberry, conversations with the author, in person, June 2003, and phone, Autumn 2004; Roberto Hernandez and Yerina Mujica, "What Works: Prodem FFP's Multilingual Smart ATMs for Microfinance" (Washington, DC: World Resources Institute, 2003).

[viii] Stuart Rutherford and Mark Staehle, email interchange with author, March 2005.

Table 8–3. Delivery Systems, Geographic Outreach, and Service Quality

Institution / delivery system	Environment	Convenience (location, hours)	Product Range
BRI Units[1] Full-service units	Moderate to densely populated urban and rural areas	Transact in offices in sub-district towns up to 30 kilometers away, open 8 hours a day, 5 days a week	Demand, time, and current account deposits
ASA[2] Collectors piggyback on existing credit groups near clients' homes	Densely populated urban and rural areas	Transact during weekly meetings near clients' homes; large and emergency withdrawals at branch, up to 8 kilometers away, 2 hours a day, 6 days a week	Mandatory-voluntary product
CVECAs[3] Small autonomous co-operatives	Sparsely populated rural areas	Transact at office in the village, open 1 day a week for 4 to 10 hours depending on seasonal demand	Time deposits and demand deposits (latter discouraged with negative real interest rate)
Kupfuma Inshungu[4] Self-managed groups	Rural areas	Transact during monthly meeting in the village; access to emergency loan at any time	Contractual product: groups decides term and amount; loan option
Prodem's[5] ATMs and full-service branches	Rural & urban commercial centers	Deposit in branches 8 hours daily; withdraw in branches or from ATMs adjacent to branches in commercial centers	Demand and time deposits
SafeSave[6] Individual collectors	Densely populated slums	Transact at home or workplace during collector's daily visits between 9:00 AM and 1:00 PM, and 2:00 and 5:00 PM; receive large withdrawals and loans at branch located within approximately ½ kilometer of client's home	Demand deposits

[1] Zaharia Zakaria, email interchange with author, 2003.

[2] Mohammed Azim Hossain and Dr. Mostaq Ahmmed, email interchange with author; "ASA at a Glance" (2002); ASA website, 2002; and Graham A. N. Wright, Robert Peck Christen, and Imran Matin, "ASA's Culture, Competition, and Choice: Introducing Savings Services into a MicroCredit Institution" (Nairobi: MicroSave, 2000).

[3] Renée Chao-Béroff, "Caisses Villageoises d'Épargne et de Crédit Autogérées (CVECA), Mali," in *Challenges of Microsavings Mobilization—Concepts and Views from the Field*, ed. Alfred Hannig and Sylvia Wisniwski (Eschborn, Germany: GTZ, 1999).

[4] Hugh Allen, Jestias Rushwaya, and Peter Koegler, "End of Term Evaluation of Kupfuma Ishungu Rural Microfinance Project (RMFP), Zimbabwe" (CARE, 2002). Alfred Hamadziripi, conversation and email with author, May 2003.

[5] Eduardo Bazoberry, "The Bolivian Experience of the Prodem Private Financial Fund S.A.," paper presented at "Paving the Way Forward for Rural Finance: An International Conference on Best Practices in Rural Financial Institutions," Washington DC, June 2003), 2–3; Eduardo Bazoberry, conversations with the author, in person, June 2003, and phone, Autumn 2004; Roberto Hernandez and Yerina Mujica, "What Works: Prodem FFP's Multilingual Smart ATMs for Microfinance" (Washington, DC: World Resources Institute, 2003).

[6] Stuart Rutherford and Mark Staehle, email interchange with the author, March 2005.

Table 8–4. Delivery Systems and Staffing

Institution / delivery system	Staffing (minimum)	Education of key staff (# years of schooling)	Product range
BRI Units[i] Full-service units in subdistrict towns	• 1 manager • 1 teller • 1 credit officer • 1 administrative officer • 1 guard	Professional and administrative staff: 12	Demand, time, and current account deposits
ASA[ii] Individual collectors piggyback on existing credit groups near clients' homes	• 1 manager • 4 credit officers • 1 office aide	Manager: 12 Credit officers: 10	Mandatory-voluntary product
CVECAs[iii] Small autonomous cooperatives in villages	• 1 part-time cashier • 1 part-time controller • volunteer management committee	Cashier and controller: 6	Time deposits and demand deposits (latter are discouraged with negative real-interest rate)
Kupfuma Inshungu[iv] Self-managed groups in villages	• field agent (trains groups) • group members (manage groups as volunteers)	Field agent: 14 Group members: none required	Contractual product: same term and deposit size for all members
Prodem's[v] ATMs and full-service branches in commercial centers	• 1 manager • 1 credit officer • 1 teller • 1 maintenance man • 1 guard—often but not always	Branch manager and credit officer: 16 Teller: 12	Demand and time deposits

SafeSave [vi]
Individual collectors at clients' homes or work places

- 1 manager
- 1 assistant manager
- 10 collectors
- 1 office cleaner

Branch managers: 14–16
Assistant managers: 12–16
Collectors: 5–10 years

Demand deposits

[i] Zaharia Zakaria, email interchange with author, 2003.

[ii] Mohammed Azim Hossain, conversation with the author, August 2002; email interchange with author, 2004.

[iii] Renée Chao-Béroff, "Caisses Villageoises d'Épargne et de Crédit Autogérées (CVECA), Mali," in *Challenges of Microsavings Mobilization—Concepts and Views from the Field*, ed. Alfred Hannig and Sylvia Wisniwski (Eschborn, Germany: GTZ, 1999).

[iv] Alfred Hamadziripi, email interchange with the author, 2003.

[v] Eduardo Bazoberry, phone conversation with the author, Fall 2004.

[vi] Stuart Rutherford and Mark Staehle, e-mail interchange with the author, March 2005.

Notes

[1] The high quality of Indonesian roads and transport can make these distances much easier to traverse than they would be in many other countries.

[2] Klaas Kuiper, email posting to MicrofinancePractice list, January 2005.

[3] Klaus Maurer, "Bank Rakyat Indonesia," in *Challenges of Microsavings Mobilization—Concepts and Views from the Field,* ed. Alfred Hannig and Sylvia Wisniwski (Eschborn, Germany: GTZ, n.d.), 115; Zakaria Zahari of BRI's International Visitors Program, email interchange with author, May 2003.

[4] José Linares Fontela, "Product Development and Marketing: Meeting the Local Demand," in *Striking the Balance in Microfinance: A Practical Guide to Mobilizing Savings,* ed. Brian Branch and Janette Klaehn (Washington, DC: PACT Publications, 2002), 144–45.

[5] Lloyd Hardy, Renee Chao-Berrof, and Prahlad Mali, "Virtual Conference on Savings Operations for Very Small or Remote Depositors," May 2002.

[6] Perhaps because collectors travel in areas where they provide a valued service, security, except in conflict zones, is often much less of an issue than might be expected. For some security guidelines, see Section 11.3.1.

[7] Stuart Rutherford, email interchange with the author, March 2005.

[8] Sergio Duchen, email interchange with the author, 2003.

[9] Geetha Nagarajan, "Going Postal to Deliver Financial Services to Microclients," *Finance for the Poor* 4, no. 1 (2003): 5–8.

[10] Craig Churchill, Madeline Hirschland, and Judith Painter, *New Directions in Village Banking* (Washington, DC: The Small Enterprise Education and Promotion Network, 2002), 32.

[11] Sergio Antezana, "Virtual Conference on Savings Operations for Very Small or Remote Depositors," May 2002.

[12] Korotoumou Ouattara, Douglas H. Graham, and Carlos E. Cuevas, "Alternative Financial Networks: The Village Savings and Credit Associations (VISACAs) in the Gambia" (Columbus: Ohio State Univ., 1993), 5.

[13] Stuart Rutherford, email interchange with the author, March 2005.

[14] The cost of promoting these groups has been likened to the subsidies provided for technical support to develop more formal MFIs. Considered in relation to the number of clients served, the costs may be comparable, but it is hard to compare the longevity, quality, and depth of outreach of SHG services with those of MFI services.

[15] SHGs differ from small cooperatives in several ways: they are smaller; the entire group meets regularly; and they have no designated staff, just volunteer elected officers who handle transactions in the presence of the entire group. SHGs typically do not receive and repay loans to the institution that promoted them, and because SHGs manage their own services, these services are simpler than those of FINCA-style village banks.

[16] Jeffrey Ashe et al., "Virtual Conference on Savings Operations for Very Small or Remote Depositors," May 2002.

[17] GTZ, *Marketing for Microfinance Depositories: A Toolkit* (Washington, DC: PACT Publications, 2000), 52.

[18] Sushila Gautam, "Virtual Conference on Savings Operations for Very Small or Remote Depositors," May 2002.

[19] Information in this section comes from Charles Waterfield, *Virtual Conference on Electronic Banking for the Poor Final Report* (Nairobi: *MicroSave*, 2004) and *CGAP IT*

Innovation Series (Washington, DC: CGAP, 2004): Laura I. Frederick, with contributions from CGAP staff and e-change, LLC, "Interactive Voice Response (IVR) Technology"; Charles Waterfield, "Personal Digital Assistants"; and Steve Whelan with contributions from CGAP staff and e-change, LLC, "Automated Teller Machines," "Biometrics Technology," and "Smart Cards."

[20] In the microfinance field, electronic banking is used to refer to a range of automated banking technologies including PDAs, ATMs, debit cards, POS devices, cell phones, and Internet banking.

[21] Waterfield, "Personal Digital Assistants," 2.

[22] This chapter uses the term *ATMs* to refer to both ATMs and cash machines. The distinction between these machines is discussed in the following section, "Cash and ATMs."

[23] David Cracknell, email interchange with the author, April 2004.

[24] Whelan, "Automated Teller Machines," 2–3.

[25] Cracknell, email interchange.

[26] Romain Y. Tougma, "Virtual Conference on Savings Operations for Very Small or Remote Depositors," May 2002.

[27] The CVECAs also have a relatively high average balance and, not coincidentally, are the only other institutions that offer time deposits.

[28] Because *Safe*Save's savings and lending services are so tightly integrated, a precise administrative cost ratio is not available; however, the ratio is higher than the others in the table.

9

Pricing

Madeline Hirschland
and John Owens

The interest rates that a deposit-taking institution pays and the fees it charges depositors will affect its profitability, its volume of deposits, and its competitive position.[1] Rates that are too high—without fees that compensate—make cost recovery difficult. Rates that are too low or fees that are too high can make it hard to attract deposits. If rates and fees are priced well, however, they can be a key to achieving goals for outreach, profitability, and liquidity. Given their importance, how should rates and fees be set?

The first task is to define what range of prices is possible. On the one hand, this range is limited by the need to be sustainable—in light of our administrative costs to mobilize deposits and our yield from performing assets, what prices will enable us to recover costs? On the other hand, this range is limited by the market—what will our potential customers accept? The prices customers will accept may be quite limited for certain types of products in competitive markets and more flexible elsewhere. In other words, to determine the range of what is possible, managers should consider two factors: (1) *the prices offered in the local financial market*, or, in an uncompetitive market, *the prices that depositors expect to receive;* and (2) *the prices at which the costs of managing deposits can be covered* (see Figure 9–1).

The second task is for management clearly to define its pricing objectives. Within the range of possible prices, which will best serve the institution's strategic objectives? Pricing might be used to maximize the institution's short-term profitability, to manage risk by attracting deposits with certain terms (see Chapter 13), to maintain or increase market share, or simply to survive in a difficult

The authors extend their sincere thanks to David Cracknell for his valuable input.

Figure 9–1. Factors for Determining the Interest Rate and Fees

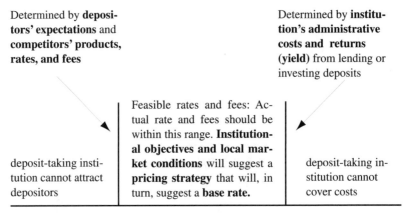

Determined by **depositors' expectations** and **competitors' products, rates, and fees**		Determined by **institution's administrative costs and returns (yield)** from lending or investing deposits
	Feasible rates and fees: Actual rate and fees should be within this range. **Institutional objectives and local market conditions** will suggest a **pricing strategy** that will, in turn, suggest a **base rate.**	
deposit-taking institution cannot attract depositors		deposit-taking institution cannot cover costs
low rate (high fees)		high rate (low fees)

market. These pricing objectives together with local market conditions will suggest a *base interest rate,* one that may then be varied for different market segments.

Finally, management must decide whether and how to vary the base rate. For example, larger accounts might receive a higher rate, or complimentary insurance might replace part of the interest rate. This chapter discusses the factors that define the range of feasible prices, identifies some common pricing strategies, and considers when to vary the base interest rate or provide non-interest returns.

9.1 DEFINING FEASIBLE PRICES

To determine feasible interest rates and fees, managers should consider two factors: first, the rates and fees for similar competing products and how these products compare to their own, or, in the absence of formal or semi-formal competition, the rates and fees clients expect; and second, the cost of administering the product and the yield from investing deposits.

9.1.1 Local Financial Market Rates

To set its interest rates and fees, an institution must first understand its position in the market. To do so, management should compare competing products, both formal and informal, that are available locally. Using market research, managers should consider not only the rates and fees of competitors' products but also how customers value those products relative to their own. In many cases customers will care much less about interest rate and fees than about other aspects of the product and institution, including how well the product meets their liquidity needs and whether the institution seems secure and convenient relative to competitors.

Competition can vary by market segment and by product. For example, a local commercial bank may compete for an MFI's large depositors, but its high minimum-balance requirements may be prohibitive for the MFI's small depositors. If so, the MFI may need to offer a competitively high interest rate for large accounts but not for small ones (see Section 9.3.1). Similarly, the physical distance from the competing institution matters a lot for products like passbook and contractual accounts that involve many transactions. It matters less for time deposits that involve just two. So, institutions that are farther away may compete more in an institution's time-deposit market than in its passbook market.

Once management identifies its competitors, it must determine whether its institution's image, delivery system, and product features make its product more or less valuable to customers than its competitors' products. For example, when they compete with large commercial banks, small deposit-taking institutions generally must offer higher rates for similar products to make up for the fact that customers see the small banks as less secure. Similarly, institutions that are new to mobilizing deposits need to pay a higher rate than their more trusted and established competitors. In contrast, a more convenient or attractive product can pay less than a competitors' rate (see Box 9–1).

Box 9–1. Pricing by a Rural Bank in the Philippines

The tables below show the full set of interest rates offered by a large rural bank, Green Bank of Caraga, and a large competing commercial bank. In the Philippines over 770 rural banks serve small farmers, cooperatives, and small merchants. These banks compete for deposits with one another and with credit cooperatives. In larger towns and cities commercial banks with ATMs also offer stiff competition. The Green Bank offers rates that are much higher than the larger commercial banks but lower than the smaller rural banks and credit cooperatives.

Green Bank of Caraga interest rates (May 2004)

Time deposit accounts	30-day	60-day	90-day	180-day	360-day
US$54,000 & above	10%	10.50%	11%	11.50%	12%
US$18,000–53,999	9.50%	9.75%	9.80%	10.50%	11%
US$9,000–17,999	8.50%	8.75%	8.80%	9%	9.25%
US$3,600–8,999	7.50%	7.75%	7.80%	8%	8.25%
US$1,800–3,599	6.25%	6.50%	6.75%	7%	7.25%
US$900–1,799	5.40%	5.45%	5.50%	5.75%	5.80%
US$180–899	4.50%	4.60%	4.80%	5%	5.50%

Passbook savings	No maturity
US$1.80–8.99	0%
US$9 & above	4%

Continued on page 196

Continued from page 195

Kiddie Savers   **Maturity: high school graduation**
US$1.80–8.99   0%
US$9 & above   6%

Contractual savings   **Maturity: preset amount or date**
US$1.80–8.99   0%
US$9 & above   4%

Bank of the Philippines Islands interest rates (May 2004)

Regular time deposits (pesos)	30-day	60-day	90-day	180-day	360-day
US$90,000 & above	4.250%	4.625%	4.750%	4.750%	5.000%
US$18,000–89,000	4.000%	4.375%	4.500%	4.500%	4.750%
US$9,000–17,999	3.750%	4.125%	4.250%	4.250%	4.500%
US$3,600–8,999	3.625%	4.000%	4.125%	4.125%	4.375%
US$900–3,599	3.500%	3.875%	4.000%	4.000%	4.250%
US$180–899	3.375%	3.750%	3.875%	3.875%	4.125%
US$18–179	3.750%	3.750%	4.000%		

Express Teller Savings[1] **No maturity**
Savings US$54 & above 1%
Checking US$180 & above   0%

Passbook and   **No maturity**
Platinum Savings[1]
US$180–449   1.00%
US$450–5,399   2.25%
US$5,400–8,999   2.50%
US$9,000–17,999   2.75%
US$18,000 & above   3.00%

---

[1] The bank charges US$1.80 each month that an account falls below the minimum average daily balance.

Assessing the competition is crucial. An institution should monitor competing products and pricing monthly and whenever it introduces a product into a new market—and it should be prepared to adjust its pricing.[2] Initially, the relative value of different products should be learned from "carefully constructed focus group discussions to compare different institutions and their products" and the use of a competition analysis matrix (see Section 6.2 and Appendix 6.1).[3] However, even where there is no competition, how much customers deposit will be affected by the interest rates that they expect to receive and the fees they expect to pay.

9.1.2 Expected Price

When deciding whether to deposit funds, potential customers consider whether they will receive what they perceive to be a fair and attractive rate of interest. This perceived rate or range of rates is known as the expected price. Customers also will consider whether the fees involved seem reasonable. In competitive environments the expected price tends to be easy to establish; it is close to competitors' rates for a similar product. Where there are no similar products, the rates that customers will accept should be determined by a market study. Where customers have no other options, they are likely to accept a lower interest rate and may pay higher bank fees.

Typically, for each interest rate, the institution would attract a different volume of deposits. How much demand changes in response to changes in interest rates is known as *interest-rate sensitivity*. Knowing customers' precise interest-rate sensitivity is usually not possible. Having a general sense of it, however, is critical to effective pricing. Market research should suggest what volume of deposits would be attracted at different rates of interest. For example, management needs to have a general sense of how much clients will withdraw if the MFI lowers its current interest rate by 1 percent. As discussed in the rest of this section, depositors' interest-rate expectations differ by product and market.

For *passbook accounts*, particularly small ones, depositors tend to be fairly insensitive to rate changes and care more about easy access. They often will accept negative real rates of interest. In the Philippines, even when they offer relatively high interest rates, small rural banks find it harder to compete where commercial banks have convenient ATMs. Furthermore, clients tend to deposit the same amount in the small passbook savings accounts regardless of small changes in interest rates; having access to their funds is more important than receiving a higher return.

For *contractual accounts*, depositors typically expect a higher interest rate than they do for passbook accounts. However, where no other institutions are offering a contractual product, the expected rate may be surprisingly low and demand may be fairly insensitive. For example, when Workers Bank in Jamaica found that the interest it was paying on its Partner Savings Plan product was harming its profitability, it lowered the rates significantly. Following the change, the number of accounts actually increased. The market turned out to be relatively insensitive to interest rates, perhaps because the product was modeled on informal-sector products that do not pay interest.[4]

For *time deposits*, which typically involve larger deposits for longer periods of time, clients expect the highest rates and may be highly rate sensitive. This is particularly true in competitive markets. Therefore, many smaller institutions peg their rates for time deposits several percentage points above the time-deposit rates of larger institutions or, in particular, government treasury bill rates.

In *uncompetitive markets*, where there are no other interest-bearing savings options, do potential clients expect to receive interest? Although only market research can tell for sure, many institutions find that they can attract depositors only if they pay some interest, but this rate can be negative in real terms.[5] Highly convenient services, such as doorstep collection or a card that provides twenty-four-hour access to an ATM, may be exceptions for which clients are willing to pay. Interest can be the key to convincing potential customers not to consume their savings or invest it in livestock, jewelry, or other goods. With small depositors, any interest or nonmonetary reward tends to be highly valued, creates goodwill, and can trigger word-of-mouth marketing.[6] At the same time, a rate that is positive in real terms usually attracts significantly more deposits.[7]

Some expectations are true across products and markets. First, many clients accept a minimum balance under which they do not earn interest if they know that they can earn interest by increasing their balance above this minimum (see Box 9–5). Second, interest rates that are too high can put off potential customers. Overly high rates may lead prospective clients to suspect that the institution is not sound. An overly high rate may also attract deposits that are highly interest-rate sensitive and volatile; these depositors will leave quickly if a competitor sets an even higher rate.

Because it is hard to know precisely what customers expect, institutions should change interest rates gradually in step with local market rates. Where demand is highly sensitive to changes in the interest rate (especially for time deposits), institutions should carefully weigh the benefits of changing interest rates against the expected change in the volume of deposits. Depending on interest rate sensitivity, any change in the interest rate can either improve or worsen cost recovery.

9.1.3 Cost Recovery

Institutions should be able to cover the financial and direct administrative costs of their deposit services with net revenues from investing or lending out these deposits and from fee income from deposit accounts. The implication for interest rates is obvious: products must be priced such that their costs overall can be recovered from fees and investment opportunities.

When thinking about cost recovery, managers usually consider the average costs of all deposits; less costly accounts are expected to cross subsidize more costly ones. In competitive markets, however, operating margins for less costly accounts also will be squeezed and significant cross subsidization may not be viable over time (see Box 9–2). Therefore, management must determine the costs for each product by account size, and these costs should guide its pricing structure. These costs of mobilizing deposits and the revenues generated from investing or lending out deposits can be determined through product costing, which is explained in Chapter 15.

The relative costs of different products and accounts lead to the following rules of thumb:

Maturity: When yield curves in the economy are normal, longer-term deposits should receive higher rates of interest because investing them yields a higher rate of return.[8] Breaking this rule makes sense if shorter-term deposits are needed to fund shorter-term loans (see Box 9–3) or if the institution wants to lower the risk posed by inflation by mobilizing more short-term deposits. For

Box 9–2. Cross Subsidies and Competition

Cross subsidization can be a key to cost recovery, but it also makes the deposit-taking institution particularly vulnerable to competition. Cross subsidies take many forms. For example,

- *Across account sizes:* Institutions that serve very small depositors typically use revenues from investing their larger accounts to cover the high costs of their smaller ones.
- *Across different products:* Small passbook accounts tend to be relatively stable but have high administrative costs, which can be offset by lower-cost products. For example, time-deposit accounts tend to be lower cost but more volatile than passbook accounts. An institution might manage costs and volatility by maintaining a mix of 30 percent time deposits to 70 percent passbook deposits.
- *Across regions:* Some institutions cover the costs of serving rural markets through their more profitable operations in urban areas.
- *"Loss leaders":* Known as loss leaders, some types of accounts cost a lot but attract or secure the loyalty of customers who then use the deposit-taking institution's more lucrative services. Rather than looking at the profitability of an individual account, deposit-taking institutions may better consider whether individual clients, including *all* of their business with the institution, are profitable.

Each of these strategies can be threatened by competition. By paying a higher interest rate, competing institutions might lure away the lower-cost accounts, leaving only the higher-cost ones. For example,

- An institution might lose its larger accounts to a competitor that pays a higher interest rate. The competitor's high minimum balance requirement may leave the institution with only its costly small accounts.
- A competitor who pays higher interest rates might take over an institution's low-cost urban market, leaving it only with its high-cost rural one.
- If a loss leader does not instill customer loyalty, an institution can find itself providing a popular but costly service to clients who go elsewhere with their more lucrative business.

To hold on to its lower-cost business, the institution might have to pay a higher rate of interest for these products and accounts, but this would squeeze its operating margin such that revenues from investing these products and accounts might no longer be able to subsidize the lower-cost ones. Therefore, in highly competitive environments the viability of managing high-cost accounts and products should be considered separately from the viability of serving low-cost ones. One tool for managing the higher costs of certain products and markets is differential pricing (see Section 9.3.1).

Box 9–3. Pricing at Teba Bank, South Africa

Established in 1976, Teba Bank's original mission was to serve mine workers. Although miners are still its primary market, in July 2000 the bank obtained the legal status to begin mobilizing deposits from the public. The bank offers four savings products that are priced as follows:

Account name	Account type and terms	# of accounts	Interest rate
Transaction	Linked to debit card, for the public	new	0%, transaction fees
Passbook	Passbook & payroll service for miners only	430,000	0.25%
Grow with Us	Passbook service for the public	10,000	1%
Fixed deposits	Time deposits for 6 months to 2 years	11,000	4.5%–5.25%

Teba's products hold different market positions that affect how it sets its interest rates. For its Grow with Us and fixed-deposit accounts, Teba is a *price taker*. Because these products are not distinct and Teba is not a market leader, it pegs its interest rates to those of its competitors. Teba uses a monthly schedule to track its competitors' rates for each account size.

In contrast, Teba's miners' passbook accounts do have a *competitive advantage*. The mines pay a payroll fee to Teba for making automatic monthly deposits into miners' accounts. Because this is a savings and convenience to the miners, Teba can pay a lower interest rate than its competitors and still hold on to miners' accounts. To earn a higher rate of interest, miners can open a Grow with Us or fixed-deposit account.

Teba monitors its interest rates monthly. It notes the number and volume of its accounts and estimates the annual financial cost of 0.25 percent, 0.5 percent, 0.75 percent, and 1 percent increases in its interest rate.

Within the constraints of competition and costs, Teba's first pricing objective is to *manage interest-rate risk* by maintaining a secure asset-liability position. For example, in 2003, when the bank introduced a housing-loan product with relatively long terms, management sought to generate more long-term fixed deposits. The bulk of Teba's fixed deposits had terms of six to nine months. Although Teba could not realistically expect large numbers of miners to demand fixed deposits with a term of more than one year, Teba did want to attract more one-year deposits. To accomplish this it set its most attractive rates, relative to its competitors, for one-year deposits and set its interest rates for deposits with terms greater or less than one year less competitively.

Within the context of managing interest-rate risk, Teba also seeks to *maximize its profitability*. The bank considers the predicted future movement of interest rates to decide whether to lock in rates on its accounts.

An interbank rate increase by the central bank that stimulated a rate increase among Teba's competitors has given Teba room to shift its own rates relative to market rates and still meet client expectations. To cover the costs of new staff incentive commissions, management wanted to lower its rates on fixed deposits, but this would not have been well received by the market. Instead, it now has the opportunity to increase its rates more slowly than its competitors.

—Jennifer Hoffmann

example, in 2003, OIBM paid 26 percent and 28 percent, respectively, for one-month and three-month fixed deposits. Because of concerns about inflation, OIBM paid progressively less for six- and nine-month deposits (22 percent and 20 percent, respectively).

Account size: Relative to their size, larger accounts cost less than smaller ones. Therefore, they can accommodate higher rates of interest (see Section 9.3).

Liquidity: Less liquid products should receive higher rates of interest because they cost less to administer and because less of these accounts must be set aside as reserves that bear no or low interest. Thus, fixed deposits earn more than passbook accounts. Paying a lower rate for more liquid accounts can also discourage frequent transactions. In 1997 BRI paid 3 percent more for a pass-book account that allowed only two withdrawals per month than for the same account with unlimited withdrawals.

Convenience: Services that cost the institution more to deliver should receive a lower interest rate or pay higher fees than less convenient services that can be provided more cheaply. Equity Bank charges a fee for transactions deliv-ered by its mobile van service but not for transactions at its branches. PRODEM charges US$4 (230 percent) more per year for an account that includes ATM access than for a passbook account that provides access at only one branch during office hours.

These guidelines are summarized in Table 9–1 and are illustrated with a case in Box 9–1. In conclusion, institutions discover their own range of feasible prices by considering the factors discussed above: local market prices, clients' expecta-tions, and costs and revenues. Within this range, an appropriate rate will flow from the institution's objectives.

Table 9–1. Guidelines for Relative Interest Rates

Lowest interest rate			Highest interest rate
Demand deposits	Contractual	Fixed deposits	Institutional deposits
Shorter term			Longer term
Smaller			Larger
More liquid			Less liquid
Daily doorstep collection		Satellite office or ATM	Branch-based
Rural			Urban
Trusted, established institution			Institution new to deposit-taking
Larger, more formal institution (for example, a commercial bank)			Smaller, less formal institu-tion (for example, rural banks, cooperatives)

9.2 PRICING OBJECTIVES AND STRATEGIES

Institutions typically try to use their interest rates and fees on deposits to manage costs or improve market outreach. Alternatively, an institution might use them to manage risk, maintain its current market position, or survive in a difficult market. Different pricing objectives call for different pricing strategies.

9.2.1 Controlling Costs and Increasing Profits

If an institution wants to control its costs or maximize profits over the short term, then it should set its rates relatively low and fees relatively high (see Box 9–4).[9] This is especially appropriate if competition is weak or the market or institution is very liquid. One particular cost control strategy is *market skimming*. Market skimming is appropriate when an institution wants to achieve high profits initially. The interest rate is set at the lowest possible level (and fees may be set at the highest level) at which a segment of clients will still make deposits. A short-term strategy, market skimming is often used for a new product to recover its development costs and to restrict initial demand to a manageable level. Management usually increases the interest rate over time, particularly as competition increases. In most competitive markets a skimming strategy will not work because potential clients will seek out the higher interest rates of competitors. A market-skimming strategy does not keep out competition.

9.2.2 Increasing the Volume of Deposits or Market Share

An institution that primarily wants to attract depositors can do so by offering relatively high rates. Institutions typically focus on increasing their market share or volume of deposits when they want to grow quickly or keep competitors out of the market. One strategy to increase market share rapidly is penetration pricing, setting interest rates well above those of competitors in order to attract a large volume of deposits and market share quickly. The resulting low profit margin can lure depositors away from existing competition, discourage other institutions from entering the market with competing products, and develop customer loyalty. Penetration pricing makes the most sense where:

- a large market exists for the product or is expected soon,
- this market is highly competitive,
- demand is highly price-sensitive, and
- the market segment willing to accept low rates is too small for a skimming strategy to work.[10]

Because it increases financial costs and limits profit margins, this strategy is generally used only for short periods. For deposits with long-term maturities, it is

Box 9–4. *Pricing Objectives at Caja Municipal de Arequipa*

Launched in 1987, Caja Municipal de Arequipa is one of Peru's leading deposit-taking institutions. The caja's primary market is savers with less than US$1,000 in deposits. In 2002 it reported a savings portfolio of approximately US$70 million. One key to its success has been sound pricing. The caja's three principal savings products are priced as follows:

Type	Terms	# of accounts	Interest rate
Current account	Unlimited term	76,918	2% per month (local currency) 1% per month (dollar)
Fixed-term deposit	Fixed term (1–36 months)	8,482	3–18% per month (local currency) 1.5–4.75% per month (dollar)
Service compensation deposits (legally required of employees)	Fixed term (1–36 months)	2,963	18% annual (local currency) 4.75% annual (dollar)

The caja has three well-defined pricing objectives. Above all, it seeks to *maximize profits;* therefore, it pays relatively low interest rates on deposits. Although the Peruvian microfinance market is highly competitive, the caja can offer low rates without losing its market position because of its brand equity, garnered through years of quality service and commitment to small savers.

The caja also aims to *increase long-term deposits* as a way to lower its costs and liquidity risk. It accomplishes this by paying substantially higher interest rates on larger long-term deposits. Getting the price right for different market segments has drawn on the caja's significant market intelligence.

The caja also uses pricing to *reduce foreign-exchange risk.* By offering far more attractive interest rates on domestic currency deposits, it encourages savings in Peruvian soles and discourages dollar-denominated deposits, reducing the risk of a currency mismatch between its loans and deposits.

Caja Municipal de Arequipa seeks to earn clients' trust through transparent pricing. Its research found that clients avoid its competitors because of their fees and commissions. By eliminating these from its own services, the caja has earned the trust of savers, who know they can take its interest rates at face value and that hidden fees will not eat away their capital. Moreover, Caja Municipal de Arequipa does not charge for fund transfers between branches, which clients view as a hidden fee.

—Hillary Miller Wise

high risk; it requires ongoing long-term opportunities for lending at a very high rate of interest.

9.2.3 *Managing Risk*

Institutions frequently use interest rates to manage risks. For example, rather than trying to increase its overall volume of deposits, an institution may seek to increase its volume of deposits that have a specific maturity or range of maturities. Its aim might be to lower interest-rate risk by matching deposit and loan volumes. If, for example, an institution begins to offer a new six-month loan product, it may need to mobilize more six-month fixed term deposits. To accomplish this, it can offer particularly attractive rates for deposits with six-month terms. Alternatively, it might seek to manage the risk associated with high or erratic inflation by attracting mostly short-term funds. Managing risk is often a major objective in setting the interest rates of fixed deposits (see Boxes 9–3 and 9–4).

9.2.4 Maintaining Market Share

A deposit-taking institution's goal might be to hold on to its current depositors or to avoid provoking the competition. So, it simply sets its rates and fees at the same levels as its competitors', making some adjustments for differences in the perceived value of its product, delivery system, or institutional image (see Box 9–2). With this competitive-pricing strategy, the institution is a price taker. For example, BAAC pays precisely the rate of its competitors for its time-deposit accounts, which typically attract an interest-rate sensitive market.[11]

Competitive pricing makes sense where the market is highly competitive, the institution is not a major provider in the market, and its product is not distinctive. However, the strategy does not take into account that cost structures may vary. What if the deposit-taking institution's cost structure is higher than that of its competitors? Then, providing services at its competitors' rates may make it difficult to cover costs unless its return on productive assets is also sufficiently higher.

9.2.5 Surviving

A struggling institution may offer interest rates that are much higher than its competitors'—and that are not financially sustainable—in order to attract a large amount of deposits over a limited time period. The institution then lowers these rates as soon as it has secured a viable share of the market. Survival pricing may make sense when an institution faces "intense competition, changing consumer wants, or high fixed costs."[12]

9.2.6 Summary

In summary, an institution's interest rates can help it achieve its objectives. These objectives and its market position will determine its pricing strategy, which, in turn, will guide it to a base rate. This rate can then be adjusted for different markets.

9.3 BEYOND THE BASE RATE

Adjusting the base interest rate or fees for different markets can help attract a larger volume of deposits and/or improve cost recovery. There are two types of adjustments: to apply different rates or fees for different market segments, and to replace part of the interest rate with in-kind returns.

9.3.1 Fees, Tiered Interest, and Other Changes to the Base Rate

The base rate can be adjusted in various ways for a variety of purposes. For example:

Levying administrative fees: Each customer transaction imposes a cost on the institution. Some of these costs can be covered with transaction fees, such as fees for withdrawals or for closing an account, which can increase revenues substantially. For example, one postal savings bank found that its savings accounts generated nearly three times as much in fee revenues as they incurred in interest expenses. In fact, these revenues were only 23 percent less than its income from investing the deposits. Similarly, in 2002 Equity Bank generated nearly 50 percent of its income from commissions and other income, a large portion of which was fees on savings accounts. By discouraging withdrawals, fees can also increase account balances. However, management should research whether fees dissuade potential customers from opening an account (see Box 9–4). For institutions that use a manual MIS, managing fees can be costly.

Tiering interest rates: Institutions that mobilize deposits should consider paying low or no interest for the smallest accounts and progressively higher rates for larger accounts (see Box 9–5). Higher rates can motivate depositors to increase their account balances. Furthermore, paying less for small accounts can compensate for their high administrative cost (relative to account size), and providing no returns on the smallest accounts avoids the costs of calculating and distributing interest. Charging a fee for accounts that fall below a minimum balance can also compensate for their high administrative costs. Because few institutions serve the costly small-depositor market, small depositors typically do not expect high interest rates (as larger depositors often do). Although tiered rates make financial and marketing sense, institutions may not have an MIS that can readily handle changing interest rates as account balances change.

Paying more in competitive markets: Some institutions have branches in both competitive and uncompetitive markets. In the Philippines some small rural banks allow managers to offer slightly higher rates on time deposits than those posted in the bank so they can quickly match rate changes offered by competitors and retain larger depositors.

Charging for convenience: Clients can be paid a lower interest rate or charged a higher fee for conveniences such as doorstep collection or ATM facilities.

Paying less in rural areas: Mobilizing deposits is typically more costly in rural areas. An institution might offset these higher costs by offering lower

---

Box 9–5. *Tiered Interest Rates at BRI*

Tiered interest rates should enable institutions to cover their costs while offering competitive rate/product combinations for each account size. For example, in 1997 the BRI unit system paid the following rates for its liquid passbook savings account: no interest for minimum monthly balances of less than US$4.20; 10 percent interest for minimum monthly balances of US$4.21 to 420; 11.5 percent for minimum monthly balances of US$421 to 2,100; and 13 percent for minimum monthly balances exceeding US$2,100.[1]

Management can set the account sizes at which the interest rate shifts by considering:

- competitors' rates for different size accounts;
- at which different interest rates the account size at which the average revenues generated from investing in productive assets covers the average cost of mobilizing deposits; and
- at what account sizes an increase in interest rate might motivate the greatest increases in the overall volume of deposits.

The deposit-taking institution can then provide a higher interest rate or some sort of reward in order to encourage an increase in the average account size to reach the break-even level.

---

[1] Klaus Maurer, "Bank Rakyat Indonesia (BRI), Indonesia (Case Study)," in *Challenges of Microsavings Mobilization—Concepts and Views from the Field,* ed. Alfred Hannig and Sylvia Wisniwski (Eschborn, Germany: GTZ, n.d.), 117.

---

interest rates. This is unlikely to compromise the volume of savings; because high costs deter most institutions from serving rural markets, rural depositors typically have fewer options and, therefore, are less sensitive to interest rates.

Discouraging early withdrawals: Fixed or contractual deposits that are withdrawn early can receive less than the rate on passbook savings accounts.[13]

Attracting institutional accounts: A deposit-taking institution might routinely pay a higher rate to large institutional accounts or might negotiate such a rate on a case-by-case basis, especially if doing so enables the institution to market deposit services to many new individual clients or if the institution requires limited liquidity.[14] Many Philippine rural banks offer slightly higher rates to large businesses or institutional depositors because these clients also demand other services, such as payroll services, that also allow the banks to reach additional customers.

9.3.2 Replacing Interest with Nonfinancial Returns

Offering savers some value-added features may attract a higher volume of deposits than an interest-rate increase of a similar value.[15] For example, clients may be lured out of saving informally by the prospect of winning a lottery (see Box 10–7). Or they may be motivated to save more by life-insurance benefits equal to their account size or by valued household items (see Section 10.3.4).

If they are awarded strategically, non-interest returns can inspire depositors to increase their account size. For example, management might set a target average balance to which it would like its current average balance to grow. It might then provide a lottery ticket to any account that maintains a minimum monthly balance of at least the target amount and an additional ticket for every multiple of that target (see Box 10–3).

9.4 CALCULATING INTEREST

Sophisticated commercial institutions typically pay interest monthly based on an account's average daily balance. This may be necessary in competitive environments. However, interest can also be calculated based on the minimum balance and can be paid quarterly or even annually. How it is calculated and paid can affect customer satisfaction as well as administrative and financial costs.

For many less sophisticated MFIs, paying interest on the minimum rather than on the average balance makes sense. It results in lower financial costs—although these translate into lower revenues for depositors—and can encourage depositors not to withdraw their funds. If MIS is manual, determining the minimum balance is much easier and quicker.

Calculating interest is demanding and costly administratively. Therefore, institutions with less management capacity may calculate it quarterly—based on the minimum monthly balance—instead of monthly. How interest is calculated and paid should hinge on the practices of competitors, customers' expectations, and the management capacity of the institution, in particular whether it uses a computerized or manual MIS.

9.5 FREQUENT PITFALLS

Despite how important pricing is, deposit-taking institutions frequently make basic mistakes in setting their interest rates and administrative fees. Most commonly, they err by:

- thinking only in terms of maintaining low costs and high profit margins,
- not varying rates and fees for different products and market segments,
- setting interest rates higher than can be covered by the returns and fee income,
- not considering the value of the service vis-à-vis the competition, and
- not changing rates frequently enough to keep them in line with market changes.[16]

These pitfalls can be avoided if the following guidelines are kept front and center:

Local financial market rates: Local financial market rates and fees should be considered before and above all else. Management should understand how customers value the institution's products relative to those of the competition, should revisit this analysis regularly, and should adjust interest rates accordingly.

Expected price: What clients expect to earn is important, especially in rural areas where there are few competitors. Even where there is no competition, interest can be a key to convincing people to deposit their savings.

Cost recovery: The financial and direct administrative costs of mobilizing deposits must be covered by fees and the revenues from investing these deposits.

Pricing objectives: Different objectives and markets call for different pricing strategies. These strategies will guide the institution to an appropriate rate.

Varying the base rate and/or charging fees: Management can vary the base rate in order to attract larger amounts of deposits or to cover costs and/or may charge fees depending on administrative costs and different market conditions.

Non-interest returns: Value-added features can attract a higher volume of deposits than interest of the same financial value. If awarded strategically, non-interest returns can motivate widespread increases in account size.

If they are set astutely, interest rates can significantly advance an institution's strategic objectives. Regular analysis to "get the prices right" is crucial to staying profitable and competitive.

Notes

[1] Many deposit-taking institutions charge fees for low balances, transactions, and early withdrawals.

[2] David Cracknell, Henry Sempangi, and Graham A. N. Wright, "Costing and Pricing of Financial Services—A Toolkit" (Nairobi: *MicroSave*, 2004), 1. Available on the *MicroSave* website.

[3] David Cracknell, email interchange with authors, May 2004.

[4] John Owens, "The Partner Savings Plan of the Workers' Bank, Jamaica: Lessons in Microsavings from ROSCAS," in *Promising Practices in Rural Finance* (Washington, DC: Inter-American Development Bank, 2003), 325.

[5] Sergio Antezana, Romain Tougma, and Alfred Hamadziripi, "Virtual Conference on Savings Operations for Very Small or Remote Depositors," May 2002.

[6] Gerry Lab-oyan, contribution to "Virtual Conference on Savings Operations for Very Small or Remote Depositors," May 2002.

[7] David C. Richardson, draft of "The Keys to Cost Recovery," *Savings Services for the Poor: An Operational Guide.*

[8] Yield curves can be reversed under certain conditions.

[9] To maximize profits over the long term, the institution may want to pay a higher rate and/or charge lower fees, thus foregoing some profits over the short term in order to increase its market share.

[10] Cracknell, Sempangi, and Wright, "Costing and Pricing of Financial Services," 43.

[11] Delbert Fitchett, "Bank for Agriculture and Agricultural Cooperatives (BAAC), Thailand," in *Challenges of Microsavings Mobilization—Concepts and View from the Field,* ed. Alfred Hannig and Sylvia Wisniwski (Eschborn, Germany: GTZ, n.d.), 88.

[12] Cracknell, Sempangi, and Wright, "Costing and Pricing of Financial Services," 9.

[13] Brian Branch, "Savings Product Management: Establishing the Framework," in *Striking the Balance in Microfinance: A Practical Guide to Mobilizing Saving*, ed. Brian Branch and Janette Klaehne (Washington, DC: PACT Publications), 94.

[14] GTZ, *Marketing for Microfinance Depositories: A Toolkit* (Washington, DC: PACT Publications, 2000), 46; Branch, "Savings Product Management," 94.

[15] Richardson, "The Keys to Cost Recovery."

[16] Cracknell, Sempangi, and Wright, "Costing and Pricing of Financial Services," 16–17.

10

Promotion

The Final Step in Marketing

Hayder Al-Bagdadi
and David Cracknell

For deposit mobilization to be financially viable, an MFI must attract a large number of depositors and a large volume of deposits. To do this, its products, pricing, and delivery systems should fit the demand of potential clients at least as well as those of the competition. Meeting demand well is not enough, however. The MFI must also effectively communicate this product to the target market. This is promotion.[1]

Promotion aims to influence buying behavior. It informs, persuades, and reminds the market of specific products. At its heart, promotion is about communicating. The MFI must translate an idea about why potential clients should want to deposit with the MFI into a message that motivates them to do so.

This chapter discusses the steps involved in developing a promotional strategy and looks in detail at two elements of this strategy: messages and promotional tools. These tools include *personal sales, advertising, word of mouth, sales promotion,* and *public relations.* It also outlines steps to implement a promotional strategy, presents some guidance for assessing the effectiveness and cost effectiveness of different promotional activities, and highlights some of the common mistakes that MFIs make with their promotion.

This chapter is drawn in part from GTZ's *Marketing for Microfinance Depositories: A Toolkit* (Washington, DC: PACT Publications, 2000). The toolkit outlines the aspects of a comprehensive marketing program for MFIs aiming to offer fully client-oriented saving products. The authors also extend their thanks to Kathryn Larcombe and Margaret Mensah for their valuable input.

10.1 DEVELOPING A PROMOTIONAL STRATEGY

A systematic approach to the design of promotional activities can increase their success. The MFI should start with a solid understanding of and plan for positioning itself within the market. Next, it should consider its objectives for promotion. Only then should it determine what tools, themes, and messages it will use. To implement this plan, it will need to develop its marketing function gradually, recognizing that expertise may need to be developed through training and consultants. Finally, it should evaluate the effectiveness and cost effectiveness of its promotional activities.

10.1.1 Market Strategy

Before developing its promotional strategy, the MFI should be clear about:

- which groups of potential clients—*market segments*—it aims to serve,
- what these market segments *demand* of an institution, delivery system, pricing, and product,
- what they are being offered by *the competition*, and, therefore,
- how it wants to distinguish itself to these market segments, that is, its *market niche*—products, delivery systems, and interest rates—and its *corporate identity* or institutional image.

These decisions and information should flow out of the MFI's market research —including research to understand how the institution is perceived by prospective clients—and strategic planning. Together, these decisions and information form the MFI's *market strategy*. The market strategy should clarify what markets to target, what institutional image to convey, and what products, delivery systems, and interest rates to promote (see Figure 10–1).

10.1.2 Promotional Objectives

Once the MFI is clear about its target markets, institutional image, products, delivery systems, and relative interest rates, it should define the objectives for its promotional activities. What does it hope to accomplish through its promotion? Promotional objectives vary—and they can change over time. An institution in one context may seek to convince the target customers of its safety and reliability. An institution in another may seek to convince the market of the benefits of its product vis-à-vis its competition.

10.1.3 Branding

Branding is an institution's deliberate attempt to influence customer perceptions. To create its brand, an institution delivers its service in an identifiable, uniform

Figure 10–1. Elements of the Marketing Cycle

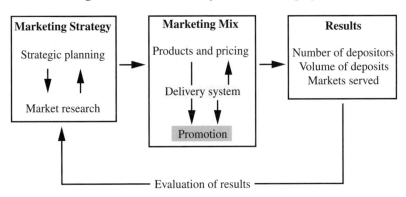

manner through a consistent infrastructure; every branch should look and feel the same.[2] By encouraging customer recognition of the financial institution, a strong brand significantly increases the return to promotional efforts; it creates confidence in the stability of the institution and develops the expectation of good service delivery.

An institution's brand is intimately related to its promotional strategy and facilitates promotion. If the brand is firmly established in the minds of potential customers, promotion efforts can spend less time on who the MFI is and more on its competitive advantages and products. A good corporate brand provides:

- *Instant recognition:* Consumers feel that they know what they can expect.
- *Warranty:* Consumers expect that services will be high quality and reliable.
- *Credibility:* Consumers believe in the organization—which is especially important with savings services.
- *Word-of-mouth marketing:* Customers easily recommend the MFI and its services; those hearing the recommendation remember the MFI's name.
- *Differentiation:* The MFI stands out from the crowd—which is especially important in a competitive market.
- *Goodwill:* The MFI is better equipped to weather problems and to talk to stakeholders who are not customers, from government officials to donors.
- *Reputation*: High-quality staff are more likely to want to work there.[3]

The promotional strategy should clearly promote the institution's brand as well as its products. For example, when the Cooperative Rural Development Bank of Tanzania promoted its ATM debit card, the promotion helped reposition the bank in the market and build the bank's brand. This stronger brand led the bank to increased sales and record profits. At the same time, the brand itself guides many aspects of promotion as discussed below.

10.1.4 Promotional Budget

The budget should be appropriate to the size of the institution, and should reflect the position of its brand and the level of competition in the market. A strong brand can lower marketing costs. For example, while experiencing rapid growth driven by word of mouth, Equity Bank was able to reduce its marketing department. In highly competitive markets, the need to inform potential clients of the institution's services is greater, but making publicity stand out can be much more difficult. For these reasons there are no absolute guidelines on how much the promotional budget should be in a particular institution.

In any case, much can be achieved at relatively low cost. Brochures and posters can be effective and are relatively inexpensive. Public relations can generate a high profile without the expense of newspaper advertising. For example, FINCA Uganda regularly receives visits from international dignitaries. Similarly, hosting a radio talk show on financial issues provides an excellent community service and should generate positive institutional publicity. A media survey that establishes which media an institution's actual and potential customers hear or read is always a good starting point in focusing promotional activities and spending.

The key is to establish the cost effectiveness of different promotional approaches. A promotional activity plan needs to be constructed and different options priced. The process is usually iterative; marketing and promotional budgets should start small and increase over time as management determines which promotional methods are most effective at generating sales (see Section 10.5). In relation to advertising objectives, management should carefully consider the cost per exposure (see Table 10–1).

10.1.5 Themes and Tools

Once management understands its objectives and budget, it can decide what themes it will convey and, within its budget constraints, what promotional tools will convey them most effectively. To determine its themes it needs to understand clearly what the target market values and what, in its eyes, can distinguish the MFI and its offerings. The MFI's promotional objectives and market strategy will determine its choice of themes and tools. For example,

> *Where potential clients are skeptical about saving in a financial institution,* such as in new markets, the objective of promotion will be to persuade people that doing so is valuable. Potential clients may believe that they cannot save or that their savings would be too small to be worthwhile. In this type of market a key to generating demand can be interacting with individuals or groups of potential clients face to face *(personal sales)* (see Box 10–1). Another key may be *primary-demand advertising,* which aims to stimulate demand for a generic category of product, such as passbook accounts, rather than for a specific product offered by a specific institution. The theme will be the value of saving in a financial institution and how even poor people can save.

Box 10–1. Promotion of a New Market: VYCCU Cooperative, Nepal

The biggest challenge that faced the founders of the VYCCU financial cooperative, twenty-six teenagers, was convincing community members that they could and should save. The prevailing attitude was, "We're poor, we can't save even one to two rupees." To persuade people to join VYCCU, the founders canvassed door to door and organized three-hour "camps" to discuss the importance of savings. The founders:

- lectured, told stories, or presented cases, and asked questions like, "How much do you spend every day?"
- pointed to the traditional practice of setting aside a handful of rice before cooking as a way to save small amounts;
- openly discussed financial and social conditions, emphasizing that "if we can save, we can improve our social status and our relatives will benefit as well"; and
- used the slogan Just Fifty Paise a Day to encourage their elders to save the monthly payment by foregoing a cup of tea or a cigarette every other day.

Several months of promotion yielded two thousand rupees from which the cooperative made its first loan. It was this loan that impressed many non-members, who then joined the cooperative. The loan showed concretely that saving fifteen rupees a month could make a difference.

—Madhav Poudyal and Khem Raj Sapkota

Where the market distrusts financial institutions, the primary promotional challenge may be to project an institutional image of safety and reliability. The MFI will want to establish this image through the demeanor of its sales force, its *institutional motto* or slogan, and each of its promotional messages. One component of an effective strategy might be *institutional advertising* that aims to create a favorable impression of the organization. The theme will be the MFI's safety and reliability.

In highly competitive environments the primary task may be distinguishing the MFI's product from those of its competitors. The highest priorities may be *sales promotions* that make a specific product more attractive and *selective-demand advertising*. Sales promotions with incentives such as coupons, gifts, contests, or lotteries stimulate short-term demand. Selective-demand advertising highlights the special features and benefits of a specific product offered by a specific MFI. This type of advertising pits the MFI's brand against the rest of the market. The theme will be the superiority of a specific product (see Box 10–2).

Where the most pressing issue is increasing the average account balance to a viable level, one key may be carefully designed *sales promotions*—such as lottery tickets or small gifts—tied to the size of the account and tailored to

Box 10–2. Operating in a Competitive Environment: VYCCU, Ten Years Later

After a decade of operation VYCCU faces very different promotional challenges than when it began. Now that people are used to saving in a financial institution, other cooperatives, commercial banks, and finance companies have entered its market. VYCCU uses all four promotional tools as well as distinctive services to attract and retain customers. It capitalizes on its home-grown image. Members may be intimidated by financial institutions that are housed in big buildings and staffed by better-off professionals. In contrast, VYCCU feels familiar. VYCCU staff continually remind members of VYCCU's promotional message: This is our bank. We are the owners and promoters. If VYCCU profits, we profit.

Personal sales:

General meetings and word of mouth: VYCCU introduces members to new services at its annual meeting. However, members are likely to have heard already by word of mouth.

Promotion by local officials: VYCCU informs the Village Development Committee (VDC), the local governing body, of new products. The VDC has the ear of the people and spreads the word effectively.

Sales promotions:

Value-added loan: All new members can receive a loan of US$66 after six months.

Members' discount card: VYCCU members can receive a 5 to 10 percent discount at five local shops. They especially appreciate the 8 percent discount at the medical shop.

Maternity allowance: After the birth of their first and second child, women receive US$4 to help cover medical costs. Women value the benefit highly; they use it to justify their hospital care to their husbands.

Accident insurance: Clients who make a fixed deposit of at least US$660 for at least one year receive accident insurance for the amount and period of the deposit.

Advertising:

Children's badges (pins): Children who open an account are given a badge or pin. When other children see them, they ask their parents if they can also join.

Slogan: The checks provided with VYCCU's current accounts carry the imprint "Starting from fifty paise," a constant reminder of its roots in the community.

Public relations:

Member education: Members can participate in training and study tours.

VYCCU also pays a higher rate of interest, provides quicker service, and is open longer than local banks. With all these promotional techniques and competitive services, VYCCU has managed to hold its own in an increasingly competitive market.

—Madhav Poudyal and Khem Raj Sapkota

potential clients who might deposit more. The theme will be the benefits of larger accounts (see Box 10–3).

Box 10–3. Aiming to Increase Account Size: The Philippines

One Philippine rural bank aimed to increase its average daily balance from US$75 to US$100 over the course of six months. To meet this goal, the bank changed the terms of the product, made the delivery system more convenient, and designed a sales promotion—a raffle –that rewarded increases in account balance. Specifically, the bank:

- established minimum balances of US$1.25 and fees on accounts that went below US$2.50;
- gave the clients lockboxes and told them to save daily and to deposit the contents at the bank when the box was full; and
- instituted a raffle. The bank provided a ticket to all clients who maintained a balance of at least US$75 and another ticket for each additional US$12.50. The quarterly raffle prize was equal to the winner's average daily balance for the past month. Hence, the raffle was called Double Your Savings. The prize limit was set at US$125 (over the US$100 target balance).

The result? In just three months the average balance of general savings accounts increased by more than 20 percent.

John Owens, email posting to DevFinance Network, April 2000.

In each of these cases the MFI must understand its market—how potential clients perceive savings services and MFIs—in order to identify appropriate objectives and themes. Together with the MFI's target market and objectives, these tools and themes form the core of an MFI's promotional plan (see Appendix 10.1).

10.1.6 Messages

Finally, in light of the target market and tools to be used, how can these themes be expressed in effective messages? Some guidelines for effective messages are discussed in Section 10.2.

10.1.7 Evaluation

Once promotion is under way, regularly evaluating the effectiveness and cost of each initiative will enable managers to assess the bottom line: what has and has not strengthened sales?

10.2 THE MESSAGE

Whatever an MFI's promotional tools and themes, its messages should be clear, simple, and compelling. For example, products should have memorable and catchy names that nearly explain themselves, such as:

- *Multiple Fortune account.* BAAC's passbook account that both yields interest and gives the depositor the chance to win attractive lottery prizes
- *Patriot Deposit.* FECECAM in Benin enables urban clients who want to contribute to the development of their region of origin to deposit funds that are then transferred and lent out in their region of choice.

This same criteria—clear, simple, compelling—apply to how the terms of the product are described to the public and how the institution itself is promoted. For example, returns might be marketed as "double your money" in some number of years rather than citing an annual interest rate. A key step in defining a compelling message is to identify and apply a unique selling proposition or "difference that makes the difference." In other words, what about the product or institution will sway potential customers to choose it over its competitors?

An institutional slogan or tag line can help the MFI convey its market niche, distinguish itself from its competitors, and reinforce the image it wants to project. For example, Centenary Rural Development Bank in Uganda bases all of its advertising on the slogan, The Bank for All Ugandans.

Researching the market before developing a message and organizing focus groups to test reactions to the proposed message—including photos and graphics—is critical to assure that the message is completely understood by potential customers and gets the results expected (see Figure 10–2, which illustrates how a message might be misinterpreted and why market research is important for honing the message; see also Chapter 6).

The effectiveness of messages can be reinforced by visual images, in particular logos for the institution or its individual products. Giving each product a symbol that is always used in its advertising can help depositors remember and feel familiar with the product. An MFI will want to ensure that all of its messages convey a consistent institutional image that is compelling to its target markets. An institutional logo or slogan can help provide this consistency.

The message will also be conveyed—or undermined—by the look and feel of each branch—its layout, upkeep, and appearance, the attitude of its staff, and all of its customer information. Whether explicit and intentional or not, customer information sends a message to customers. This is true of every single communication, not only brochures and posters but also price lists, signs, and notice boards. All information should be written in clear, concise language that clients can understand. Where the market is semi-literate, words should be complemented by graphics and photographs. Customer information should always be available.

Figure 10–2. Promotion as Communication

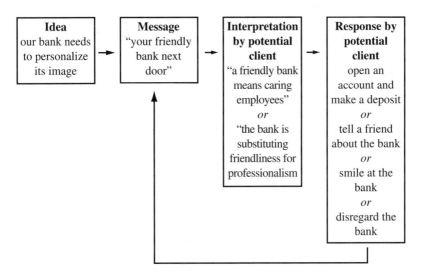

Signs must be visible in a crowded banking hall, so that customers know that they are in the right place. For this reason, hanging signs may be more effective than smaller signs placed on the tellers' windows. By doing all this, management sends a powerful message that the institution is attentive and responsive to its customers.

Information that is poorly presented can undermine the message management intends to convey and can greatly impede communication. Many banking halls contain out-of-date posters and brochures, which can be disastrous when prices or product features change. When customers are presented with too much information, they may not be able to determine what is important to read. Casually handwritten materials lessen the impact of the corporate brand; the corporate brand should be used to signal the information's importance. Of course, the message itself should vary according to the target market and the promotional tool.

10.3 PROMOTIONAL TOOLS

An MFI has five tools with which it can promote itself and its products: personal sales, advertising, word of mouth, sales promotions, and public relations. These tools reinforce one another, particularly when their messages are well coordinated. Together with the MFI's target-market objectives and messages, the tools form the basis of the MFI's promotional plan (see Appendix 10.1).

10.3.1 Personal Sales

Personal sales means a personal communication of information to persuade some-body to buy something. Personal sales tends to work best when it informs potential customers of the product at the same time it gives them an immediate opportunity to open an account. Because personal sales usually takes place face to face, it can be one of the most effective ways to promote a product and to build a customer relationship. Personal sales can be undertaken in a variety of ways:

When staff interact with potential clients for other reasons: Staff can promote products and open accounts when they conduct field research about where to locate a new branch, open the branch, or interact with borrowers about loans.

Through door-to-door canvassing: Particularly in new markets where saving in cash is unusual, field agents may initially need to solicit clients during informal visits to their homes or work places. Staff might engage in a "sales walk," soliciting new customers along the way.

By going where groups already are: Many MFIs recruit large numbers of clients at a time by introducing them to products in places where they congregate. For example, the Burkinabe MFI Sonapost holds an annual sales campaign during which its staff members visit water plants, schools, health clinics, flour mills, agricultural cooperatives, and government agencies. During the campaign staff open accounts on the spot. MFIs also promote services at army barracks, police stations, temples, markets, and community gatherings.

By bringing groups together during promotional campaigns: MFIs may call a community gathering specifically to promote their services. To promote its new contractual product, BURO, Tangail conducted a weeklong Savings for Future campaign. It organized large meetings, small meetings, and rallies with songs, clapping, and speeches in which new members declared that they had signed up. It expected to recruit eight thousand new clients; fourteen thousand signed up.

By approaching better-off individuals and institutions: To bring in larger depositors, MFI staff often identify better-off individuals and institutions, particularly those who employ large numbers of potential customers to approach on an individual basis. BRI's training teaches staff to identify promising potential clients (see Box 10–4).

When others interact with clients: Some MFIs use government bureaucrats or community leaders with great success to promote new products during anything from community meetings to census surveys. Because potential clients may perceive these people as disinterested third parties, potential clients may trust them more than the MFI's sales force. (In some places, however, promotion by someone associated with the government might taint the product in the eyes of potential customers.) This method has two disadvantages: accounts

---

Box 10–4. A Systematic Approach to Mobilizing Deposits:
Personal Sales at BRI

To expand and deepen its outreach, the BRI unit system developed a book of case studies to use in training its staff—examples of mobilizing savings from a wide range of individuals, groups, private institutions, and government offices. They demonstrated different types of household savings to help staff understand how households save and how to explain the savings instruments in ways that would attract these clients. The cases also demonstrated how staff might locate potential depositors.

Each case highlighted specific lessons about mobilizing deposits. For example,

- Staff should listen carefully to what clients want instead of assuming that they already know. It is easy to assume the opposite of what a saver actually wants.
- Staff can pursue specific high-potential clients. For example, rural land sales can be the source of large deposits, and remittances can be captured as savings.
- Word-of-mouth advertising from satisfied clients is the best form of promotion.
- Deposits can be mobilized from a wide range of public and private institutions. Staff should identify institutions in their service areas, meet with their heads, and explain how the unit's savings services could benefit them.

To ensure that the units applied the lessons of the cases methodically, BRI developed the Systematic Approach to Savings Mobilization. Staff were taught a system for identifying the hundred largest depositors in their service areas. First, staff were to visit government and village officials, heads of local institutions and government offices, better-off residents, and other local leaders and contacts. From talking to these people, staff compiled lists of potential large savers. After the unit noted their locations on a large map, each staff member was assigned names and dates for visiting these potential clients. Staff were taught how to talk to these people, including how to explain the uses and advantages of each savings product. They were also taught how to record the visits and the next steps needed for each potential client. Through talking with potential clients, managers and staff learned about their market in general as well as about individuals.

Marguerite Robinson, *The Microfinance Revolution*, vol. 2, *Lessons from Indonesia* (Washington, DC: World Bank, 2002), 279–97.

---

cannot be opened on the spot, and the MFI cannot control how the product is described.

When clients interact with potential clients: For many MFIs, word of mouth may be the most far-reaching, inexpensive, and effective form of promotion (see Section 10.3.3). As with the previous method, however, accounts cannot be opened on the spot, and promotion leaves the MFI with even less control over how the product is described.

Face-to-face communication can do more harm than good if the potential client leaves with a negative impression. Most MFIs rely on their existing field staff to be their sales force. If staff members are unclear, unfriendly, or simply off-putting, personal sales can turn potential customers away as quickly as a positive interaction can attract them. Therefore, developing a strong product description is not enough. MFIs must ensure that their field agents actually describe products in clear, simple, and compelling terms and appear inviting and friendly. Effective personal sales hinges on:

- recruiting the right staff,
- ensuring that they internalize the MFI's vision and objectives,
- training them adequately, and
- providing appropriate incentives, supervision, and performance evaluation.

Managers must remember that every contact with actual and potential customers is important—as is every staff member who contacts them. When customers enter a branch, they do not immediately distinguish between tellers and loan officers; they expect all staff to be able to answer simple questions. In fact, a customer often encounters the security guard before any other staff person. In customer-focused banks, the security guard is able to direct customers to the appropriate officer and answer frequently asked questions.

Should credit staff be used to promote savings? The cost of using credit staff is negligible. In comparison, using staff specifically dedicated to promoting savings is very costly—and not financially feasible for most MFIs. But can credit staff handle another function? Credit staff are likely to promote savings effectively only if they are motivated to do so. Will providing them with incentives to promote savings products divert them from their other important priorities? These are questions management must consider.

Head office staff and branch managers often have the opportunity to meet clients during their activities outside the bank. When Equity Bank was opening a branch in Nyeri, more than a dozen branch managers from around Kenya visited the town for a week and spoke to business leaders and individuals. Once the branch opened, it broke even in record time.

10.3.2 Advertising

Advertising is impersonal mass communication designed and paid for by an MFI. It includes short spots on radio, placement in newspapers, billboards, leaflets and brochures, posters distributed to clients or exhibited in the MFI's offices, banners displayed at branches, public events, sales campaigns, and announcements and songs broadcast in public places by loudspeaker. Advertising can be used to:

- Support personal sales;
- Inform customers about a new product, product line, or brand names;

- Expand the use of a product to new markets; and
- Prevent substitution, motivating existing customers to stay with the MFI.

Vital to a market-led MFI, posters and brochures are the cheapest form of mass communication. They support personal interactions between the MFI and its clients, to communicate key product features and benefits, and to close sales. For example, every branch of Teba Bank displays a full range of product posters that are framed to highlight their significance and that meet strict color and logo guidelines. They effectively communicate the bank's full range of products to customers and staff alike and thereby promote additional sales to existing customers.

Brochures and posters should be simple. Because posters have much greater longevity than brochures, they should be of higher quality. If all posters and brochures have the same theme, corporate colors, and logo, they help to communicate the institution's brand. A good example of this is Western Union, whose black and yellow publicity materials are instantly recognizable worldwide.

Where services are delivered through branches, the branch is probably the most important venue for advertising to existing clients. Given its strategic importance, managers pay remarkably little attention to maximizing its communication potential. A simple example is name tags. Requiring staff to wear name tags conveys that the institution is transparent and accountable and encourages staff to provide excellent service. If staff do not have them—which is surprisingly common—customers will identify poor service as an institutional failing rather than an individual one.

Advertisements should be designed in the context of an *advertising campaign*, a coordinated advertising program intended to accomplish specific target goals for a product or brand. As with an overall promotional strategy, the first step in an advertising campaign is to define target markets, objectives, budgets, and themes clearly. The MFI then translates the themes into an advertising message and selects the media to convey it.

Advertisements are sales messages; their ultimate purpose is to sell something. An advertising message should do two things:

- Attract and hold the attention of the intended audience. Techniques to gain attention include surprise, shock, amusement, and arousing curiosity.
- Influence that audience in the desired way. First, the message should express how the individual will benefit from the product (or other subject of the message). This is called the *appeal* of the message, and it can be demonstrated in various ways such as data, the endorsement of a respected person, or the testimony of satisfied users. Second, these benefits need to be convincingly tied to features of the product; that is, the advertisement must persuade the audience that it will receive these benefits by using the product. This is called the *execution* of the message.

The message should be shaped by the benefits of the product to the target market. For example, when the target audience is the customer, the message should be short, clear, and, often, connected to a picture that enhances the message. In contrast, when the target audience is a business, advertising should provide more detailed information, such as performance data. In all cases a catchy and meaningful message is the key to a successful campaign.

The message and media through which it is transmitted should be selected at the same time (see Box 10–5). When choosing a medium, the MFI should consider:

Advertising objectives: The media should match the purpose of the advertisement. For example, if the objective is to increase general awareness, a radio spot might be the best choice. In contrast, if the objective is to create immediate awareness in a rural town about the arrival of a mobile savings unit, loudspeakers on top of the mobile unit vehicle may be the best medium.

Target market: The market reached by the medium should match the geographic distribution of the product and socioeconomic profile of the target clientele. Moreover, the medium should reach the market with a minimum of wasted coverage. This is the case if the number of people who are not targeted customers is limited. For example, for many less educated markets the most effective advertising medium is the radio, rather than a newspaper. Many countries have an annual media survey that details which media reach which socioeconomic groups.

Message: The medium should depend on the message. For example, if an MFI has a very brief message, perhaps six words, a billboard may the best medium.

Time and location: The medium should reach prospective customers when and where they are about to make their buying decision. For example, advertising for a savings plan targeting farmers should reach them before harvest

---

Box 10–5. Advertising: Union Bank in Jamaica and BAAC in Thailand

To promote a product for the low-income market, Union Bank hired a popular local reggae artist to sing a catchy single, which played both on radio and television. Promotional materials and advertisements in the press used cartoon characters and Jamaican dialect to appeal to the low-income market segment. In three years the bank amassed over US$3 million in Partner Savings deposits.

BAAC uses brochures, posters, banners, and radio broadcasts to advertise its products. It also advertises its individual saving products by loudspeaker at branch offices during peak hours, at temples when there are religious ceremonies, and at district events. The "BAAC Song" is popular among clients; each mobile savings unit is equipped with powerful loudspeakers that play the catchy advertising jingle as soon as it arrives at a stop. These promotional efforts have proven very successful.

time. Posters or brochures placed in the waiting areas of branches are an excellent medium for advertising available products to existing customers.

How much is the right amount of advertising? There is no uniform answer. Decisions on advertising must be based on the market and the MFI's position within it. While some MFIs spend considerable sums to advertise, others fear that too much advertising will give the impression that their institution is unstable or in dire need of new deposits. Some institutions advertise on a very limited budget. For example, BURO, Tangail, which operates in an extremely competitive market, keeps advertising costs low by limiting its advertising activities to passing out brochures, using public address systems in marketplaces, and erecting billboards at strategic locations. Still others promote themselves very successfully without advertising. Instead, they rely solely on word of mouth.

10.3.3 Word of Mouth

In the mass market, word of mouth—informal communication among clients and potential clients—is the single most significant driver of sales in financial services. Potential clients often trust their neighbors and friends more than any other source of promotion. For example, the Bangladeshi NGO ASA has grown massively without advertising. Instead, it relies on personal sales by its field staff, the quality of its services, and word of mouth. Similarly, Equity Bank of Kenya has experienced phenomenal growth based almost solely on being responsive to clients and the resulting word of mouth (see Box 10–6).

Word of mouth grows from being responsive to customers and is maintained by continuing to deliver services that customers value:

Design and communication of services: The best way to influence word of mouth is to deliver easy-to-understand services that clients want in the manner they want them (see Chapter 6) and *to communicate these services carefully.* If these services are also backed up by *Frequently Asked Questions*—prepared responses to customers' common questions—staff will be able to explain them easily to potential customers. Marketing teams also must ensure that each staff member fully understands the benefits to customers of each financial service. To help accomplish this, they may train and test staff on their product knowledge.

Service delivery: Excellent service is critical to developing strong word of mouth. A customer-focused banking environment is carefully planned to provide a pleasant, effective, and efficient banking experience. A customer-focused branch often has significant front-office staff presence, including specialized customer-service staff and sales staff.

Completing the feedback loop: Implementing a complete feedback loop— understanding customer needs, responding to these needs, and informing

---

Box 10–6. Word of Mouth: The Key to Growth at Equity Bank

In late 2001 Equity Bank in Kenya had 100,000 depositors. Growth since 1995 had been significant but modest, peaking after the introduction of a new computer system in 2000. Equity was searching for what to do next to become more responsive to its clients. Three years later Equity had 375,000 depositors, was growing rapidly, and did very little formal marketing. How was this achieved?

Equity gradually built very positive word of mouth among potential customers. Equity started by training thirty of its staff in market research. Then, with technical support from *MicroSave,* these staff conducted research that uncovered product features that customers disliked. In particular, customers felt Equity was expensive and not transparent due to a myriad of small charges. In response, Equity modified its product range and simplified and published its charges. It then clearly displayed these in its banking hall.

In 2002 Equity continued to perform client research and modify its services. Each time, it communicated carefully with its clients; in one case it printed more than 150,000 letters telling customers how it had listened, what it had learned, and the changes it was making. It also created a consistent look and feel for all its physical infrastructure. Counters were made from the same laminate, signage was made consistent, and lighting was improved. New branches were built with the same physical layout. Word of mouth continued to build, and the number of new accounts per month increased to eight thousand. In August 2003 Equity celebrated its twentieth anniversary with national publicity and public-relations exercises from which it received extensive free media coverage. Once again, the rate of growth increased, peaking at twenty thousand accounts per month.

Months later Equity was still benefiting from positive word of mouth. While growth moderated to approximately fourteen thousand new accounts per month, it continues to open new branches and to extend its services.

---

customers of positive change—is essential. Successful marketing teams use various tools to monitor continually the quality of their service delivery: management reviews of branches, branch statistics, mystery shopping, customer-satisfaction surveys, focus groups, and suggestion boxes.[4] An example of completing the loop is Equity Bank's use of letters to customers advising them that Equity had listened to their concerns, how it was responding, and why some suggestions were not taken up.

Corporate branding: Branding is key to developing potential customers' expectations that the MFI will provide high-quality, reliable, and professional services.

Public relations: Stimulating others to champion the institution creates powerful and trusted endorsements. For example, FINCA Tanzania employed a journalist as a marketing manager to help it gain positive publicity (see Section 10.3.5).

Living up to promises: Institutions should think very carefully about what they promise their customers. Consistently under-promising and over-delivering is far better than continually disappointing customers. For example, institutions should be careful about promising access to new technologies, such as ATMs, which frequently take longer to introduce than anticipated. Failing to deliver on brand promises creates strong negative word of mouth.

10.3.4 Sales Promotion

From coupons to lotteries (see Box 10–7), sales promotions may be used to:

- create awareness about a new or improved product,
- attract new customers,
- encourage greater use of a product by existing customers, or
- combat a competitor's promotional activities.

Some MFIs use sales promotion as an ongoing means to promote their products. In many environments regularly scheduled lotteries with prizes have proven highly successful at attracting new savers, motivating existing clients to increase the sizes of their accounts, and drawing clients closer to the institution. Typically, any saver with a minimum balance is eligible for a ticket and, for each multiple of this balance, receives an additional ticket. Prizes can be awarded at a public event at which information on products and services is available. Life insurance can be another ongoing sales promotion that builds client loyalty. Many credit unions provide all depositors with a free policy that, in the event of death, pays the family a sum equal to the savings balance.[5] However, management should be careful about using sales promotions to compete, as the cost can be unmanageable.

The objectives of the overall marketing program should dictate what sales promotion technique to employ. Factors to consider include:

- *Costs:* How much would the promotion cost if it succeeded in attracting many customers? Give-aways to a large audience may be prohibitively expensive.
- *The target market:* Is the target group loyal to a competing product? If so, a high-value coupon may be necessary to disrupt customer-purchasing patterns.
- *Promotional objectives:* Is the aim to increase the depositor base? If so, giving out a lottery coupon for each new savings account may be appropriate.
- *Current economic conditions:* Are customers particularly price conscious because of a recession or inflation? If so, coupons are a good option.

Box 10–7. Sales Promotions from Africa to Latin America

Gifts: Sonopost in Burkina Faso offer depositors a range of popular small gifts, from T-shirts to folders, calendars, key chains, and hats. These gifts increase client loyalty to the bank.

In-kind returns: For deposits over a minimum size and maturity, the Cooperative Bank of Benguet in the Philippines offers a combination of in-kind and cash returns. The in-kind return is determined by a market survey of what kind of kitchenwares, small farm or carpentry tools, and equipment are desired by the target market. Samples of the prizes are displayed at the branch office and by field staff when they meet with clients. For example, for a US$50 CD with a one-year term the bank offers a rate of return of 7 percent per annum. The bank uses half of the 7 percent interest earnings, US$1.75, to buy good quality kitchenware that it gives to clients outright when they make their deposit. It gives the remaining 3.5 percent interest upon maturity of the deposit. Some depositors prefer to receive their entire return in-kind.[1]

Promotional incentives: Banco Solidario in Ecuador offers promotional incentives to both staff and clients. Every depositor who introduces a new client receives US$2 in cash and a food gift basket. In addition, when clients or staff members motivate friends to deposit a minimum of US$5,000, they earn a commission ranging from 0.2 percent of the amount (for a period of thirty to fifty-nine days) to 1.2 percent of the amount (for a period of more than 179 days). Banco Solidario reports that these promotional incentives have been very successful.

Lotteries: Research conducted by BRI revealed that games of chance were popular among rural Indonesians and that informal savings mechanisms often involved randomly choosing whose turn it was to receive funds at a meeting that doubled as an important social event. Therefore, BRI introduced a semi-annual lottery to promote its liquid savings products. The lotteries are popular and effective promotional events. Both cash and in-kind prizes (autos, motorcycle, television, radios, refrigerators, and clocks) are awarded in public ceremonies. In 1995 the aggregate value of prizes for regular savings depositors was about 0.7 percent of account balances, and 0.16 percent of account holders won a prize. For less liquid accounts with a higher interest rate, the aggregate value of prizes totaled less than 0.15 percent of annual account balances. BRI's overall cost for the lottery was about 1 percent of its outstanding deposit balance, as compared to its interest rate of 4 percent of account balances and administrative costs for savings of 2.9 percent.[2]

---

[1]Gerry Lab-oyan, Sergio Antezana, "Virtual Conference on Savings Operations for Very Small or Remote Depositors," May 2002.
[2]Marguerite Robinson, *The Microfinance Revolution*, vol. 2, *Lessons from Indonesia*, (Washington, DC: World Bank, 2002), 299–300.

10.3.5 Public Relations

Public-relations activities aim to build or maintain a favorable image of an organization and a favorable relationship with its customers, prospective customers, owners, employees, the local community, and the government. Good public relations can be achieved by supporting charitable projects, supplying volunteer labor or other resources, participating in community service events, sponsoring sport teams, funding events, producing an employee or customer newsletter, and disseminating information through exhibits and displays.

Unlike most advertising and personal sales, public relations does not include a specific sales message. Nevertheless, positive exposure through the media or as a result of community involvement can produce a high return on the investment of time and resources. Two types of public relations deserve particular mention: publicity and sponsorship.

Publicity is a relatively inexpensive and powerful form of public relations. Publicity is any communication about an organization, its products, or its policies through the media that is not paid for by the organization. It usually takes the form of a news story appearing in a mass medium. MFIs can generate good publicity by:

- *Preparing a news story (press release),* and circulating it to selected newspapers, radio stations, or other media who can report the story as news.
- *Personally communicating with a group.* For example, if the subject is of public interest, a press conference can attract media representatives.
- *Personally communicating with influential individuals.* An organization can lobby powerful people in order to influence their opinions and decisions.
- *Interacting with prominent people,* especially those with media representatives, in order to generate press coverage. For example, an MFI could invite the governor of the central bank for a tour. Especially if the MFI distributes a press-information kit well in advance, media representatives may include information about the MFI and its products in their coverage of the event.

What distinguishes publicity from advertising is that a third party reports the information. This gives positive publicity much more credibility than advertising, in which the MFI reports positively about itself. Since publicity appears as objective editorial material or news, prospective customers are more likely to pay attention to it than they are to advertising, which they may ignore. Because a third party pays most of the costs, publicity costs the MFI less than advertising and may contain more detailed information. Another advantage is that preparing a news release is quick.

Publicity also has its limitations. There is no guarantee that a news release will appear in the media, and if it does, it will usually appear just once. Furthermore, the MFI cannot control how the media presents the message. Even a small miscommunication can cause the message to have unintended negative consequences. For example, many postal savings banks would like to develop a range of credit products, especially when treasury bill rates are low. However, the banks' expressed desire to develop a range of credit products could be misinterpreted by customers to mean that it is about to introduce these products.

Sponsorship is a mixture of advertising and publicity. An MFI might sponsor a sporting event, concert, parade, or scholarship program. The MFI should choose an event or program that affects its target market and that transmits the image it seeks to project (see Box 10–8).

These tools—personal sales, advertising, sales promotions, and public relations—are summarized in Table 10–1. Whichever one is used, management should be very careful not to promise too much or otherwise promote the product inappropriately.

Box 10–8. Public Relations: People's Bank of Sri Lanka

In 1992 People's Bank began sponsoring a scholarship program in schools throughout the country. Each year the bank awards forty-three two-year scholarships to student account holders with the best "O" level grades in order to pursue their "A" level education. Award lists are published in all of the big newspapers, and the scholarships are presented in a public ceremony. Client interviews conducted in January 2000 demonstrated that People's Bank sponsoring of bright young students has endeared the bank to local communities and greatly enhanced its reputation.

10.4 PUTTING PROMOTION INTO PRACTICE

Within a financial institution, promotion should be managed by the marketing team. In small institutions this might include senior managers as well as one or two branch managers. Ideally, however, it will include staff who are dedicated to marketing. Of course, marketing activities, including promotion, should be the part of the job responsibilities of all staff.

In many MFIs the marketing function is weak, in part because marketing requires skills that are difficult and expensive to acquire. To develop or strengthen its marketing function, management should take the following steps:

1. Commit financial and human resources to building a marketing function.
2. Develop the market research, product marketing, branding, and customer-service skills that are needed. Because MFIs often cannot find or afford people with these skills, many use existing staff who learn these skills progressively through training and on the job.

Table 10–1. Summary of Promotional Tools

	Techniques	Cost per exposure[1]	Keys to success
Personal sales	During routine operations Door-to-door campaigns Going where groups congregate Bringing people together for a campaign Soliciting institutions Soliciting larger depositors Using government officials Word of mouth	Moderate unless using a dedicated task force (then very high)	Highly effective if staff is properly recruited, trained, and motivated
Advertising	Radio, loudspeakers Written news media Billboards, posters, and banners Leaflets and brochures Jingles and songs	Relatively low	Effectiveness depends on catchy, meaningful message and reach to target audience
Word of mouth	Customer-focused product design and delivery Excellent customer service Successful branding Good public relations	Very low	Fulfilling promises Completing feedback loops
Sales promotions	Gifts Interest-rate premiums Incentives for bringing in new clients Contests Lotteries	Can be high or negligible	Should be closely tied to immediate objectives; lotteries can be especially effective, even over long term
Public relations	Community service; charitable projects Staff /client newsletter; exhibits Funding events Press releases and press conferences Lobbying or interacting with powerful people Sponsoring events, teams or programs	Low or very low	Publicity can be especially effective because third party is trusted more than MFI promoting itself.

[1] Cost divided by the number of people that are expected to be reached.

3. Start with market research and promotion activities.
4. Develop "Frequently Asked Question Guides" and other materials to communicate products to staff and customers.
5. Have the marketing department and front-line staff agree about the services the marketing department will provide, the local promotional activities front line staff will conduct, and sales targets.
6. Broaden the focus of marketing to include customer service and branding.
7. Periodically hire consultants to help with advertising, publicity, research, branding, and customer service. Invest in gradually deepening the skills of existing staff.

As the marketing function grows and expands in influence, it is likely to meet resistance from more established departments. Because of this, an evolving marketing function usually involves an institutional transition to a market-led approach to delivering services. Long-term success in the marketing function requires excellence in operations, efficiency, and information systems.[6]

10.5 EVALUATING THE EFFECTIVENESS OF MARKETING

Evaluating the effectiveness of marketing initiatives can be uncertain because it is difficult to attribute specific sales to particular marketing activities. However, several approaches to measuring the effectiveness of marketing are commonly used.

- *Plotting growth statistics for the branch or institution against particular marketing initiatives:* Branch statistics are used to evaluate local initiatives; institution-wide statistics are used for national ones.
- *Account opening questionnaires:* When customers open an account or take out a loan, they respond to a questionnaire that asks how they heard about the institution and/or product.
- *Focus-group discussions:* Discussions review the messages actually communicated to customers by different publicity and promotional materials.
- *Product-knowledge tests (clients):* These are used where marketing initiatives depend on personal sales.

Some marketing initiatives are intended to improve the image of the institution and only indirectly influence sales. In this case it is appropriate to measure through quantitative and qualitative research how market perceptions of the institution are changing. Market perceptions strongly influence word of mouth.

Another mechanism that is commonly used to improve the effectiveness of the marketing function, rather than of specific marketing events, is a marketing audit. During a marketing audit, experienced marketing professionals review the functioning and impact of the institution's marketing, identify issues, and recommend solutions.

10.6 SOME COMMON MISTAKES

Institutions will do well to avoid the following common marketing mistakes:

Treating marketing as a department: Marketing is not just a department; it is a key and integral function of the business. As such, it is a responsibility of every employee. For example, in Equity Bank, head-office staff operate the bank's stands at trade shows, branch managers attend public functions at which they can be recognized and approached by potential clients, and tellers market services during slack mid-month periods. In postal savings banks the marketing challenges often are to empower branches to market their services and to ensure that all staff are familiar with products, have clear sales targets, and are continually supplied with promotional material.

Over-promising: In an attempt to "clinch the sale," marketing teams and chief executives often make promises that the institution cannot fulfill. Or they over-emphasize potential developments that are only delivered much later.

Failing to coordinate marketing campaigns: Marketing campaigns must be coordinated within the financial institution. Operations need to know when and where the marketing campaign is going to take place so that additional staff are positioned to take advantage of increased public interest. If the campaign centers on a new product, all staff need to receive training in the product before the campaign takes place.

Failing to focus on benefits: Frequently, marketing materials fail to communicate key benefits that customers will derive or experience from the financial service. To avoid this mistake, carefully analyze benefits and test marketing materials on potential clients.

Failing to control the quality of marketing documentation: Senior management, specifically operations managers, must ensure the quality of marketing documentation such as frequently asked question guides and advertising materials. Quality control reduces factual mistakes and over-promising.

10.7 CONCLUSION

This chapter has provided a framework and some guidelines for deciding how to promote products. It also has illustrated the wealth of ways that innovative MFIs attract their customers. Finally, it has highlighted a few important lessons:

Promotion should never take place in a vacuum; it should be shaped entirely by the MFI's objectives and the demand of the target market. Understanding what customers want and how they hear is essential; whatever the promotional tool, the message they receive must be clear, simple, and compelling.

Table 10–2. Savings for the Future: Promotional Plan for New Contractual Product

Target market	Objective	Activity/tool	Schedule	Responsible	Cost
All staff	Every employee has an account	Introduce new product	Jan.–March	Human Resources and Savings Departments	50,000
All field agents	Agents well trained to market product: agents can explain advantages relative to customer needs	Two-day training in selling product and handling its operations.	Jan.–March	Human Resources Department	50,000
Urban markets	Introduce new product; 1,000 new accounts	Personal sales campaign at bus & taxi parks	Apr.–June	Marketing Manager	300,000
Established families, middle-aged	Inform them of new product; 750 new accounts	Advertising campaign: daily paper and radio stations with the best acceptance in the target groups	May–July	Marketing Manager	1,500,000
Established families	Introduce new product; 500 new accounts	Personally contact prospective customers. Staff bonus for new accounts.	May–Dec.	Savings Department	Promotion bonus 200,000
Middle-aged couples, no at-home children	Introduce new product; 500 new accounts	Personally contact prospective customers. Staff bonus for new accounts.	Sept.–Dec.	Savings Department	Promotion bonus

Notes

[1] Microfinance practitioners often think that promotion is the same as marketing. In fact, promotion is only the final element of the "marketing mix," which also includes its products, pricing, and delivery (or distribution) systems. An MFI's volume of deposits will depend on all of these elements. The success of the entire mix will depend, in turn, on whether the MFI has done its homework: market research and strategic planning. Marketing refers to this entire cycle: market research, strategic planning, and the development of the marketing mix (see Figure 10–1).

[2] See *MicroSave*'s *Corporate Brand and Identity* (Nairobi: *MicroSave*, 2004). This toolkit is available at the *MicroSave* website.

[3] Graham A. N. Wright et al., "Corporate Branding and Identity: Why They Are Important for MFIs," *MicroSave,* Briefing Note 27 (Nairobi: *MicroSave*, n.d.).

[4] See *MicroSave's Customer Service Toolkit* for pro forma survey instruments.

[5] See David C. Richardson, Chapter 3 herein.

[6] See the *MicroSave* website for marketing tools and guidance.

PART III

SYSTEMS

Managing Risk, Maximizing Productivity

11

Maintaining the Security of Client Funds

Monnie Markel Biety

Guarding against fraud, theft, and the mismanagement of funds is always important. When these funds are the savings of poor people, guarding them well becomes imperative. At the same time, the unpredictable size and timing of deposits make MFIs vulnerable to fraud and error. These risks are magnified when, in order to serve small or rural depositors, transactions are handled by a single staff person in the field or by staff with little education.

The first line of defense against fraud and errors is strong management. This includes, of course, internal controls and internal audits backed up by a strong board. Controls and audits have the potential to prevent and detect operating problems and the risk of such problems. But, by themselves, controls and audits are not sufficient.

Audits and controls will be effective only if they are reinforced by the MFI's culture and by its policies and procedures, including training and supervision of staff and information systems. In short, clients' deposits will be secure only if an MFI makes security an integral part of its operations. Accordingly, this chapter discusses:

- How errors can lead to fraud, and why internal controls must focus on both;

The author greatly appreciates the valuable feedback of Jenny Hoffman, Nthenya Mule, Meryl Hirschland, and Ismail Adams. She gives heartfelt thanks to the following individuals, whose help, explanations, patience, and translations made this chapter possible: Mohammed Azim Hossain, Mohammed Jamilur Rahman Chy, Mohammed Shafiqual Choudhury, Mosharrof Hossain, S. K. Sinha, Mohammed Hossin Islam, and Mark Staehle.

Box 11–1. Some Useful Definitions

Audit: A systematic review of internal controls as well as of an institution's finances, operations, and computer systems.

Audit trail: The evidence of the transactions created by the paper documentation that allows an auditor to trace a transaction from inception (for example, a cash deposit or withdrawal slip) to the financial statements.

Authorization: Designated by policy, the power given to an individual or body to approve a transaction, procedure, and/or policy.

Compliance: To follow or act in accordance with government regulations, rules, financial standards, and MFI policies and procedures.

Discrepancies: Differences or errors that occur, accidentally or intentionally, in the processing of transactions in the MFI or between the MFI and its clients.

Dual control: The separation of transaction responsibilities between at least two employees. Ideally, one employee originates the transaction, another records it, and a third audits or verifies its authenticity and correctness.

External audit: An audit, generally performed on an annual basis, by a qualified, independent third party. Its objective is to determine that the financial statements fully and fairly disclose the true value of the MFI's assets, liabilities, and equity.

Fraud: An act of deceiving or misrepresenting, usually perpetuated by falsifying or altering documents, embezzling funds, omitting the effects of transactions, recording nonexistent transactions, and/or incorrectly using accounting policies and procedures.

Internal audit: For the MFI's use only, an audit performed by an MFI employee, volunteer, appointed committee, or outside professional auditor to help determine the effectiveness of the internal control structure, promote operational efficiencies, safeguard the MFI's assets, and ensure that the MFI is producing accurate and reliable information. These reports discuss operational areas and recommend improvements in internal controls.

Internal controls: Policies and procedures designed to minimize and monitor operational risks, in particular the risks of fraud and mismanagement.

Mismanagement: Bad or improper management.

Reconciliation: The process used to identify the differences between the subsidiary ledger balance (for example, bank statement, investment statement, and asset depreciation schedule) and the month-end balance stated in the MFI's general ledger.

Signatories: People who sign a document.

- How an MFI should enhance the security of its funds and other physical assets through its culture and its operational policies and procedures;
- How internal controls should be selected, and which ones are relevant for all MFIs that mobilize deposits; and
- Additional controls for institutions that increase their risk of fraud and errors by the way that they deliver services to small or rural depositors.

The appendices illustrate systems and tools that help MFIs safeguard their funds.

11.1 FRAUD AND ERRORS

In deposit mobilization fraud is usually perpetrated by falsifying or altering documents, not recording transactions, recording nonexistent transactions, or incorrectly using accounting policies and procedures. Regardless of the form fraud takes, the problem is clear: it threatens the savings of the poor, undermines the client's trust in the MFI, and can put the long-term future of the MFI at risk.

Although errors and fraud can look alike, errors are unintentional. Furthermore, they usually involve small amounts of money. A certain number of errors is inevitable. Indeed, although the goal of internal controls regarding fraud is to eliminate it, the goal regarding errors is to detect and correct them.

Although individual errors usually do not represent a large amount of funds, their cumulative total and the time needed to correct them can be significant. Even more important, where the error rate is high, staff know that they can easily disguise fraud as error. When confronted with a high error rate, branch managers might have to spend much time checking passbooks and fixing problems that would be better spent spot checking good clients and larger clients, activities critical for preventing fraud.

A culture that permits errors is a culture that invites fraud. Therefore, internal controls to detect errors, though costly to implement, should ultimately provide a net benefit to the institution. MFIs should establish expectations and procedures from the outset for sound collection and reporting. They should use training, policies, and incentives not only to prevent fraud but also to create a relatively error-free environment.

11.2 THE INTERNAL CONTROL ENVIRONMENT

Managing risk must be an integral part of an MFI's organizational culture and operations at all levels. Internal controls should constitute a system of checks and balances that hold individuals responsible for their actions. To be effective, these checks and balances should be supported by:

- A culture that strongly discourages fraud and mismanagement;
- Clear and concise *written* policies and procedures; job descriptions that clearly allocate responsibilities and accountabilities;
- Accepted, transparent accounting practices;
- An adequate MIS that provides accurate and timely information;
- Effective internal supervision, including routine spot checking; and
- Internal audit functions performed by a qualified individual(s) who reports to a strong board of directors or other independent management body.

Each of these items is discussed below.

External audits and government supervision also contribute to the control environment by identifying errors and irregularities. However, because the focus of their contacts is not fraud, neither external audits nor supervision can be relied on to uncover the problems in systems and operations that could lead to financial loss or to the reporting of false information. This is the role of internal controls.

11.2.1 Institutional Culture

First and foremost, to control the risks of fraud and mismanagement, the MFI's leadership must establish a culture that promotes control, honesty, and proper management. Management must model integrity and transparency and demonstrate with words and actions that support for internal controls, discouragement of errors, and intolerance of fraud are essential institutional values (see Box 11–2).

Leadership can promote these values with the following policies:

Severe consequences for fraud and for consistently high error rates: Penalties or punishments should be written, conveyed verbally, and strictly enforced. Even small acts of fraud should meet with "swift and permanent action." Publicizing these actions through memos or staff newsletters will clearly signal to staff that fraud is not tolerated.[1] Punishments for high error rates should be applied fairly and should reflect the severity of the errors or omissions. Error rates greater than 5 percent should be considered excessive. Staff should be informed that if data is not recorded in the passbooks and/or collection sheets, then the staff person will be presumed negligent, at the least, and at the worst, guilty of fraud until the contrary is proven (see Appendix 11.7).

Competitive salaries that reduce the motivation to commit fraud and *performance-based incentives* that motivate high productivity and low error rates: Staff should be expected and motivated to complete all of their tasks quickly and without error. BURO, Tangail branch managers receives their salary only if their branch portfolio management report, progress report, and financial statements are correct and complete by the seventh of the next month. Nirdhan Bank checks all passbooks regularly and fines its credit officers for mistakes. Teba Bank gives a bonus for an error-free month.

Box 11–2. A Culture of Internal Control: ASA

When it comes to internal controls, few MFIs are as vigilant as ASA. ASA serves 2 million members during weekly group meetings. Except at its central office, it uses a manual MIS. ASA's institutional culture is unique. Its management is passionate about simplicity, standardization, internal controls, and routine auditing. This commitment can be seen throughout its operations:

Routine auditing by supervisors: Nearly every position in ASA is involved in some form of auditing. All employees audit the transactions of those immediately below them through random spot checks. For example, area managers, who supervise the branch managers, spend much of their time visiting branches and groups to perform audit functions. They check all calculations and compare the totals to those in each branch's monthly report. They also check that credit officers made the entries. Finally, they verify that the proper signature is next to each entry and total. Area managers and their supervisors use an internal control document, the *monitoring register*, that serves as an audit work plan.

Passbook verification: The branch manager visits two groups a day to observe the credit officer and perform surprise passbook verifications. In this way the branch manager verifies all members' accounts within a two-month period. If the system is effective, any fraud at the credit officer/member level should be discovered within that period. The groups to be verified are chosen at random by the branch managers. The branch manager uses an audit form to record differences between the passbooks and the credit officer register and immediately investigates all differences. The branch manager also verbally confirms each transaction with each client. Area managers also verify the records of one group in each branch each week; thus, they verify the passbooks of all groups in their areas every nine months.

Simplicity and transparency: ASA's systems and record keeping are transparent and simple. Policies like restricting member deposits or withdrawals to multiples of five *taka* reduce credit-officer errors. Posting visibly in the branch the groups' meeting locations, meeting times, and credit officers ensures that the branch manager always knows where each credit officer is and can visit his or her groups at random.

Standardization: Every policy and procedure in ASA is prescribed, standardized, and written. For this reason, exceptions are easy to catch.

Internal audits: ASA's internal audit office reviews the area and division-manager reports. Each of its five members spends at least fifteen days a month auditing the branches on site.

Rotation of duties: Credit officers work with the same member group for only one year and in a particular branch no longer than three years.

Security deposits: New credit officers must make a US$9 security deposit for which they receive interest. Losses due to their errors or fraud are deducted from this security deposit.

Staff training that emphasizes the organization's values: These values include zero tolerance for fraud, dishonesty, corruption, and bribery; that the integrity of records is paramount and how errors hurt the institution and its clients; and the reasoning behind specific internal controls. Where fraud or bribery is a norm, training must clarify that what is tolerated "out there" is not tolerated "in here." During training the MFI might make an example of employees who have committed fraud.[2] Regarding errors, staff must understand the importance of clear handwriting, correct arithmetic, the use of documents in their correct numbered order, and the like.

Encouragement of staff reporting of suspected fraud: Reporting fraud must be easy, costless, and, if necessary, anonymous.[3] This is important because fraud is usually detected by co-workers rather than auditors.

Visible strict implementation of an internal controls system: This system should be easily understood and cover all areas.

11.2.2 Clear Written Policies, Procedures, and Job Descriptions

The potential for fraud and error is lessened by procedures that are simple, clear, and communicated effectively to employees and clients. Regardless of an MFI's size, written policies and procedures are imperative. Policies, procedures, and job descriptions let all employees know what is expected of them, how they should perform their job, and what the consequences are if they do not perform as required.

Policies and procedures should be included in one or more regularly updated *operations manuals*. The manuals should include the disciplinary actions that can be taken against employees, detailed guidance on how to undertake transactions and handle exceptions,[4] and a job description for each position that clearly defines its duties (see Appendices 11.7 and 11.6) and that can serve as the basis for *written performance reviews*. Job descriptions should detail supervisory duties, how the internal audit will be managed, and which individuals are responsible for responding to uncontrolled risks and for implementing, monitoring, and evaluating the effectiveness of internal controls.[5]

The MFI should require employees to review all policies that pertain to their position during initial job training and on an annual basis. Manuals should also be accessible to employees at all times, and knowledge of their contents should be considered part of the performance reviews of employees.

11.2.3 Effective Internal Supervision

Supervisors should be strong, well trained, and detail oriented. All supervisors should routinely check whether their staff adhere to policies and procedures. Supervisors should also regularly spot check operations for errors and fraud. A key to the supervision of savings mobilization is a *narrow control span;* that is, one manager should supervise only a small number of staff. The precise number will depend, in part, on how many clients each staff member manages, but a rule of thumb is one supervisor to five to ten employees. Furthermore, each level of management should be clearly accountable for operations at the next level closer to the field.

11.2.4 Transparent Adequate Accounting and MIS

The MFI should use transparent accounting practices that are accepted by accounting professionals within the country and that provide for full and fair disclosure of assets and their values. The MIS should provide timely, accurate, and useful data to all employees. The system should not overwhelm staff with data. Instead, it should focus their attention on a few key indicators. A transparent MIS is crucial to deter and detect fraud.

11.2.5 Routine Internal Audit Functions

MFIs should develop an annual internal audit plan.[6] Current risks and previous audit findings should determine how many branches to visit, which branches must be included, the overall focus of the audits, and the extent of the audit for each branch.[7] Internal audits should systematically:

- appraise the effectiveness of the MFI's internal controls,
- confirm that financial and operating information is correct,
- check that the computer systems are secure and sound,
- check that MFI policies and government regulations are followed, and
- identify and alert management to uncontrolled risks.[8]

Appendices 11.2 and 11.3 provide a list of steps for an internal audit and a simple internal audit checklist. The audit should focus on headquarters reporting and branch operations. The internal auditor should also visit clients, another common way that MFIs uncover fraud.[9]

For MFIs with fewer than one hundred employees, employing an internal auditor may not be cost effective.[10] Instead, internal auditing may be performed by another employee, a paid external party, or a trustworthy volunteer. In any case the auditor must have enough "authority and administrative autonomy to execute his or her control duties." As well as reporting the results and recommendations to management, the auditor should periodically report directly to the board—or another management body that is independent of daily operations—and should always have access to them.[11]

Within the organizational structure the internal auditor should never report to management, as there are times when an audit might uncover fraud, errors, or mistakes made by management. If the internal auditor were to report these types of findings to management, management would be tempted to hide the findings and recommendations. If the internal auditor reports directly to an independent body not involved in daily operations, then the findings and recommendation are more likely to be properly addressed.

For an internal audit to be useful, the MFI must have a strong board that understands what strategic decisions to make when it receives the audit results. A weak board of directors weakens the MFI's ability to have strong internal controls.

11.3 INTERNAL CONTROLS

Internal controls are policies and procedures specifically designed to minimize and monitor operational risks, in particular the risks of fraud and mismanagement. The primary objectives of internal controls are to:

- confirm the efficiency and effectiveness of the operations;
- ensure that financial and management information are reliable and complete;
- deter and detect fraud, errors, and theft; and
- comply with applicable laws and regulations.[12]

There are three types of internal controls. *Operational or administrative controls* are policies and procedures that establish lines of authority and responsibility, segregate the operating and recording functions, and provide for the hiring of qualified individuals. They are a managerial responsibility that directly affects the MFI's success. *Physical controls* are measures that physically safeguard the MFI's assets and records against theft, problems with the information system, or calamities such as a fire. *Accounting controls* include the organizational plan, procedures, and records needed to safeguard the assets and the reliability of financial records. Their purpose is to provide reasonable assurance that staff carries out transactions according to management's authorization and records transactions to permit preparation of financial statements according to local accounting standards.

This section describes the operational, physical, and accounting controls that should be implemented by all MFIs and discusses some additional controls, the implementation of which should depend on the individual MFI. Before doing this, it suggests guidelines for how an MFI should select what controls to implement. Appendix 11.1 provides a checklist for senior management of recommended internal controls.

11.3.1 Selecting Cost-effective Controls

The internal controls that are appropriate to a particular MFI will depend on the risks facing it, the costs and benefits of addressing them, and the MFI's capacity to implement controls. To select controls, management should first identify potential areas of risk. When considering whether to institute particular controls, managers should weigh the cost of instituting each control against the potential loss from not doing so and then choose the most cost-effective controls. When considering cost effectiveness, managers should keep in mind that when fraud and mismanagement are unchecked, they grow quickly.[13] For any particular MFI, however, not all possible controls are cost effective. It will make sense for some risks to be managed through the internal audit process. For example, internal auditing can be used to spot check transactions in small MFIs without enough employees to segregate the duties within the daily processes.

What controls are appropriate will also hinge on how the MFI chooses to balance the security, convenience, and attractiveness of services. For example, limiting the amount of cash held in a satellite office or in the field may increase security but may decrease convenience for clients who must either wait or travel to a main office to withdraw funds.

Management must choose the MFI's internal controls, but an outside expert may be able to identify control weaknesses more objectively than an insider. In particular, a technology expert may be best suited to improving information-technology controls. Audits, feedback from staff and clients, external auditors, and incidents of fraud and mismanagement can also provide important feedback on whether existing or proposed controls are sufficient and appropriate.[14]

11.3.2 Operational Controls

The following internal controls should be built into the daily operations of any MFI no matter what its size and sophistication:

Board approval and monitoring of information. In addition to using the policies below to establish control, the board establishes control and direction through the annual budget and the longer-term business plan that it is a part of developing, approving, and reviewing on a periodic basis. The board should request, at least monthly, the following reports to monitor the financial condition of the MFI: balance sheet, income statement, investment report, liquidity analysis, delinquent-loan report, and comparison of actual results to budgeted figures.

Rotation of duties of all employees that handle client transactions. Rotation of duties refers to temporarily shifting the job duties of a permanent employee to another staff person. The objective is to uncover fraud. Without control over their job duties, employees will be unable to hide their fraudulent activities. Rotating duties also helps to cross train employees in others' jobs. The cross-trained employee can substitute when employees take vacations, are absent, or are rotated. Duties should always be rotated on a surprise basis so that employees do not have the opportunity to hide their fraudulent activities. *Compulsory vacations* serve the same purpose as rotating duties except that they are not conducted on a surprise basis.

Segregation of duties or *dual control* refers to the separation of transaction responsibilities between at least two employees. Ideally, one employee should originate the transaction, another employee should record it, and a third should audit or confirm its authenticity and correctness. One employee should not have control over the entire process as fraud can go undiscovered for a very long time, causing a large financial loss to the MFI and a loss in client trust. For example, a person handling cash should not post to the accounting records, a loan officer should not disburse loan proceeds for loans he or she approves, and those having authority to sign checks should not reconcile bank accounts. In small, thinly staffed institutions, this may not be possible. At a minimum, at least one of the steps must be performed by a different individual. *Most small MFIs have a serious lapse of internal controls because they cannot afford to hire several employees in the same functional area.* This can be resolved by having supervisors confirm the correctness of transactions as soon as possible and by using knowledgeable clients and trustworthy volunteers to fill this role (see Section 11.4).

Establishing limits on expenditures. Expenses can be controlled by:

- authorizing only expenses that are included in the budget, requiring a supervisor's approval prior to making any purchase over a set amount, and requiring board of director approval for purchases over a set higher amount;
- requiring joint signatures for all expense checks; and
- requiring managers to get several quotes for any expense over a certain amount.

Signature requirements for who can sign and how many signatories are needed are normally established in written policy for any transaction above a predetermined amount. An MFI can have one set amount that management is not allowed to exceed without approval from a higher authority, or there may be expenditure limits based on the various types of operating expenses. Requiring two signatories to check cash counts also can help with accuracy.[15]

11.3.3 Physical Controls

Regardless of their size and operating environment, all MFIs should:

- *set limits on how much cash* any individual staff person and any branch are permitted to hold;
- *ensure cashier control* by requiring cashiers to balance the contents of their cash drawers with the general ledger daily. Additionally, cashiers should not be allowed to leave the MFI until the drawer balances or the difference has been paid by the cashier or recorded as income or expense;
- *require documentation of all transactions by and between cashiers with a receipt* and require immediate verification under dual control of cash upon receipt and when cashiers buy or sell funds to the safe or another cashier;

- *restrict access to offices and assets* and lock doors and windows;
- *conduct a periodic physical inventory of assets* such as registers and supplies; and
- *conduct cash counts* whereby branch managers check actual cash against branch records daily and supervisors check the same during frequent surprise visits.

Other typical safeguards include safes that can only be opened by two people with different keys or combinations, burglar alarms, fire extinguishers, the insurance of deposits against theft or disaster, and security guards who might be uniformed, armed, accompanied by a watchdog, or connected by radio to the police station. To manage costs, a guard might double as a janitor. If possible, MFIs should regularly back up computer databases, make duplicate copies of MISs, and store the copies off-site.

11.3.4 Accounting Controls

Accounting controls may differ with the size and complexity of the MFI. The following accounting controls, however, should assist any MFI:

Internal reports need to be timely, easy to understand, and concise, they should review and summarize the key areas of operations. Reports that meet these standards assist management to identify problematic operational areas and negative trends.

Recording of accounting transactions complies with local accounting law and is consistent from one period to the next.

All instruments are sequentially numbered, including checks, cash-receipt vouchers, journal vouchers, certificates of deposit, and loan notes. All unused, prenumbered instruments are kept under dual control.

An adequate audit trail makes it possible to trace each transaction from its inception to its completion (see Appendices 11.3 and 11.4). To provide this:

- If a manual system is used, all accounting entries must be written clearly, contain the date and the initials of the individual who performed the transaction, and describe the transaction in detail;
- Each step of the transaction, from the source document (such as the client deposit or withdrawal receipt) to the final entry in the general ledger must be documented clearly in writing;
- Individuals handling cash must prepare a detailed report that shows all daily transactions and provides space to calculate that they are in balance;

- Bank reconciliations should be timely and should clearly identify all items, the amounts, and the date of the transactions;
- The records should be prepared using a pen, as should any corrections made; if the system is computerized, there should be a record or report of the corrections made; and
- Books and records should be kept current and closed at the end of each accounting period.

A secure MIS. The MIS identifies the individual making the transaction, limits the number of employees who have access to records, and limits the types of transactions they can make. If the system is automated, confidential passwords are used and are routinely changed at least every six months. The passwords of individual staff are disabled while they are on vacation. *If possible, transactions are posted daily* to the accounting system. Keeping each day's activities separate and distinct from another day's makes it easier to find errors. (See Box 11–3.)

Reconciliations. Managers regularly confirm that general ledger totals are reconciled with bank statements or other subsidiary ledgers. A bank reconciliation identifies the differences between the bank-account balance per the bank and the MFI's month-end balance stated in its general ledger. Periodically the reconciling entries are checked to ensure that they are truly outstanding and that funds have not been misappropriated. Any reconciling entries that do not clear in a timely manner (thirty days or less) should be researched to ensure that the items are valid.

Box 11–3. Controlling the Interface between Manual and Computerized MIS

A computerized MIS can generate accurate information efficiently and quickly. However, computers do not magically eliminate field-based error and fraud. A number of internal control measures can help MFIs that use both a manual and a computerized information system or that use one computerized system for their accounting and another for their client's loans and savings accounts:

- Check and correct data prior to entering it into the computer system.
- Use a computer system with adequate checks and balances. A computerized financial information system can provide quick and inexpensive reports to check balances and totals.
- If the accounting and deposit/portfolio management system are not linked, compare and reconcile the two systems at least monthly.
- Perform a daily reconciliation to ensure that the net value of all transactions entered in the database for the day is equal to the total cash amounts remitted to the branch office for that day.

11.4 INTERNAL CONTROLS WHEN SERVING SMALL AND RURAL DEPOSITORS

Serving small or rural depositors can raise three additional internal control challenges. First, because small and rural depositors may not be willing to travel to a branch, many MFIs that serve these markets provide services in the field. This means that staff must carry cash outside the office, which requires additional physical controls. Second, to manage the costs of serving very small or remote depositors in their communities, some institutions deploy individuals rather than teams to handle transactions with clients. Allowing cash and transactions to be handled by just one person creates opportunities for fraud and errors, which MFIs must guard against with additional controls and policies. Finally, small community-based organizations whose managers have little education often are the only institutions that can afford to serve remote areas. These organizations pose particular culture, capacity, and security challenges for internal controls that must be met with training, appropriate systems, and alternative physical controls.

11.4.1 Managing the Risk of Field-based Transactions: Physical Safeguards

Making transactions outside the office increases the risk of theft, particularly in conflict and post-conflict environments. MFIs reduce the risk of loss due to theft by:

- varying the staff members' schedules or routes for carrying money and never communicating these to clients or staff who are not directly involved in the transfer;[16]
- assuring that staff do not wear identifying clothes, such as a uniform or t-shirt, or expensive items, such as jewelry;
- having staff travel at safer times of day;
- having clients accompany staff and having them walk far enough apart that one can get help if the other is accosted;
- training staff to be vigilant about their environment as they walk and to contact the appropriate authority if they see evidence of a problem;
- taking out insurance for theft from staff, and
- minimizing the amount of cash that field staff must carry.[17]

MFIs minimize cash held by staff in a number of ways. ASA minimizes cash held by carefully ordering which groups field agents visit when. The agent might first visit a net-savings group and then a net-borrowing one. Excess cash from the first group is used to fund loan disbursements for the second.[18] At *Safe*Save collectors are given a personal locker to which they have the only key, so that they rarely need to hold more than US$50 to US$100 when in the field.

The Small Farmers Cooperative Limited in Kumroj, Nepal, is vulnerable to attacks by Maoists. To protect its funds, the SFCL stores a minimum amount of cash and documents in the office. Because the closest bank branch is not convenient to Kumroj, managers distribute the cooperative's ledgers and cash on hand to board members. Finally, it stores excess cash at the closest bank branch. The cooperative also insures its members' savings up to approximately US$2,700.

11.4.2 Managing the Risk of Collection by Individuals: Some Alternative Controls

When a single staff person both handles the cash and records the transaction, he or she can more easily commit errors or fraud. The point of greatest vulnerability is when the staff person records the transaction on the MFI's collection sheet and in the client's passbook. MFIs compensate for the lack of standard dual control with a number of procedures and policies.

Employee Identification and Client Vigilance

One way that collectors misappropriate funds is by continuing to collect deposits for their own benefit after they have quit or been fired. To guard against this, the MFI must:

- Require collectors to wear an identification badge whenever they are with clients, which they must return immediately when they terminate their employment (see Appendix 11.6), and
- Instruct clients to transact business only during regular hours with someone who has a proper identification badge.

Transparency and Client Vigilance

Misrecording a transaction in the passbook is a simple and very common way for an employee to commit fraud. Misrecording can also be a result of carelessness. To commit fraud, an employee simply records the same incorrect amount in the passbook and on the collection sheet—a smaller deposit than the employee actually received or a larger withdrawal than he or she actually dispensed—and pockets the difference. Alternatively, the employee can not record a transaction at all or can record the wrong type of transaction. This type of fraud or mistake can only be caught by the client.

To prevent and detect misrecording, MFIs should require employees to work with one client at a time, record transactions in pen immediately, read aloud the amount and type of transaction(s) and the new passbook balance, and have customers initial the passbook and transaction sheet. The MFI then relies on clients to serve as the dual control by training them to:

- expect to hear, check, and sign for the amount and type of transaction(s) and the new passbook balance—as well as the date—while still in the presence of the employee,
- demand an official, pre-numbered receipt whenever money changes hands,[19] and
- contact the branch manager to voice complaints and concerns.[20]

Here and with employee identification, the key is that the MFI imposes requirements on employees and then trains clients to use these requirements to check for fraud. The combination of policies and client training enables clients to serve as the dual control. This can work only if the MFI convinces clients to be vigilant and outspoken.

Passbook Verification

Employees can also commit fraud by recording a different amount or type of transaction in the passbook than on the collection sheet or recording the transaction on the transaction sheet under the wrong person's account. Misrecording can also be a mistake. In fact, making mistakes—reversing the digits in a number, recording the wrong type of transaction, attributing a transaction to the wrong account, dropping a zero or calculating incorrectly[21]—is easy, particularly when an employee is handling transactions from many clients at once and may not perceive errors as a problem.

One effective method to discover this type of fraud or error is to check client passbooks. The objective is to verify that the client's passbook balance is equal to the balance on record at the financial institution. *Passbook verification* should also sample selected transactions and their dates to check that they are authentic and correct.

A branch manager or supervisor should personally check all transactions in each passbook every two to three months (see Box 11–4 and Appendix 11.5). Discrepancies between passbooks and office records should be systematically noted and immediately investigated. The branch manager's work should also be checked. To help guard against collusion between the employee and the branch manager, the MFI can hold branch managers liable for any discrepancies that they do not detect.

Passbook verification should be carried out on a surprise basis. Staff should not be given an opportunity to manipulate the balances in order to hide fraud. For this reason, the branch manager should collect the passbooks directly from the clients, appoint a third party to pick up their passbooks, or visit the clients to perform the verification.

---

*Box 11–4. Field-based Collection and Internal Controls:
In Their Own Words*

"We never have problems [of fraud] at the level of the office. The problems are always at the level of the passbook to collection sheet. . . . You can catch fraud [by verifying passbooks], but you cannot prevent it. We will always catch fraud within two to three months. But, a lot can happen in two to three months."

—Mohammed Azim Hossain, head of Finance and MIS, ASA

"Assuring that the MFI's office and field records agree is not enough to prevent fraud. Fieldworkers can trick unsuspecting or illiterate clients or simply delay the submission of deposits and payments to the office. The only way to prevent this behavior is to conduct unannounced 'spot checks' of client accounts, which are chosen at random. Once assigned, these checks must be completed, even at great effort. A spot-checking program is expensive but essential."

—Mark Staehle, technical advisor, *Safe*Save

Spot Checking through Client Visits

Clients selected should be chosen at random for visits; "good" clients should be checked as often as "bad" clients. The manager should:

- discuss the client's experience with the MFI, with special attention to the employee's behavior and adherence to policies such as transaction recording, reading aloud of balances, and frequency of visits.
- verify that the amounts, dates, and types of transactions in the passbook match those in the records from the office. Different dates in the passbooks and collection sheets may indicate fraud.
- confirm with the client that he or she actually made the withdrawals on record.
- thank the client and explain that the spot check is a procedure intended to maintain reliability and to protect his or her money.[22]

Stamps for Cash

A simple, effective accounting control to improve the likelihood that the employees record the proper amount and that illiterate clients can detect fraud is the stamp system developed by Self-Help Development Foundation in Zimbabwe. The employee goes out in the morning with a certain number of stamps and must return at the end of the afternoon with the remaining stamps and the cash equivalent to the difference, which must match the total deposits recorded on the collection sheet. Rather than recording the amount of a deposit, the employee applies stamps to the passbook. Deposits therefore must be made in increments equal to the amount of a single stamp. When savings are withdrawn, the stamps get canceled with a mark.

Staff Security Deposits

Many MFIs require staff to guarantee their good performance with a security deposit. If fraud is discovered, the MFI deducts the amount stolen from the security deposit and severely sanctions or terminates the employment of the field staff. This combination of security deposit and severe consequences pressures field staff to perform well and discourages low-level fraud.

Typically, the MFI requires employees to make a one-time security deposit when they are hired. For example, ASA requires a one-time security deposit of US$88 from new hires and pays a market rate of interest on the funds. Alternatively, an MFI might also require ongoing deposits. For example, *Safe*Save staff must deposit US$16 when they join, and a minimum of US$1.60 per month thereafter. They may elect to deposit up to US$8 per month. This money is put into a special savings account that earns 12 percent interest, from which staff may not withdraw, but against which senior staff may borrow up to 70 percent (without cost). The account serves as a benefit to the employee as well as a security deposit to protect *Safe*Save. When an employee resigns or is terminated from *Safe*Save employment, *Safe*Save retains the security deposit for up to three months, until the general manager is sure that the employee did not make errors or commit fraud. Staff members who give one month's notice can have their security deposit the day they depart.

11.4.3 Small Community-based Organizations: Training and Physical Controls

Small community-based organizations may face three particular challenges in relation to internal controls. First, these institutions typically rely solely on staff members and/or a management committee comprising individuals who may have just a few years of schooling or may not be numerate. In this context, training the management committee in numeracy with a specific focus on internal control procedures is a costly but vital investment in overall safety. Committee members and staff must understand the rationale for internal controls and why they must be strictly applied. Furthermore, records must be very simple yet reliable enough to prepare budgets and financial statements and to generate the indicators needed to monitor performance (see Box 11.5 and Appendix 11.4).

Second, because cooperatives are built on the principle of solidarity, members often do not consider the possibility of fraud. Training clients to be vigilant can be particularly important. For example, it is common for a trusting member to chat and look around rather than watching carefully as a familiar collector opens the lockbox and counts and records its contents.

Box 11–5. Internal Controls in the CVECAs, Mali

The CVECAs in rural Mali are autonomous community associations managed by people with little schooling. The CVECAs are loosely federated village banks open a few hours a week staffed by a cashier. The CVECAs safeguard deposits through the following written policies and procedures:

Joint custody: The two CVECA employees, the cashier and the controller, are jointly responsible for managing transactions and bookkeeping. They are chosen by the villagers based on their integrity and numeracy. The controller is trained in internal control procedures. At the end of each banking day, the controller closes the journal, verifies procedures such as customer signatures, calculates the total accounts and balance, and checks that the theoretical balance corresponds to the actual balance and cash in hand.

Dual control: Each time the bank opens, a member of the management committee verifies the accounting journal, cash settlements, and cash in hand. At the end of the day a committee member compares the loan ledger with cash disbursements. Committee members are provided with training in numeracy with a specific focus on their roles.

Audits: A controller from a neighboring CVECA serves as an *internal auditor*, verifying the bank's accounts quarterly. The CVECA Federation compiles a list of capable CVECA controllers. One of these must approve the CVECA in order for it to be refinanced through the Federation. Each CVECA also has a contract with the Service Commun, a technical-assistance provider that primarily serves the CVECAs. The Service Commun performs mid-year, end-year, and unannounced *external audits*, including passbook verification.

Despite these controls, the CVECAs encountered operational problems when they started managing larger deposits and loans from outside their villages. In response, the French NGO CIDR is instituting a training-and-certification program in Mali for managers of community-based financial institutions.

—Renée Chao-Béroff

Finally, some community-based organizations—particularly informal groups such as self-help groups—do not have a secure office where they can store funds. These organizations can safeguard their funds by:

- *Choosing carefully who holds the funds between meetings or after office hours:* Organizations often find that funds are kept most reliably by a respected chairperson or treasurer, who is wealthy enough to resist misusing the funds.

- *Storing funds in a locked box that can be opened only with two different keys:* At the end of the meeting the keys and box are distributed to three different people. Members take turns without making it generally known who has them. Key holders are recorded in a register so that the persons responsible for the keys at any point in time can be determined. At the start

of the next meeting the box is opened in public, the money is counted, and the total is checked against the record.
- *Storing funds in a bank:* Excess funds might be regularly deposited in a bank or other financial institution. A member other than the signatories to the transaction should keep the passbook.

11.5 SUMMARY

The importance of safeguarding clients' savings deposits cannot be stressed enough. Effective internal controls and an internal control environment that reinforces these are the keys to keeping deposits secure. What internal controls are appropriate will depend on the risks within the MFI, how able it is to implement controls, and how it chooses to balance security and convenience of services. Management must recognize that written policies and procedures are useless unless the staff understands and implements them. Finally, a culture that prioritizes security and integrity from top to bottom is crucial.

APPENDIX 11.1 INTERNAL CONTROL CHECKLIST
FOR SENIOR MANAGEMENT

The questions below summarize the internal controls that any MFI that uses pass-books to record savings transactions should have. If all of the questions can be answered in the affirmative, the internal control environment would be accept-able for most MFIs.

Note: Tellers process clients' deposits and withdrawals. *Cashiers* handle the cash during transactions. In many thinly staffed organizations, the teller and cashier are one person. Similarly, in field-based services, a *collector* typically serves both as teller and cashier.

Client Passbooks

1. Are clients required to present their passbook in order to deposit or with-draw funds?
2. Are the client transactions recorded immediately in the passbooks?
3. Is it easy to identify the passbook owner through the use of a photo or signature?
4. Does the passbook identify the account by an account number specific to the client or by a national identification number?
5. Is the passbook owner the only person who is allowed to withdraw from the account?
6. Does the passbook include the following information: date of transaction, amount of deposit, amount of withdrawal, current balance, and signature of the staff member performing the transaction?
7. Are the clients instructed not to transfer the passbook under any circum-stances?

Client Passbook Transactions

1. Does the client review the transaction information and the current balance recorded in the passbook in the presence of the teller immediately after each transaction?
2. Does the teller read aloud to the client the transaction(s) made for the day and the current passbook balance(s)?
3. Does the teller initial each transaction?
4. If a passbook is not used, are withdrawal transactions initiated by the client with a withdrawal form or receipt?
5. Are the withdrawal forms at least in duplicate?
6. Does the client retain one copy of the withdrawal form and the teller the other, which is kept by the branch office with the collection sheet?
6. Does the teller record each client transaction immediately (in the passbook and on the collection sheet), and does the teller complete one transaction prior to starting another?

7. Does the teller verify (check) that the addition and subtraction is correct before beginning the next transaction?
8. Are clients encouraged to report any passbook discrepancies to someone other than the teller?
9. If the financial institution is using mobile collectors, does the institution alert the members immediately after a collector has quit or been terminated?
10. Are tellers expected to perform their job with a low error rate (for example, an error rate of less than 5 percent of total transactions)?
11. Is the teller's pay partially based on his or her level of errors?
12. Are maximums established for the amount of cash that a cashier may have under his or her control or for the amount of cash a collector can physically carry?
13. Is this amount reasonable?
14. Does the maximum amount sufficiently limit the risk of loss to the MFI?

Client Passbook Verifications

1. Are verifications performed frequently enough to find errors and fraud so that the clients and the financial institution are not negatively affected by the actions of the employees? Are client passbook verifications performed on a surprise basis?
2. Is the verification performed by someone other than the individual who is responsible for recording the transactions in the passbooks?
3. Is access to the passbook limited to the client and the individual performing the verification?
4. Does the financial institution have a form or a procedure that is used to document any differences between the passbooks and collection sheets?
5. Are the differences researched and corrected immediately?
6. Do supervisors track the passbook errors made by each employee? Are cumulative totals kept of the number and amount of the errors made by each employee?
7. Are the employees held financially responsible for any errors or discrepancies in their clients' passbooks that result in a loss to the MFI?

Cash

1. Do all individuals handling cash have sole access to the cash for which they are responsible?
2. Are the individuals handling cash required to balance the actual amount held with the official records daily?
3. Are cash counts of individuals responsible for cash performed on a periodic but surprise basis?
4. Are deposits made to the bank frequently in order as to reduce the amount of cash kept on the premises?

5. Does someone who is not involved in cash functions prepare the reconciliation of the bank account?
6. Is there a procedure to ensure that the bank account is reconciled on a timely basis each month?
7. Is a policy in place that states that all differences between the bank balance and the institution's cash balance are to be researched and corrected immediately?
8. Is signing blank checks against the institution's policy?
9. Are there levels of authority for signing checks? (For example, any check for an amount above US$300 must be signed by two individuals.)

Record Keeping

1. Are employees required to post records daily in order to maintain each day's work separate and distinct from another day's work?
2. Are written, independent subsidiary records kept for each general ledger account?
3. Are the subsidiary records (such as savings and loan ledgers, bank and investment statements, and fixed asset depreciation records) balanced with the respective general ledger accounts monthly?
4. Does the MIS provide internal reports (such as loan-delinquency reports, dormant savings accounts, and negative savings accounts)?
5. If so, are these reports reviewed by an individual not responsible for making the initial transactions?
6. Does the MFI use accounting practices that are prescribed by accepted accounting principles to record all transactions?
7. Does the MFI use all numbered instruments—such as checks, cash receipt and journal vouchers, or share certificates in sequential order?

Miscellaneous

1. If single employees serve as both teller and cashier, are these employees transferred or moved annually so that they do not consistently work with the same clients and have sole control over those clients' transactions?
2. Are client accounts in which there has been no activity for one year or more adequately supervised to prevent unauthorized access to these accounts?
3. Is a supervisor's approval required prior to making any purchase over a set amount?
4. Is a supervisor's approval required for any credit entries into staff accounts other than salaries and allowances?
5. Are at least two authorized signatures required on all expense checks?
6. Is management required to get at least two bids for any purchase over a set amount?
7. Is access to the office and valuable assets (such as a computer, vehicle, and copy machine) restricted to those employees or officials who require access to perform their duties?

8. Is a physical inventory performed no less than annually to ascertain that all of the MFI's assets are present and in working order?
9. Does the MIS identify individuals making transactions by their initials, name, or employee number?
10. Does the MIS limit the types of transactions that employees may make based on their job and user profile?
11. Does the MIS require the use of passwords to access the system?
12. Are these passwords confidential and not shared among the employees?
13. Are the passwords changed at least quarterly?
14. Are there written policies and procedures for the major operational areas such as lending, savings, investments, collection of delinquent loans, personnel?
15. Are there written position descriptions that define the duties, responsibilities, and performance standards for each position?
16. Does each employee receive a written performance appraisal annually?
17. Are there limits on how many individuals are authorized to (1) handle cash and valuables, (2) handle client records, and (3) sign checks or withdraw funds from the financial institution where the MFI deposits excess funds?
18. Is there dual control (two individuals with two keys, combinations, and/or passwords to gain access) or a modified system (due to a small number of employees) that limits employees so they cannot completely control any process or transaction?
19. Is there adequate segregation of duties (no individual can process a transaction from inception to completion) or a modified system (due to the limited number of employees) that limits employees so that they cannot completely control any process or transaction?
20. Are employees required to take at least five consecutive working days of vacation?
21. Does the MFI have a culture that does not tolerate excessive error or fraud?
22. Do MFI records and systems provide an audit trail or adequate paper documentation that allows for the tracing of each transaction from inception to completion?
23. Is there an adequate internal audit program in place?
24. Does the board or official body act upon the recommendations of the internal audit report?
25. Is there adequate follow-up to ensure that the recommendations are put into place by management?
26. Is an external audit performed on a reasonable basis (preferably annually) by a qualified independent party?
27. Does the board or official body act upon the recommendations of the external auditor?
28. Is there adequate follow-up to ensure that the external audit recommendations are put into place by management?

APPENDIX 11.2 A SIMPLE INTERNAL AUDIT CHECKLIST

(*Note:* This checklist does not contain items pertaining to loans)

Cash

❑ On the first day of the audit, arrive before the branch opens to witness the opening of the safe. Check that the amount of cash balances with the previous day's closing entry.

❑ Check that the amount of cash is within the MFI's policies for maximum cash held on site and minimum cash reserves.

❑ Ensure that only authorized employees have access to the cash in the safe by checking the cash transfer register and identifying who has the keys or security code.

❑ Check that all authorized employees have properly signed off on the cash count in the cash register.

❑ Check that all transactions were conducted according to policy and were recorded properly.

❑ Reconcile cash transfer vouchers against the general ledger (also known as the transactions register). Verify that transfers of cash to and from the safe all have supporting records, such as an official receipt or voucher, that can be reconciled to the general ledger, which, if automated, is printed from the computer. (This ensures that the cash transactions are properly recorded and no accounts have been manipulated.)

Savings Accounts

❑ Check that the dates and amounts of deposits and withdrawals in the field agent's records match those in the branch records.

❑ Check that the client's savings file contains all the documents it should.

❑ Check that the receipts in the client's file match the transactions register.

❑ Check that the client's signature matches the signature card.

❑ Check that interest is correctly posted to the account.

❑ For term savings accounts, check that the early withdrawal penalty was applied consistently and calculated correctly.

Transfers

❑ Review client transfers from one account to another.

❑ Review interoffice transfers by bringing records of funds transfers from other branches and reconciling those with the records at the branch being audited.

Computer Systems

- ❑ Check that employee passwords are regularly changed to maintain their secrecy.
- ❑ Check that employees log on and off properly and are not using a computer that was logged onto by another employee.
- ❑ Ensure that employees are not able to access information outside their scope of work.
- ❑ Check that employees ask clients to present proper identification before providing them with information on their account.
- ❑ Ensure that backup files are made frequently and that they are stored in a location that is relatively safe from physical damage.
- ❑ Check that the computers are scanned for viruses regularly and that the virus software is up to date.
- ❑ Using either a hand calculator or audit software, check that the computer makes accurate calculations and stores the information properly.

Fixed Assets

- ❑ Check that all major fixed assets exist.
- ❑ Check that their condition matches the reported level of use.
- ❑ Check that depreciation is properly recorded on the balance sheet.

Financial Statements

- ❑ Check that the amount of revenues and expenses are reasonable and within budget.
- ❑ Check receipts for purchases, check items, amounts, and dates.
- ❑ Ensure that purchases conform to policies. For example, check to see that large purchases have proper authorizations (signatures).
- ❑ Check that this period's opening balance matches last period's closing balance.
- ❑ Check the amounts of all assets, liabilities, and retained earnings recorded.
- ❑ Check allocation of incentive pay and whether it was paid in a timely fashion.

Client Records

- ❑ Check depositors' name, address, date, and amount for all transactions. Reconcile these with client receipts and transactions recorded in the branch records. (If they are not consistent, identify the source of the discrepancy and assess whether it resulted from unintentional error or intent to deceive by speaking with employees and clients.)

Group Management (where groups handle tasks that would otherwise be carried out by an employee)

- ❏ Attend a group meeting to see that the group exists, is cohesive, and can properly perform its roles.
- ❏ Check the group's records for proper calculations and accurate reporting. Assess whether discrepancies result from poor training, intent to deceive, or other reasons.
- ❏ Check whether the group adheres to the MFI's policies and the group's bylaws.[23]

APPENDIX 11.3 INTERNAL CONTROLS WITH DOORSTEP COLLECTION AND FLEXIBLE SERVICES

*Safe*Save collectors visit clients daily to accept payments and to provide withdrawals. Because clients decide on the spot whether to make a transaction and its size, sound internal controls are imperative. This flowchart indicates the controls that are part of the routine daily job duties of *Safe*Save's branch staff.

Figure 11–1. SafeSave.

During client visits, collectors perform transactions, enter them into client passbooks, and update the outstanding balance. They then enter the transaction information into the collection sheet. Collectors remit collection sheets and cash to the branch manager at the branch office at the end of the day.

The cash received by the branch manager must balance with the collection sheet totals. Upon receiving the cash and collection sheets, branch managers check to see that the cash balances with the collection sheet totals and issues the collector a pre-numbered Field Transaction Cash Voucher for the amount of cash received. This is the collectors' proof that they gave the branch manager funds equal to the total on their collection sheets. The branch manager retains a copy of the voucher and gives the collection sheets to the assistant manager for data entry.

The assistant manager checks the database balances against the passbook balances (as noted on the collection sheet) before entering the transaction data from the collection sheet into the Access database. Before any transaction is entered, all discrepancies must be corrected by the branch manager.

The assistant manager enters the totals from the field transaction cash voucher into *Money Manager.*

At the end of the day, the branch manager and assistant manager perform a reconciliation to ensure that the transactions entered in the database for the day are equal to the cash amounts remitted to the branch office. They generate the Statement of Daily Affairs that reconciles the net value of all transactions for the day with the total amounts remitted by the collectors.

At the end of the month, the branch manager generates the trial balance, balance sheet, and income statement. The balances on these reports should equal the State-ment of Daily Affairs generated by *Access.*

At the end of the month, the Branch Manager compares the end of the month Statement of Daily Affairs to the end of month trial balance, income statement, and balance sheet generated by Money Manager. The account balances should be equal.

APPENDIX 11.4 INTERNAL CONTROLS
IN A SMALL COMMUNITY-BASED COOPERATIVE

Community-based savings-and-credit cooperatives often are managed by village members without much education. They require simple, transparent systems such as the one below. These records are kept by well-known village women who own homes and farms in the community, and are elected by the members.

1. Members deposit money at monthly meetings of their cooperative.
2. The cashier counts the money and confirms the amount, writing the member's name, account number, and deposit amount in the *Cash Ledger for Deposits*. The accountant recounts the money and signs beside the member's name. The member signs to confirm that the information is correct.
3. The accountant records the deposit in the member's passbook and signs it. To confirm that the entry is correct, the member co-signs the passbook.
4. The accountant records the deposit in and signs the *Record of Transactions.*
5. The cashier adds up the total deposits recorded for the day in the *Cash Ledger for Deposits.* The treasurer counts the cash deposited and confirms that it matches the calculation recorded by the cashier.
6. If the totals match, the cashier completes a *Bank Transaction Record,* a record of member funds that will be deposited in the bank. The accountant co-signs after confirming the amount is correct. This record stays within the cooperative.
7. The accountant and cashier deposit the money in the bank. By signing a *Bank Transaction Record* that matches the amount of the deposit, the accountant, cashier, and bank manager confirm that the deposit amount is correct.
8. A copy of this record is returned to the cooperative. The total recorded in this deposit record must match the amount recorded in the *Bank Transaction Record,* in the *Cash Ledger for Deposits,* in the individual member passbooks, and in the *Record of Transactions.*
9. The accountant records the total deposits for the day in the *Accounting Records,* which again must match the above records.

To ensure transparency, all the records except the individual savings passbooks and the *Record of Transactions* are open to all members. Each member can cross reference her passbook with the transactions recorded in the *Bank Transaction Record* at the cooperative. Field staff regularly review these records, and an external auditor confirms their accuracy and completeness.

—Lloyd Hardy

APPENDIX 11.5 PASSBOOK VERIFICATION PROCEDURES AND VERIFICATION FORM

Step-by-step Procedures at One MFI

Using the computerized branch records, the branch manager prepares the *Client Balance Sheet,* which shows the balances of client accounts for the previous month. The branch manager compares the savings balances in the passbooks to those on the *Client Balance Sheet.* Those that match are considered verified—checked—and require no further work. For all others, the following must be done:

1. *Check the addition and subtraction in the passbook.* If there is no mistake in the arithmetic, go to step 2. If there is a mistake in the passbook,

- correct it and sign it.
- If the passbook now agrees with the *Client Balance Sheet,* then no further work is required.
- If the passbook still does not agree with the *Client Balance Sheet,* go to step 2.

2. *Determine if the passbook agrees with the* Collection Sheet. If it does, the mistake is in the computer, so go to step 4. If the passbook does not agree with the *Collection Sheet,* the mistake was made in the field. In this case the client must be visited and the collector, branch manager, and data processor must agree on the correct figure. If there is any doubt, the client will be favored.

- If, after this agreement, the passbook is changed, so that the passbook now agrees with the *Client Balance Sheet,* no further work is required.
- If, after this agreement, it is decided that there is a mistake in the *Collection Sheet,* do not correct the original *Collection Sheet.* Make an entry in the current day's *Collection Sheet.* At the same time, correct the cash collection by bringing more money from the field or returning money to the field, so that the cash record in the current *Collection Sheet* is correct. Return to the office, and go to step 3.

3. *Correct mistakes in the* Collection Sheet. (A mistake was found in the field in the original *Collection Sheet.* The mistake has been corrected by making an entry in the current day's *Collection Sheet,* and the amount of cash brought from the field today now agrees with today's *Collection Sheet.*)

- Now the data processor should enter today's *Collection Sheet* into the computer, under today's date, as usual. At the end of this month, the balances for that client will agree in all three documents: passbook, *Collection Sheet,* and next month's *Client Balance Sheet.*

- However, the date of a particular transaction may be different in the passbook than in the *Collection Sheet.* To avoid future confusion, make a note in these documents.

4. Correct mistakes in the computer. It was determined in the field that the passbook and the *Collection Sheet* agree, but the *Client Balance Sheet* disagrees. This means the mistake is in the computer and must be corrected. All corrections must be made in this month's file. Sometimes the correction will involve just one account. In some cases, however, the correction may involve two accounts (if the data processor entered an amount against the wrong account number). The branch manager must record all the computer corrections in a ledger.

BURO, Tangail Account Verification Form

Established in 1990, BURO, Tangail provides over 185,000 customers with credit and savings services through groups of up to forty members. BURO is a pioneer in the area of flexible community-based voluntary savings. At BURO, Tangail one of the branch manager's principal duties is account verification. The branch manager checks the passbooks of two or three groups each week, thus verifying all passbooks every six months. The passbook checking takes between five and nine hours weekly. For each group checked, the branch manager completes and signs the *Savings and Loan Passbook Verification Report* (see Table 11–1), noting differences between the passbook and register. He or she then follows up on all differences with the village development worker.

Upon signing and dating the verification form below, the branch manager becomes personally and solely responsible for any other discrepancies found during passbook verifications performed by other, more senior BURO, Tangail staff members. The area manager examines the passbooks on a sample basis. If discrepancies are found that result in a loss to the institution, the branch manager must reimburse BURO for these losses.

Table 11–1. BURO, Tangail Savings and Loan Passbook Verification Report

Branch:_____   Kendra #_____   Village development worker: _____   Verification date: _____

1. Account Number	2. Client Name	Savings			6. Cash in Hand (3-4)	Credit			10. Cash In Hand (7-8)	11. Village Development Worker Responses
		3. Passbook Balance	4. Collection Sheet Balance	5. Subsidiary Ledger Balance		7. Passbook Loan Balance	8. Collection Sheet Loan Balance	9. Subsidiary Ledger Loan Balance		
Totals	---									---

APPENDIX 11.6 JOB DESCRIPTION FOR SAVINGS COLLECTORS

The following procedures are the core of the collectors' duties to the client. They are not to be deviated from, despite the development of a close working relationship with the client. These basic daily procedures *must* be followed without exception by all collectors:

Clients:

1. Enter loan disbursements or large savings withdrawals[24] on the *Collection Sheet* in the presence of the branch manager; obtain the branch manager's signature in red on the collection sheet next to the notation.
2. At the client's doorstep record any new savings deposits, small withdrawals, and fee payments on the *Collection Sheet*.
3. Record any new loan disbursements or delivery of large savings withdrawals in the passbook as they appear on the *Collection Sheet*.
4. Record today's savings deposits, small withdrawals, and fee payments in the clients' passbooks.
5. Issue a withdrawal slip if any small withdrawal is made, obtaining the client's signature. Give one copy to the client and attach one copy to the *Collection Sheet*.
6. Check to see that the entries on the *Collection Sheet* and the entries in the passbooks are the same, and review the handwriting to be sure that others will be able to read the entries.
7. Read aloud to the client the previous and new balances: savings (including contract savings, if there is a long-term savings account open), loan outstanding, and fees due.

Accounts: Settle accounts with the branch manager who visits the collector's place of work at least once every other working day; store safely the cash receipt voucher issued by the branch manager.

MIS: Recognize and correct passbook errors.

Other: All employees shall use and maintain an identity badge when they are in contact with clients. Employees may not handle transactions with clients unless they are wearing their identity badge in a visible location. Collectors who are suspended from duty will have their badges confiscated by their supervisor. Lost badges must be reported to the branch manager immediately and a new badge issued. In the meantime, the collector will carry a letter, issued and signed by the branch manager, stating that he or she is an employee of this institution and is awaiting the issuance of a security badge. This, in combination with another form of picture identification, will serve as a temporary badge.

Clients will be instructed not to transact with employees who are not wearing a security badge, whether they know them or not.

APPENDIX 11.7 DISCIPLINARY ACTIONS FROM *SAFE*SAVE'S 2001 OPERATIONAL MANUAL

All employees are subject to immediate termination for these offenses upon sufficient evidence:

- misappropriation of funds,
- use of *Safe*Save cash for personal purposes,
- actions that jeopardize the financial stability of *Safe*Save,
- entry into personal transactions with clients involving *Safe*Save funds, or
- violation or misrepresentation of *Safe*Save policies for personal gain.

The following actions can be taken against an employee:

Suspension of Duties: Any employee suspected of misappropriating funds for personal gain is immediately suspended from duty by the supervisor, pending investigation. The supervisor holds the employee's identity badge and instructs the person to cease all activities with clients pending further notice. If misappropriation occurs, the manager will communicate to clients that:

- *Safe*Save's key value is reliability. Dishonesty and manipulation by a *Safe*Save employee, including managers, is never tolerated.
- *Safe*Save is a commercial institution with its own funds. Both *Safe*Save and its clients' funds are managed carefully.
- If there is a discrepancy between *Safe*Save records and a client's passbook, *Safe*Save will always favor the client if alterations have been made to *Safe*Save documents.
- *Safe*Save will favor the client if there is any appearance of fraud by a *Safe*Save employee, except for money lost by a client in a personal transaction with the employee.

Show Cause Notice: This official notice to the employee of pending termination requires a written response from the employee within twenty-four hours of receipt. A show cause notice is issued for all cases involving suspected misappropriation and suspension of duties or irresolvable under-performance leading to termination. The notice relates to the seriousness with which *Safe*Save must consider the reliability of staff members who work on a daily basis with clients' funds. It gives the employee an opportunity to respond in writing to evidence of actions leading to dismissal. The general manager, general secretary, and vice-chairman must agree upon the issue of a show cause notice and record their decision in the resolution book.

Letter of Warning: A letter of warning is issued to highlight poor performance or to document a serious violation of policy by an employee when the employee is expected to continue in *Safe*Save's employment. The letter is issued by the employee's supervisor with prior approval of the general manager, general secretary, and vice-chairman. A letter of warning requires the employee to respond in writing within forty-eight hours of receipt. The supervisor will prepare a remediation plan. At the end of the remediation period the supervisor will submit a written progress appraisal to the general manager.

Letter of Dismissal: A letter of dismissal will be issued any time an employee is terminated for poor performance or acts leading to termination. The letter will state the reason for the employee's dismissal and will be approved by the general manager, general secretary, and vice-chairman, with the corresponding entry made in the resolution book.[25]

Notes

[1] Craig Churchill, "Virtual Conference on Savings Operations for Very Small or Remote Depositors," May 2002.

[2] Churchill, "Virtual Conference."

[3] Ibid.; and Jenny Hoffman, email interchange with editor, June 2004.

[4] Anita Campion, *Improving Internal Control: A Practical Guide for Microfinance Institutions* (Washington, DC: Microfinance Network, 2000), 13, 37.

[5] Ibid., 21.

[6] This section does not include information pertaining to the auditing of loans, which is also crucial.

[7] Campion, *Improving Internal Control*, 22.

[8] Ibid., 53.

[9] Ibid., 21.

[10] CGAP, *External Audits of Microfinance Institutions: A Handbook* (Washington, DC: CGAP, 1998).

[11] Campion, *Improving Internal Control*, 53–55.

[12] Basel Committee on Banking Supervision, *Framework for the Evaluation of Internal Control Systems* (Basel: BIS, 1998). Available from the BIS website.

[13] Campion, *Improving Internal Control*, 17–18.

[14] Ibid., 19, 62, 68.

[15] Ibid., 19, 25.

[16] Romain Tougma, "Virtual Conference on Savings Operations for Very Small or Remote Depositors," May 2002.

[17] This list is based on Kenneth Graber, "Security Issues for Microfinance Following Conflict," Brief No. 6 (Washington, DC: USAID/MBP, 2004).

[18] Campion, *Improving Internal Control*, 24–25.

[19] Churchill, "Virtual Conference."

[20] Ibid.

[21] Campion, *Improving Internal Control*, 26–28.

[22] *Safe*Save operations manual, 2001.

[23] This checklist was adapted from Campion, *Improving Internal Control*, 24–39.

[24] The operations manual prescribes different procedures for larger withdrawals of more than US$10.

[25] These procedures have been revised in response to *Safe*Save's experience and current operations.

12

Liquidity Management

Monnie Markel Biety

When an MFI takes voluntary deposits and uses them to fund the loan portfolio, it faces a complex financial-management challenge. The MFI must manage erratic cash flows from deposits and withdrawals, changes in market interest rates, as well as the varied terms, interest rates, and demand for loans and deposits. Managers are confronted with these questions: (1) Do we have enough liquidity to meet the demands for our funds, that is, operating expenses, client loan demand, and savings withdrawals? (2) If we do not have enough liquidity,

- do we have access to a liquidity source?
- how can we best meet client needs without making the problem worse?
- how can we avoid this problem in the future?

And (3), if we have more liquidity than we need to meet these demands, how can we manage our funds so as to maximize profit without unduly increasing the risk of having insufficient liquidity?[1]

Liquidity risk is the danger that an MFI will be unable to meet the demands for its funds—that it will not have the cash to honor requests for withdrawal of deposits or to disburse new loans. Lack of liquidity can put a quick end to an MFI's efforts to mobilize deposits and, in the worst case, can cause it to collapse. An MFI cannot afford to send away a customer who wants to withdraw cash with a "perhaps tomorrow." If clients cannot withdraw their funds, the word will spread rapidly. Large numbers of clients may then also try to withdraw their savings, and the liquidity situation can worsen.

Many thanks to Michael Kasibante, Constance Larmie, Rochus Mommartz, Jalal Sharma, and John Takacsy for their valuable feedback. Responsibility for the final content is my own.

275

Even if the MFI finds a way to remain open, a liquidity crisis can be devastating. Mobilizing deposits requires clients to trust that they will always be able to access their savings. Building this trust takes a long time, yet a liquidity crisis can destroy it instantly. A liquidity crisis is also costly if the MFI must borrow funds at a high rate of interest and/or sell assets at a loss because they are not easily converted into cash.

If experiencing a lack of sufficient liquidity is so damaging, why doesn't an MFI simply hold a large amount of its assets in a liquid form, that is, in cash or assets that are easily converted into cash? Since cash and convertible assets earn little or no interest, holding too large a percentage of assets in these forms limits net income and undermines profitability. Therefore, managing liquidity involves continually balancing between two requirements:

1. *Being able to satisfy all cash outflow requests:* An MFI's cash plus convertible assets must be able to satisfy the current demand for savings withdrawals, expense payments, and loans. The MFI should hold enough liquid assets to meet all government regulations regarding liquidity and to avoid having to sell assets at a loss or to borrow at a high cost.
2. *Profitability:* Enough of the MFI's assets must be earning enough interest to ensure the viability of its current and future operations. The MFI should seek to maximize revenue from interest-bearing accounts and minimize the amount of cash kept in non-interest-bearing accounts (for reasons of security as well as profitability) on site.

To meet these objectives, an MFI will need:

- tools for projecting and monitoring liquidity,
- reliable ways to obtain liquid funds quickly when needed and to invest excess funds safely at a reasonable rate of return, and
- strategies, policies, and procedures for using these tools and options to manage liquidity.

This chapter assists the reader in meeting these objectives and offers guidance for managing liquidity crises and excess liquidity. Before providing a set of tools and strategies for managing liquidity in a small- to medium-scale MFI, however, the chapter briefly describes an option for the least sophisticated institutions.

12.1 THE SIMPLEST APPROACH TO MANAGING LIQUIDITY

The simplest way to manage liquidity risk is to avoid it altogether. Many organizations that serve solely remote areas or small depositors manage their costs by using staff or volunteers who have little education. For these institutions the most

---

Box 12–1. Definitions

Core deposits: The volume of deposits that are unlikely to be withdrawn, even in response to changes in market interest rates or seasonal swings.

Fixed rate: An interest rate that is set and cannot be changed for the duration of the loan or deposit.

Liquid assets: Assets with a maturity of less than thirty days. This includes both earning (savings and current accounts) and non-earning (cash) assets.

Liquidity risk: The possibility that the MFI will not be able to meet its obligations: that its cash inflows will not meet the demand for cash outflows presented by saving withdrawals, new loan demand, and operating expenses.

Material: Large enough to have a significant impact. A given volume of delinquent loans may be material to a small portfolio and not material to a large one.

Rate-sensitive assets and liabilities: Assets and liabilities with yields that change with market interest rates during a specified period of time. Liability examples include term or saving deposits that have no maturity and can be re-priced (at a higher or lower interest rate) at any moment due to changes in the market. Asset examples include variable rate loans.

Re-priceable, re-priceability: Assets or liabilities that either mature or have a variable interest rate or pricing component that allows the financial institution to change the interest rate during the time period under consideration.

Stable deposits: Deposits that are unlikely to be withdrawn from the MFI in response to changes in market interest rates.

Variable rate: An interest rate that by contract can be adjusted in response to changes in market interest rates.

Volatile deposits: Deposits that will move in search of the most competitive interest rate.

---

feasible way to manage liquidity may be to eliminate the risk by ensuring that no deposits that can be withdrawn are used to fund loans. This low-risk strategy makes it feasible for staff with minimal education to manage deposit services. However, it severely limits the range and terms of services that clients can receive.

This strategy often is employed by small community-based cooperatives and by self-help groups. The latter couple mandatory inaccessible savings services with access to emergency loans. The groups do not have to manage liquidity and, to the extent that resources permit, the members can access savings in the form of a loan. Another possibility is to precisely match the terms of loans and savings (see Box 12.2). An alternate strategy is to provide liquid savings services but no loans. However, recovering the high costs of mobilizing small deposits without the high returns from small loans can be very difficult.

Many MFIs do have the capacity to manage liquid savings. Section 12.2 looks at the tools needed to help them maintain sufficient liquidity when offering these products.

---

*Box 12–2. Managing Liquidity with Limited Management Capacity:
CVECAs, Mali*

The CVECAs are a group of autonomous local village banks that are owned and operated by their members in a sparsely populated region of Mali. Each bank is managed by two part-time local staff and a board composed of members, all of whom have minimal education. Consequently, the CVECAs manage liquidity very conservatively and simply.

The CVECAs manage liquidity based on the two types of savings products they offer, passbook savings accounts, which they do not use for lending, and time deposits, which they use in full, taking into account maturity. The CVECAs pay no interest on passbook accounts and 20 percent interest on time deposits. The volume of passbook accounts is very low, and depositors are free to withdraw these funds at any time without prior notification. Time deposits have a contractually agreed term of three to twelve months. The CVECA reprocesses these deposits as loans with a slightly shorter duration. With the exception of its guarantee fund, the bank also uses its own equity to provide credit. The passbook account deposits and the guarantee funds are held in the bank as a small liquidity reserve.

There are no liquidity exchange mechanisms between the village banks, because the banks lend all their available funds on site. In addition, establishing a central cash facility would be very costly in terms of qualified personnel and would create a risk of fraud that is not justified in a network where the need for such an institution is rare. On the other hand, being able to access refinancing from the national agricultural development bank, the BNDA, eases the chronic shortages of funds. BNDA refinancing makes it possible to respond to the many loan applications. The CVECAs leverage the BNDA funds with their passbook account deposits and equity. The CVECAs tend to ration loans in line with local management capacity.

This system limits the range of the CVECAs' services; the CVECAs can only offer term deposits and loans with terms that precisely match. However, it nearly eliminates liquidity risk.

—Renée Chao-Béroff

12.2 TOOLS FOR MONITORING AND PROJECTING LIQUIDITY

To avoid a liquidity crisis in an institution that offers liquid savings services, managers must project and monitor their liquidity requirements. In many small MFIs, however, inadequate time to plan, lack of expertise, lack of a long-term plan, or a volatile, unpredictable economic situation lead to management styles that are reactive. This section offers four simple tools management can use to be more aggressive in ensuring that liquidity is adequate but not excessive: *daily cash forecasting, cash-flow budgeting, sources-and-uses analysis,* and *ratio analysis.* Together, they meet the MFI's need to monitor liquidity risk and excess liquidity and project liquidity needs. These tools are neither costly nor time-consuming. They do, however, require that the MFI be able to produce some basic information.

12.2.1 Information Needed for Effective Monitoring and Projections

Whether manual or computerized, an MFI's information system must be sophisticated enough to generate the following information in a timely manner:

- A monthly balance sheet and income statement;
- A report detailing the amount of the MFI's deposit liabilities as of a certain date according to maturities, interest rate, and type of account; and
- A history of daily cash demands of all types, including deposit and loan inflows and outflows. (At least a year of data is needed in order to consider seasonal cash flows.)

But this information alone is not enough. Management must also make realistic projections for the growth of loans, the likelihood of their repayment or restructuring, the growth in the different types of deposits, and the probability and timing of withdrawals. These projections should be a part of the MFI's business plan, no matter how simple. Management should constantly watch for changes in lending and borrowing habits, economic changes (such as inflation, changes in interest rates, or a recession), and other developments that could affect the MFI and its liquidity. This information is essential to forecasting liquidity needs.

12.2.2 Cash Forecasting: Two Tools for Projecting Short-term Liquidity Needs

On a daily basis, managers should estimate in detail the size and timing of cash inflows and outflows over the next thirty days. Short-term cash forecasting is based on a review of past cash needs. Although the future does not always reflect the past, historical data gives management a fairly good idea of future liquidity needs under normal operating conditions. Because MFIs just starting to mobilize savings do not have historical data, they must proceed with caution until information on cash inflows and outflows can be collected and analyzed. This section provides two alternative tools for forecasting short-term cash needs, *daily cash forecasting* and *cash sufficiency forecasting*.[2]

Tool 1: Daily Cash Forecasting

Daily cash forecasting involves three steps: choosing the historical data, charting cash inflows and outflows, and modifying these in light of the MFI's current activity to project more accurately current liquidity needs.

Step One: Choosing the Sample of Historical Data. The objective of the first two steps is to determine the MFI's net cash inflow or outflow each day for a given period in the past. Because no day is typical, a cash analysis survey should use historical data from various time periods. For example, looking at every day of the month for one month out of each of four consecutive quarters can ensure that fluctuations related to the day of the week, holidays, and seasons are included. Or if managers have the time to perform such an analysis, they may look at daily cash flow over the last twelve months so as not to miss a critical seasonal period or fluctuation. The cash survey must take special seasonal factors into account, either by putting an appropriate number of days from the special season into the analysis or by remembering to take the expected fluctuation into account in planning monthly cash requirements.

Step Two: Charting Cash Inflows and Outflows. The manager should now examine daily liquidity needs and cash balances for the periods decided upon in step one. Examining these past trends using a graph is a key to understanding future liquidity needs (see Figure 12–1). To chart past liquidity needs:

1. Set up a graph (use a separate graph for each month charted). The vertical axis represents the units of cash. The horizontal axis shows days and dates of the week. Having both the day and the date will help identify trends for days when cash demands are high and low.
2. Chart the daily net cash inflow or outflow. This line represents the change in the MFI's liquidity for each day. To calculate it, take each day's total cash outflow minus each day's total cash inflow. A negative result means that the MFI increased its liquidity; a positive figure indicates that the MFI had to dip into its cash reserves to cover the difference.
3. Chart a second line that represents the balance for the cash ledger account at the close of each business day. This *net cash balance* is the total liquidity the MFI has at the end of the day (after having received the net cash inflow or outflow). This line will be above the first unless the MFI is in a negative cash-flow position (see Figure 12–1).

The space on the graph between the net cash balance line and the net cash inflow/outflow line represents additional liquidity that was not needed to meet the daily liquidity demands. As it plans for future liquidity, management must determine how close it wants the net cash inflow/outflow line to come to the net cash balance line, taking into consideration any government reserve requirements and how much it wants to risk having the two lines cross. If the two lines cross, the net demand for cash outflows (cash outflows minus cash inflows) is greater than the institution's liquid assets; in other words, the institution cannot meet the demands for its funds and faces a liquidity crisis.

Step Three: Using the Historical Data to Project Current Liquidity Needs. Using the graph as an initial approximation of future liquidity needs, management should then modify this projection of short-term needs using a detailed and up-to-date business plan and cash budget (see Section 12.2.3). The business plan and cash budget should be developed from input obtained from all the MFI's operational levels, from front-line employees to top management. Information should also be gathered on macroeconomic issues that may have a substantial impact on liquidity.

Figure 12–1. Sample Cash-Flow Forecasting

The liquidity information represented in this chart is from Ashoka Credit Union, a small credit union in the United States. At the end of 2003 Ashoka had $1,921,250 in assets and substantial liquidity. Because the loan demand did not use all the available liquidity, Ashoka placed the excess in time deposits, money-market accounts, and other low-risk investments of varying maturities.

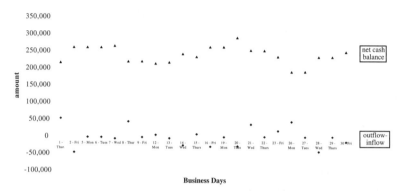

Tool Two: Cash Sufficiency Forecasting

In addition to performing daily cash forecasts, management can determine the amount of liquidity needed to meet demands in the coming weeks or months (in the absence of loan repayments) by performing the quick analysis described below. This simple analysis is intended to forecast cash needs in a time of rapid growth of the loan portfolio and can be performed by management for any period of time (one to three months is probably the most common).

1. Calculate the loan disbursements over the past three months.
2. Calculate the net savings withdrawals (savings withdrawals minus savings deposits) over the past three months.
3. Project the cash disbursements to meet expenditure, fixed asset purchase, liabilities repayment, or other obligations over the next three months.
4. Add the results from steps 1 through 3 to obtain the total liquidity requirement for the period.
5. Divide the result of step 4 by the number of weeks in the three-month period. This gives the weekly cash requirement.
6. Calculate the value of cash on hand and other short-term liquid assets.
7. Divide the result of step 6 by the result of step 5. This tells us how many weeks our current sources of funds can support the projected disbursement requirements.[3]

This analysis yields a rough estimate of the time period that can be covered by current liquidity. Managers should modify this estimate by considering "both cyclical and seasonal loan demand, growth in new clients, drop-out rates, rates of increase in average loan size and term, and the effect of general economic conditions on demand. Beyond six months this technique becomes more difficult if the loan portfolio has a rapid turnover due to very short average loan maturities."[4]

From this analysis, the MFI can determine how much cash it needs to have on hand to meet daily demands over the near term. It enables the MFI to react to current trends to ensure that it remains sufficiently but not overly liquid. Of course, the MFI should also engage in longer-term measures to anticipate and actively to shape its liquidity position. This is the role of a cash-flow budget.

12.2.3 Cash-flow Budgeting: A Tool for Anticipating Long-term Liquidity Needs

A cash-flow budget is part of the annual budgeting process. If management is very realistic in developing the cash-flow budget and makes every attempt to adhere to it, the budget can be an effective tool for avoiding liquidity problems. Used in conjunction with daily cash forecasting, the cash-flow budget gives management short-term and longer-term information on liquidity requirements.

Management should develop its cash-flow budget from its operating budget—both the balance sheet and the income statement—and from the assumptions used to develop the operating budget. Both budgets should have the same monthly or quarterly intervals (see Table 12.1) and should be based on management's assumptions about future operations and cash flows. For example: How quickly will loans and savings increase? Will this be affected by seasonal demands? With experience, management can make relatively accurate cash budgets that give a realistic picture of upcoming cash needs or surpluses.

The cash-flow budget should be monitored monthly, updated throughout the year as needed, and used as a part of monthly financial forecasting. The cash-flow budget can help management highlight and manage excess liquidity. Another simple way to manage excess liquidity is to perform a sources-and-uses analysis.

12.2.4 Sources-and-Uses Analysis: A Tool for Monitoring Relative Costs of Funds

In assessing the liquidity position of an institution, management should regularly consider its sources and uses of funds and the financial costs or income it generates. While the previous tools focused on availability of funds, this tool focuses on relative cost and is particularly important in ensuring profitability. The sources of funds are the liabilities and equity. The MFI must pay for many of these funds. The uses of funds are the assets. These are funds for which the MFI may receive interest. The sources and uses of funds can be easily analyzed by reviewing the

Table 12–1. Format for Annual Cash-flow Budget

	3/31/06	6/30/06	9/30/06	12/31/06	2006 cumulative
Beginning cash balance (including cash on site and in bank accounts)[1]					
Operating activities:					
Net income					
Add: Depreciation					
Provision for loan loss					
Liability (increases only)					
Less: Other assets (increases only)					
Cash from operations					
Lending and investing activities:					
Add: Investments maturing					
Loan repayments					
Less: Investment purchases					
Loans issued					
Cash from lending and investing activities					
Funding Activities:					
Add: Savings and deposits					
External borrowings					
Less: Savings withdrawals					
Borrowed funds repayments					
Cash from funding activities					
Ending cash balance[2]					

[1] The ending cash balance for the previous period is the beginning cash balance for the next period.
[2] The ending cash balance represents the sum of beginning cash plus the net result of each of the three activity areas. If the ending cash balance is positive, this amount may be invested during the period. If it is negative, this amount needs to be borrowed to meet cash requirements

balance sheet. The cost of each source of funds and the revenues from each use of funds may be known or can be calculated from the income statement. With the findings from this analysis management can make better decisions about managing excess liquidity.

Managers will want to consider a few simple but critical questions:

- What are the sources of our funds (for example, borrowed funds, customer time deposits, customer demand deposits, or MFI equity)? What rate of interest do we pay for each of these sources? Identify each source, the interest rate, and (from the income statement) the amount of interest paid for the period.
- Are we using our sources of funds in the best way that we can? How are our sources of funds being invested on the asset side? Are loans being made and/or investments purchased?
- What rate of interest do we receive for each of our uses of funds? Management should look at both the stated interest rate and the amount of interest actually received for our loans and investments (see the income statement).
- Are our uses of funds profitable enough to cover the costs of our sources? The answer to this question can be found on the income statement (interest income—cost of funds). Do loans and investments yield a return (interest yield) high enough to pay for the cost of attracting the funds (interest paid), operating expenses, and contributions to capital?

The findings from this analysis can be important. The institution described in Box 12.3 found that it was using large amounts of relatively costly external credit for investments that were yielding far less than it was paying for this credit. Taking external credit and then investing it was hurting its profitability. Another institution realized that because it could use subsidized low-cost credit to fund its loan portfolio, using higher-cost deposits to do so was not a good business decision. Deposit mobilization undermined its profitability. In short, it is critical that management compare the costs of its sources of funds with the yields from its uses.

12.2.5 Ratios: Analysis Is a Key to Managing Liquidity

As MFI management becomes more aggressive in monitoring liquidity, ratio analysis can help clarify what types of changes are needed to maintain a sound liquidity position. For every ratio management should determine the range of values or *target ratios* that represent, for its institution, a reasonable balance between pursuing profitability and limiting liquidity risk. The institution then monitors its liquidity position by regularly comparing its actual ratios against these targets. For example, an institution should monitor the proportion of assets that are not earning interest and therefore are not contributing to profitability. If the actual proportion is higher than the target proportion, managers will know that more of the institution's assets should be invested to earn interest.

Box 12–3. Discovering the Cost of Excess Liquidity: Sources and Uses

A financial institution will undermine its profitability if its sources of funds cost more than its uses of funds yield. The MFI may be able to see this clearly only if it analyzes its sources and uses of funds. For example, the following monthly balance sheet (amounts stated in local currency) came from an MFI that could access external credit easily and was unaware that borrowing externally—and therefore having more liquidity than was needed to meet demands—was hurting its profitability.

Assets (in millions)		Liabilities and Equity (in millions)	
Cash	30	External Credit	64
Investments	43	Internal Credit	32
Loans	331	Savings	249
Fixed Assets	10	Equity	53
Other	11	Other	27
TOTAL	425	TOTAL	425

Examining the balance sheet showed management that the MFI was using the external and internal credit mainly to fund cash and investments, while most loans were covered by deposits and equity. In fact, its external credit cost more than its investments were yielding. The average cost of the external credit was 9.5 percent per annum, compared to the average return on investments of 3.7 percent. The MFI was losing money by borrowing and investing funds.

A closer look showed that the vast majority of investments were in short-term investments with, at most, a one-month maturity, even though the funds were not needed to meet daily liquidity demands and the external credit was not due in the near term. The following table breaks out the investment portfolio by maturity.

	Maturity (in months)					
Investments	Overnight	1	2 to 3	4 to 6	7 to 12	> 12
Demand Deposits	14,330,531					
Required Reserves	1,658,712					
Fixed Income Fund		1,000,098				
Other Funds		1,000,000				
Government Bills		12,988,775	5,799,584			
Bank CDs		14,966,866	3,413,178			3,005,000
Totals	15,989,243	29,955,739	9,212,762	0	0	13,005,000

With the majority of the investments having a maturity of one month or less, the MFI's investment portfolio was very liquid. Although this excess liquidity made it easy for the MFI to meet all liquidity needs, it also meant that it was earning lower returns. Furthermore, the investment portfolio was not diversified and was largely subject to changes in short-term interest rates. Finally, reinvesting two-thirds of it every month was labor intensive. The sources-and-uses analysis showed that this MFI should have repaid some of this credit or invested the excess funds in longer-term investments that yielded more than the credit cost.

Box 12–4. The Stability and Rate Sensitivity
of Different Sources of Funds

Stable sources of funds

MFI equity, especially retained earnings, is a permanent source of funds for institutions operating profitably. Therefore, it can be used to fund longer-term assets, including fixed assets, long-term investments, and loans. Some special-purpose equity accounts, such as regulatory reserves, should not be used to fund longer-term assets.

Fixed deposits and *contractual savings* can be stable until their maturities if the interest rate is competitive and sufficiently rewarding, and if early withdrawals are not allowed or are penalized severely enough to discourage withdrawals. These funds can be used to fund assets with maturities shorter or equal to their own maturities and do not pose serious liquidity concerns during this period. A liquidity crisis can arise if deposit maturities all come due within a similar time period, clients do not renew deposits, and there are not new deposits. This can be prevented by structuring deposits so that they come due consistently over time. Some portion of such deposits may be used to fund longer-term assets that have maturity beyond the stated maturity of the deposits as long as the clients remain loyal and continue to renew their deposits.

Demand deposits with small balances. Although clients can withdraw their funds at any time, small demand-deposit accounts tend to be very stable if clients trust that they can access this money as needed and if no unforeseen natural disaster or economic event occurs. However, relatively high interest rates can make these funds much less stable by attracting clients who move with high returns. Management must have sufficient liquidity to fund withdrawals from these accounts, but a percentage of these funds may be used to fund longer-term assets.

Volatile sources of funds

Money market accounts offer high interest rates to attract large interest-rate-sensitive deposits. These accounts have no maturity date. If the MFI cannot continue to pay relatively high rates, these clients are likely to leave. Therefore, the MFI must always have enough liquidity to pay all withdrawal demands immediately. By attracting rate-sensitive deposits away from regular savings accounts, money market accounts can make ALM easier; they can enable management to identify funds that are rate-sensitive and unstable.

Demand deposits with large balances typically do not receive as high a rate of interest as accounts specifically designed for larger depositors. Because the MFI has no way of determining which clients will withdraw their funds when they find an investment with a better return, the MFI should have sufficient liquidity to meet all withdrawal demands by clients in this category. These accounts should never be used to fund longer-term assets, unless management has compelling information based on experience, actual client behavior, or historical analysis that indicates some accounts will remain in the MFI.

Continued on page 287

Continued from page 286

Short-term commercial borrowings can be instrumental in solving a sudden liquidity shortage but should be used only as a last resort in the event of a liquidity crisis for several reasons: the lending institution controls the loan terms, the funds are often vulnerable to interest-rate changes and market trends, and they usually cost more than mobilizing deposits.

Donor funds are not reliable income and often arrive later than anticipated. Once they arrive, though, donors rarely withdraw them. Thus, they are volatile in terms of projecting future income but not in terms of existing funds.

Ratios are easy to calculate from the most recent set of financial statements. By analyzing ratios over time, management can detect positive and negative liquidity trends. If trends are negative, management should respond promptly.

For a small MFI that can devote only limited time and resources to liquidity management, we recommend monitoring the six ratios detailed in Table 12.2. Initially, these ratios should be reviewed monthly or more frequently as needed. If after one year's time, it becomes clear that the ratios change very little, then management may want to calculate the ratios and analyze their trends quarterly. Although no one ratio is sufficient by itself, together these six ratios enable an MFI to adequately track the key factors that affect liquidity.

12.3 MANAGING LIQUIDITY

Ratio analysis, cash forecasting, cash-flow budgeting, and sources-and-uses analysis are important tools for projecting and monitoring liquidity. Managers also need ways to manage liquidity. In addition to knowing their liquidity position, they must have ways to steer their institutions on a safe and profitable course between excess and insufficient liquidity. In case they lose course, they must also know how to manage a liquidity crisis and excess liquidity.

12.3.1 Maintaining a Balanced Liquidity Position

Daily cash forecasting will assist an MFI in determining the minimum cash it wishes to maintain on-site. The MFI should keep this minimum on hand and deposit the rest in a deposit-taking institution. Where such institutions are not available, management must hold its own cash reserves and work to keep excess funds at a minimum in order to maximize profitability and minimize the potential for fraud or theft. Strategies for maintaining a sound liquidity balance include:

Adhering to the operating budget: Once an MFI has set a realistic cash-flow budget, management should make every effort to adhere to it.

Table 12–2. Ratios for Monitoring Liquidity

Ratio	Significance	Suggested target values
(short term assets – short term payables) /total deposits *Short-term assets:* liquid or mature within 30 days *Short-term payables:* due within 30 days	Measures adequacy of liquid cash reserve to satisfy client savings withdrawals after paying all immediate obligations.	Normally, between 10% and 15%. Higher if: (1) the maximum client deposit size is larger, (2) it is more likely that large deposits may be withdrawn, or (3) future funding needs are expected to increase.
net loans total assets *Net loans:* Total gross loan portfolio – total provision for loan losses	Shows whether there are enough assets outside the loan portfolio to provide short-term liquidity to meet future demands.	Not more than 85% if all assets other than net loans are liquid and can be used to meet client demand. Less than 85% if some of these assets—such as fixed assets or investments with longer maturities—are not considered liquid.
Core deposit ratio: core deposits / (total loans and investments with a maturity greater than x months) *Core deposits:* see Box 12–5	Measures the portion of longer-term loans and investments funded with stable deposits. A higher value indicates a more solid financial institution for which liquidity and ALM are easier to control.	No suggested range. However, the higher the result the more stable the liquidity.
liquid assets total assets	Because liquid assets generally have a lower yield, a high value can reduce profitability yet increase liquidity. Only enough funds to meet liquidity needs should be maintained in these accounts.	15% or less under normal operating conditions. More when demand for loans or withdrawals increases significantly.

non-earning assets total assets *Non-earning assets:* cash on hand + non-interest-bearing current account + accounts receivable + assets in liquidation (repossessed collateral awaiting sale) + fixed assets (land, building, equipment) + prepaid expenses	Measures the percentage of total assets that do not contribute to net income or capital. These assets should be kept at a minimum needed to meet liquidity needs and operate effectively. If investment in the less liquid of such assets is excessive (especially fixed assets), the MFI may not have sufficient liquidity.	Between 5% and 10% under normal operating conditions.
Loan turnover ratio: average loans outstanding during the month / loan repayments for the month The result is the average loan maturity in months: a result of 4 means that the entire loan portfolio matures on average every four months. Refinancing and one-payment loans should not be included if they are material and if the information system makes it possible to exclude them.	Measures how quickly the loan portfolio matures and, therefore, how quickly loan funds will be made available to meet liquidity needs. A lower value—that is, a faster-maturing loan portfolio—should make liquidity and ALM easier. Refinancing and one-payment loans can distort this ratio: Loan refinancing will reduce it because these loans seem to be paid in full. One-payment loans (loans with a single balloon payment) increase it because no payments are made during the loan period.	No suggested range. However, the lower the result, the greater the liquidity.

Box 12–5. Core Deposits

Certain types of funds are considered *stable* because they are rarely withdrawn. For this reason, different sources of funds pose different levels of liquidity risk to the MFI (see Box 12–4). Stable types of funds include MFI equity, fixed deposits, contractual savings, and savings accounts with small balances. Unstable or volatile sources of funds are money market accounts, large-balance savings accounts, and short-term borrowings from financial institutions.

Some portion of the account types that are stable can be considered core deposits. Core deposits are the volume of deposits that are unlikely to be withdrawn, even in response to changes in market interest rates or seasonal swings. Thus, core deposits can be treated as longer-term funds. A portion of core deposits, in addition to the other stable sources of funds, may be used to fund longer-term fixed-rate loans and investments.

To determine the total amount of core deposits, management should estimate the core deposits for each type of account and then add these estimates together. For savings accounts that have no stated maturity and for which withdrawals may be made on any business day, the volume of the core deposits of these accounts must be estimated from the MFI's historical data. Management may choose to examine one month in each quarter or look at the entire year, taking into consideration any seasonal demands for savings, changes in interest rates within the MFI, and interest changes in the market. A conservative estimate of core deposits uses the lowest savings balance for the months analyzed; alternatively, the average of all the low points can be used.

Graphing this can help in estimating core deposits. It enables managers to see trends over time, especially when a long period of time is analyzed. For each product, set up a graph with monetary increments on the vertical axis and days of the month on the horizontal axis. Then plot "the volume of total deposits . . . over time and draw a horizontal line through the low point(s) of the graph. This line through the low points represents the trend in the minimum or core deposits, below which in all likelihood the actual deposit level will not fall."[1]

---

[1] Bankakademie, *Liquidity Management: A Toolkit for Microfinance Institutions* (Eschborn, Germany: GTZ, 2000), 32.

Adhering to targets for liquidity ratios: Similarly, once management has determined its target policy ranges for liquidity ratios, it should stay within these ranges. To do this, the MFI should regularly monitor its actual performance and, when indicated, take action to regain its desired position. For example, for the non-earning assets to total assets ratio, an MFI might determine that a maximum of 5 to 10 percent of its total assets should not earn interest. If its monthly ratio analysis found its actual ratio above 10 percent, it would immediately look into why this is and how it could safely invest more of its assets to earn interest.

Establishing a liquidity pool and similar sources for backup liquidity: A key to liquidity management is access to safe and liquid investment options to cope with unexpected changes in cash flow. Institutions need a means to invest some of their cash profitably and a source of additional cash should demand outstrip or outpace supply. Access to a liquidity backup enables an MFI to avoid holding large amounts of cash as non-earning assets. Some options are:

- establishing a line of credit/overdraft facility with a commercial bank to make short-term borrowing possible,
- accessing or helping to establish a liquidity pool through a second-tier organization like a credit-union federation,
- arranging for another MFI or cooperative to serve as a liquidity pool,
- accessing the rediscount window of the central bank, and
- developing an equity or capital base, which is accumulated through past profitable operations, allowing MFIs to meet unanticipated costs or losses.

Controlling unpredictable cash outflows: An MFI can institute incentives or restrictions that reduce the number and volume of unpredictable withdrawals. For example, an MFI might:

- prohibit withdrawals over a certain amount or frequency,
- charge a service fee on all or certain withdrawals,
- require advance notice for withdrawals over a certain amount,
- charge a fee to withdraw large amounts without advance notice,
- pay a higher interest rate for accounts with restrictions on withdrawals, or
- require new members to make deposits for a certain period before they can become eligible for a loan.

In all these cases, however, the MFI reduces its liquidity risk at the cost of client satisfaction, possibly with serious repercussions to the MFI.

Improving cash management: Cash that is held on-site by an MFI earns no return; it is like a fixed or non-earning asset. In order to improve cash management and MFI profitability, management must limit the time the cash is not "working" or earning interest. On a day-to-day basis, an MFI can:

- improve how it collects cash coming into the MFI (for example, loan officers might coordinate loan disbursements with the receipt of client savings deposits),
- identify ways to ensure that cash is not disbursed any faster than it has to be (for example, it might pay expenses only on their due date), and

- implement methods to earn the best return on cash while the cash is in the MFI's control, if only for the day (for example, the MFI might seek to deposit excess funds in short-term, interest-earning money-market or demand-deposit accounts).

12.3.2 Managing a Liquidity Crisis

Despite sound policies and careful planning, an MFI might find itself in a liquidity crisis. In this event, it can pursue several options, even simultaneously (see Box 12–6):

- borrow short-term funds using its line of credit or liquidity pool;
- borrow from another MFI;
- sell investments to meet liquidity needs or to generate collateral in order to borrow funds (before doing this, management should consider the loss that might be incurred);
- sell loans to other MFIs or financial institutions;
- mobilize more savings by increasing the interest rate (management must be careful not to attract any more funds than are necessary; increasing interest rates will have a negative effect on profitability and could attract rate-sensitive, unstable funds);
- slow the demand for loans by restricting loans to new clients, making smaller loans, temporarily discontinuing making certain types of loans such as larger loans with longer terms, or increasing interest rates on loans; and/or
- place limits on withdrawals such as daily limits or requirements for prior notice of withdrawal.

The latter two strategies can have a serious long-term impact on the MFI's business because they reduce client confidence in the institution.

12.3.3 Managing Excess Liquidity

An MFI is overly liquid when it has more than enough cash and convertible assets to meet liquidity demands, central bank requirements, and emergencies. However, when an MFI concentrates its excess funds in cash and short-term investments, it can face numerous difficulties, including:

- a lower return on investments,[5]
- exposure to changes in short-term interest rates,
- an investment portfolio that is not well diversified according to maturity, and
- the frequent need to reinvest the portfolio—which can be labor-intensive.

Box 12–6. Managing a Liquidity Crisis: ASA

In 1997 ASA introduced more flexible savings features and services to meet client needs. Above all, it allowed members to withdraw funds from their mandatory savings accounts so long as they maintained in the account an amount equal to 10 percent of their loan amount and continued the mandatory weekly savings deposit of US$0.17 to US$0.34. It also established the Associate Members' Savings Account for relatives of ASA members. Owners of these accounts did not have loans and could deposit and withdraw any amount with no minimum balance requirements.

These changes greatly increased the challenge of managing ASA's liquidity. Although ASA had planned for the initial high level of withdrawals that inevitably follow opening up of locked-in savings, it was surprised by the withdrawals associated with the two Eid festivals and the cultivation season that coincided at the beginning of 1998. ASA suddenly faced a liquidity crisis. The institution responded with speed and effectiveness by

- slowing the disbursement of loans (by a few weeks here and there),
- reducing loan amounts (for example, honoring a US$102 request with a US$85 loan),
- borrowing from the national apex microfinance funding institution,
- borrowing from a local commercial bank,
- negotiating with suppliers to lend it money should the need arise, and
- as a last resort, temporarily liquidating its staff retirement fund.

With these measures ASA was able to ride out the crisis. It quickly amended its liquidity planning to ensure that the crisis is not repeated. ASA had previously planned liquidity from the top down. Now liquidity planning starts at the credit-officer level and flows up to central-office planning staff. (See Appendix 12.1 for the liquidity management tool ASA uses.) Credit officers project liquidity needs for their groups for the upcoming six months. They give these to their branch manager, who develops a branch liquidity plan for the area manager, and so on. Since the crisis, ASA's liquidity management system is based on input from the employees that are most in touch with client needs.[1]

---

[1] Graham A. N. Wright, Robert Peck Christen, and Imran Matin, "ASA's Culture, Competition and Choice: Introducing Savings Services into a MicroCredit Institution" (Nairobi: *MicroSave*, 2000).

Although excess liquidity will not cause a sudden crisis, it can erode profitability. Like a liquidity shortfall, excess liquidity requires rigorous management.

Excess liquidity should be invested so that it is secure and does not negatively influence profitability. In other words, investments should be made in entities that are safe and sound and that provide interest rates above what the MFI is paying to attract the funds. In some countries such entities are hard to find. In any case, when an MFI has excess liquidity, the investment portfolio needs to be actively managed.

One simple portfolio management method that provides a yield reflecting average market returns is known as *laddered investing*. The goal of laddered investing is to limit interest-rate risk[6] by investing similar amounts in each maturity time frame; this ensures that equal-sized investments mature at set intervals over a desired time period. The laddered portfolio is easy to maintain because maturing investments are continually reinvested to maintain the laddered structure. In this way, they are intentionally invested without regard to current market conditions. This technique has numerous advantages:

- Maintaining it requires little time.
- MFI managers need not guess how interest rates will change because investments are made based on maturity not interest rates.
- Although MFI managers do not choose investments based on their returns, the long-term outcome of the strategy should still mirror the general market performance.

Appendix 12.2 illustrates how the laddered investment technique works.

Laddering notwithstanding, management must be mindful not to think of the investment portfolio in isolation. The investment strategy is part of managing liquidity; managers must consider future liquidity needs when making longer-term investments so that the MFI does not have to sell longer-term investments at a loss in the future to meet liquidity demands.

12.4 PUTTING IT ALL TOGETHER:
LIQUIDITY MANAGEMENT POLICY

The tools and strategies discussed so far are the building blocks of effective liquidity management. To ensure that they work, management should develop and adhere to a written liquidity-management policy. Because written policies require managers to think through potential problems or issues ahead of time, they ensure that management is taking action rather than merely reacting. By spelling out rules or guidelines, written policies and procedures also provide employees with a concise and reliable directive from management and make it possible for employees to act consistently.

Decisions on lending, investments, liabilities, and equity will greatly affect both ALM and liquidity. Therefore, developing the liquidity and asset liability management policies as one policy or alongside each other is imperative. The liquidity policy should be flexible enough to enable management to react quickly to unforeseen events. At the same time, it should specifically state the following:

Responsibility and Authority

- Who is responsible for liquidity management.
- Who may access or establish a line of credit for short-term liquidity needs.
- If excess cash is kept on deposit at another institution, limits to the signatory authority of the liquidity manager. Often liquidity decisions need to be made rapidly to avoid a liquidity crisis. Therefore, the liquidity manager should have some authority. However, this authority should not be excessive. For unusually large transactions, at least two signatures should be required.

Tools for Liquidity Management

- How liquidity will be monitored: what liquidity management systems will be used, what time frames will be used in cash-flow analysis, their level of detail, and the intervals for updating ratio and cash-flow analysis.

Targets for Liquidity Management

- What MFI assets are considered liquid. This can vary greatly depending on the composition of the MFI's balance sheet.
- Minimums and maximums for total cash assets and for the amount to be kept on-site at the MFI relative to total assets and member deposits.
- Minimums and maximums for other liquidity-related ratios.

Managing Excess Funds and Obtaining Additional Funds

- The maximum amount to be deposited in any one bank to limit exposure to a bank failure. The ratio is usually no more than 20 percent of the investment portfolio or a percentage of institutional capital, but it is dependent on the number of financial institutions that are considered financially sound.
- Acceptable reasons, benchmarks, or scenarios for accessing the line of credit or alternative source of liquidity.
- If liquid funds are not placed in another financial institution or investment, how excess funds are to be handled, who has access to them, and where they are to be kept.
- Which institutions, types of investments, and terms are acceptable (see Table 12–3).

Review of Policies

- How often management will review this policy's key parameters.

This policy should be reviewed and revised as needed, no less than annually.

Table 12–3. Sample Table of Investment Policies

	Maximum amount or % to be invested in the institution or investment	**Maturity terms that are acceptable**
Name of Institution		
Arab Bank	50% of investment portfolio	State range in months
Bank of Palestine	50% of investment portfolio	State range in months
Type of Investment		
Certificates of deposit	40%	State range in months
Savings accounts	30%	State range in months
Government securities	20%	State range in months

Table 12–4. Credit Officer Monthly Summary

Name of Credit Officer: Name of Branch: Name of

Month	Total fully repaid previous loan cycle		Credit disbursements		Drop -out	Savings withdrawals		Savings refunds (liquidation of accounts)				
		Prin-cipal amount	Disbursement (principal)			Members	Assoc-iates	Members	Associate	Long-term	Term	
	No. of mem-bers		No. of mem-bers	Amount	No. of mem-bers	Amount	Amount	Amount	Amount	Amount	Amount	
1	2	3	4 = 2- 6	5	6	7	8	9	10	11	12	
Total												

Name of Credit Officer: Code No.:   Signature: Date:

APPENDIX 12.1 SIX-MONTH CASH FORECASTING: ASA'S SYSTEM

Liquidity can be forecasted in a variety of ways. After experiencing a serious liquidity crisis, ASA recognized that it needed to improve the way in which it collected information on liquidity. It decided that the information should flow up from the field to the central office. To do this, ASA started liquidity forecasting at the field level, using a spreadsheet (see Table 12–4). The spreadsheet information is collected year round at the credit-officer, branch-manager, regional, and area-manager levels. The previous six months of data are used to forecast future liquidity needs, keeping in mind holidays and cyclical occurrences such as the rainy season.

Sheet of Half-yearly Liquidity Plan

Area: Outstanding loan at start of 6-month period:

Total cash out	Loan install-ments in	Savings collection						Insurance & fees received	Total cash in
		Collect-ion of loans	Member required	Member volun-tary	Assoc-iate	Long-term	Term	fees & other	
Amount	Amount	Amount	Amount	Amount	Amount	Amount	Amount	Amount	Amount
13=5+7 +8 +9+10 +11+12	14	15	16	17	18	19	20	21=14+ 15+16+ 17+18+ 19+20

Name of Branch   Code No.:   Signature: Date:
Manager:

Spreadsheet provided by Azim Mohammed Hossain, ASA's head of Finance and Management Information Systems, 2001.

APPENDIX 12.2 A LADDERED PORTFOLIO REINVESTMENT TABLE

Table 12–5. Laddering Time Table

m = million
month or months = time left until the security reaches maturity

Month	Overnight funds	1-month security	3-month security	6-month security	12-month security	Total
Initial Purchases	$1 m	$1m: 1 month	$1 m: 3 months	$1 m: 6 months	$1 m: 12 months	$5 m
End of 1	$2 m	Buy $1 m	$1 m: 2 months	$1 m: 5 months	$1 m: 11 months	$5 m
End of 2	$2 m	Buy $1 m	$1 m: 1 month	$1 m: 4 months	$1 m: 10 months	$5 m
End of 3	$3 m	Buy $1 m	$1 m: 3 months	Buy $1 m	$1 m: 9 months	$5 m
End of 4	$2 m	Buy $1 m	$1 m: 2 months	$1 m: 5 months	$1 m: 8 months	$5 m
End of 5	$2 m	Buy $1 m	$1 m: 1 month	$1 m: 4 months	$1 m: 7 months	$5 m
End of 6	$3 m	Buy $1 m	$1 m: 3 months	$1 m: 6 months	Buy $1 m	$5 m
End of 7	$2 m	Buy $1 m	$1 m: 2 months	$1 m: 5 months	$1 m: 11 months	$5 m
End of 8	$2 m	Buy $1 m	$1 m: 1 month	$1 m: 4 months	$1 m: 10 months	$5 m
End of 9	$3 m	Buy $1 m	$1 m: 3 months	Buy $1 m	$1 m: 9 months	$5 m
End of 10	$2 m	Buy $1 m	$1 m: 2 months	$1 m: 5 months	$1 m: 8 months	$5 m
End of 11	$2 m	Buy $1 m	$1 m: 1 month	$1 m: 4 months	$1 m: 7 months	$5 m
End of 12	$3 m	Buy $1 m	$1 m: 3 months	$1 m: 6 months	Buy $1 m	$5 m

Explanation:

Table 12–5 shows the portfolio at the end of each month with the number of months remaining to maturity for each security. The initial purchases represent the desired ladder, which the MFI will maintain as closely as possible. When a security reaches maturity, the proceeds are deposited into the overnight funds and then are used to buy a new security with a maturity that will keep the ladder balanced, in other words, that will make the portfolio resemble as closely as possible the initial balanced portfolio. A new US$1 million security must be bought regularly—in this case, monthly—so that the portfolio earns an average interest rate over the time period. This takes the guesswork out of interest rates and investing.

1. At the end of each month, the one-month security reaches maturity. The proceeds are deposited into the overnight funds and used to purchase a new one-month security.

2. At the end of the third month, the three-month security matures and the six-month security has three months left to maturity. Therefore, the original six-month security takes the place in the ladder of a three-month security. The proceeds from the three-month security are used to purchase a six-month security. (The twelve-month security still has nine months to maturity. It maintains the twelve-month place in the ladder.)

3. At the end of the sixth month, the original six-month security matures, and the six-month security purchased at the end of the third month now occupies the three-month maturity slot. The original twelve-month security now has six months to maturity and occupies the six-month maturity time frame. Therefore, a new twelve-month security is purchased.

4. At the end of the ninth month, the six-month security bought at the end of the third month matures. The six-month security bought at the end of the sixth month occupies the three-month time frame. The twelve-month security bought at the end of the sixth month stays in the twelve-month slot. A six-month security is bought to fill the six-month time frame.

5. At the end of the twelfth month, the original twelve-month security matures, and the twelve-month security bought at the end of the sixth month takes the six-month time frame in the ladder. The six-month security bought at the end of the ninth month takes the three-month time frame in the ladder. A twelve-month security is purchased.

Notes

¹ It also faces *interest-rate risk*, the risk that changes in market interest rates will harm the MFI's profitability. Interest-rate risk is managed by planning, monitoring, and controlling asset and liability volumes, maturities, rates, and yields. This process is called *asset liability management* (ALM), which is discussed in Chapter 13. ALM and liquidity management are closely related and must be highly coordinated.

² The Microfin business planning tool (a spreadsheet) also forecasts liquidity (see the microfin website).

³ Adapted from Robert Peck Christen, *Banking Services for the Poor: Managing for Financial Success* (Washington, DC: ACCION International, 1997), 158–59.

⁴ Ibid.

⁵ This is true as long as the yield curve is not *inverted*, that is, as long as short-term interest rates are lower than long-term ones.

⁶ Interest-rate risk is the risk that changes in market interest rates will harm the MFI's profitability. It is discussed in detail in Section 13.1.

13

Managing Interest-rate Risk

Asset Liability Management

Monnie Markel Biety

When a financial institution mobilizes deposits at one interest rate and lends them out at another, it exposes itself to *interest-rate risk*. Interest-rate risk is the risk associated with changes in market interest rates that can harm a financial institution's profitability.

For example, changes in the market might force an institution to increase its interest rate on deposits in order to remain competitive; if it does not increase its rate, depositors may withdraw their funds. At the same time, if its earning assets are concentrated in long-term, fixed-rate loans, it does not immediately have the option of increasing the interest rate on these loans. Because the institution will not be able to increase its interest income from loans as fast as its cost of funds is increasing, it can face a serious shortfall in its operating funds. In this way a change in market interest rates can undermine the institution's viability.

A financial institution can avoid this kind of interest-rate squeeze by carefully maintaining a balance among different types and volumes of assets (in particular, loans) and liabilities (in particular, savings). This balancing of assets and liabilities is known as asset liability management (ALM). ALM is the process of planning, monitoring, and controlling asset and liability volumes, maturities, rates, and yields. One goal of ALM is to minimize interest-rate risk while still earning sufficient profits.[1] Managing interest risk through ALM is the focus of this chapter. The chapter

- describes the circumstances that increase interest-rate risk,
- offers an overview of ALM,

The author expresses her thanks to Carlos Danel, Mahendra Giri, Fabian Kasi, and Nthenya Mule for their valuable comments on this chapter.

- describes three types of monitoring that comprise ALM: analysis of the *gap*, the *net interest margin* (NIM), and *core deposits*,
- identifies the policy decisions required for effective ALM, and
- recommends a process for liquidity and ALM.

13.1 VOLUNTARY SAVINGS AND INTEREST-RATE RISK

When a microcredit institution funds its loan portfolio with interest-free grants, loans, or compulsory savings (that clients must deposit and cannot access), interest-rate risk is fairly low. These sources of funds are unlikely to be interest-rate sensitive; that is, the volume of compulsory savings or grants is unlikely to change in response to changes in market interest rates. Interest-rate risk increases when an MFI begins to mobilize voluntary savings and to use these to fund its loan portfolio. Voluntary savings will be more sensitive to changes in market rates. In order to hold on to voluntary savings, the MFI will need to respond to increases in market rates by increasing the rates on its savings products. *Interest-rate risk is primarily an issue for MFIs that extend loans and have investments with maturities greater than six months, that have fixed interest rates, and that fund their assets with short-term client deposits with differing maturities and interest rates.*

Interest-rate risk can increase dramatically in any of the following scenarios:

- Longer-term *fixed-rate* loans and investments are funded with savings and deposits that either are short-term and can be *re-priced* quickly or have

---

Box 13–1. Definitions

Asset liability management (ALM): The process of planning, monitoring, and controlling asset and liability volumes, maturities, rates and yields. The primary goal of ALM is to minimize interest rate risk while maintaining an acceptable profitability level.

Gap: The volume of rate-sensitive assets (RSAs) minus the volume of rate-sensitive liabilities (RSLs). (See Box 12-1.) The larger the gap, the greater the interest-rate risk. For any given time period, the gap is managed by matching the volume of RSAs with that of RSLs.

Interest-rate spread: The difference between the interest rate paid on deposits and the interest rate charged on loans. Along with the volume of deposits and loans, the spread is a major determinant of the net interest margin.

Interest-rate risk: The risk that changes in market interest rates will harm the financial institution's profitability.

Net interest margin (NIM): Gross interest, fees, and other operating income minus the cost of funds. The minimum NIM is the minimum amount needed to cover operating expenses and target equity contributions.

Re-priceable, re-priceability: Assets or liabilities that either mature or have a variable interest rate or pricing component that allows the financial institution to change the interest rate during the time period under consideration.

variable-rate interest with short-term adjustment periods.[2] For example, a one-year fixed-rate loan is funded by certificates of deposit with a three-month maturity or with a one-year maturity but a variable interest rate that adjusts quarterly.

- There is high or unpredictable inflation. Even when inflation is high, depositors expect to earn a "real" rate of return, that is, a return equal to the inflation rate (to make up for the loss of value of their deposit due to inflation) plus a return for depositing funds in the MFI. In order to pay a real rate of return on liabilities, management must earn a correspondingly high real rate of return on assets. Inflationary environments require that management monitor interest rates constantly and adjust assets and liabilities in a timely fashion.

- Some or all of the assets and liabilities are highly sensitive to interest-rate changes (see Box 12.2). Assets and liabilities that are considered highly sensitive to interest changes include lines of credit and bank loans, large deposits, and any deposits being paid above market interest rates. Low interest-rate sensitivity is common among small balance savings accounts.

- The microfinance environment is competitive. Competition usually compels MFIs to reduce the margin between the interest rate they charge on loans and the rate they pay on deposits. In a competitive environment the MFI may not be able to increase rates earned on loans or lower the rate paid on deposits without affecting consumer demand and profitability.

To some degree interest-rate risk is unavoidable; however, it is manageable.

13.2 ALM: AN OVERVIEW

MFIs manage or reduce the risk that changes in interest rates will hurt their profitability by properly balancing their assets and liabilities. An example can illustrate how this works:

Suppose that an MFI offers both passbook savings accounts and certificates of deposit. If competitors increase their interest rate on time deposits and the MFI does not, as the time deposits reach maturity, time-deposit holders may well withdraw their funds and place them with a competing institution that offers a higher interest rate. To hold onto these rate-sensitive deposits, the MFI must increase its interest rate for this type of account. *To do so and still maintain the same level of profitability, however, it must be able to receive simultaneously a higher rate of interest on a similar volume of loans or other assets.*

The core of managing interest-rate risk is to maintain the *interest-rate spread* (the difference between the rate the MFI pays for deposits and the rate it charges for loans). Changes in interest rates for a given volume of assets must be matched in time with changes in interest rates for a similar volume of liabilities. This requires the MFI to match the volume and maturities of rate-sensitive assets with rate-sensitive liabilities. It is this process of matching RSAs with RSLs that is called ALM.

ALM is another form of planning. It allows management to be active or anticipate change rather than merely to react to unanticipated change. The objective of ALM is to maintain a match of the terms of RSAs with their funding source (deposits, equity, and external credit) *while maximizing profitability*. Tools to match assets and liabilities while maximizing profitability are discussed in Section 13.4.

To meet these objectives, an MFI needs to

- adopt an overall strategy for managing its interest-rate risk,
- develop a system—a set of tools—for monitoring its interest-rate risk and its match between RSAs and RSLs,
- be prepared to alter the terms and mix of its assets and liabilities, in line with its ALM policy and in response to the results of monitoring,
- develop a written policy regarding how it will perform its ALM, and
- establish a process by which ALM is carried out, in line with its policy.

The following sections will address each of these elements in detail.

13.3 ALM STRATEGIES

Management can reduce interest-rate risk in a number of ways. Some of these ways are more complex but enable the MFI to offer a range of services. Others are simpler but limit the services that can be offered. Management should choose an option that is commensurate with its management capacity:

Simplest, most restrictive option: The maturities of loans, investments, and deposits can be limited to between one and three months. Loans and investments can be matched against deposits of a similar maturity. As loans are repaid and deposits mature, the interest rates can be changed as needed to maintain profitability. The only management concern would be that profitability is adequate. This approach is by far the simplest because the short-term maturities greatly reduce interest-rate risk. However, this approach reduces the type of loans and savings products that may be offered to clients. Furthermore, in a competitive environment, it might not be feasible (see Box 12–2).

Most complex option: If the MFI's financial managers and information system are sophisticated enough, variable interest rates can be used. This allows management to grant longer-term loans as long as it can change interest rates on a monthly or quarterly basis. The interest rates on variable-interest loans and deposits will change at nearly the same time. Therefore, if management responds quickly to changes on both sides of the balance sheet, variable interest rates can greatly reduce interest-rate risk.

For most MFIs, this approach has several drawbacks. First, changes in the interest rate will either increase the size of the payment or extend the life of the loan. Most MFIs are likely to find these record-keeping changes to be prohibitively labor intensive. Second, variable interest rates enable MFIs to match the terms of assets and liabilities perfectly, in theory. In reality, this will only work if management responds quickly to changes in the market by changing its rates both on loans and on deposits—which is hard for many MFIs. Third, if there is a maximum percentage to which interest rates on loans can be increased, then when this limit is reached, loans become fixed rate. At this point interest-rate risk again becomes a concern.

Finally, with variable interest rates the institution passes interest-rate risk on to the client. Many clients will not be willing to accept this risk, especially if competitors offer fixed-rate loans, and so variable rates can damage the relationship to clients. Moreover, when clients bear interest-rate risk, credit risk increases for the MFI because when rates go up loan payments also rise.

Middle option: Interest-rate risk can also be managed by matching the maturities and interest rates of loans and investments with the maturities and interest rates of deposits, equity, and external credit in order to maintain adequate profitability. Because this option is the most appropriate for many MFIs, it is discussed in detail in Section 13.4.

For most MFIs, whatever option they choose, all savings and loans should be exclusively in local currency. Alternatively, if an MFI accepts deposits in other currencies, it must also be able to lend or invest those funds in assets in the same foreign currency. If not, then foreign-exchange risk becomes a problem. "The devaluation/revaluation of such assets and liabilities acts the same way as interest rates in exposing the institution to potential gain or loss. In both cases, assets and liabilities can re-price over time and give rise to interest-rate risk, even though, strictly speaking, the extra income or loss from exchange rate fluctuations would not be considered as interest."[3] There are many ways of mitigating foreign-exchange risk, and MFIs face different situations, depending on their country. Monitoring and managing this risk is beyond the capabilities of most small MFIs.[4]

Once management has determined its overall strategy for managing interest-rate risk, it should develop a set of tools commensurate with the size and sophistication of the MFI to guide ALM.

13.4 TOOLS FOR MANAGING INTEREST-RATE RISK

This chapter recommends that management monitor and manage three items: its *core deposits, net interest margin* (NIM), and *gap.* Each of these management tools is explained in detail below. Monitoring and managing these items requires that management have the following in place:

- effective liquidity management;
- historical and current information on deposits and withdrawals from different types of deposit accounts over time, on current income and the cost of funds, and on the projected difference between gross income and the cost of funds;
- a written ALM policy (discussed below); and
- a commitment to change both deposit and loan interest rates as changes occur in the local market. The interest-rate changes on both sides of the balance sheet must be equal.

13.4.1 Monitoring and Managing Core Deposits

As discussed in Box 12.5, core deposits are the volume of deposits that are unlikely to be withdrawn, even in response to changes in market interest rates or seasonal swings. For purposes of ALM, management should determine what proportion of the core deposits they are willing to use to fund longer-term assets, that is, longer-term, fixed-rate loans and investments.

A conservative observation is that approximately 50 percent of the low average monthly savings balance of the core deposits may be used to fund longer-term assets. Once management sets a maximum amount for this percentage, it should use it regularly to determine the amount of funds it has available for lending or investing in longer-term assets. It should then adhere to this limit.

13.4.2 Monitoring and Managing the NIM

NIM is defined as gross interest, fee, and other operating income minus the cost of funds. It is strongly affected by the *interest-rate spread*, that is, the difference between the interest rate paid on deposits and the interest rate charged on loans. NIM is the funds that an MFI can use to cover operating expenses and equity contributions to meet equity goals and regulatory requirements. The MFI must maintain a NIM that is large enough to cover these costs in order to be financially viable (see Box 13–2). This is a key to managing interest-rate risk.

To ensure the MFI's viability, management must both monitor and actively manage its NIM. First, management must determine the minimum NIM needed to fund operating expenses and increase equity. This information is easily obtainable from the annual budgeting process. The annual budget should project a gross interest, fee, and other operating income that is large enough to cover operating expenses, the cost of funds, and capital increases. If the gross income is not large enough to cover all of these demands for cash, then the MFI will not be profitable.

Box 13–2. NIM Illustration

The Ashoka Credit Union is a small credit union located in the United States. On December 31, 2003, the credit union had $1,921,250 in assets and $161,076 in capital. The capital-to-assets ratio was, therefore, 8.38 percent. In the 2004 annual budget the manager and board members wanted to increase the capital-to-assets ratio to 8.79 percent with the longer-term goal being a ratio of greater than 9 percent. The credit-union manager and officials therefore developed a 2004 budget that allowed them to meet this goal. With their projected 2004 operating-budget information, the minimum NIM is easily calculated:

Gross income	$195,600
(minus) Cost of funds	$46,000
Minimum NIM	$149,600
(minus) Operating expenses	$128,370
Contribution to capital (net income)	$21,230
Total assets projected for 12/31/04	$2,073,875
Capital projected as of 12/31/03	$161,076
(plus) Projected net income for 2004	$21,230
Total capital projected for 12/31/04	$182,306
Total capital-to-assets ratio 12/31/04	8.79%

Therefore, the minimum NIM needed is $149,600 for the year or $12,467 a month to cover operating expenses and the contribution to capital to increase the capital-to-assets ratio to the desired level. The officials have to act quickly when the NIM is trending downward so that it does not fall below the minimum. If it is allowed to fall below the minimum amount, then the capital ratio will not meet the established goal.

Then, with this minimum NIM in mind, management should monitor and manage the MFI's actual NIM. If the MFI's actual NIM begins to approach its minimum NIM, management should make changes so that profitability is not adversely affected. An MFI can increase its NIM to the necessary level by employing any of the following strategies (or a combination of them):

- The MFI can enhance its income by increasing its interest rates or fees on loans. The effect of this change takes time because the lower-interest-rate loans must mature so that the funds may be lent again at the new higher interest rates. In order to maintain profitability, management must respond to changes in the local market by changing interest rates on loans as well as deposits. Frequently, officials are eager to increase deposit rates and are less enthusiastic about increasing loan rates. This is a recipe for a profitability problem.

- The MFI can reduce its cost of funds by decreasing the interest rates paid on savings and deposit accounts. This is always the quickest way to decrease expenses because the effect is immediate on all deposit accounts except those that have a fixed interest rate for a stated time period, such as certificates of deposit.

- The MFI can reduce its operating expenses, although this tends to be very difficult.

13.4.3 Monitoring and Managing the Gap

The third tool for managing interest-rate risk is *gap management*, matching RSAs with RSLs. The goal of gap management is to decrease the effects of interest-rate changes.

RSAs and RSLs are those assets and liabilities that can and are likely to respond to changes in market interest rates during a given period. These assets and liabilities either mature or can be priced either upward or downward during the given period. More specifically, RSAs are loans or investments with yields that respond to changing short-term interest rates. The change may be contractual in nature (such as with variable-rate loans) or due to maturity of the asset (the loan will be repaid and new loans will be given at the new interest rate). RSLs have terms that respond to changing short-term interest rates. Examples include certificates of deposit that mature or non-core savings that have no maturity and could be re-priced (increasing or decreasing interest rates) at any moment in response to changes in the market.

The objective of gap management is to have RSAs and RSLs fairly well matched. Ideally, for any given time period the amount of RSAs would be equal to the amount of RSLs. If RSAs minus RSLs is equal to zero, this means that RSAs and RSLs are evenly matched over a specific period of time. In other words, both assets and liabilities could be re-priced at exactly the same moment. For example, if interest rates have increased in the local economy, the MFI will take the new rates into consideration in re-pricing both its assets and liabilities at the same time. In theory, this will allow the MFI to maintain its spread and to eliminate interest-rate risk.

When RSAs and RSLs are not exactly matched, the difference is called a *gap*. A positive gap, when RSAs exceed RSLs, signifies that more RSAs are able to re-price at the new interest rates than RSLs. As a result, higher interest rates will result in an increase in the NIM. The NIM improves because the asset yield is more responsive to changing short-term rates than is the cost of funds. For the same reason, an MFI with a positive gap would see a drop in the NIM when market interest rates fall.

A negative gap, where RSLs exceed RSAs, signifies that more RSLs can be re-priced in a time period than RSAs. In this case higher interest rates will result in a smaller NIM. An increase in short-term rates increases the cost of funds faster than asset yield, reducing profitability. Likewise, for an MFI with a negative gap NIM goes up when market interest rates fall. MFI management should never try to guess which direction interest rates will move; instead, management should keep RSAs and RSLs fairly well matched. This is known as "managing the gap."

Calculating the Gap

How well RSAs and RSLs are matched can only be analyzed with the aid of a spreadsheet known as gap management report (see Appendices 13.1 and 13.2). The gap management report should be commensurate with the MFI's size and sophistication. The report should include all of the MFI's assets and liabilities divided into time periods based on when they can be re-priced. The totals for each asset and liability should be equal to the totals on the balance sheet.

For each time period the report should provide two important calculations: the gap (RSAs minus RSLs), and the gap divided by total assets (also known as the *gap ratio*). The gap ratio is a key ratio for monitoring interest-rate risk.

The gap report is driven by the assumptions made about RSAs and RSLs. If the assumptions are wrong, so too is the report. It is straightforward to categorize deposit accounts and investments with a specific maturity, such as fixed-rate certificates of deposit. The time of re-pricing is the same as the maturity. It is harder to categorize savings accounts with no maturity and variable-rate loans, given uncertainty about when they might be re-priced.

Fixed rate loans: Except for loans that have a single payment, loans generate a stream of repayments over the life of the loan. They do not have a specified one-time maturity. In the gap report, a loan is distributed across time periods according to its repayment stream. Furthermore, because loans can be prepaid or delinquent, the loan maturity does not indicate when the loan will come due for re-pricing. For purposes of calculating the gap, the simplest way to allocate fixed-rate loans is to use the loan turnover. (For how to calculate loan turnover, see Table 12.2.) Using this calculation, loans are entered into the spreadsheet based on how quickly they turn over. For example, if the loan turnover ratio is 8, the outstanding total loan balance will be divided equally over eight months in the gap report.

Deposits with no maturity: For demand deposits (where withdrawals are made according to the customers' demand) the core savings deposit analysis previously discussed will assist in determining the timing of re-pricing. Non-core deposits should be considered re-priceable in the current period or in the first category (less than one month) of the gap report; if external interest rates increase and the MFI does not increase its interest rate, these funds are likely to be withdrawn and placed elsewhere. In contrast, core deposits, although they can be re-priced at any time, should be considered non-rate-sensitive, longer-term deposits.

Variable-rate loans and deposits: To determine when variable-rate loans and deposits should be considered re-priceable, managers should consider the following set of questions:

- What are the terms/maturities of the variable-rate loans or deposits? Specifically, under what conditions and how frequently can interest rates be changed?
- Does the MFI respond to changes in the market by changing the variable rates? If not, loans or deposits should be considered as fixed rate for purposes of calculating the gap. If so, how long does it take for the MFI to respond to changes in the market? This period should be considered the period of re-priceability for purposes of calculating the gap.
- Is there a maximum percentage that interest rates can increase in a year and over the life of the loan or deposit? If the loan or deposit reaches the lifetime maximum interest rate, it then becomes fixed rate for purposes of calculating the gap.

Monitoring the Gap

The gap ratio is helpful in monitoring the match between RSAs and RSLs. In addition, the MFI can also monitor its interest-rate risk by analyzing how the gap would be affected by changes in interest rates. This is known as "what if" analysis.

Gap ratio: *(RSAs – RSLs)/total assets:* The gap ratio has a dimension that the gap does not. The gap ratio for a particular time period measures the MFI's exposure to interest-rate risk during that time period. It relates the gap to the size of the MFI. A US$500,000 gap would be material—significant—for an MFI with US$1.5 million in assets but not for an MFI with US$5 million in assets. The general goal for gap ratios for MFIs in which voluntary savings deposits represent more than half of the MFI's volume of funding is between +10 percent and –10 percent. A ratio within this range usually indicates low exposure to interest-rate risk. Any ratio greater than +10 percent or –10 percent is considered to be of moderate or high risk. However, if an MFI has a large source of very stable funds, as does the MFI in Appendix 13.2, the acceptable range might increase to +15 percent to –15 percent. A larger range is tolerable because the funding sources (internal loan between the NGO and the MFI, compulsory savings, donations, and institutional capital) are not interest-rate sensitive.

The magnitude rather than the sign (positive or negative) of a gap ratio is the important factor to consider when assessing rate sensitivity. A 2 percent interest-rate decline can be just as damaging to the net margin of an MFI with a +20 percent gap ratio as a 2 percent interest-rate increase would be to an MFI with a –20 percent gap ratio. Ratios outside the acceptable range indicate that interest-rate changes could adversely affect profitability.

"What if" analysis: Changes in interest rates can profoundly affect profitability. Management should project these effects. This can be done using "what if" analysis. "What if" analysis answers questions like this: If interest rates increase 2 percent, what will be the impact on profitability? Most small MFIs do not have access to the sophisticated software packages that perform this type of analysis. Instead, they can estimate the effect of interest-rate changes on the MFI's NIM. To do this for a selected time period, they can multiply the anticipated interest-rate change for this period by the difference between RSAs and RSLs for the period.

For example, if within the three- to six-months time frame,

$$RSAs - RSLs = -US\$1,000,000$$

then an increase in interest rates of 1 percent per annum will decrease earnings by approximately US$10,000 on an annualized basis:

$$-US\$1,000,000 \times 0.01 = -US\$10,000$$

The results of "what if" analysis should be considered as a general indication of magnitude and direction. They are not exact.

Of course, monitoring the gap is only valuable if senior managers are prepared to take corrective action as needed.

Managing the Gap

The gap report is similar to the balance sheet. It is a "snapshot" in time. The next business day the numbers have changed. For small MFIs, the gap report may be prepared and analyzed monthly or quarterly. If very little changes in the MFI annually, then the report could be produced semi-annually.

After analyzing the gap report, management must develop strategies to change the mix of RSAs and RSLs within specific time frames that are outside of the acceptable ranges. For instance, if the gap ratio for the two- to three-months time period was +30 percent, then management would want to change the mix in that time frame so that the gap ratio fell in the acceptable range. This could be done by increasing the amount of savings deposits that come due in that time frame or decreasing the amount of loans maturing in the time frame. This must be done keeping in mind established goals and objectives and the impact on profitability, liquidity, and customer service.

13.5 ALM POLICY

ALM should be guided by a written policy that is reviewed annually and revised as needed. ALM and liquidity management are closely related and operationally inseparable. ALM decisions affect liquidity in several ways:

- Any changes in the maturity structure of the assets and liabilities can change the cash requirements and flows, therefore affecting liquidity. Historical data on liquidity may not be sufficient to project the impact of material changes.
- Loan or savings promotions to better serve clients or change the ALM mix could harm liquidity, if not monitored closely; it is crucial that financial and marketing managers work together closely.
- Changes in interest rates could affect liquidity. If savings rates are lowered, clients might withdraw their funds. Higher interest rates on loans could make it difficult for some clients to meet interest payments. Either change could cause a liquidity shortage.

Management must always analyze the impact that any ALM policy or decision has on liquidity. Therefore, the policy should address both ALM and liquidity management. The ALM policy should discuss:

- What tools will be used to monitor ALM.
- What are the acceptable parameters or ranges for ALM indicators, including the proportion of core deposits used to fund longer-term assets, the minimum NIM, and the target range for the gap ratio.
- Who is responsible for monitoring the MFI's ALM position.
- How often the ALM position will be analyzed and discussed.

Interest-rate risk is just one of the risks affected by how the institution manages its assets and liabilities. There are other risks, and no risk stands alone. Sound financial and operational management are crucial to managing interest-rate risk. Management should establish the following policies[5] to strengthen its ALM:

- *Goals for short-term and long-term minimum equity to total assets ratios.* Equity is defined as regulatory reserves, other reserves, donations, and undivided earnings. For example, an appropriate goal for this long-term ratio is no less than 10 percent. If the MFI is short of this amount, then it should set short-term goals that move toward it. Equity serves as a cushion to absorb unforeseen losses; it is crucial to an institution's survival.
- *The maximum percentage of assets to be held by any one client.* An appropriate goal is no more than 10 percent of the loan portfolio or assets if the loan is collateralized and no more than 10 percent of equity if the loan is uncollateralized. By diversifying the portfolio and assets, the institution avoids undue concentration risk, the risk that any one non-performing individual can have a strongly negative effect on financial performance.
- *Adequate diversification in the types of loans and investments made to reduce loan and investment portfolio risk.* This also avoids the possibility

that one poorly performing sector or type of investment can have a strongly negative effect on financial performance.

- *The maximum percentage of total assets to be held in fixed-rate investments.* An appropriate limit is no more than 5 percent of total assets. Holding too large a proportion of assets in fixed-rate investment increases interest-rate risk by making it difficult to adjust interest rates.
- *The maximum amount of loans with a fixed rate of interest and a maturity greater than one year.* Holding too much in long-term fixed rate loans increases both interest-rate risk and liquidity risk.
- *The desired diversification of savings and deposits by account type and client to reduce concentration risk.*
- *The maximum maturities for all types of loans, investments, and deposits.* Again, holdings that have very long terms increase interest-rate risk.
- *If management and the MIS are capable, the offering of variable-rate loans and deposits that adjust in a timely manner to market rate changes.* This can greatly reduce interest-rate risk.
- *Pricing strategies for loans and savings products based on what it costs to offer the product and what the local market will bear.* Getting the prices right is crucial not only for viability but also for managing liquidity and interest-rate risk.

13.6 THE PROCESS OF LIQUIDITY MANAGEMENT AND ALM

Policies and tools have meaning only if they are implemented. An MFI should monitor all ALM and liquidity information on a monthly or periodic basis depending on the activity and sophistication of the MFI. Monitoring can be performed by individual staff members or by an asset liability management committee (ALCO) composed of staff members in senior, decision-making positions, such as the heads of lending, finance, accounting, and marketing. If this committee is formed, its responsibility should be to oversee the ALM process. Based on the review of ALM reports and local market conditions, it would make recommendations to the executive director of the MFI. The ALCO can meet monthly, quarterly, or as needed. Written minutes should be maintained for all meetings.

A typical ALCO meeting might include:

- a review of policies concerning the diversification of loans and deposits, goals for minimum equity to total assets ratios, and pricing (interest rate) strategy;
- a review of the gap management report, daily cash needs, cash-flow budget, and the pertinent ratios presented in a trend-analysis format;
- a discussion on anticipated interest-rate changes and other market changes that could affect the MFI's profitability, ALM, and liquidity;

- suggestions concerning any changes in interest rates or terms for loans and deposits;
- review of any new investments, unusual loan or deposit activity in loans or deposits, and the activity in new loan or savings products;
- review of the maturity and types of investments and client savings and deposits to ensure that there are no concentrations with regards to maturity and type; and
- review of the loan report or trial balance to ensure that the loan portfolio is well diversified with regard to maturity, collateral securing the loans, and loan type.

13.7 SUMMARY

Liquidity and ALM are complex, and their complexity grows as the MFI offers deposit services. No matter what the size and sophistication of the institution, policies and procedures to handle these complexities are essential. These policies and procedures should be reflective of the MFI's sophistication and responsive, so that they grow and increase in complexity as the MFI does. Furthermore, management must thoroughly understand how to perform the procedures and interpret the results of all analysis. To this end, management must:

- Develop specific written procedures to monitor liquidity, determine the stability and liquidity of the sources of funds, determine the NIM, and ensure that RSAs and RSLs are properly matched.
- Develop a written liquidity and ALM policy. Ensure that it is coordinated with other MFI policies and that their objectives do not conflict.
- Establish an ALCO or appoint those responsible for monitoring liquidity and ALM.
- Hold ALCO meetings monthly or as needed to review the liquidity and ALM position of the MFI and make changes and/or recommendations.
- Perform and review monthly, quarterly, or as needed (if there is little or no change) ratio analysis, cash forecasting, cash-flow budgeting, analysis to identify stable sources of funds, adequacy of NIM, and gap analysis of RSAs and RSLs.
- Establish a funding source when liquidity drops below the minimum level.
- Identify any other available options to resolve a liquidity and/or ALM problem.

APPENDIX 13.1 GAP MANAGEMENT

Table 13–1. Report Form with Comments

GAP MANAGEMENT REPORT AS OF _____	< 1	2 - 3	4-6	7-9	10-12	>12	NRS or no maturity	totals
				months				
RATE SENSITIVE ASSETS								
Cash and deposits earning no interest	$ -	$ -	$ -	$ -	$ -	$ -	$ -	$ -
Interest-earning demand deposits in other institutions	$ -	$ -	$ -	$ -	$ -	$ -	$ -	$ -
Fixed-term deposits in other institutions	$ -	$ -	$ -	$ -	$ -	$ -	$ -	$ -
Investments	$ -	$ -	$ -	$ -	$ -	$ -	$ -	$ -
Current loans	$ -	$ -	$ -	$ -	$ -	$ -	$ -	$ -
Fixed assets	$ -	$ -	$ -	$ -	$ -	$ -	$ -	$ -
Asset totals	$ -	$ -	$ -	$ -	$ -	$ -	$ -	$ -
RATE SENSITIVE LIABILITIES & CAPITAL								
External credit	$ -	$ -	$ -	$ -	$ -	$ -	$ -	$ -
Core regular savings accounts	$ -	$ -	$ -	$ -	$ -	$ -	$ -	$ -
Non-core regular savings accounts	$ -	$ -	$ -	$ -	$ -	$ -	$ -	$ -
Certificates of deposit	$ -	$ -	$ -	$ -	$ -	$ -	$ -	$ -
Core current accounts	$ -	$ -	$ -	$ -	$ -	$ -	$ -	$ -
Non-core current accounts	$ -	$ -	$ -	$ -	$ -	$ -	$ -	$ -
Core retirement savings	$ -	$ -	$ -	$ -	$ -	$ -	$ -	$ -
Non-core retirement savings	$ -	$ -	$ -	$ -	$ -	$ -	$ -	$ -
Core savings accounts with a stated purpose	$ -	$ -	$ -	$ -	$ -	$ -	$ -	$ -
Non-core savings accounts with a stated purpose	$ -	$ -	$ -	$ -	$ -	$ -	$ -	$ -
Other types of deposit accounts:								
Institutional capital:								
Statutory reserve fund	$ -	$ -	$ -	$ -	$ -	$ -	$ -	$ -
Retained earnings	$ -	$ -	$ -	$ -	$ -	$ -	$ -	$ -
Contingency reserve (maturity related to purpose)	$ -	$ -	$ -	$ -	$ -	$ -	$ -	$ -
Charity and donations	$ -	$ -	$ -	$ -	$ -	$ -	$ -	$ -
Totals for liabilities and capital	$ -	$ -	$ -	$ -	$ -	$ -	$ -	$ -
1. Gap: assets - (liabilities + capital)	$ -	$ -	$ -	$ -	$ -	$ -	$ -	$ -
2. Gap ratio: gap / total assets	0%	0%	0%	0%	0%	0%	0%	0%

The goal for the gap ratio is between +10 percent and –10 percent. This range indicates that there are no material problems with liquidity or interest-rate risk. If the ratios in the time frames are outside the acceptable range, a change in the interest rates could affect the profitability of the MFI. For example, if the MFI has a ratio of –20 percent in the four- to six-months category, this indicates that more liabilities will mature than assets. If interest rates were to increase, the profitability of the MFI would decrease. This is because the liabilities and deposits that will mature in this time period will earn interest at the new higher rates while the assets earn interest at the previous lower rate.

Comments:

1. The bolded cells represent the only cell or maturity option for this type of asset, liability, or capital account.
2. The assets, liabilities, and capital are distributed in the time periods according to re-priceability and maturity. The re-pricing time for some assets and liabilities, such as fixed-rate term deposits, is the maturity date; for other assets and liabilities, such as rate-sensitive, large-balance regular savings accounts that can re-price at any time, the criteria for distribution to a time period is strictly re-priceability. For example, the amount of loans in the four- to six-month category represents the total of all outstanding loan balances that will re-price or mature in that time frame.
3. Each category is from the date of the analysis. For example, if the date of the analysis is March 31, 2005, the certificates of deposit that are in the category four- to six-months will mature and be available for re-pricing between June 30 and September 30, 2005.
4. This analysis is similar to the MFI's balance sheet. It is a "snapshot" of the ALM position after the close of business for the month. The next day the information will change.
5. Cash earning no interest is not considered rate sensitive, so it is placed in the no-maturity or non-rate-sensitive category.
6. Demand-deposit accounts that earn minimal or no interest are considered non–rate sensitive because clients are likely to have their funds in the account not for its interest rate but for its transactional convenience. Demand-deposit accounts that do earn a competitive interest rate should be entered into the next time period in which interest is to be paid or the interest rate changed.
7. Loans should be entered into the spreadsheet using the result of the loan turnover calculation, if the calculation is indicative of how loans mature (see Table 12–2). If the result of the loan turnover is fourteen months, then the loan portfolio amount should be evenly distributed over fourteen months. If management has better information than the loan turnover provides, that should be used to distribute the loan portfolio over the time periods.
8. External credit should be entered based on its terms. If the interest rate can be changed at any time, then it should be entered in the time period "less than one month."
9. Savings and deposit accounts should be split to identify core and non-core deposit accounts if the breakdown is available and the data dependable. The non-core accounts should be placed in the time frame in which they can re-price. For example, non-core regular savings accounts usually re-price whenever interest is calculated.

This could be daily, monthly, quarterly, or some other interval. Core regular savings accounts are considered non–rate sensitive and matched against assets with a longer maturity. The time frames in which these funds will be placed are up to management's judgment.

Table 13–2. A Bank with Mostly Short-term, Stable Funds

figures in millions

ASSETS	1 month or <	2-3 months	4-6 months	7-9 months	10-12 months	> 1 year	non-rate-sensitive	Totals
Cash and deposits (earn no interest)	0	0	0	0	0	0	5.2	5.2
Demand deposits (earn interest)	15.9	0	0	0	0	0	0	15.9
Fixed term deposits	8.9	0	0	0	0	0	0	8.9
Investments	21	9.2	0	0	0	13.	0	43.2
Group loans	45.2	90.5	90.5	0	0	0	0	226.2
Emergency loans	30.7	46.0	0	0	0	0	0	76.7
Salary loan	.8	1.7	.8					3.3
Seasonal loan	1.6	1.6						3.2
Restructured loan	7	1.4	2.2	2.2	2.2	23.7		32.4
Fixed assets	0	0	0	0	0	0	10.5	10.5
Asset totals	125.8	149.4	93.5	2.2	2.2	36.7	15.7	425.5
LIABILITIES								
External credit	0	0	8.9	1.9	2.5	47.3	0	60.6
Internal loan	0	0	0	0	0	0	35.7	35.7
Checking deposits (earn no interest)	0	0	0	0	0	0	.1	.1
Term deposit—type 1	2.2							2.2
Regular savings	25.9	0	0	0	0	0	0	25.9
Term deposits—type 2	74.9	22.4	2.9	4.8	31.2	0	0	136.2
Compulsory savings	0	0	0	0	0	0	96.5	96.5
EQUITY								0
Paid-in equity	0	0	0	0	0	0	37.1	37.1
Retained earnings	0	0	0	0	0	0	10	10
Current net income	0	0	0	0	0	0	6	6
Other:	0	0	0	0	0	0	15.2	15.2
Liabilities and equity totals	103.0	22.4	11.8	6.7	33.7	47.3	200.6	425.5
Gap: assets - (liabilities + equity)	22.8	127	81.7	-4.5	-31.5	-10.6	-	
Gap ratio: gap/total assets (all periods)	5%	30%	19%	-1%	-7%	-2%		
What if: Impact on net income of 1% increase in interest rates	.23	1.27	.82	-.05	-.32	-.11		
What if: Same, as a % of net income	4%	21%	14%	-1%	-5%	-2%		

Note: This bank has a sound ALM position. Its goal for the gap ratio is between +15% and -15%. This is larger than the -10% to +10% suggested in the chapter because the bank's funding sources are very stable. Even the 30% gap ratio in the 2-3 month time frame is not of great concern because the difference between assets and liabilities can be funded with liabilities that are stable and non-rate sensitive. Therefore, the interest rate risk is manageable and profitability will not be adversely affected by a change in interest rates. Gap reports become increasingly important as MFIs attract more RSLs and make more longer-term loans.

Notes

[1] ALM refers to the actions taken to manage all risks related to assets and liabilities. This chapter focuses solely on interest-rate risk. Liquidity risk is discussed in Chapter 12 and new product risks are covered in Chapter 6. Other risks, such as credit risk and foreign-exchange risk, are outside the purview of this book.

[2] With a *fixed-rate* loan, the interest rate is set for the duration of the loan; with a *variable-rate* loan, it can be changed with changes in market rates.

[3] Robert Peck Christen, *Banking Services for the Poor: Managing for Financial Success* (Washington, DC: ACCION International, 1997), 134.

[4] For strategies for managing foreign-exchange risk, see Peter R. Crabb, "Foreign Exchange Risk Management Practices of Microfinance Institutions," *Journal of Microfinance* 6, no. 2 (2004).

[5] In some places, regulators will impose ALM restrictions and limits to gaps. Management should study these, and they should be the "minimal" policy of the institution.

14

Product Costing

Lorna Grace
and Brigit Helms

Product costing is a powerful tool. Determining the costs of products can enable management to discern which of its products are viable, which cost more, and which contribute most to the bottom line. In fact, understanding what savings products cost can be a key to improving their viability. A costing exercise can help managers make key decisions about product design, delivery mechanisms, and pricing. It can also can raise awareness of the cost components of different products, reveal hidden costs, instill cost-consciousness in staff, and uncover operational problems.

Product costing sheds light on fundamental questions about a product's future viability, efficiency, and customer segments, such as:

- Is the product likely to be profitable over time?
- What are the sources of costs—inefficiencies? excess capacity? How might the costs per account be reduced?
- How should pricing and minimum requirements vary by size of account?

Product costing is fairly new to microfinance, although it has been used in the broader business world for years. Experience to date suggests that product costing

This chapter was abstracted from the "CGAP Product Costing Tool" developed by Brigit Helms and Lorna Grace in collaboration with *MicroSave* and Bankakademie. For the tool (which provides more in-depth guidance, particularly on activity-based costing) and related information on product costing, see www.cgap.org/productcosting. The views expressed and mistakes made are attributed solely to the authors. The authors express their appreciation to David Cracknell, Kathryn Larcombe, and Gokul Pyakurel for their useful feedback, along with the several MFIs that have tested the tool to make sure it's useful in practice as well as in theory.

is demanding. It delves into nearly every aspect of an MFI's operations and can uncover inefficiencies and other operational problems. It therefore requires top management and staff to be highly committed to the process and open to improving operations and efficiency.

This chapter presents two methods for determining the administrative costs of individual savings products, *traditional cost allocation* and *activity-based costing* (ABC). Traditional cost allocation distributes administrative costs directly to products. ABC traces administrative costs first through activities and then to products. By first assigning costs to activities, ABC allows managers to understand more fully the costs of each product, identify excess capacity, and make informed decisions to improve efficiency.

This chapter

- compares the two methods,
- describes the steps involved in each,
- explains how each can be used to understand the marginal costs of a product, and
- details how to use the results to calculate the viability of savings products.

14.1 TRADITIONAL COST ALLOCATION VERSUS ABC

The purpose of product costing is to assign shared or *indirect* administrative costs to individual products. Many if not most of an MFI's nonfinancial (administrative) costs are indirect. Staff or resources rarely work solely on one product, so nearly all costs must be distributed among products. If management wants to analyze what a product costs, these indirect costs must be allocated. This section describes two ways to do this, traditional cost allocation and ABC.

Traditional cost allocation distributes indirect costs among products using allocation bases. An allocation basis might be the proportion of direct labor hours spent on a product or its total account balances relative to that of other products. The allocation process can provide insight into the total cost of each product and, ultimately, its profitability. Furthermore, because the traditional cost allocation method uses the MFI's existing accounting categories, after costing is implemented the first time, the information system can be adapted to generate costing information as part of regular monthly budget reports (as long as staff time information is also collected regularly).

However, traditional cost allocation normally uses allocation bases that are related to volume. These can overestimate the per unit costs of the larger products and underestimate the costs of smaller ones. Another drawback is that traditional cost allocation distributes costs according to accounting categories like salaries or office rent. These provide managers with few insights into *how* costs are incurred and *why* one product costs more than another (see Figure 14–1).

Box 14–1. The Basics: Cost Accounting Terms

The language of cost accounting can be confusing. Some important definitions follow:

Administrative costs: All recurring costs except the cost of funds and loan losses.

Allocation basis: Method of assigning indirect costs to cost objects.

Cost allocation: The assignment of identifiable cost items (direct or indirect) to cost objects.

Cost objects: Cost units being studied, in this case, products. (Alternative cost objects could be branches or customer segments.)

Cost drivers: An event or action that triggers a unit of activity to which costs are assigned, such as the number of deposit transactions.

Direct costs: Costs that can be directly traced to a given cost object.

Indirect costs: Costs that are not directly related to one cost object but are shared among cost objects.

Fixed costs: Costs that remain constant regardless of activity or output levels.

Marginal costs: The amount that costs increase when adding another product or product line (or decrease when eliminating a product or product line).

Unit costs: Cost per unit produced or per transaction.

Variable costs: Costs that change in proportion to levels of activity or output.

ABC traces costs to specific activities undertaken by the MFI (such as processing a loan application or opening a savings account) before *driving* them to products. These activities are "used" or "consumed" by the different products depending on specific attributes that trigger activity costs (for example, the number of housing loan applications received or the number of passbook savings accounts opened). A given product consumes many different activities. Adding up the costs of these activities reveals the total costs of delivering the product.

Instead of trying to allocate time to the abstract idea of a product, asking staff to think about the time spent on particular activities is more intuitive and provides a powerful tool for understanding and managing costs. Because sources of product costs can be traced back to very specific activities, this approach provides richer information about how or why costs are incurred than traditional cost allocation methods. For example, one MFI that undertook an ABC exercise discovered several sources of inefficiency: correcting routine errors in data entry absorbed nearly one-sixth of its branch managers' time; its monthly cost of collecting a payment nearly tripled once the payment became overdue; and large office-based withdrawals cost significantly more than smaller withdrawals in the field.

ABC also has drawbacks. Above all, it demands more time, technical expertise, and analysis than traditional cost allocation. An MFI should undertake ABC only if it has capable managers who have been trained in ABC and/or should utilize technical assistance from someone with ABC expertise. A full ABC model

Figure 14–1. Results of Traditional Cost Allocation versus ABC

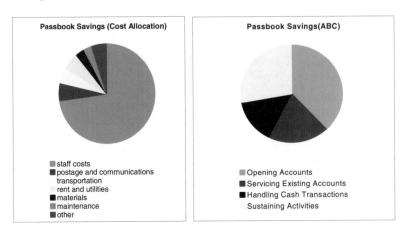

also requires a significant amount of detailed process-level information and may lie beyond the scope of many MFIs' information systems. Table 14–1 summarizes the pros and cons of traditional cost allocation and ABC.

14.2 COSTING EXERCISES: FREQUENCY AND PREPARATION

Product costing is most effective when it is done at least once a year. Although a one-time study will provide important insights, tracking performance over time will help managers see whether the actions they take to increase efficiency succeed in doing so. More frequent product costing can also provide better insight into seasonality issues and may not require a full costing exercise.

The effort required for product costing exercises depends on the size and complexity of the organization and the quality of its information system. Product costing exercises entail two phases: preparation and implementation. The first phase, which involves planning, selecting a costing team, and developing a questionnaire, takes up to two days for everyone on the costing team (described below). Implementation takes a few weeks, depending on the MFI. Data gathering (for example, validating and using a staff questionnaire and organizing data from the MIS into the preferred format) can be done at the same time by different team members. Developing or modifying the database model and analyzing the data takes two to three days. Subsequent costing exercises demand less time, as much of the work will have been completed during the initial exercise.

Costing requires an understanding of how staff members spend their time. This can be estimated in three ways: (1) they can record the time they spend on each product or activity in a journal or time sheet, (2) a member of the costing

Table 14–1. An Assessment of Traditional Cost Allocation and ABC

	Traditional cost allocation	**ABC**
Pros	• Fewer steps • Simpler, less expensive • Consistent with the chart of accounts: allows costs to be monitored regularly • Can be powerful when used to identify and focus additional investigation	• By tracing (rather than allocating) costs, allows management to understand how and why costs are incurred and where to reduce costs • Focuses on activities that are meaningful to staff and management • Helps management better understand business processes • Useful for projections and introducing new products • Useful for designing staff and client incentives
Cons	• Relies on subjective input • Allocates costs simplistically: can over-allocate costs to large-volume products • Presents costs using general ledger accounts that are not meaningful for most staff • Can focus managers on allocating costs rather than on managing them	• Complex, time consuming, and expensive • Relies on subjective input • MIS may not provide sufficient information • Requires expertise in ABC, either from a consultant or from well-trained managers

team can observe them, or (3) a member of the costing team can conduct in-depth interviews with staff members. Time sheets are forms that enable staff to track the amount of time they spend on different activities. A grid with activities on one axis and dates on the other axis allows staff members or technical-assistance providers to note the number of hours and minutes spent each day on each activity. Where using time sheets is not feasible, staff can simply estimate the percentage of time spent on each activity. In practice, percentage estimates can be accurate at the head-office level but may be less so at the branch level, so care should be taken to verify information by cross checking estimates among staff members at the same level.

To make sure that the results of different costing exercises can be compared, MFIs should follow the same costing model and steps each time. During its first costing exercise, the MFI should tailor the process and tools to its own circumstances. Managers may also need to modify the model in response to new products or changes in operations.

Before either a traditional cost allocation or an ABC exercise, MFIs should take the following steps:

1. *Clarify purpose and process for senior managers:* From the beginning, senior managers themselves must understand the purpose and process clearly. A short workshop may be helpful.
2. *Communicate the purpose to staff:* Senior management should thoroughly explain the purpose and importance of the costing exercise to the rest of staff. Management should reassure staff that the findings from the exercise will not be used against them but will help them make better decisions.
3. *Choose a team leader:* Because leading a serious costing exercise is time-consuming, the executive director should delegate the task to another senior manager who should report to the executive director.
4. *Assemble the costing team:* Management should assemble a costing team of three to five members. At a minimum, the costing team should include members from operations (if possible, both branch and head office), accounting, and MIS departments. Representatives from human resources and internal audit could also be included. A comprehensive team will enrich the analysis and make recommendations that incorporate the points of view of all elements of the MFI. The senior manager or consultant with expertise should train the team in the purpose, process, and specifically in how to observe and collect data on how staff use their time.
5. *Choose the period:* The team should choose a specific period of time for analysis that is as recent as possible. All data should come from that time period. A full year is ideal as it can even out swings in business cycles, but shorter periods may be more practical.
6. *Choose the representative branch site(s):* Especially for large MFIs, gathering data from all branches may not be possible. One or two representative branches will usually be enough. The branches should be considered mature, or fairly stable, by the MFI, should not be located in the headquarters office, and should offer all the products that the costing study is investigating.
7. *Assemble necessary information:* Senior management should ensure that the team has adequate access to information. For example, it will need a chart of accounts, income statement, staff costs and numbers by grade and location, operational manuals, organizational charts, product balances, and transaction statistics. The team should start gathering this information at the same time it gathers information on staff time usage.
8. *Complete time sheets or time estimates:* If time sheets or journals are used, the costing team may want to have staff fill these out before the costing exercise begins. However, staff can find these very difficult to fill in and may need outside help.

9. *Prepare the work plan:* The team should identify the major steps involved in the costing exercise. For each step it should estimate the amount of time needed, indicate the person(s) responsible for implementation, and estimate the nature and quantity of resources required. The plan should note the prerequisites for each step, and these should be included in the plan. The team leader should obtain formal approval from the executive director for the plan. The plan should be converted into a checklist used by the team as it proceeds with the costing exercise in order to ensure that the costing exercise goes smoothly. The team should focus on keeping the work cost effective and simple as well as on producing useful analytic results.

10. *Identify products for costing:* Many MFIs have several products, such as housing, loans, microenterprise loans, emergency loans, passbook savings, and time deposits.[1]

14.3 METHOD ONE: TRADITIONAL COST ALLOCATION

After the preparatory work is complete, traditional cost allocation can be accomplished with the following three steps. These steps are illustrated with an example of an extremely simple cost allocation exercise in Box 14–2.[2]

Step One: Identify Costs to Allocate

The costing team must first decide which nonfinancial line items to consider individually and which to aggregate or combine. In general, line items that represent a large portion of total administrative costs—over 15 percent—should be considered individually. Line items that represent a smaller portion—less than 5 percent—should be combined with other line items. For instance, costs related to purchasing individual stationery items and other office supplies could be combined into one category named supplies. An MFI should decide how detailed an allocation to perform based on its needs and the resources it can expend on the costing exercise. Items that are not treated individually should be combined with other items that "act" similarly; assigning the same allocation basis to these combined items should be reasonable. For example, the rationale for allocating rent and utilities might be similar when deciding on allocation bases. The number of product transactions or accounts, for instance, could be used.

Step Two: Decide and Calculate Allocation Bases for Each Type of Cost

The team must decide what basis to use to allocate indirect costs to individual products. The allocation bases should be objective and reasonable; they should represent as closely as possible how much each product "consumes" indirect costs. For example, staff salaries usually are allocated based on the percentage of time staff spend on each product. Computer costs might be allocated based on the

Box 14–2. Example of Cost Allocation Method

A. Cost allocation: total costs

Step 1: Identify costs to allocate		**Step 2: Decide and calculate allocation bases** allocation basis	**calculation of allocation basis**			**Step 3: Use bases to distribute costs** allocation of costs		
			Loan 1	**Loan 2**	**Savings**	**Loan 1**	**Loan 2**	**Savings**
Head office	**206,038**	same as BM time	53%	20%	27%	**109,200**	**41,208**	**55,630**
Branch								
Branch manager	66,000	time analysis	53%	20%	27%	34,980	13,200	17,820
Collectors	369,360	time analysis	60%	15%	25%	221,616	55,404	92,340
Data entry staff	50,000	transactions	42%	15%	43%	21,000	7,500	21,500
Total salaries	485,360					277,596	76,104	131,660
Rent	50,400	(see note)	49%	16%	35%	21,168	7,560	21,672
Paper	41,038	transactions	42%	15%	43%	17,236	6,156	17,646
Other	29,976	transactions	42%	15%	43%	12,590	4,496	12,890
Travel	12,292	same as BM time	53%	20%	27%	6,515	2,458	3,319
Depreciation	22,108	transactions	42%	15%	43%	9,285	3,316	9,506
Total branch	**641,174**					**344,390**	**100,091**	**196,693**
Total costs	**847,212**					**453,590**	**141,299**	**252,323**

BM = branch manager

Note: Area of space is allocated according to time analysis of staff who use offices.

B. Cost allocation: marginal costs
(see Box 14–1 for an explanation of marginal costs)

Step 1: Identify costs to allocate

Step 2: Decide and calculate allocation bases

Step 3: Use bases to distribute costs

costs to allocate		allocation basis	calculation of allocation basis		allocation of costs	
			All core products	Marginal product Savings	All core products	Marginal product Savings
	Amount					
Head office	206,038	fixed cost	100%	0%	206,038	0
Branch						
Branch manager	66,000	fixed cost	100%	0%	66,000	0
Collectors	369,360	fixed cost	100%	0%	369,360	0
Data entry staff	50,000	transactions	57%	43%	28,500	21,500
Total salaries	485,360				463,860	21,500
Rent	50,400	fixed cost (see note)	100%	0%	50,400	0
Paper	41,038	transactions	57%	43%	23,392	17,646
Other	29,976	fixed cost	100%	0%	29,976	0
Travel	12,292	same as BM time	73%	27%	8,973	3,319
Depreciation	22,108	fixed cost	100%	0%	22,108	0
Total branch	641,174				598,709	42,465
Total costs	847,212				804,747	42,465

Note: Area of space is allocated according to time analysis of staff who use offices.

Table 14–2. Some Possible Allocation Bases

Allocation basis	Application
Staff time	The proportion of staff time spent on each product over a defined period of time, based on timesheet data or other estimation techniques.
Number of transactions	The number of transactions per product as a percentage of all transactions over a defined period of time.
Number of accounts	The average number of accounts for a product as a proportion of the average total number of accounts over a defined period of time.
Volume of accounts	The average volume of accounts for a product as a proportion of the average total volume of accounts over a defined period of time.
Equal	When the resource used is generic, each product is given an equal share.

percentage of total transactions that relate to each product (see Table 14–2). Of course, some costs are directly allocated to a product, for example, marketing costs for a specific savings product. The choice of bases can significantly affect the results of the costing exercise.

Once the team decides on the allocation bases, it must assemble the data needed to calculate these bases. For example, the costing team may already have had branch staff use time sheets to track and record the amount of time they spend on each product over a week or a month. The team uses these time sheets to determine the percentage of time each staff position spends on each product. The team then uses these percentages to allocate the costs of branch staff to different products. For head-office staff, the team might use allocation bases that relate to volume, such as account balances or number of transactions per product. The team might determine that head-office staff, who operate farther away from the products, would have a hard time recording time spent per product and that volume-related allocation bases would more fairly distribute head-office staff costs to products. To use transactions as an allocation basis, the team must be able to obtain this information from the MIS.

Achieving 100 percent accuracy in traditional cost allocation is impossible. Often one of the most valuable benefits of a traditional cost allocation exercise is the discussions with staff members throughout the costing process. The costing team should be ready to discuss and change its decisions on allocation bases as a result of consulting with staff. For example, where MFI experiences seasonality in its operations, the team may want to ensure that the figures represent a typical period. Box 14–3 illustrates how one institution chose a very simple allocation process to estimate the cost of savings operations.

Step Three: Use Allocation Bases to Distribute Costs among Products

Finally, the team should apply the allocation bases to the costs and add each element of a product's costs together to calculate its total costs. For example, in example A in Box 14–2, the branch manager costs US$66,000 and spends 53 percent of his time on loan product one. Therefore the branch manager costs for loan product one is 53 percent of 66,000, or 34,980. This figure is added to each of the other administrative costs of loan product one to arrive at its total administrative costs (US$453,590 out of a total cost of US$847,212, or 54 percent).

14.4 ABC

ABC involves a few more steps than traditional cost allocation. Instead of allocating costs directly to products, ABC first determines the cost of an MFI's core processes and activities. It then allocates costs to products based on how much each product "consumes" these activities, as explained below.[3]

The preparation required for ABC is the same as for the traditional cost allocation model (see Section 14.2). The next five steps, however, differ somewhat from traditional cost allocation methods.

Step One: Determine Core Processes and Activities

Every MFI will have different core processes. Processes typically include originating loans, servicing existing loans, opening deposit accounts, servicing deposits and withdrawals from savings accounts, identifying clients, and/or forming groups. In addition to these operational processes, MFIs also have *sustaining activities*, activities that are not easily traced to products. These activities include general management, accounting, secretarial tasks, information-technology support, human resource management, and marketing. Both core processes and sustaining activities can take place at headquarters and branch levels.

For each major process the costing team will identify the main activities performed by staff at the branch and headquarters levels. Activities will include things like accepting and approving loan applications, booking deposits in the accounting system, and performing general reporting functions (see Table 14–3).

Most MFIs have neither identified nor documented their core business processes. ABC gives them an ideal opportunity to do so. The act of documenting processes and activities can assist management to better understand the microfinance business and help it improve its MFI's efficiency. Process mapping, a management tool to streamline business processes, may also be a logical outcome of an ABC exercise.

Box 14–3. Estimating the Costs of Services: Traditional Cost Allocation at WOCCU

Sometimes an institution seeks a rough estimate of the costs of its services. In 2001, WOCCU sought to determine the administrative cost of savings services for fifteen of its Latin American affiliates. To do this, it used a traditional cost allocation method.

Allocating direct administrative costs was straightforward. These costs included the salaries, bonuses, and fringe benefits paid to staff primarily engaged in savings mobilization (marketing staff, tellers, and security guards) and the costs of publicity, promotion, such as raffles, and feasibility studies for savings services. These were allocated directly to savings.

The challenge was to find a reasonable way to allocate administrative costs that were indirect: the costs of staff, administrative services, depreciation, and protection that were only partly dedicated to savings operations. Indirect human resource costs included the remuneration of personnel who spend just a portion of their time in savings-related activities. Indirect administrative services included utilities, communications, office and vehicle maintenance, MIS support, and supplies. Depreciation included buildings, furniture, vehicles, computers, and the cost of remodeling rented facilities. Finally, protection included the cost of insurance premiums to protect against property damage, theft, and general liabilities; external audit and supervision fees; and certification and rating quotas.

WOCCU wanted to allocate costs using bases that relied on verifiable, quantitative data and that were simple enough for managers to calculate without sophisticated computer software. It ultimately chose three:

Transaction-based allocation. WOCCU used this basis for costs related to the volume of savings transactions such as supplies, insurance for robbery, and computer maintenance and depreciation. To calculate the allocation basis, managers needed to know the numbers of savings transactions and total transactions during the year.

Physical space-based allocation. Each of the credit unions serves clients solely in its office. Therefore, as a basis for allocating expenses like telephone, utilities, janitorial services, office maintenance, and building depreciation, WOCCU calculated the building's square footage that was dedicated to savings mobilization and divided it by the building's total square footage.

Time-based allocation. Finally, the cost of employees who were only indirectly or partly involved in savings mobilization was allocated according to the percentage of time they spent on savings-related activities. Staff estimated the time they spend on different services. Where more than one person holds the same type of position—for example, tellers—their responses were averaged. The result was also used to allocate administrative and protection costs such as depreciation and other expenses related to vehicles; external audit and supervision; and rating and certification quotas.

With these three allocation bases, WOCCU calculated the cost of savings operations in each credit union. Their ratios of administrative costs to total volume of savings ranged from 3 percent to 8.5 percent. The higher ratios belonged to credit unions with less than US$1 million in deposits.

David C. Richardson and Oswaldo Oliva V., "Counting the Costs of Savings Mobilization," in *Striking the Balance in Microfinance: A Practical Guide to Mobilizing Savings,* ed. Brian Branch and Janette Klaehn (Washington, DC: PACT, 2002), 155–84.

Step Two: Conduct Staff Time Estimates for Each Activity

Next, the team studies the costs of each activity, starting with estimates of the time all staff spend on the activity (see Table 14–3). This process is the same as the traditional cost allocation process for estimating staff time except that instead of estimating time per product, staff members estimate their time per activity. This may be easier because it focuses on what staff actually do every day. Measuring their use of time can generate discussions that motivate and enable staff to become more efficient.

Step Three: Calculate Costs per Activity

The team must now determine the monthly or annual cost for each activity. First, staff salaries and benefits are distributed to the activities based on the time estimates already completed. Next, the costing team allocates all non-staff administrative costs to the activities. Non-staff costs can be distributed among activities in the same proportion as total staff time (see Table 14–4).[4]

The total figures for all core processes and sustaining activities should exactly match those in the income statement. They are organized, however, according to activities and processes rather than according to ledger accounts. This makes it easier to understand how and why costs are incurred.

Step Four: Assign Cost Drivers and Determine Unit Activity Costs

Now, the team identifies cost drivers for each activity. This enables the calculation of a per unit or per transaction cost for each activity. A good cost driver is an event or action that triggers the activity. For example, a cost driver for the activity "collect and record cash in" could be the total number of cash transactions from loan repayments and savings deposits; each loan repayment or savings deposit requires the MFI to perform the activity "collect and record cash in" one time.

To calculate the per unit costs of the activity, the total costs of the activity are divided by the volume of the cost driver. For example, dividing the total costs of "collecting and recording cash in" by the total number of loan repayments and savings deposits yields the cost per transaction of "collecting and recording cash in."

These unit costs can then be distributed among the various products based on how intensively each product uses or demands each activity (or expects to use or demand it, for future-looking cost models) over the selected period, in this case a month (see Table 14–5). For example, the cost of "collecting and recording cash in" for the savings deposit product can be calculated by multiplying the cost per transaction of "collecting and recording cash in" by the number of savings deposits for that product.

Even before using them to determine individual product costs, unit costs can be a powerful tool to help managers identify the source of inefficiencies and track

Table 14–3. Example of ABC Steps One and Two

Step 1: Define processes and activities   **Step 2: Estimate time each staff position spends on each activity per month**

Core processes and activities	Branch Manager		Collector		Other positions[1]		Total	
	Hours	%	Hours	%	Hours	%	Hours	%
Core process: servicing existing loans	**51**	**24.6**	**50**	**25.3**	---	-	**277**	**19.9**
Follow up with delinquent clients	24	11.6	6	3	---	-	182	13.1
Analyze repayment performance	14	6.7	2	1	---	-	28	2.0
Collect current payments	13	6.3	42	21.2	---	-	67	4.8
Core process: making new loans	**3.8**	**1.8**	**11.1**	**5.6**	---	-	**14.9**	**1.1**
Process requests	1.8	1	4.6	2.3	---	-	6.3	.5
Disburse and record	2	1.8	6.6	3.3	---	-	8.6	.6
Core process: opening deposit accounts	**15**	**7.2**	**3.5**	**1.8**	---	-	**58.5**	**4.2**
Explain rules	7	3.4	2.8	1.4	---	-	49.8	3.6
Prepare application and passbooks	8	3.7	.8	.4	---	-	8.8	.6
Core process: servicing deposit accounts	**48**	**23.1**	**5.7**	**2.9**	---	-	**161.7**	**11.6**
Routine checking and updating	35	16.4	2.5	1.2	---	-	44.5	3.2
Close accounts	5	2.4	1.3	.6	---	-	10.3	.7

Activity							
Process large withdrawals	5	2.4	2	1	---	.6	9
Client visits and spot checks	2	1.0	0	0	---	4.6	6
Correct errors	2	1.0	0	0	---	2.4	34
Core process: handling cash transactions	**60.8**	**29.3**	**119**	**60.2**	---	**24.4**	**339.8**
Collect and record cash in	24	11.6	108	54.6	---	19.8	276
Collect and record cash out	24	11.6	5	2.5	---	2.1	29
General cash administration	12.8	6.1	6	3	---	2.5	34.8
Sustaining activities	**29.1**	**14.0**	**8.5**	**4.3**	---	**38.8**	**541.1**
Area selection and promotion	2.3	1.1	0	0	---	.4	6.3
Staff meetings	9	4.3	8	4	---	2.5	35
Month-end accounting and reporting / MIS	3	1.4	.5	.3	---	.9	12.5
Recruit and train	4	1.9	0	0	---	1.9	26
General administration	.8	.4	0	0	---	28.3	393.8
Fraud prevention	8.3	4.0	0	0	---	1.5	21.3
External relations	1.8	.8	0	0	---	3.3	46.3
All activities	**207.6**	**100**	**197.8**	**100**	---	**100**	**1,392.9**

[1]Each branch and head office staff position should have a column.

Table 14–4. Example of ABC Step Three (for one process only)

Step 3: Calculate staff and non-staff costs per activity

Process / Activity	Branch manager	Other positions[1]	Total Staff Costs	Total Hours (number)	Total Hours (%[2])	Total Non-Staff Costs[3]	Total Costs
Core Process: Servicing Deposit Accounts	**6,868**	---	**197,692**	**661**	**6.1%**	**51,789**	**249,481**
Routine checking and updating	4,865	---	80,409	271	2.5%	21,253	101,662
Close accounts	715	---	19,792	77	.7%	5,997	25,789
Process large withdrawals	715	---	24,649	103	.9%	8,075	32,724
Client visits and spot checks	286	---	38,242	72	.7%	5,645	43,886
Correct errors	286	---	34,601	138	1.3%	10,819	45,420

[1] Each branch and head office staff position should have a column. Formula: total salary x proportion of time spent on activity = staff cost per activity. Proportion of time comes from step 2 (see Table 14–3).

[2] Total hours spent on this activity as a percentage of total work hours of this staff person.

[3] Non-staff costs are allocated to each activity using the percent of total staff time spent on the activity as the allocation basis. Formula: MFI's total non-staff costs x % of total staff time spent on activity = non-staff costs per activity.

progress over time. Managers can also *benchmark* unit costs of a specific activity among branches. For instance, if the activity "open deposit accounts" costs US$0.15 per account in one branch, but US$0.40 in another, managers can dig behind the numbers to understand why it costs so much at the second branch. Another option is to use the low-cost branch cost as the performance target for all other branches.

Cost drivers should be assigned early in the costing exercise because their collection can be time-consuming. Selecting cost drivers for all activities can be difficult. Sustaining activities that support the institution as a whole may require a more traditional cost allocation (see Step Five below). Other activities may have multiple cost drivers, or individual tasks within an activity may have different cost drivers. In any case, all drivers must be divided by product. For example, if a driver is "number of loan applications," then, for each product, the MFI should have available the number of loan applications. If the MIS is unable to come up with a driver, it is possible to use a "proxy." For example, if the most suitable driver is number of loan repayments per month, but the system does not give a ready count, a proxy can be used by taking the number of loans outstanding multiplied by the expected payment frequency (such as weekly, or biweekly) for each loan product. The costing team must build a model that reflects reality as well as possible without becoming too complex with too many activities and cost drivers.

Step Five: Drive Unit Activity Costs to Products

Finally, the team must apply the unit costs for each activity to the MFI's products. First, the costing team must split the average volume or value of each cost driver for every product (see Table 14–6). Then, it must multiply the value for the cost driver for this product and activity times the unit cost for this activity to get the cost of this activity for this product. For instance, if a particular cost driver is the number of outstanding accounts, then the team determines how many outstanding accounts each product has during the period being considered. Then the costs are "driven" to each product by multiplying the number of outstanding accounts for the product by the activity unit cost. The formula for driving unit activity costs to a specific product is:

cost driver per product *x* unit cost = activity cost per product

For instance, if a particular cost driver is the number of loan applications, then the costs are driven to each loan product by multiplying the number of loan applications for that product by the unit cost.

This final step will yield the costs of each product, not including the costs of sustaining activities, by process and activity (see Table 14–7). Expressing sustaining activities in terms of unit costs for a particular product may not make sense. Instead, these activities can be allocated directly to products using allocation bases similar to the ones outlined in Section 14.3.

Table 14–5. Example of ABC Step Four (for one process and sustaining activities only)

Step 4: Assign cost drivers. Divide total costs of activity by volume of cost drivers to calculate unit cost

Processes and activities	Total monthly costs	Cost drivers	# of cost drivers per month	Unit cost
Core process: servicing existing loans	62,313	No. of delinquent clients	1,032	17.19
Follow up with delinquent clients	17,745	No. of outstanding loans	3,137	1.51
Analyze repayment performance	4,728	No. of outstanding loans	3,137	12.70
Collect current payments	39,841			
Core process: making new loans	10,452	No. of loan applications	327	13.20
Process requests	4,322	No. of loan applications	327	18.75
Disburse and record	6,130			
Core process: opening deposit accounts	8,136	No. of new deposit accounts	2,435	0.14
Explain rules	6,068	No. of new deposit accounts	2,435	
Prepare application and passbooks	2,068			
Core process: servicing deposit accounts	20,790	No. of outstanding accounts	6,402	1.32
Routine checking and updating	8,472	No. of accounts closing	2,329	.92
Close accounts	2,149	No. of large withdrawals	226	12.07
Process large withdrawals	2,727	No. of outstanding accounts	6,402	.57
Client visits and spot checks	3,657	No. of outstanding accounts	6,402	.59
Correct errors	3,785			

Core process: handle cash transactions	135,968			
Collect and record cash in	118,088	No. of cash receipt journal entries	52,704	2.24
Collect and record cash out	8,629	No. of cash disbursement journal entries	1,499	5.76
General cash administration	9,251	No. of cash transaction journal entries	54,203	0.17
Sustaining activities				
Area selection and promotion	563		1	563
Staff meetings	9,394		1	9,394
Month-end accounting and reporting/MIS	1,557		1	1,557
Recruit and train	2,676		1	2,676
General administration	14,523		1	14,523
Fraud prevention	2,770		1	2,770
External relations	3741		1	3,741

Table 14–6. Example of ABC Step Five (for one process and one product)

Process / activity	Cost drivers	Unit cost	Monthly cost drivers: passbook product	Monthly cost of passbook product
Core process: servicing deposit accounts				**11,262**
Routine checking and updating	No. of outstanding accounts	1.32	3,251	4,302
Close accounts	No. of accounts closing	.92	1,407	1,298
Process large withdrawals	No. of large withdrawals	12.07	156	1,882
Client visits / spot checks	No. of outstanding accounts	.57	3,251	1,857
Correct errors	No. of outstanding accounts	.59	3,251	1,922

Table 14–7. Example of ABC Results: Monthly Product Costs by Core Processes

Processes	Loans			Savings			Total
	Micro	Housing	Total	Passbook	Time	Total	
Servicing existing loans	14,960	10,660	25,620				25,620
Making loans	33,120	3,840	36,960				36,960
Opening deposit accounts				12,420	6,400	18,820	18,820
Servicing deposit accounts				11,262	22,400	33,662	33,662
Handling cash transactions	11,360	1,200	12,560	11,000	8,400	19,400	31,960
Monthly cost before sustaining activities	59,440	15,700	75,140	34,682	37,200	71,882	147,022

14.5 MARGINAL COSTS, COST ALLOCATION, AND ABC

The chapter thus far has discussed a product's total costs—the costs of all the resources related to a particular product. However, understanding total costs will not help answer some important cost questions: What costs will my MFI save if we drop our contractual savings product? What additional costs will we incur if we add a new time deposit product? Questions like these are answered by looking at *marginal costs*—additional costs incurred by adding a product or saved by dropping a product.

Because some costs will be incurred whether an institution offers one product or four, the marginal costs of a product are not the same as its total costs. For example, an MFI will need branches regardless of the number of products it offers. A proportion of these fixed costs are part of the total costs of a new product. They would not be marginal costs of this product, because the MFI incurs these costs whether or not the product is added.

In fact, in MFIs nearly all administrative costs are fixed, at least in the short term; very few costs, outside of some materials, communications, and transportation costs, increase in proportion to the level of output or the number of products. Because most costs are fixed, marginal costs can be very small for individual products.

Determining the marginal costs of a product requires the same process as determining its total costs. With traditional cost allocation methods, managers must first determine which costs they consider to be fixed. They then must decide which products are core or primary, and which product(s) is marginal. Marginal cost allocation distributes fixed costs only to core products.

When determining marginal costs, costs are allocated according to the same basis as when determining total costs, with one exception: fixed costs are not allocated to marginal products. (Since allocating the fixed costs among multiple core products can be arbitrary, core products are lumped together: the point is not to determine the costs of the core products but to understand the marginal costs of the marginal product.) Thus, marginal cost allocation imposes an additional allocation basis that can replace other allocation bases (see Box 14–2).

Allocation basis	Application
Fixed cost	Because the cost item is fixed, it should not be allocated to marginal products.

With ABC, managers can gain insight into marginal costs in three ways. First, ABC allows them to understand which activities will no longer be undertaken when a given product is eliminated. Second, in cases when some staff members are dismissed, the impact on the remaining staff members can be analyzed. For instance, when a fired staff member had spent some proportion of his or her time on activities not uniquely related to the marginal product, other staff members will have to take up the slack. Third, ABC enables managers to identify and quantify excess capacity of staff members retained after eliminating a product. The ABC framework allows managers to understand more fully the day-to-day operational implications of a marginal product.

The marginal costs of *existing* products are usually very low because most MFI costs are fixed with respect to individual products. This is particularly the case for the costs of MFI staff that deliver more than one product. Most MFIs find it difficult to terminate staff that are under-utilized because the MFI has eliminated a product. When a product is terminated, dismissing staff may be possible only if there are many similar employees, for example, data clerks. A few costs, such as materials, postage, and communications, and some transportation costs may be marginal because they are variable costs that are linked to the number of accounts or transactions.

On the other hand, *adding* a new product will likely involve extra costs, both start-up costs like staff training, new systems, and fixed assets, and ongoing costs such as new staff, materials, and transportation. Because costing an existing product may not uncover the marginal costs of adding a new product, adding a new product requires a separate forecasting exercise.

14.6 CALCULATING THE VIABILITY OF SAVINGS PRODUCTS

Both costing methodologies provide information only on administrative costs. To understand the viability of a product, fees and interest also need to be taken into account. Calculating viability is a critical final step because the results can spur MFIs to action. In particular, seeing that a product is running at a loss is a surefire way to motivate senior management to explore how to improve its efficiency or marketing. And since many MFIs do find that one or more of their products are running at a loss, undertaking this final set of calculations is crucial.[5]

MFIs typically charge fees on savings products to offset some of the administrative costs of processing and handling these accounts. To understand the viability of a savings product, these fees should be subtracted from the product's administrative costs.

Next, the cost of funds—interest paid to clients—should be added. This will give the total administrative and financial costs of the product. Expressing each of these costs as a percentage of the product's average portfolio can make them easier to analyze than using raw cost data (see Table 14–8).

Since savings products do not directly earn income, how can product viability be measured? In analyzing the financial viability of savings, savings products are treated as a funding source. The total cost of savings (administrative costs *plus* interest paid *less* fees received) must make it an affordable source of funds. The question is how to define affordable. One way is to compare the total costs of

Table 14–8. Example of Total Cost Calculation for Two Savings Products

		Passbook		Time	
		Annual figures	Cost / average balance	Annual figures	Cost / average balance
a.	Average outstanding balance	382,284		94,974	
b.	Transfer price		9.5%		11.5%
c.	minus finance costs (interest paid)	15,314	4.0%	5,700	6.0%
d.	Interest contribution (b – c)		5.5%		5.5%
e.	minus total administrative costs	36,317	9.5%	3,609	3.8%
f.	plus fees	3,828	1.0%	952	1.0%
g.	minus implicit cost of reserves		.44%		.67%
h.	Total admin. and reserve costs net of fees ([e – f] + g)		8.94%		3.47%
i.	Total costs (c + h)		12.94%		9.47%
j.	Bottom line (b – i)		(3.44%)		+2.03%

savings to the cost of alternative sources of funds that have similar terms and negligible administrative costs. This alternative source price is often referred to as the *transfer price.*

To make this comparison, the total costs of the savings product should include the implicit cost of holding savings in reserve. While all funds received from an alternative source can be invested, some percentage of savings must be held in reserves. This reserve cost is calculated by using the formula:

reserve cost = (financial cost/[1 − reserve rate]) − financial cost

(where the financial cost is the interest rate).

If the next best alternative for raising funds is commercial loans at 9.5 percent for a short-term loan and 11.5 percent for a long-term one, and the interest rate paid on passbook savings and time deposits equals 4 percent and 6 percent, respectively, then the viability analysis would look like Table 14–8.

In this case, the time-deposit product is viable while the passbook product is not. The total cost of the time-deposit product is about 2 percent cheaper than the alternative (9.47 percent versus 11.5 percent). On the other hand, the passbook savings product in this case is more expensive than the alternative short-term funding option (12.94 percent versus 9.5 percent). The MFI would be better off from a purely financial perspective if it accessed funds from this alternative source. When a product is not viable, as in this case, MFI managers need to decide whether to continue, discontinue, or seriously modify it.

14.7 COMPILING AND USING THE RESULTS

Regardless of which costing method is used, once the costing team has conducted the exercise, it will need to compile and present the results. The team should present its assumptions, allocation bases, findings, and suggestions for follow-up to senior management. The results of either type of costing exercise, but particularly traditional cost allocation, typically highlight the need for further investigation. For example, the results may raise the question of why a particular staff position spends so much time on a particular product or activity. (ABC typically requires less follow-up study because it already provides a significant amount of information about processes and activities.)

The benefit of the costing exercise will be limited unless senior management follows up on the results with changes in policies or operations. A follow-up costing within a year can enable management to see the impact of the changes it has made. Adjusting time sheets, accounting systems, and budgeting systems so that they automatically generate much of the product-costing data can enable management to keep a constant eye on the efficiency and profitability of different products. Typically, time sheets will still need to be facilitated and verified, especially initially. An alternative, therefore, is to redo the time sheet or staff interview process at more lengthy intervals than the costing exercise, updating only the non-staff time more frequently. Once the costing spreadsheet is refined to reflect the institution's needs, it may only require minor adjustments for subsequent costing exercises.

The MFI may seek to improve the viability of an unprofitable product. It may find ways to reduce the costs of the activities involved in offering the product (see Box 14–4). It might also lower the interest paid on deposits (see Chapter 9). Management might also choose to continue offering a product that is not viable because it:

- recognizes that an alternate source of funds may not be available or may not be available in sufficient volume to meet the needs of the MFI;
- understands that the product provides a much-needed service to customers;

Box 14–4. ABC in a Peruvian Institution

In 2004, Mennonite Economic Development Associates worked with a regulated financial institution in Peru to conduct an ABC exercise. The aim was to understand the costs and profitability of the institution's savings and loan products. As of June 2004, the institution served nearly thirty-six depositors with an average account size of US$531.

The costing exercise took one month. It was carried out by two external consultants and nine staff members working in two teams, as well as one staff person from the MIS department and one from accounting. Each team member spent four to six days each on the exercise. In addition, consultants spent a total of fifteen days on the project. To carry out the exercise, the teams needed information on the number and volume of accounts of each type, salaries, and how staff use their time. They also developed a list of activities that consume staff time.

On the savings side, the costing exercise showed the institution that it needed to reduce the interest rates on savings products. It also showed that front-end staff were spending a portion of time just waiting for clients. These findings motivated the institution to look into some issues more deeply. Were its high interest rates necessary to attract savers? Could it afford to lower interest rates? To answer these questions, the institution developed surveys to look at client satisfaction with its products and services. It also developed a cost-of-funds analysis that compared the cost of the institution's savings products with the cost of commercial long-term and short-term loans. It found that the cost to the institution of lottery prizes was much too high. Learning that cashiers were under-utilized led management to look more carefully at usage and reduce the hours of some of the cashiers.

Overall, management learned that a costing exercise does not give quick answers. Rather, it is part of a bigger process to improve operating efficiency and the quality of products and services. All of this takes time.

—Cherie Tan

- accepts that larger accounts will cross subsidize smaller ones. This should be based on a "customer segment analysis" that examines the viability of different size accounts;[6]
- determines that, for this newly introduced product, unit costs will decrease over time as the systems and delivery are refined and become more efficient. This assessment should be based on sensitivity analysis that uses future expected costs instead of actual costs to see whether the product might be more viable if expectations turn into reality; or
- uses this product as a loss leader to attract and retain clients who will use more profitable products, which may be the case with passbook savings.

Beyond costing products, managers can also use ABC to look more closely at operating costs and sources of inefficiency at both the institutional and branch levels (rather than the product level). Indeed, operating-cost information can be at least as useful as product-level cost information, if not more useful. At the institutional level managers can identify inefficiencies by analyzing data on how staff spend their time and unit costs for activities. Splitting the ABC data by branch (time sheets, expenses, and cost drivers) allows a detailed analysis of branch costs. This analysis can be helpful to ensure adherence to procedures and standards for the organization as a whole. It also supports an MFI's process of decentralization, giving the branches themselves the tools to identify and manage their costs.

14.8 CONCLUSION

Product costing is an important tool to increase efficiency and profitability. Product costing helps managers determine the full costs of their products, including savings for the poor. Costing helps them make decisions that can improve delivery mechanisms and customer service, contribute to better product design, reveal hidden costs, and provide a basis for business planning and investment.

This chapter has presented both traditional cost allocation and ABC. An MFI that wants to cost its products should think carefully about whether the more simple traditional cost allocation or the more complex ABC costing will serve it best. Whatever method MFI managers choose, they should be aware of the ever-present tension among accuracy, complexity, and cost. More complex and expensive costing approaches will not necessarily lead to more accurate results. In fact, simpler models may provide enough information to help managers begin thinking about product costs. On the other hand, MFIs should know that costing models that are too simple or general might not provide the depth of information they need to make sound decisions.

NOTES

[1] This list of preparatory steps is adapted from David Cracknell, Henry Sempangani, and Graham A. N. Wright, *Costing and Pricing of Financial Service—A Toolkit for MFIs* (Nairobi: *MicroSave*, 2004). The toolkit also includes guidance from field-testing experience.

[2] An actual allocation might break down the line items further. For example, head office might be broken down into numerous line items such as salaries, communications, and insurance.

[3] This section provides an overview to the main steps of ABC. For detailed guidance, see Brigit Helms and Lorna Grace, "CGAP Product Costing Tool" (Washington, DC: CGAP, 2004). The tool can be downloaded from CGAP's Product Costing Resource Center at www.cgap.org/productcosting.

[4] The reason for doing this is that resources are consumed in the process of completing specific activities. Therefore, the amount of effort spent on each activity, as approximated by total staff time, will reflect how much each activity consumes different resources. Thus, allocating non-staff costs according to total effort expended (time spent) on each activity makes sense.

[5] David Cracknell and Henry Sempangi, "Product Costing In Practice: The Experience of *MicroSave*" (Nairobi: *MicroSave*, 2002), 12–13. The paper is available from the *MicroSave* website.

[6] If the MIS is sophisticated enough for cost drivers to be split according to different types of accounts, then ABC customer-segment analysis can be used to gain insight into the cost structure of different client segments within each product line.

15

Financial Incentive Schemes for Staff Engaged in Savings Mobilization

*Martin Holtmann
and Mattias Grammling*

Because the savings of the poor are at risk, institutional sustainability is even more important for deposit-taking entities than for pure lenders. Savers also strongly prefer to entrust their money to organizations that they expect will survive over the long term. Thus, for deposit-taking MFIs, managing costs and achieving a high level of efficiency and productivity is essential. And, since personnel costs usually account for 60 to 70 percent of a microfinance provider's total operating costs, looking at ways to maximize staff productivity makes sense.

To achieve this goal, staff incentive schemes can play a useful role. Staff incentives are rewards that are granted for achieving certain targets or for making a certain effort. They are usually paid as part of the salary, but nonmonetary staff incentives also are possible.

Within the field of microfinance, incentive schemes for savings are quite new. Successfully attracting savings depends on many factors, from effective communication to queue management and fast computer systems. We do not yet know how much incentive schemes for staff and managers can influence the environment for attracting savings. Neither are we certain which factors will most affect savings mobilization in different environments. Nevertheless, we do have some principles to guide our way.

At the same time, if not carefully designed, a staff incentive scheme may improve efficiency and profitability over the short term at the expense of responsiveness

The authors thank Monnie Biety and David Cracknell for their valuable feedback.

to client demand. This can have serious long-term consequences. If the objective is to stimulate the mobilization of savings from poor clients, the scheme must be carefully tailored to align the interests of the MFI with those of its customers and employees.

This chapter alerts readers to how financial incentive systems can enhance staff and organizational performance. After discussing the role of an incentive scheme, we present general guidelines and steps for designing such incentive systems. We then design a simple bonus system that can boost savings mobilization. We look at how this system might be refined to suit different contexts and institutional missions, most notably the aim to reach small or rural depositors. Finally, we discuss some common mistakes and recap key points regarding schemes to strengthen savings mobilization.

15.1 PERSONNEL IS KEY: THE REASON FOR AN INCENTIVE SYSTEM

The quality and commitment of staff are probably the most important success factors in MFI operations. Managers should devote significant effort to selecting, training, and motivating staff. Many factors contribute to the motivation and commitment of staff. Among these are:

- *Job satisfaction:* Is the job interesting and does it provide enough opportunities to use one's own judgment rather than following simple and repetitive instructions?
- *Prospects for professional growth:* Are there learning opportunities, and will it be possible to be assigned more responsibility in the future?
- *Possibilities for promotion:* Is it possible to advance one's career by being promoted to a higher level in the organization?
- *Sense of identification and belonging:* Is it easy to identify with the mission of the organization, and is it fun to work hard as part of the team?

Managers who want to recruit and retain committed, hard-working, and loyal staff should consider these organizational and psychological issues and provide a working environment that will foster excellence and productivity.

At the same time, for most people, the remuneration attached to a particular job is a decisive factor in determining their effort and commitment. Very few people would like to work for a measly salary, particularly if there is no prospect for improvement. MFIs all over the world have found that paying staff members well helps to keep them motivated and to prevent unnecessary staff turnover.[1]

But why a variable component—an incentive system? MFIs seek to serve as many customers as possible, and operational staff are the "agents" responsible for contacting clients and delivering services. Paying these staff members variable bonuses that are linked to their performance makes sense because these bonuses can strongly influence productivity and job performance. Indeed, loan-officer bonus systems are already widely used to enhance performance.[2] Much less is known about effective incentive systems for staff who mobilize savings. Before we consider how to design a system for savings, let us first look at some general guidelines.

15.2 GUIDELINES FOR THE DESIGN OF BONUS SYSTEMS

By linking pay to performance, bonus systems provide a strong incentive for staff to improve effort and performance.[3] The goal of a financial incentive system is to align the interests (desired outputs) of the organization with those of the individual staff members. In other words, the system should ensure that the objectives of the employees are the same as those of the organization as a whole. To accomplish this, three characteristics are important:

- *Measurability:* It must be possible to measure accurately the desired outputs. A person cannot be held accountable for results that cannot be properly measured.
- *Transparency:* Staff members affected by the system should be able to understand easily how the bonus is calculated. The system should not be overly complex. Furthermore, the rules should be made known to everyone and should not be changed arbitrarily or without notice.
- *Fairness:* Everybody should perceive that better performers are indeed rewarded with higher salaries, and that anyone can achieve a higher bonus by working better and harder.[4] This might mean, for example, that the incentive system is varied for geographic areas that are more challenging.[5]

When designing a bonus system, managers should also carefully consider these critical issues:

Timing: In general, a financial incentive scheme should be introduced only after staff has received sufficient training. Otherwise the system may "penalize" mistakes. Making and correcting mistakes is an essential part of the learning process. In the authors' experience, most staff members should become eligible for bonuses approximately six months after they have joined the organization. If new members are added to existing teams (for instance, in a branch involved in savings mobilization) this guideline may be safely discarded.

Frequency of bonus: Above all, personnel should not see the bonus as an entitlement, that is, a fixed and regular part of the monthly salary. However, bonus pay will affect staff productivity more if intervals are fairly short. Indeed, personnel will find it very difficult to relate a bonus payment that is annual to any particular actions or effort. In practice, the most effective bonus payments are probably monthly or quarterly.

Portion of total remuneration that is bonus: On average, what part of the total remuneration should be salary and what part bonus? The bonus portion should be big enough that participants in the scheme feel that it really makes a difference; otherwise, they are unlikely to increase their effort. But, it should not be too big; if it is, the job might only attract those who enjoy risk. Staff need to be confident of earning an acceptable minimum.

What does this mean in practical terms? In lending operations, bonuses often make up about 50 percent of the total compensation that a loan officer can receive. For staff engaged solely in savings, a maximum of 20–30 percent may be more appropriate. With savings, even the best efforts often will not immediately produce new deposits. Savings mobilization is a long-term effort. It requires the building of trust. Excessive bonuses based on short-term performance send the wrong signal to staff members.

Base salary: The base salary should be high enough to enable staff members to manage with it if they do not earn a bonus. It generally is not feasible to lower salaries in order to institute an incentive system. So, if salaries are too high to add bonuses, the MFI may need to wait until the value of salaries drops in real terms before initiating an incentive system.[6]

Duration: Will the scheme be ongoing or short term? A short-term bonus system, lasting from one to six months, can be used to promote new products. To be fair, everyone affected by the scheme should be made aware that it is temporary.

Participants: Which staff members will be involved in the scheme, and how will this affect those not receiving incentives? Often, the introduction of a scheme at one organizational level or function may create a need to implement schemes at other levels as well. If other staff members are not covered by some kind of incentive scheme within a reasonable time frame, they may simply stop working as hard. To the extent that MFIs thrive on excellent performance in all departments and units, managers are well advised to consider more comprehensive incentive schemes.

Individual or team basis: Will the bonus be received by individuals or by a team, such as the entire branch? Individual-based incentive schemes are appropriate if individual output is easy to measure; employees have enough autonomy that they can decide themselves how much effort they will put into their job; there is no need for close cooperation among staff members—and competition between them is even beneficial for the whole organization; and the organizational culture favors individual achievement.[7] As discussed below, this is usually not the case for savings. Bonuses for savings should generally be awarded to a team rather than an individual. If they are awarded to a team, should they be divided equally among the team or proportionally according to the size of each member's salary? Management should decide this based on the MFI's corporate culture and circumstances.

With these guidelines and issues in mind, we will now look at the steps involved in designing an incentive scheme.

15.3 STEPS IN DESIGNING AN INCENTIVE SCHEME

Whether designing a new scheme or making changes to an existing one, it pays to be systematic. Following these critical steps will help assure that the scheme is effective.[8]

Step 1: Define the incentive scheme's objectives. Management—and the board—should be clear about what they are trying to achieve with the incentive system. What results are expected? What problem are we trying to fix? For instance, the goal might be to increase overall staff motivation and long-term commitment, or it might be to increase branch productivity. Be as precise as possible.

Step 2: Analyze the culture and clientele. Senior management should consider the MFI's clients and operations as well as its staff's mentality and concerns. How important is money for our field staff? How would clients react if staff tried to be more productive (which might result in reduced attention to each existing customer)? Including staff in the design process can help with this and with the acceptance of the scheme once it is ready to be implemented. The same holds for times when the scheme is adjusted. Adjustments can cause resentment, which can be lessened by working closely with staff.[9]

Step 3: Decide how much the MFI is willing to spend. This is the point at which we need to conduct a proper cost-benefit analysis to estimate the impact that the planned scheme will have on operating costs and the organization's financial performance. In the short run, a bonus scheme will increase total staff costs. If the system is designed well, these costs will later be compensated for by increased staff productivity and output.

Step 4: Conduct the technical design work. The design work involves developing, calibrating, testing, and adjusting the bonus formula. How this is done is discussed in detail in Section 15.4. However, three points are worth noting here: First, and above all, do not underestimate the power of spreadsheet testing. Many problems in the implementation of staff incentive schemes could have been avoided if the designers had spent time testing and adjusting the bonus formula at this stage. Second, using a participatory process can help a lot. Finally, it is useful to imagine ourselves in the position of the employees who will eventually be affected by the scheme. We imagine what we would do if we were asked to work according to this scheme. By predicting behavior in this way, we can often weed out negative incentives and side effects before the scheme is implemented.

Step 5: Run a pilot test. Testing the scheme on a limited basis is very important. Imagine that we overlooked a small but significant detail that rendered our scheme useless. And imagine that we had introduced the scheme in twenty-seven branches at the same time! It is far more sensible to implement the scheme in one or two representative branches on a trial basis and to monitor its performance over a certain period, for instance, three months. Based on the results, we could adjust the scheme. Only then should we implement it in the entire network.

Step 6: Sell the scheme to the staff. Like everything that affects the daily lives of our staff members, new incentive schemes (or changes in existing ones) will be critically reviewed by everyone. So we need to think about how to sell the scheme. If staff members participated in the scheme's design, this task will be easier. Do not underestimate the intelligence of your employees; if the scheme results in any disadvantages or hardships (such as lower pay or harder work), they will quickly figure it out. It usually helps to explain the reasons for changes, for example, "Our average productivity has increased by 50 percent over the past year, so we raised the benchmark performance levels in the bonus formula," or "Our owners and directors want us to increase outreach, so we now pay a higher bonus for new clients than for repeat customers."

In many cultures the concept of a salary bonus based on performance may be foreign, and implementation can be challenging. There is no one answer to this issue. Managers need to debate carefully the issues with all those who will be affected. They might "sell" the bonus system as an innovation that will benefit both the institution and the individual staff members.

Some schemes, however, clearly make work more difficult for the affected staff members. In such cases it can help to calibrate the scheme in such a way that initially even the lowest performers will be as well off with the new scheme as they were under the previous one. However, when introducing the new scheme, management should announce that the scheme's current performance standards will apply only for a certain temporary period. This provides everyone with a fair opportunity to bring performance up to the new standards and makes introducing the new scheme easier.

Step 7: Monitor and adjust the scheme's performance as necessary. Senior management should monitor and review the scheme's performance regularly, for example, semi-annually, and more frequently at first. Are the organization's objectives still the same? Does the scheme still produce the desired outcomes? If not, it should be adjusted.[10] A badly designed bonus system can produce "perverse"—unwanted—incentives (see Box 15–1). For example, staff might be motivated to coerce depositors to save more than depositors would choose. Furthermore, a system can lose its effectiveness or become unnecessary over time (see Box 15–2). Having a deficient system is worse than having no system at all.

15.4 TECHNICAL DESIGN FOR A SIMPLE SAVINGS SCHEME

Let us now consider the specific requirements for a bonus system to motivate staff to increase their efforts to mobilize savings.[11]

Box 15–1. Possible Negative Effects: Safe*Save*'s Decision Not to Use Financial Incentives

*Safe*Save operates in the densely populated slums of Bangladesh's capital, Dhaka. Its mission is to provide commercially viable financial services that poor and very poor individuals value. Collectors live in the same slums as their clients and visit them daily to collect savings and loan payments and to provide withdrawals. They also are responsible for recruiting new clients and promoting *Safe*Save's products. In other words, *Safe*Save collectors offer multiple services to clients and potential clients with whom they are in close contact.

A financial incentive scheme for savings would boost the productivity of *Safe*Save collectors. Indeed, *Safe*Save already benefits from its bonus system for lending. Nevertheless, *Safe*Save's management does not implement a scheme for savings for one reason: it predicts that collectors would pressure their clients to save. Clients might then save because of a sense of obligation to the collector or to *Safe*Save. Alternatively, they might believe that if they did not save, they would not receive loans in the future. Collectors might also provide clients with wrong information, such as claiming that *Safe*Save now requires regular deposits or larger amounts of savings—neither of which is supported by rules. Therefore, management decided to refrain from introducing an incentive scheme.

Carefully predicting all potential effects of a new incentive scheme is essential. *Safe*Save did this well and had the courage to decide not to introduce a bonus system for savings.

15.4.1 Choosing the Output Variables

First, management must choose output variables for which staff performance will be rewarded. Remember, if we want staff to be accountable for certain results, then these outputs must be measurable. If management is interested in growth or boosting productivity, then it may be interested in several variables, such as the number of new clients or the average deposit volume (which is an indicator of the depth of outreach). For our simple example, we choose two variables:

- number of new accounts opened during the period, and
- volume of funds deposited during the period.

Both variables are strategic "drivers" if an organization is serious about mobilizing savings from (poor) people. Opening many new accounts is a reflection of the desire to offer services to the largest possible number of customers. At the same time, the volume of deposits collected is also important; the higher the volume of savings, the more the organization will be able to engage in lending operations and decrease its dependence on external (and often foreign) funding.

Box 15–2. The Changing Need for Incentives over Time:
BURO, Tangail

BURO, Tangail is an NGO that operates in Bangladesh, primarily in rural areas. It offers numerous savings and loan products using a group methodology. Village development workers attend weekly group meetings and are responsible for both loans and savings. In 1999 BURO, Tangail's management implemented a bonus system for its contractual savings products in order to make them better known among its clients. The scheme included a bonus scheme for lending activities and offered village development workers between US$0.10 and US$1.20 for each new contractual savings account. The exact bonus size depended on the type of the contract and the savings amount. In 2002 BURO, Tangail eliminated the scheme entirely—because it was so successful!

While the scheme operated, many members opened accounts. As account holders talked about their positive experiences and recommended the product to their peers, it became widely known among their groups. Consequently, village development workers no longer needed to promote it extensively.

Of course, such client-to-client promotion works best in communities where people interact with each other a lot. The scheme seemed to motivate the staff members to promote the product to those clients for whom it would provide real value. The BURO, Tangail experience shows that the parameters of bonus formulas should be adjusted and that some schemes can even be eliminated once they have achieved their goals. It also highlights the fact that it is not always necessary to motivate staff members with lots of money. The variable incentives paid out by BURO, Tangail were actually rather modest. Regardless of the size and impact of any changes, they should always be well communicated to staff.

With these two simple indicators, we can devise a simple bonus system that effectively resembles the piece-rate systems widely used in manufacturing. For instance, for each account opened by a customer, an absolute amount X would be paid, and per US$100 deposited, an amount Y would be added to the bonus of the responsible staff member. If X and Y are sufficiently large, we could certainly expect our staff to seek new clients. Such a crude system would also have two clear disadvantages: it would produce unintended negative consequences, and it would not be fair.

If bonuses are awarded only for bringing in new customers, staff members will feel that it is not worthwhile to provide good service to existing clients. But retaining deposits and clients is also important.[12] This flaw can be fixed by replacing one of the indicators: instead of including the number of new accounts and the *volume deposited during the period*, the bonus formula could use the number of new accounts and *the total outstanding balance at the end of the period*. With this combination of indicators, staff have an incentive not merely to attract new clients but also to provide efficient and friendly service in order to induce existing clients to maintain their accounts and deposit funds on an ongoing basis.

To be fair, the output variable used to calculate the bonus must clearly be related to the effort exerted on the job. But, in savings mobilization, discerning exactly what (and who) caused the customer to entrust the institution with his or her funds can be difficult.[13] Some clients may be actively recruited by extension workers; others will simply walk in to one of the branches. Who deals with the new walk-in customer is often a matter of chance; usually it is the next available desk officer or teller. Furthermore, branch operations are usually organized in such a way that it is difficult to match the results achieved by the unit with the individual efforts of each staff member.

For these reasons, it makes much more sense to base incentives on the performance of teams rather than of individuals. This can easily be done at the branch level, where results are measurable. Branch bonuses have the additional benefit of rewarding cooperation among all those who attend to savings clients, even if individual actions are not directly related to generating a new deposit.

With the outputs chosen, let us now construct a simple bonus system for those branch staff who mobilize and handle deposits. The first variable is the net increase in the number of accounts held at the branch during the period (for instance, one month). However, we will want to reward branch staff with a bonus only for the number of accounts *greater* than a minimum number—*base value*—of net new accounts. Let us call this base value V_{1a}, the base value over which a bonus is earned.

$$V_1 = \text{(number of accounts at end of period} - \text{number of accounts at beginning of period)} - V_{1a}$$

A second variable reflects the volume of funds that savings clients have deposited in their accounts. Again, we will reward staff with a bonus only for the amount *greater* than a minimum volume that we set as a base value. We will call this base value V_{2a}:

$$V_2 = \text{total volume of savings deposits held at the branch at the end of period} - V_{2a}$$

Now we need two factors, P_1 and P_2, which will be used to convert the output variables into a financial bonus. In our example,

$$P_1 = \text{amount received as a bonus for net increase of one account (as absolute monetary value, for example, US\$1)}$$

$$P_2 = \text{percentage of total value of deposits branch staff receive as a bonus (for example, 1 percent)}$$

The total bonus B is then calculated:

$$B = (V_1 \times P_1) + (V_2 \times P_2)$$

Let's try this with some real numbers. Assume that the branch increased the number of savings accounts during the period by 300 and the base value, V_{2a}, has been set at 250. The branch has 50 net new accounts over the base value for the net number of new accounts:

$$V_1 = 300 - 250 = 50$$

Assume also that the deposit volume at the end of the period amounts to US$459,000 and the base value, V_{2a}, has been set at US$450,000. Then, the branch has US$9,000 over the base value:

$$V_2 = US\$459,000 - US\$450,000 = US\$9,000$$

In this case, the bonus would be:

$$B = (50 \times US\$1) + (US\$9,000 \times 0.01) = US\$140$$

If three people work at the branch, each person would receive a bonus of:

$$US\$140/3 = US\$46.67$$

This bonus system is used by a number of MFIs with very favorable results. The most important benefit is that staff members feel rewarded for working harder. In many MFIs loan officers receive bonuses while other staff in operations— including in savings—do not. Paying a regular bonus to staff engaged in savings helps to ease this tension. Also important, the variable "outstanding volume of deposits" rewards not only attracting new clients but also keeping existing clients happy (reflected in stable or growing deposit volumes). Finally, the scheme is very simple, making it easy to understand and implement.

15.4.2 Calibrating the Scheme

We now have a simple bonus formula, but how does a specific institution determine appropriate values for each of the variables? First, senior management must decide base values, V_{1a} and V_{2a}, above which staff members will start to earn a bonus. Second, management must decide the values for P_1 and P_2, the rates at which staff are rewarded for exceeding these base values. Setting these values is known as *calibrating* the scheme. To calibrate the scheme, management should estimate the impact that different proposed values will have on staff remuneration, operating costs, and the organization's financial performance. It is very useful to use a simple spreadsheet to help set these values.

The values for V_{1a} and V_{2a} should be standards—the minimum expectations of what staff must achieve in order to earn their salary without a bonus. The exact value of the factors P_1 and P_2 depends on the incentives that management wants to provide as well as on the total bonus amount that the institution is prepared to pay. Clearly, both issues depend on the local situation. However, in setting these values managers should keep the following in mind:

- For staff engaged solely in savings mobilization, about 20–30 percent of their total remuneration should be earnable from the bonus system. In the author's experience with numerous banks and MFIs this suggested range represents a "safe bet" in terms of making the incentive portion of the salary truly rewarding while avoiding excessive risk for the employees. The salary portion of remuneration should cover at least the employee's subsistence needs. This can be estimated by using the minimum pay level offered by other microfinance providers for similar jobs.
- In the short run, a well-designed bonus scheme will increase total staff costs. If MFI managers really expect staff to increase their effort levels significantly, they should set these values such that staff costs will initially increase between 15 and 25 percent. Experience in a variety of organizations suggests that smaller increases will be considered marginal by employees and will not elicit much of a response.
- If the system is designed well, these costs should be offset by increased staff productivity and output, typically in a period of approximately one year.
- Initially, even the lowest performers should be as well off with the new scheme as they were under the previous one. However, these performance standards should be raised after an introductory period of, for example, three to six months.

One simple way to test different values for the components of the bonus formula is to enter into the spreadsheet the bonus formula, existing productivity data (such as total volume of deposits and number of new accounts), and monthly salaries for the targeted staff for some period of time (for instance, using data from all branch staff for the last three months) (see Table 15–1A). The spreadsheet then calculates the hypothetical income that each employee would have received if the scheme were already in place. This can be compared to the income they did receive. Outliers (extreme values) will be immediately obvious. Likewise, this process will help to identify who (or which groups of persons) would benefit from the new scheme and how much, who the potential "losers" are, and those who probably will not like the scheme.

Table 15–1. Using a Spreadsheet to Test the Bonus Formula and Scenarios: Example of a Simple Savings Scheme

Table A. Testing the initial bonus formula based on recent past performance (typical recent month)[1]

1) Branch[1]	Actuals without the scheme			Bonus calculations if scheme had been in place						
	2) Salary	3) Net increase in # of accounts	4) Volume of deposits end of period	5) Base salary (usually equal to col. 2)[2]	6) Base value for net increase in # accounts ($V_{1a} = 80$ per staff member * # of staff members)	7) Base value for volume of deposits end of period ($V_{2a} = \$180,000$ per staff member * # of staff members)	8) Bonus[3] (B = (column 3 – col. 6) * \$2) + ((col. 4 – col. 7) * 1%)	9) Total remuneration[4] (col. 5 + col. 8)	10) % change in total remuneration (col. 8/col. 2)	11) % of remuneration earned from bonus (col. 8 / col. 9)
Total	$5,040	1,015	$2,179,000	$5,040	960	$2,160,000	$300	$5,340	6%	6%
Branch A	$2,100	420	$910,000	$2,100	400	$900,000	$140	$2,240	7%	6%
Branch B	$2,940	595	$1,269,000	$2,940	560	$1,260,000	$160	$3,100	5%	5%

Table B. Testing the revised bonus scheme based on projected future performance, three scenarios (seventh month of scheme)[7]

1) Branch[1]	2) Salary for period[5]	3) Net increase in # of accounts[5]	4) Volume of deposits end of period[5]	5) Base salary (usually equal to col. 2)[2]	6) Base value for net increase in # accounts ($V_{1a} = 85$ per staff member * # of staff members)	7) Base value for vol. of deposits end of period ($V_{2a} = \$218,333$ per staff member * # of staff members)	8) Net increase in # of accounts	9) Volume of deposits end of period	10) Bonus[3] (B = (col. 8 – col. 6) * \$2) + ((col. 9 – col. 7) * 1%)	11) Total remuneration (col. 5 + col. 10)[4]	12) % of total remuneration earned from bonus (col. 10 / col. 11)[6]
Without the scheme											
Total	$5,040	1030	$2,631,130								
Branch A	$2,100	425	$1,101,100								
Branch B	$2,940	605	$1,530,030								
With the scheme: conservative scenario											
Total				$5,040	1,020	$2,620,000	1,071	$2,657,441	$476	$5,516	9%
Branch A				$2,100	425	$1,091,667	442	$1,112,111	$238	$2,338	10%
Branch B				$2,940	595	$1,528,333	629	$1,545,330	$238	$3,178	7%
Without the scheme											
Total	$5,040	1030	$2,631,130								
Branch A	$2,100	425	$1,101,100								
Branch B	$2,940	605	$1,530,030								
With the scheme: expected scenario											
Total				$5,040	1,020	$2,620,000	1,134	$2,683,753	$866	$5,906	15%
Branch A				$2,100	425	$1,091,665	468	$1,123,122	$401	$2,501	16%
Branch B				$2,940	595	$1,528,331	666	$1,560,631	$465	$3,405	14%
Without the scheme											
Total	$5,040	1030	$2,631,130								
Branch A	$2,100	425	$1,101,100								
Branch B	$2,940	605	$1,530,030								
With the scheme: optimistic scenario											
Total				$5,040	1,020	$2,620,000	1,185	$2,715,326	$1,284	$6,324	20%
Branch A				$2,100	425	$1,091,667	489	$1,136,335	$575	$2,675	21%
Branch B				$2,940	595	$1,528,333	696	1,578,991	$709	$3,649	19%

Table C. Summary: Impact of bonus scheme on three branches' net revenues, three scenarios (one month)

Projected scenario	1) Total salary without the scheme (Table B, col. 2)	2) Vol. of deposits end of period without the scheme (Table B, col. 4)	3) Total remuneration with the scheme (Table B, col. 11)	4) Vol. of deposits end of period with the scheme (Table B, col. 9)	5) Increase in deposits end of period due to scheme (col. 4 – col. 2)	6) Increase in non-staff expenses due to scheme [7]	7) Revenues associated with change in deposit vol. (R = 6% * (col. 5 * (1-10%)) 8	8) Net revenues due to bonus system [9] (col. 7 – (col. 6 + (col. 3 – col. 1))
Conservative	$5,040	$2,631,130	$5,516	$2,657,441	$26,311	$210	$1,421	$735
Expected	$5,040	$2,631,130	$5,906	$2,683,753	$52,623	$421	$2,842	$1,555
Optimistic	$5,040	$2,631,130	$6,324	$2,715,326	$84,196	$674	$4,547	$2,589

NOTES

Overall explanation: Table A: For the first six months, the MFI sets the base values at just the level that the least productive branch is achieving without the scheme. With these base values, even if the branches' performance remains the same, all staff will receive slightly higher salaries than they did without the scheme. Table B: After six months, the MFI resets the base values above or equal to what the branches would be projected to achieve without the scheme. To earn a bonus, the branches must perform better than they would without the scheme. In Table B, even the starting figures without the scheme are higher than in Table A because of natural growth in productivity and volume during the at least six months that have elapsed between Table A and Table B.

Footnotes

[1] In this example, branch A has 5 and branch B has 7 staff members who participate in the incentive scheme.

[2] At a minimum, base salary should provide for subsistence.

[3] Bonus = $(V_1 * P_1) + (V_2 * P_2)$ See explanation of variables below.

[4] In a well-designed scheme, total remuneration with the scheme should always be equal to or greater than without the scheme.

[5] Projected figures should be based on historical data.

[6] Bonus should be no more than 20% to 30% of total remuneration.

[7] Business plan projections should be used to calculate non-salary expenses that arise from the larger volume of deposits resulting from the scheme.

[8] Formula: R = T * (increase in volume of deposits * (1- r)). See explanation of variables and results below.

[9] Formula: increase in revenues associated with increase in deposit volume – (increase in non-staff expenses + increase in staff expenses)

Variables set by management:
P_1 = amount received as a bonus for net increase of one account = US$2
P_2 = % of total value of deposits branch staff receive as a bonus = 1%

Base salaries = US$ 5,040 total for branch staff involved in savings mobilization
r = reserves rate = 10%
V_{1a} = base value, maximum net increase in # of accounts for which no bonus is earned. In Table A, V_{1a} is equal to number of staff members * 80 net increase in accounts per staff member. So, for Branch A in Table A: V_{1a} = 5 staff members * 80 net increase in accounts per staff member = 400
V_{2a} = base value, maximum volume of deposits for which no bonus is earned. In Table A, V_{2a} = number of staff members * US$ 180,000 increase in volume of deposits. For Branch A in Table A, V_{2a} is equal to 5 staff members * US$ 180,000 per staff member = US$ 900,000

Variables set externally: T = transfer price = 6%

Results calculated by spreadsheet:
V_1 = net increase in the number of accounts during period – V_{1a}
V_2 = volume of deposits at end of period – V_{2a}
B = Bonus = $(V_1 * P_1) + (V_2 * P_2)$
R = revenues associated with change in deposit volume
T * increase in volume of deposits * (1- r)

15.4.3 Testing and Adjusting the Scheme

Next, we conduct scenario analyses to calculate the possible financial effects of the scheme. What will happen to costs and revenues if average productivity and/ or deposit size are affected by the scheme? This should also be considered through the use of a spreadsheet (see Tables 15–1b and 15–1c). Costs should include not only the salaries and bonuses but also additional costs that result from the increased number and/or volume of new accounts.

As discussed in Section 14.6, revenues should be calculated using the *transfer price* that management has assigned for savings. The transfer price is the cost of alternative sources of funds that have similar terms and negligible administrative costs. It is used to calculate the revenues that should be allocated to savings. For example, if the next best alternative to mobilizing deposits for raising funds is commercial loans at an interest rate of 9.5 percent, then this should be used as the transfer price. We will call the transfer price T. The calculation of revenues should also take into account that a percentage of savings must be set aside as liquid reserves. These reserves do not earn interest. We call this percentage the reserves rate, r. Therefore, the revenues associated with the increase in the volume of deposits—R—will be equal to:

$$R = \text{increase in volume of deposits associated with bonus system} \times$$
$$(1 - r) \times T$$

Testing should also consider whether the scheme will affect the volume of transactions per account, as this can also affect productivity and costs.

The spreadsheet should generate data on net revenues for at least three possible scenarios: the scheme's impact on performance is less, the same, or more than expected. The net revenues under each scenario should be compared to the predicted net revenues without the scheme.

In order to calculate costs, the spreadsheet model should be built on estimates of key variables in the bonus formula (such as the number of new accounts and the average volume of deposits) and should include the assigned values in the bonus formula (for example, P_1 and P_2 in the example above). Management should try calibrating the bonus formula with different values to see which produce bonuses equal to 20–30% of total remuneration and generate greater revenues than without the scheme. Developing this type of sensitivity and scenario analyses is essential. Proper spreadsheet testing can help avoid costly mistakes in practice.

In summary, the technical design for an incentive scheme includes three steps: (1) developing the bonus formula, which will depend on what outputs the MFI wants to reward; (2) calibrating the formula, that is, determining at what level of outputs staff members will start to receive the bonus and the absolute amount or percentage reward that will be associated with a unit of output; and (3) testing and adjusting the formula with a spreadsheet using scenario analyses.

15.5 REFINEMENTS FOR A SCHEME FOR SAVINGS

The very simple system described above could be refined further:

Conveying savings product priorities: Different types of savings accounts could have different weights in the bonus formula to reflect management's evaluation of their relative importance. For example, management might wish to pay a bigger bonus for the opening of new term deposits (which would generate funds for the MFI for longer periods of time than regular savings). Thus, the formula might be refined to:

$$B = (V_{lt} \times P_{lt}) + (V_{lr} \times P_{lr}) + (V_2 \times P_2)$$

with *t* standing for term deposits and *r* for regular savings and with P_{lt} larger than P_{lr}.

Promoting both strong lending and savings operations: If staff members are engaged in lending and deposit mobilization at the same time, management could combine an individual incentive scheme for lending operations with a group-based scheme rewarding deposit mobilization.[14]

Preventing dormancy: To prevent staff members from encouraging new accounts that will not be active, the variable "number of accounts" could be replaced by a variable "number of active accounts," which would have to be defined with care.

Avoiding cannibalization: If management predicts that rewarding the "number of active accounts" might result in staff members encouraging customers to open new accounts with funds that they withdraw from their existing accounts, management might change this variable to "number of active savers."

Promoting intra-bank competition: To create a spirit of competition among different branches, a special bonus could also be paid according to the results of regular branch rankings. Experience shows that such "tournaments" have a very positive effect on staff motivation (see Box 15–3). Tournaments can instill a healthy sense of competition and help to disseminate information among branches and staff members. It would be a good idea to reward not only the best branch (which might be the same one again and again) but also other good branches or branches that have managed to improve their performance considerably. Rewards may be for increases in volume or number of new accounts. They might be of a monetary nature or simply consist of a special recognition or nonmonetary benefit.

Box 15–3. Motivating Both Credit and Savings:
Banco Caja Social

When Banco Caja Social shifted from partly mandatory to fully voluntary savings and converted itself into a full commercial bank, it instituted a monthly bonus system for branch staff by which they receive a base salary and variable bonus. The system rewards the performance of each branch relative to other branches in its region, based on previously established commercial goals. Within the branches, individuals are rewarded according to their position and performance. In addition, based on accumulated monthly results, the best-performing branches attend an annual sales convention held at a resort. The "best teller," "best financial advisors," and "best office managers" also are invited to attend. There, they are honored by senior management.

Banco Caja Social's incentive system is closely tied to its strategic and business plans. For senior managers and headquarters administrative staff, goals are aligned with the business strategy twice a year. For branch staff, the amounts of the bonuses, indicators on which they are based, and how much weight each product carries in the bonus formula can be revised quarterly—also in accordance with the business plan.

The branch bonus formula is based on ten to fifteen criteria that include the net number of new savings accounts, the value of deposits, loan repayment, administrative income from transaction services, and the quality of customer service. Each criterion translates into points, and those points translate to cash bonuses. The quality of customer-service measurement is based on semiannual "hidden" client reports that assess performance in four categories: image, sales techniques, product knowledge, and service. The incentive formula weights different types of savings products—for example, savings accounts, current accounts, and term deposits—differently. It does not explicitly reward mobilizing savings from certain market segments, for example, the poor.

—Elsa Patricia Manrique and Hillary Miller Wise

Encouraging money transfers: Where MFI staff handle money transfers as well as savings, the volume of money transfers could also be factored into the bonus formula.

Promoting good customer service: The system outlined above factors customer satisfaction only indirectly (through the proxy variables of net increase in accounts and/or volumes outstanding). Using a more direct and precise measurement would be more efficient. For example, clients could be given questionnaires to rate the quality of service they receive. The average rating could be another variable in the bonus formula (see Box 15–3). In the long run, excellent customer service is perhaps the single most important driver or determinant of successful savings mobilization.

Encouraging outreach to small savers: If the potential clients are poor people who are likely to deposit very small amounts of money, the bonus formula should have

- a higher weight for the variable "net change in number of accounts," and
- a lower weight to the variable "volume of deposits."

For a limited period of time, it may even be useful to drop the variable "volume of deposits" completely from the formula and to focus exclusively on the number of depositors and accounts. This would ensure that even the smallest account would count equally toward the bonus of the staff member. Again, it would be useful to combine the regular incentive scheme with special "tournaments" that might pay out special prizes (not necessarily monetary ones). For example, one could give special awards to branches that managed to open a certain number of new accounts.

Providing incentives to branches with uneven market prospects: When client demand varies widely among branches (such as between urban and rural branches, and also often between the capital city and other towns), the formula can be adjusted for these inequalities. A higher reward can be given for new accounts in one branch than in another.

In some environments, such as government-run postal savings banks, the opportunity to pay monetary bonuses may be limited. If that is the case, management should consider the use of nonmonetary incentives such as branch tournaments that give public recognition to the best performers. Sometimes the fact that performance is measured and compared in a transparent way can serve as a powerful incentive.

15.6 COMMON MISTAKES

In practice, some problems seem to occur rather frequently:

Failure to analyze how the scheme would fit into the internal culture. This problem usually leads to a clash with the organizational culture. As a result, staff members may not accept the incentive scheme. For example, the introduction of an individual incentive scheme may create problems in an organization that has previously had a policy of pay equality.

Bad internal promotion. Because management did not effectively communicate the reasons for developing the scheme, its advantages, and its potential disadvantages, the affected employees react negatively to the scheme. This may sound obvious, but there are countless examples where changes in the staff incentive scheme were only announced to staff on the day of implementation. In some cases this led to labor unrest and strikes, and the new scheme failed.

Failure to think thoroughly through the scheme and its likely effects. The result of this management failure can be that staff's behavior changes in unanticipated ways, producing undesirable side effects. For example, if a scheme rewards the opening of new accounts by clients and does not take into consideration the quality of services rendered, it should not come as a surprise if staff members recruit many new clients whose accounts then quickly become inactive. The best insurance against this potential problem is to thoroughly test the proposed scheme, both by discussing it with experienced operations managers (who can usually anticipate quite well how their staff are likely to react) and by field testing the scheme in a small number of outlets.

Failure to calibrate the incentives properly. Incentives awarded by the scheme are too small so staff do not behave much differently than before the scheme. Or, monetary rewards become too big, which makes the scheme less effective and the MFI less profitable. Proper spreadsheet modeling can help avoid this problem.

Faulty bonus formula. Because the formula has a technical problem or is inconsistently applied, the incentive scheme does not work as efficiently as intended. Again, careful spreadsheet work can reduce this risk.

Failure to align incentives properly among different organizational levels. The formula for different members of a team are inconsistent, so staff work toward conflicting goals instead of supporting one another. This is one of the most common problems, especially at the branch level, and can result in inefficiency. In team-based situations it is important to use a coherent set of goals and performance measurements for all team members. For instance, one would want to avoid a scheme in which branch staff members receive an incentive based on number of accounts opened and the branch manager is paid according to the volume deposited in the branch. In this case the manager would be interested in larger customers only, and conflicts would arise between the manager and the staff members.

15.7 CONCLUSION

Clearly, there is no simple recipe for designing a perfect incentive formula for savings mobilization. Nevertheless, a well-designed system can powerfully affect productivity and staff morale. MFI managers should design and/or adapt systems to their specific situation. At the same time, these simple design features will be appropriate for many MFIs:

- In most cases, a simple formula-based scheme taking into account outreach (that is, the development of the number of accounts) and deposit volume will be sufficient.
- When deposits are mobilized through branches, the incentive awards (such as monthly bonuses) should be based on group performance and should be shared equally among the staff members.
- Setting regular targets and conducting "tournaments" for the branch network can help to enhance deposit mobilization performance.
- Successful deposit mobilization depends on trust. Cooperation among all MFI employees is a necessary condition for generating trust among potential savings customers, but it is not sufficient. Other factors such as ownership and the MFI's image in the market also play a major role. It would not be fair to allocate the full burden and risk of deposit mobilization on the staff members by paying large bonuses, and correspondingly small base salaries, for attracting new deposits.

Remember that every system will create incentives to behave in certain ways, so it is very important to think ahead and predict what will happen. This will help to avoid completely unwanted and counterproductive behavior. Management also needs to estimate the impact that the planned scheme will have on operating costs and the organization's financial performance. In the short run, a bonus scheme will increase total staff costs. If the system is designed well, these costs will later be compensated for by increased staff productivity and output. Likewise, it is always a good idea to field-test a new system before rolling it out to the whole system.

In summary, implementing a financial incentive scheme for savings mobilization staff may well be worthwhile. Remember to keep the system simple, so that operating it will not be unnecessarily costly, and fair, so that employees accept it. Also keep in mind that salary level is not the only factor that influences staff motivation and morale: there are many other factors, and probably some more important ones. And finally, never operate an obviously deficient financial incentive scheme. It would be better to have none at all!

Notes

[1] See, for instance, Martin Holtmann, "Staff Incentive Schemes: The International Experience," in *Developing Staff Incentive Schemes* (Nairobi: *MicroSave,* 2003), 48–52. This is available on the *MicroSave* website.

[2] See the case studies in *Challenges of Microsavings Mobilization—Concepts and Views from the Field,* ed. Alfred Hannig and Sylvia Wisniwski (Eschborn, Germany: GTZ, n.d.); and Martin Holtmann, "Designing Financial Incentives to Increase Loan Officer Productivity—Handle with Care," *The MicroBanking Bulletin* 6 (April 2001). Several short papers on the issue of staff motivation are contained in "Moving Microfinance Forward," ed. Craig Churchill (Washington, DC: MicroFinance Network, 1998). "Moving Microfinance Forward" is available online.

[3] On designing bonus systems, see also Martin Holtmann, "Principles for Designing Staff Incentive Schemes," in *Developing Staff Incentive Schemes* (Nairobi: *MicroSave,* 2003), 53–61; and Holtmann, "Toolkit for the Design of Staff Incentive Schemes" (Nairobi: *MicroSave*). Both are available at the *MicroSave* website.

[4] For example, in microlending this requirement suggests that portfolios should not be reassigned between loan officers too often.

[5] Robert Peck Christen, *Banking Services for the Poor: Managing for Financial Success* (Washington, DC: ACCION International, 1997), 6.

[6] Ibid., 188.

[7] Luis R. Gomez-Mejia and David B. Balkin, *Compensation, Organizational Strategy, and Firm Performance* (Cincinnati: South-Western Publishing Co., 1992), 260–61.

[8] See Holtmann, "Toolkit," 45–47.

[9] Katherine Stearns, *Monetary Incentive Schemes for Staff,* GEMINI Tools for Microenterprise Programs (Washington, DC: USAID, 1993), 18.

[10] The same rules that apply to designing the bonus system must also be adhered to when adjusting it. Management should calculate the probable effects of the planned adjustments on the affected staff members, and staff members need to be convinced that the changes will not create any unfair burdens. All new staff should be informed that the incentive formula will be regularly reviewed as the MFI moves up the learning curve. Management should also closely monitor seasonal and unexpected patterns in savings behavior at the branch level in order to adjust the scheme as needed.

[11] In the following, we assume that savings are voluntary rather than forced. With voluntary savings mobilization, there is a positive correlation between staff efforts and savings collected.

[12] Remember that good MFIs want to provide services for their customers for a long period of time. This is especially important on the savings side. Customer retention is heavily dependent on high-quality service over the long run.

[13] Also, potential clients often will not entrust their money to an institution before a considerable period of time. The author has come across situations where clients wait for two years after the opening of a new branch before opening an account.

[14] The indicators for microlending alone typically consist of the number and volume of loans issued during a period, the number of accounts and size of the outstanding loan portfolio managed by the loan officer, and an indicator measuring the quality of the loan portfolio (typically, the portfolio-at-risk ratio). Individual bonuses are then calculated as a function of the loan officer's performance in these three basic categories. The bonus

formula for lending might contain base values for each of the main variables. Depending on how well the loan officer performed against these base values, he or she receives a bonus composed of the three main components. See Holtmann, "Principles for Designing Staff Incentive Schemes."

Contributors

Hayder Al-Bagdadi is a project coordinator in a GTZ project in Bosnia and Herzegovina to promote small and medium enterprises. Prior to this he worked as a member of GTZ's Head Office Financial Systems Development Team, which authored *Marketing for Microfinance Depositories: A Toolkit.* As a recipient of the Carl-Duisberg Gesellschaft Scholarship, he conducted a study of rural financial systems in Zambia. Al-Bagdadi has a degree in economics with a focus on microfinance and financial systems development from the Free University in Berlin.

Monnie Markel Biety is a long-time consultant specializing in the development, operations, and regulation of credit unions and microfinance institutions. She consults for WOCCU, ACDI/VOCA, FFH, Asian Development Bank, Canadian Cooperative Association, World Bank, and the National Federation of Community Development Credit Unions. She routinely works with project staff, credit union and MFI staff, and government agencies in the areas of institutional internal controls and liquidity/asset liability management. Biety has an MBA from the University of Colorado, Boulder and a BA in journalism from Creighton University in Omaha, Nebraska. She resides in Golden, Colorado.

Robert Peck Christen is the director of the Boulder Microfinance Training Program and the senior editor of the Microbanking Bulletin, an industry-wide publication devoted to financial sustainability. As an international consultant, Christen has advised commercial banks that were interested in microfinance, central banks and banking superintendencies interested in the regulatory framework for microfinance, and donor agencies interested in performance standards. Prior to his work as an independent consultant, Christen worked for ACCION International, where he established successful microcredit NGOs in Costa Rica and Chile. More recently, he worked for CGAP as a senior technical advisor. In addition, Mr Christen is the author of several publications related to sustainable microfinance.

David Cracknell has more than eleven years of experience in microfinance in Asia and Africa. After working at an advisory level within a leading Sri Lankan MFI, he worked for DFID in Bangladesh managing its enterprise development portfolio, which included investments in BRAC, Proshika, BURO, Tangail, and CARE INCOME. He was chair of Bangladesh's Donor Consortia for Microfinance and the Proshika Donor Consortia. Currently, he manages *MicroSave*'s Action Research Partnership, investigating supply-side issues of product and institutional development within ten MFIs in East and South Africa. The Action Research Partnership covers a diverse range of issues including market

371

research, product development, pilot testing, product costing, incentive schemes, marketing, electronic banking, branding, and customer service. He writes regularly on microfinance issues.

Lorna Grace is an independent microfinance consultant, focusing on financial management and capacity building of MFIs worldwide. In 1992, after a brief stint as a financial analyst in one of the top investment houses in Canada, she started her microfinance career with Calmeadow Foundation. Grace has a BA from Harvard University, an MBA from the University of Alberta, and is a chartered financial analyst. A co-author of CGAP's costing tool, she has trained and worked with several MFIs to implement the tool in their institutions.

Mattias Grammling works as an independent consultant in the field of microfinance. As a member of a team of researchers and senior specialists currently researching the staff incentive schemes of MFIs, he has reviewed the incentive schemes of more than twenty organizations in Latin America, Asia, and Africa. The team is supported by the MicroFinance Network, CGAP, and *MicroSave*. Grammling holds a master's level degree in international development economics from Trier University, where, as a PhD student, he currently explores the cross-cultural differences in the design and effectiveness of staff incentive schemes for MFIs.

Brigit Helms is a lead microfinance specialist at CGAP. She recently launched a new Savings Mobilization Initiative that focuses on learning about innovations at the country, institutional, and global levels. She founded CGAP's Donor Team to promote aid effectiveness in microfinance, specializes in microfinance capacity building, and has conducted several institutional appraisals of MFIs in Latin America, Asia, and Africa. She is also the author or co-author of several CGAP technical publications, including a costing toolkit. Before joining CGAP, Helms worked in IFAD's Latin America and the Caribbean Division, as a desk officer for Central America at the US Department of Commerce, and as an independent consultant. In her eighteen years of experience in economic development, she has worked in over thirty-five countries throughout the developing world. Helms holds the PhD from Stanford University in development and agricultural economics and speaks fluent Spanish, intermediate French, and passable Italian.

Madeline Hirschland has been engaged in microfinance since 1989. As director of Save the Children's Microenterprise Office, she catalyzed MFIs that are now industry leaders in Jordan, Lebanon, and Palestine. In that capacity and as a freelance consultant she has also provided strategic direction and technical assistance to MFIs in Africa, Asia, and Latin America. An instructor in the Boulder Microfinance Training Program since 1998, Hirschland has facilitated numerous international microfinance conferences, both face to face and virtual. She is the author of CGAP's *Deposit Services for the Poor: Preliminary Guidance for Donors* and a coauthor of the book *New Directions in Poverty Finance*. She holds a BA and MPA from Harvard University.

Martin Holtmann, now lead financial specialist at CGAP, started his career in commercial banking and management consulting. For twelve years he worked as a staff member and managing director of IPC, a firm specializing in microfinance consulting and management services for microfinance banks. He was the Moscow-based manager of the EBRD

Russia Small Business Fund and helped in the design and implementation of several bank down-scaling programs and "greenfield banks." Holtmann has taught finance and personnel economics at the University of Trier (Germany) and is a regular instructor at the Boulder Microfinance Training Program. He has done extensive action research on staff incentives with *MicroSave* and is the author of *MicroSave*'s *Toolkit on the Design of Staff Incentive Schemes*. He co-manages CGAP's cooperation with commercial banks.

Mohammed Azim Hossain joined ASA in 1984 and is the head of Finance and Management Information Systems. He obtained a master's degree in commerce with a major in accounting, management, economics, finance, and business communication from Dhaka University. Before joining ASA, he worked in a chartered accountants' firm in Bangladesh. Hossain completed a course in project management in Denmark and holds a diploma in computer science and system analysis. His work relates to ASA's policy formulation, decision-making, and business planning. Hossain reviews ASA's simple and innovative record keeping, auditing, and MIS; he is involved in developing key policies of the ASA-NGO partnership program, whereby ASA provides technical support to twenty-four small NGOs in Bangladesh. He has consulted in the Philippines, Indonesia, India, Yemen, and Ethiopia, and he has produced several international training materials. He has also contributed to publications on ASA and has participated in various international seminars.

Gerry Lab-oyan is one of the pioneers and general manager of the Cooperative Bank of Benguet, a rural bank in the Philippines. Lab-oyan developed and manages the bank's deposit mobilization from low-income tribal peoples in a rural area in the Philippines. He is also the president of the New Benguet Chamber of Commerce and Industry, Inc., and a member of the board of regents of the Benguet State University.

Kathryn Larcombe is the deputy director of Tchuma, an MFI in Mozambique that is an affiliate of ACCION International and the Fundácio Un Sol Món of the Caixa Catalunya. Larcombe has played a key role in overseeing Tchuma's development of savings operations. Prior to joining Tchuma, she worked as a management consultant in the UK and in Mozambique.

Katharine McKee is the director of USAID's Office of Microenterprise Development, which is charged with helping the agency implement its Microenterprise Initiative, which provides about US$185 million annually to improve the earnings and assets of poor entrepreneurs and their households in over sixty countries. It invests in applied research and experimentation, provides technical support to USAID programs, and promotes high-quality donor engagement in this field. McKee's professional background includes eight years with the Ford Foundation in West Africa and New York and twelve years as associate director of Self-Help in North Carolina, the largest nonprofit community development financial institution in the United States. She is an economist, with a master's from the Woodrow Wilson School at Princeton and an undergraduate degree from Bowdoin College in Maine. She has co-authored a book and written articles and chapters on microenterprise and development finance.

John Owens is the chief of party for the Microenterprise Access to Banking Services program in the Philippines, which works with more than seventy-two rural banks with over two hundred branches. By creating a systematic approach for introducing microfinance to rural banks, the program has facilitated the rapid expansion of commercial microfinance in the Philippines. Owens has worked in the field of microenterprise development and microfinance for eighteen years in the Caribbean, Latin America, Africa, and Asia. As well as working directly with banks, credit unions, specialized MFIs, and regulators, Owens has written and lectured on various aspects of microfinance. He specializes in working with banks to develop profitable microfinance services including loans, deposits, and money-transfer services. Owens earned a law degree from the University of Notre Dame and a BA in accounting and philosophy from the Gustavus Adolphus College.

David C. Richardson is senior manager of technical development for WOCCU. He is responsible for developing and integrating new credit-union financial products and services into all development programs. Richardson was instrumental in defining WOCCU's model credit-union building methodology and created the PEARLS financial performance monitoring system that WOCCU uses worldwide to monitor credit-union financial performance. He has extensive field experience in Latin America, Africa, Eastern Europe, and Asia, and has published various articles on credit unions as MFIs. At WOCCU since 1987, Richardson served as regional manager for Latin America, supervisor for Central America, and chief financial advisor/chief of party in Guatemala. He holds a graduate degree in agri-banking and business management from Texas A & M University and an undergraduate degree in university studies from Brigham Young University.

Stuart Rutherford, originally from London, is a microfinance practitioner, researcher, writer, and teacher. His interest is in understanding how poor people manage their money, hence the title of his best-known work, *The Poor and Their Money.* He has taught at the Boulder Colorado Microfinance Training Course and IDPM at the University of Manchester, UK, where he is a senior visiting fellow. He lived for many years in Bangladesh, where he founded *Safe*Save, an MFI that seeks to provide highly flexible basic financial services to very poor slum dwellers. He is currently researching how clients and fieldworkers in Bangladesh are responding to Grameen Bank II—Grameen's recent major reworking of its products. Rutherford now lives in Japan.

Khem Raj Sapkota is a founder, chairman, and member of the board of directors in VYCCU savings and Credit Cooperative Ltd., one of the largest and most successful savings and credit cooperatives in Nepal. Sapkota saw the cooperative through its infancy and transformation from an institution that served only its members to one that legally mobilizes deposits from the general public and a large number of clients. He has written several papers on what is required to make this transition. Sapkota is also the chairman of Vijaya F.M., a community radio station managed as a cooperative, and the manager of Vijaya Development Resource Center, one of the renowned NGOs in Nepal.

N. Srinivasan is a senior executive of NABARD, an apex development finance institution focused on agriculture and rural development in India. It is involved in Indian rural finance from policy to implementation levels, supporting and facilitating innovations in deepening and widening financial services in under-served rural areas. It has been working with banks and NGOs to organize self-help groups that provide over sixteen million low-income families with microfinance services. He has a master's degree in economics from the Madurai Kamaraj University and is an associate of the Indian Institute of Bankers. He has wide-ranging interests in development economics, and rural development in particular. Srinivasan has been with NABARD for the last twenty-two years. In his present capacity as chief general manager, he has handled the corporate planning function of the bank and is now in charge of the Maharashtra Regional Office in Western India.

Rodger Voorhies is the chief operating officer of Opportunity International Bank of Malawi, a new microfinance bank in Lilongwe Malawi that has developed satellite offices to serve rural areas and urban markets. Voorhies has managed the bank from its founding to the present. Prior to his work in Malawi, he served as project advisor of CETZAM in Zambia, assistant regional director for Africa for the Opportunity International Network, and director of Initiative Mikro, an MFI in Poland. He has written on impact assessment as well as down-scaling. Voorhies has a master's of management from the Kellogg School at Northwestern University and has done postgraduate work in organizational behavior at Northwestern.

Graham A. N. Wright is program director for *MicroSave*, the CGAP/DFID/Norwegian and Austrian Government–funded program that promotes the development and implementation of high-quality financial services for the poor. He is also chair of the CGAP Savings Mobilization Working Group, member of the CGAP Product Development Taskforce and a research associate at IDPM, University of Manchester, UK. Author of numerous papers and a book entitled *MicroFinance Systems: Designing Quality Financial Services for the Poor*, Wright has sixteen years of experience providing technical assistance, training, and research for a variety of MFIs in Bangladesh, the Philippines, and throughout Africa. Prior to this, he spent five years in management consultancy, training, and audit with Arthur Andersen & Co. He is a reformed chartered accountant and holds a master's in economics and psychology.

Index

Examples by Region

Note—Page numbers in bold refer to text box examples; regular page numbers refer to references or a single line of data.

Also from Kumarian Press...

Microfinance

The New World of Microenterprise Finances
Building Healthy Financial Institutions for the Poor
Edited by Maria Otero and Elisabeth Rhyne

Defying the Odds
Banking for the Poor
Eugene Versluysen

Mainstreaming Microfinance
How Lending to the Poor Began, Grew, and Came of Age in Bolivia
Elisabeth Rhyne

Housing Microfinance
A Guide to Practice
Edited by Franck Daphnis and Bruce Ferguson

The Commercialization of Microfinance
Balancing Business and Development
Deborah Drake and Elisabeth Rhyne

Pathways Out of Poverty
Innovations in Microfinance for the Poorest Families
Edited by Sam Daley-Harris

New Kumarian Press Titles

Building Democratic Institutions
Governance Reform in Developing Countries
G. Shabbir Cheema

Reducing Poverty, Building Peace
Coralie Bryant and Christina Kappaz

Working for Change
Making a Career in International Public Service
Derick W. Brinkerhoff and Jennifer M. Brinkerhoff

Visit Kumarian Press at **www.kpbooks.com** or
call **toll-free 800.289.2664** for a complete catalog.

Kumarian Press, located in Bloomfield, Connecticut, is a forward-looking, scholarly press that promotes active international engagement and an awareness of global connectedness.